PHP 8 Programr Tips, Tricks and Best Practices

A practical guide to PHP 8 features, usage changes, and advanced programming techniques

Doug Bierer

BIRMINGHAM—MUMBAI

PHP 8 Programming Tips, Tricks and Best Practices

Copyright © 2021 Packt Publishing

All rights reserved. No part of this book may be reproduced, stored in a retrieval system, or transmitted in any form or by any means, without the prior written permission of the publisher, except in the case of brief quotations embedded in critical articles or reviews.

Every effort has been made in the preparation of this book to ensure the accuracy of the information presented. However, the information contained in this book is sold without warranty, either express or implied. Neither the author, nor Packt Publishing or its dealers and distributors, will be held liable for any damages caused or alleged to have been caused directly or indirectly by this book.

Packt Publishing has endeavored to provide trademark information about all of the companies and products mentioned in this book by the appropriate use of capitals. However, Packt Publishing cannot guarantee the accuracy of this information.

Group Product Managers: Richa Tripathi

Publishing Product Manager: Sathyanarayanan Ellapulli

Senior Editor: Storm Mann

Content Development Editor: Nithya Sadanandan

Technical Editor: Pradeep Sahu

Copy Editor: Safis Editing

Project Coordinator: Deeksha Thakkar

Proofreader: Safis Editing

Indexer: Vinayak Purushotham

Production Designer: Jyoti Chauhan

First published: July 2021

Production reference: 1280721

Published by Packt Publishing Ltd.

Livery Place

35 Livery Street

Birmingham

B3 2PB, UK.

ISBN 978-1-80107-187-1

www.packt.com

Foreword

I've known Doug Bierer for many years now. It has been my great privilege to work with him on training new PHP developers and helping existing ones to grow their skills. I have even had the distinct privilege of butchering the pronunciation of his name many times. Through the years, though, I've come to respect Doug's ability to take technical concepts and put them in a language that just about anyone can understand. That's why when he wrote and asked me whether I would write the foreword for this book, I was excited to say *yes*.

Technical training is not easy. Not only does a trainer have to have a thorough understanding of the topic being discussed, but they also have to have the ability to convey ideas and concepts to others in clear language. I've spent a large part of my career struggling with how to best combine these two unrelated skills. Doug makes it look easy and this book is just the latest proof of that. From the language used to the examples given, everything is clearly laid out for you.

PHP 8 is a huge leap forward. Even as we write about PHP 8.0, PHP 8.1 is in the alpha stages of testing, and the tools and concepts embodied in PHP today are as good as they are in any language built for web development. When you add the speed increases that we have enjoyed with each new version for the past few years, you can begin to see why PHP is still a powerhouse of web development.

By purchasing this book, you are taking the first step in being able to harness the power of PHP 8 in your own projects. When you combine the knowledge you will gain from this book and Doug's skill at making the concepts understandable and immediately applicable to your problems, you will have lit the fuse on a rocket that will propel your skills and your career to new heights.

Strap in and hold on – this is going to be a fun ride!

Cal Evans (cal@calevans.com)

Senior Consultant, EICC, Inc.

Contributors

About the author

Doug Bierer has been hooked on computers since his first program, written on a DEC PDP-8, in 1971. In his wide-ranging career, he has been a professional contract programmer since 1978, having written applications in BASIC, PL/I, Assembler, FORTH, C, C++, dBase/FoxBase/Clipper, Pascal, Perl, Java, and PHP. He deployed his first website in 1993 while living in San Francisco. He speaks four languages, has traveled extensively, and now resides in Thailand. He also spent some years doing system administration and TCP/IP networking. Some of his technical works include *PHP 7 Programming Cookbook* and *Learning MongoDB 4.x* (Packt), as well as *Learning PHP and MySQL*, *Learning PHP Security*, and *Learning Doctrine* (O'Reilly Media).

About the reviewer

Matthew Setter is a highly skilled senior backend software engineer, specializing in PHP and web-based applications, with 20 years' experience. Matthew has worked for small start-ups, in academia, and for Fortune 500 companies.

He has worked on PHP, Go, Bash, TDD and BDD, MySQL, PostgreSQL, MSSQL Server, HTML5, CSS, JavaScript, Docker, Git, Slim, Laminas, Mezzio, Zend Expressive, Zend Framework, Laravel, PHPUnit, Codeception, GoConvey, JUnit, Pico, Nano, Vim, Alpine Linux, Debian, Linux Mint, Ubuntu, Apache, NGINX, ufw, and iptables, with a focus on Laminas/Mezzio and Linux.

Table of Contents

Preface

Section 1: PHP 8 Tips

1
Introducing New PHP 8 OOP Features

Technical requirements	4
Using constructor property promotion	7
Property promotion syntax	7
Using property promotion for code reduction	8
Working with attributes	10
Overview of PHP comments	10
PHP DocBlock considerations	11
Hidden dangers associated with the misuse of DocBlocks	12
The Attribute class	12
Attribute syntax	13
Incorporating match expressions into your program code	18
Match expression general syntax	18
Understanding named arguments	24
Named argument generic syntax	24
Calling core functions using named arguments	24
Order independence and documentation	25
Exploring new data types	27
Union types	27
mixed type	30
The effect of a mixed type on inheritance	31
Improving code using typed properties	33
What are typed properties?	33
Property typing can lead to a reduction in code	35
Summary	38

2
Learning about PHP 8's Functional Additions

Technical requirements	40	Defining uniform variable syntax	61
Working with new PHP 8 operators	40	How does uniform variable syntax affect PHP 8?	62
Using the variadics operator	41	Learning new array- and string-handling techniques	67
Using the nullsafe operator	46		
The concatenation operator has been demoted	51	Working with array_splice()	67
Using nested ternary operators	53	Using array_slice()	69
		Detecting string beginning, middle, and end	71
Using arrow functions	56		
Generic syntax	56	Securing SQLite databases with the authorizer	75
Arrow functions versus anonymous functions	56	Wait a minute… no security?	75
Variable inheritance	57	What's a SQLite authorization callback?	76
Practical example: Using arrow functions	58	What gets sent to the callback?	76
		Authorizer usage example	77
Understanding uniform variable syntax	61	Summary	83

3
Taking Advantage of Error-Handling Enhancements

Technical requirements	86	Promoted warnings in array handling	91
Understanding PHP 8 error handling	86	Promoted warnings in string handling	98
Undefined variable handling	87	Understanding notices promoted to warnings	100
Undefined constant handling	88		
Error-level defaults	89	Non-existent object property access handling	101
Dealing with warnings that are now errors	89	Non-existent offset handling	102
		Misusing resource IDs as array offsets	103
Promoted warnings in object error handling	90	Ambiguous string offset cast	104
		Uninitialized or non-existent string offsets	105

Handling the @ error control operator	106	@ operator and error_reporting()	107
@ operator usage	106	Summary	109

4
Making Direct C-Language Calls

Technical requirements	112	Working with FFI creational methods	119
Understanding FFI	112	Comparing data using FFI	124
Relationship between PHP and the C language	113	Using FFI infrastructural methods	131
Understanding PHP extensions	113	Using FFI in an application	137
Learning where to use FFI	115	Integrating an external C library into a PHP script	137
Adopting FFI into PHP	116	Working with PHP callbacks	139
Do not use FFI for speed	117	Summary	142
Why use the FFI extension?	117		
Examining the FFI class	118		

Section 2: PHP 8 Tricks

5
Discovering Potential OOP Backward-Compatibility Breaks

Technical requirements	146	Taking control of serialization	164
Discovering core OOP coding differences	147	Understanding PHP serialization	164
		Understanding the __sleep() magic method	166
Handling static calls in PHP 8	147	Understanding a potential code break in the __sleep() method	167
Dealing with object property handling changes	148	Learning about __wakeup()	169
Working with PHP 8 autoloading	149	Introducing the Serializable interface	171
Navigating changes in magic methods	156	Examining PHP serializable interface issues	173
Dealing with constructor changes	156	New magic methods to control PHP serialization	174
Working with changes to __toString()	162		

Understanding PHP 8 expanded variance support	177	Understanding changes to SplFileObject	183
Understanding covariant returns	177	Examining changes to SplHeap	185
Using contravariant parameters	180	Handling changes in SplDoublyLinkedList	188
Handling Standard PHP Library (SPL) changes	183	Summary	192

6

Understanding PHP 8 Functional Differences

Technical requirements	194	arithmetic, bitwise, and concatenation operations	214
Learning key advanced string handling differences	194	Handling non-scalar data types in arithmetic and bitwise operations	215
Handling changes to the needle argument	195	Examining changes in the order of precedence	217
Dealing with v*printf() changes	200		
Working with null length arguments in PHP 8	203	Taking advantage of locale independence	219
Examining changes to implode()	204	Understanding the problems associated with locale dependence	220
Learning about constants usage in PHP 8	206	Reviewing functions and operations affected by locale independence	220
Understanding PHP 8 string-to-numeric comparison improvements	207	Handling arrays in PHP 8	223
		Dealing with negative offsets	223
Learning about strict and non-strict comparisons	207	Handling curly brace usage changes	225
Examining numeric strings	208	Mastering changes in security functions and settings	227
Detecting backward-compatible breaks involving numeric strings	210	Understanding changes in disabled functions handling	228
Dealing with inconsistent string-to-numeric comparison results	212	Learning about changes to the crypt() function	230
Understanding comparison changes made in PHP 8	213	Dealing with changes to password_hash()	232
Avoiding problems during a PHP 8 upgrade	213	Learning about changes to assert()	233
Handling differences in		Summary	236

7
Avoiding Traps When Using PHP 8 Extensions

Technical requirements	238	extension	262
Understanding the shift from resources to objects	239	GD extension resource-to-object migration	263
PHP 8 extension resource-to-object migration	239	GD extension compile flag changes	264
		Other GD extension changes	265
Potential code break involving is_resource()	240	**Discovering changes to the Reflection extension**	**266**
Advantages of objects over resources	242	Reflection extension usage	267
Traversable to IteratorAggregate migration	245	Learning about Reflection extension improvements	270
Learning about changes to XML extensions	**246**	**Working with other extension gotchas**	**274**
Examining XMLWriter extension differences	247	New database extension operating system library requirements	274
Working with changes to the SimpleXML extension	248	Reviewing changes to the ZIP extension	275
Understanding other XML extension changes	253	Examining PCRE extension changes	279
		Working with Intl extension changes	281
Avoiding problems with the updated mbstring extension	**255**	Understanding cURL extension changes	282
Discovering needle-argument differences in mb_str*() functions	256	Reviewing COM extension changes	282
Examining changes to mb_ereg*() functions	260	Examining other extension changes	283
Dealing with changes to the GD		**Summary**	**283**

8
Learning about PHP 8's Deprecated or Removed Functionality

Technical requirements	286	Discovering other PHP 8 usage changes	297
Discovering what has been removed from the core	**287**	**Examining core deprecations**	**301**
Examining functions removed in PHP 8	287	Deprecated usage in parameter order	302

Working with removed functionality in PHP 8 extensions — 303

Discovering mbstring extension changes — 304
Reworking code that uses Reflection*::export() — 307
Discovering other deprecated PHP 8 extension functionality — 307
Changes to the XML-RPC extension — 307
Changes made to the DOM extension — 308

Dealing with deprecated or removed security-related functionality — 312

Examining PHP 8 stream-filter changes — 312
Dealing with custom error-handling changes — 314
Dealing with changes to backtraces — 316
PDO error-handling mode default changed — 316
Examining the track_errors php.ini setting — 317

Summary — 318

Section 3: PHP 8 Best Practices

9
Mastering PHP 8 Best Practices

Technical requirements — 324

Discovering method signature changes — 324

Managing magic method signatures — 324
Examining Reflection method signature changes — 328
Dealing with PDO extension signature changes — 328
Dealing with newly defined static methods — 330
Working with the static return type — 333
Extending the use of the ::class constant — 335
Taking advantage of trailing commas — 339
Learning about methods that are no longer required — 340

Working with interfaces and traits — 341

Discovering new DOM extension interfaces — 341
Using new DateTime methods — 347
Understanding PHP 8 trait handling refinements — 350

Dealing with private methods — 355

Controlling anonymous class usage — 357

Understanding changes in namespaces — 360

Discovering differences in tokenization — 360
Using reserved keywords in a namespace — 361
Exposing bad namespace naming practices — 362

Summary — 363

10
Improving Performance

Technical requirements	366	Examining the effect of stable sorting on keys	391
Working with the JIT compiler	366	Handling illegal sort functions	393
Discovering how PHP works without JIT	367		
Enabling the JIT compiler	372	**Using weak references to improve efficiency**	**394**
Configuring the tracing mode	373		
Using the JIT compiler	375	Taking advantage of weak references	395
Debugging with the JIT compiler	378	Reviewing the WeakReference class definition	395
Discovering additional JIT compiler settings	381	Using weak references	396
Speeding up array handling	**381**	Working with WeakMap	397
Working with SplFixedArray in PHP 8	382	Implementing a container class using SplObjectStorage	398
Implementing stable sort	**385**	Understanding the benefits of WeakMap over SplObjectStorage	402
Understanding stable sorts	386		
Contrasting stable and non-stable sorting	387	**Summary**	**405**

11
Migrating Existing PHP Apps to PHP 8

Technical requirements	408	works	432
Understanding development, staging, and production environments	408	Step 3 – Back up everything	432
		Step 4 – Create a version control branch	432
Defining an environment	409	Step 5 – Scan for BC breaks	433
Learning how to spot BC breaks before a migration	**411**	Step 6 – Fix incompatibilities	433
		Step 7 – Repeat steps 5 and 6 as needed	433
Gaining an overview of BC breaks	412	Step 8 – Commit changes to the repository	434
Creating a BC break scan configuration file	412	Step 9 – Test in a simulated virtual environment	434
Developing a BC break scan class	417	Step 10 – Return to step 5 if the test is unsuccessful	434
Performing the migration	**430**		
Step 1 – Review the migration guide	432	Step 11 – Install PHP 8 on the staging environment	434
Step 2 – Make sure the current code			

xiv Table of Contents

Step 12 – Test and clone the staging environment to production	439	Testing and troubleshooting tools	440
		Handling issues with Composer	443
Testing and troubleshooting the migration	440	Working with unit tests	445
		Summary	447

12

Creating PHP 8 Applications Using Asynchronous Programming

Technical requirements	450	application performance	467
Understanding the PHP async programming model	451	Using selected PHP frameworks in async mode	470
Developing synchronous programming code	451	Working with ReactPHP	470
		Implementing PHP async using Amp	473
Understanding the asynchronous programming model	452	Using Mezzio with Swoole	473
Working with async coroutine support	453	Working with the parallel extension	474
Creating a PHP async application	454	Learning about PHP 8.1 fibers	476
Using the Swoole extension	457	Discovering the Fiber class	476
Examining the Swoole extension	457	Using fibers	478
Installing the Swoole extension	458	Examining the effect of fibers on ReactPHP and Swoole	481
Testing the installation	461		
Examining a sample I/O-intensive application	463	Summary	483
Using the Swoole extension to improve		Why subscribe?	485

Other Books You May Enjoy

Index

Preface

PHP 8 represents the culmination of the PHP core development team's work to maximize efficiency in the core language. Your application code will immediately see a boost in speed as well as having a smaller memory footprint just by migrating to PHP 8. Further, in PHP 8, developers notice that a tremendous effort has gone into normalizing syntax and language usage. In short, programming in PHP 8 is a joy to developers who appreciate adherence to good coding practices.

However, this inevitably leads to the question: where does the PHP language go from here? PHP 8 provides the answer to this question as well, in the form of the Just-In-Time compiler and support for fibers. The latter forms the foundation of asynchronous programming and has been announced for PHP 8.1. PHP 8 gives you a glimpse of the future of the language, and that future is looking extremely bright!

If you put all this together, it becomes clear that understanding and mastering the new features and stricter coding practices implemented in PHP 8 is vital to those who wish to pursue a serious career as a PHP developer. This book is exactly the tool you need to get up and running with PHP 8 quickly. Not only do we cover new features, but we also show you how to avoid traps that could lead to code failure after a PHP 8 migration. In addition, we give you a glimpse into the future of PHP via thorough coverage of the JIT compiler and PHP asynchronous programming.

Who this book is for

This book is for PHP developers at all levels who have experience in PHP 5 or above. If you're just getting started with PHP, you'll find the code examples useful for learning to use the language more effectively. Developers who have worked for a few months on one or more PHP projects will be able to apply the tips and techniques to the code at hand, while those with many years of PHP experience are sure to appreciate the concise coverage of new PHP 8 features.

What this book covers

Chapter 1, Introducing New PHP 8 OOP Features, introduces you to new PHP 8 features specific to Object-Oriented Programming (OOP). The chapter features plenty of short code examples that clearly illustrate the new features and concepts. This chapter is critical in helping you quickly take advantage of the power of PHP 8 and adapt the code examples to your own practice.

Chapter 2, Learning about PHP 8's Functional Additions, covers important additions and enhancements introduced to PHP 8 at the procedural level. It includes plenty of code examples that show new PHP 8 features and techniques to facilitate procedural programming. This chapter teaches you how to write faster and cleaner application code.

Chapter 3, Taking Advantage of Error-Handling Enhancements, explores one of the key improvements in PHP 8, its advanced error handling capabilities. In this chapter, you learn which Notices have been upgraded to Warnings, as well as which Warnings have now been promoted to Errors. This chapter will give you an excellent understanding of the background and intent of security enhancements allowing you to better control the use of your code. In addition, it's critical to be aware of error conditions that formerly only generated Warnings, but now generate Errors, so that you take measures to prevent your applications from failing following an upgrade to PHP 8.

Chapter 4, Making Direct C-Language Calls, helps you to learn what the Foreign Function Interface (FFI) is all about, what it's good for, and how to use it. The information in this chapter is important for developers interested in rapid custom prototyping using direct C language calls. This chapter shows you how to incorporate C language structures and functions directly into your code, opening the doors to an entire world of functionality hitherto unavailable to PHP.

Chapter 5, Discovering Potential OOP Backward-Compatibility Breaks, introduces you to new PHP 8 features specific to OOP. The chapter features plenty of short code examples that clearly illustrate the new features and concepts. This chapter is critical in helping you quickly take advantage of the power of PHP 8 by adapting the code examples into your own practice. In addition, this chapter highlights situations where object-oriented code might break after a PHP 8 migration.

Chapter 6, Understanding PHP 8 Functional Differences, covers potential backwards d-compatibility breaks at the PHP 8 command or functional level. This chapter presents important information that highlights potential pitfalls when migrating existing code to PHP 8. The information presented in this chapter enables you to produce reliable PHP code. After working through the concepts in this chapter, you'll be in a better position to write code that produces precise results and avoids inconsistencies.

Chapter 7, Avoiding Traps When Using PHP 8 Extensions, takes you through the major changes to extensions that have been made and how to avoid traps when updating an existing application to PHP 8. Once you finish reviewing the sample code and topics presented, you'll be able to prepare any existing PHP code for migration to PHP 8. In addition to learning about the changes to the various extensions, you'll also gain deep insight into their operation. This will allow you to make informed decisions when using extensions in PHP 8.

Chapter 8, Learning about PHP 8's Deprecated or Removed Functionality, walks you through functionality that has been deprecated or removed in PHP 8. After you have read the material in this chapter and followed the example application code, you will be able to detect and rewrite code that has been deprecated. You will also learn how to develop workarounds for functionality that has been removed as well as how to refactor code that uses removed functionality involving extensions. Another important skill you will learn in this chapter is how to improve application security by rewriting code depending on functions that have been entirely removed in PHP 8.

Chapter 9, Mastering PHP 8 Best Practices, introduces you to best practices now enforced in PHP 8. It covers a number of significant method signature changes and how their new usage continues the general PHP trend of helping you to produce better code. You will also learn about changes in the use of private methods, interfaces, traits, and anonymous classes, and how namespaces are now parsed. Mastering the best practices covered in this chapter will not only move you toward writing better code but will help you avoid the potential code breaks that might arise if you fail to grasp these new practices.

Chapter 10, Improving Performance, introduces you to a number of new PHP 8 features that have a positive effect on performance, with a special focus on the new Just-In-Time compiler. This chapter also includes thorough coverage of weak references whose proper use results in applications that use far less memory. By carefully reviewing the material covered in this chapter and by studying the code examples, you will be able to write faster and more efficient code.

Chapter 11, Migrating Existing PHP Apps to PHP 8, introduces a set of classes that form the basis of a PHP 8 backward-compatible break scanner. Throughout the book, you are shown potential code breaks that might follow a PHP 8 update. In addition, you will learn about the recommended process for migrating an existing customer PHP application to PHP 8. This chapter will leave you much better equipped to handle a PHP 8 migration, giving you the ability to perform PHP 8 migrations with greater confidence and a minimum number of problems.

Chapter 12, Creating PHP 8 Applications Using Asynchronous Programming, explains the difference between the traditional synchronous and asynchronous programming models. In recent years, an exciting new technology has taken the PHP community by storm: asynchronous programming, also known as PHP async. In addition, popular PHP async extensions and frameworks, including the Swoole extension and ReactPHP are covered, with plenty of examples to get you started. By the time you are done working through this chapter, you will be in a position to improve the performance of your applications, making them anywhere from 5 times up to a staggering 40 times faster!

To get the most out of this book

To get the most out of this book, you must have a basic understanding of PHP syntax, variables, control structures (for example, `if {} else {}`), looping structures (for example, `for () {}`), arrays, and functions. You must also have a basic idea of PHP OOP: classes, inheritance, and namespaces.

If you have not received formal PHP training, or are unsure that you have the necessary knowledge, please review these two sections of the online PHP reference manual:

- PHP language reference:

    https://www.php.net/manual/en/langref.php

- PHP OOP:

    https://www.php.net/manual/en/language.oop5.php

Here is a summary of the software covered in this book:

Software/hardware covered in the book	Operating system requirements
PHP 8.x	Windows, macOS, or Linux
Key PHP extensions	
Docker and docker-compose	

> **Note**
> If you are using the digital version of this book, we advise you to type the code yourself or access the code from the book's GitHub repository (a link is available in the next section). Doing so will help you avoid any potential errors related to the copying and pasting of code.

Download the example code files

You can download the example code files for this book from GitHub at `https://github.com/PacktPublishing/PHP-8-Programming-Tips-Tricks-and-Best-Practices`. If there's an update to the code, it will be updated in the GitHub repository.

We also have other code bundles from our rich catalog of books and videos available at `https://github.com/PacktPublishing/`. Check them out!

Download the color images

We also provide a PDF file that has color images of the screenshots and diagrams used in this book. You can download it here: `https://static.packt-cdn.com/downloads/9781801071871_ColorImages.pdf`.

Conventions used

There are a number of text conventions used throughout this book.

`Code in text`: Indicates code words in text, database table names, folder names, filenames, file extensions, pathnames, dummy URLs, user input, and Twitter handles. Here is an example: "This chapter also taught you how the new `Attribute` class can be used as an eventual replacement for PHP DocBlocks."

A block of code is set as follows:

```
// /repo/ch01/php7_prop_reduce.php
declare(strict_types=1);
class Test {
  protected $id = 0;
  protected $token = 0;
  protected $name = '';o
```

When we wish to draw your attention to a particular part of a code block, the relevant lines or items are set in bold:

```
$result = match(<EXPRESSION>) {
    <ITEM> => <EXPRESSION>,
    [<ITEM> => <EXPRESSION>,]
    default => <DEFAULT EXPRESSION>
};
```

Any command-line input or output is written as follows:

```
Fatal error: Uncaught TypeError: Cannot assign string to property Test::$token of type int in /repo/ch01/php8_prop_danger.php:12
```

> **Tips or important notes**
> Appear like this.

Get in touch

Feedback from our readers is always welcome.

General feedback: If you have questions about any aspect of this book, email us at customercare@packtpub.com and mention the book title in the subject of your message.

Errata: Although we have taken every care to ensure the accuracy of our content, mistakes do happen. If you have found a mistake in this book, we would be grateful if you would report this to us. Please visit www.packtpub.com/support/errata and fill in the form.

Piracy: If you come across any illegal copies of our works in any form on the internet, we would be grateful if you would provide us with the location address or website name. Please contact us at copyright@packt.com with a link to the material.

If you are interested in becoming an author: If there is a topic that you have expertise in and you are interested in either writing or contributing to a book, please visit authors.packtpub.com.

Share Your Thoughts

Once you've read *PHP 8 Programming Tips, Tricks and Best Practices*, we'd love to hear your thoughts! Scan the QR code below to go straight to the Amazon review page for this book and share your feedback.

`https://packt.link/r/180107187X`

Your review is important to us and the tech community and will help us make sure we're delivering excellent quality content.

Section 1: PHP 8 Tips

This section introduces cool stuff never seen before, new to PHP 8. The chapters discuss new features, first in Object-Oriented Programming, followed by new things at the functional and extension level. The last chapter in this section covers direct C language prototyping.

In this section, the following chapters are included:

- *Chapter 1, Introducing New PHP 8 OOP Features*
- *Chapter 2, Learning about PHP 8's Functional Additions*
- *Chapter 3, Taking Advantage of Error-Handling Enhancements*
- *Chapter 4, Making Direct C-Language Calls*

1
Introducing New PHP 8 OOP Features

In this chapter, you are introduced to new **PHP: Hypertext Preprocessor 8** (**PHP 8**) features specific to **Object-Oriented Programming** (**OOP**). The chapter features a set of classes that can be used to generate CAPTCHA images (**CAPTCHA** is an acronym for **Completely Automated Public Turing test to tell Computers and Humans Apart**), clearly illustrating new PHP 8 features and concepts. This chapter is critical in helping you quickly incorporate new PHP 8 features into your own practice. In doing so, your code will run faster and more efficiently, with fewer bugs.

The following topics are covered in this chapter:

- Using constructor property promotion
- Working with attributes
- Incorporating match expressions into your program code
- Understanding named arguments
- Exploring new data types
- Improving code using typed properties

Technical requirements

To examine and run the code examples provided in this chapter, the minimum recommended hardware is listed here:

- x86_64-based desktop PC or laptop
- 1 gigabyte (**GB**) free disk space
- 4 GB of **random-access memory** (**RAM**)
- 500 **kilobits per second** (**Kbps**) or faster internet connection

In addition, you will need to install the following software:

- Docker
- Docker Compose

This book uses a pre-built Docker image that contains all the needed software to create and run the PHP 8 code examples covered in this book. You do not need to install PHP, Apache, or MySQL on your computer: just use Docker and the provided image.

To set up a test environment to run the code examples, proceed as follows:

1. Install Docker.

   If you are running Windows, start here:

   `https://docs.docker.com/docker-for-windows/install/`

   If you are on a Mac, start here:

   `https://docs.docker.com/docker-for-mac/install/`

   If you are on Linux, have a look here:

   `https://docs.docker.com/engine/install/`

2. Install Docker Compose. For all operating systems, start here:

   `https://docs.docker.com/compose/install/`

3. Install the source code associated with this book onto your local computer.

   If you have installed Git, use the following command:

   ```
   git clone https://github.com/PacktPublishing/PHP-8-Programming-Tips-Tricks-and-Best-Practices.git ~/repo
   ```

Otherwise, you can simply download the source code from this **Uniform Resource Locator (URL)**: `https://github.com/PacktPublishing/PHP-8-Programming-Tips-Tricks-and-Best-Practices/archive/main.zip`. You can then unzip into a folder you create, which we refer to as `/repo` in this book.

4. You can now start the Docker daemon running. For Windows or Mac, all you need to do is to activate the Docker Desktop app.

   If you are running Ubuntu or Debian Linux, issue this command:

   `sudo service docker start`

   For Red Hat, Fedora, or CentOS, use this command:

   `sudo systemctl start docker`

5. Build a Docker container associated with this book and bring it online. To do so, proceed as follows.

   From your local computer, open Command Prompt (terminal window). Change the directory to `/repo`. For the first time only, issue the `docker-compose build` command to *build* the environment. Note that you might need `root` (administrator) privileges to run Docker commands. If this is the case, either run as administrator (for Windows) or preface the command with `sudo`. Depending on your connection speed, the initial build might take quite a bit of time to complete!

6. To bring the container up, proceed as follows

7. From your local computer, open Command Prompt (terminal window). Change the directory to `/repo`. Bring the Docker container online in background mode by running the following command:

   ```
   docker-compose up -d
   ```

   Note that you actually don't need to build the container separately. If the container is not built when you issue the `docker-compose up` command, it will be built automatically. On the other hand, it might be convenient to build the container separately, in which case `docker build` will suffice.

   Here's a useful command to ensure all containers are running:

   ```
   docker-compose ps
   ```

8. To access the running Docker container web server, proceed as follows.

   Open the browser on your local computer. Enter this URL to access PHP 8 code:

   `http://localhost:8888`

   Enter this URL to access PHP 7 code:

   `http://localhost:7777`

9. To open a command shell into the running Docker container, proceed as follows.

   From your local computer, open Command Prompt (terminal window). Issue this command to access the PHP 8 container:

   ```
   docker exec -it php8_tips_php8 /bin/bash
   ```

   Issue this command to access the PHP 7 container:

   ```
   docker exec -it php8_tips_php7 /bin/bash
   ```

10. When you are finished working with the container, to take it offline open Command Prompt (terminal window) from your local computer and issue this command:

    ```
    docker-compose down
    ```

The source code for this chapter is located here:

`https://github.com/PacktPublishing/PHP-8-Programming-Tips-Tricks-and-Best-Practices`

> **Important note**
> If your host computer uses **Advanced RISC Machines** (**ARM**) architecture (for example, Raspberry Pi), you will need to use a modified Dockerfile.

> **Tip**
> It would be an excellent idea to get a quick overview of Docker technology and terms by reviewing this article: `https://docs.docker.com/get-started/`.

We can now begin our discussion by having a look at constructor property promotion.

Using constructor property promotion

Aside from the **Just-In-Time (JIT)** compiler, one of the greatest new features introduced in PHP 8 is **constructor property promotion**. This new feature combines property declarations and argument lists in the __construct() method signature, as well as assigning defaults. In this section, you will learn how to substantially reduce the amount of coding required in property declarations as well as in the __construct() method signature and body.

Property promotion syntax

The syntax needed to invoke constructor property promotion is identical to that used in PHP 7 and earlier, with the following differences:

- You need to define a **visibility level**
- You do not have to explicitly declare the properties in advance
- You do not need to make assignments in the body of the __construct() method

Here is a bare-bones example of code that uses constructor property promotion:

```php
// /repo/ch01/php8_prop_promo.php
declare(strict_types=1);
class Test {
    public function __construct(
        public int $id,
        public int $token = 0,
        public string $name = '')
    { }
}
$test = new Test(999);
var_dump($test);
```

When the preceding code block is executed, this is the output:

```
object(Test)#1 (3) {
  ["id"]=> int(999)
  ["token"]=> int(0)
  ["name"]=> string(0) ""
}
```

This shows that an instance of Test type has been created using default values. Now, let's have a look at how this feature might save a substantial amount of coding.

Using property promotion for code reduction

In a conventional OOP PHP class, the following three things need to be done:

1. Declare the properties, as follows:

   ```
   /repo/src/Php8/Image/SingleChar.php
   namespace Php7\Image;
   class SingleChar {
       public $text     = '';
       public $fontFile = '';
       public $width    = 100;
       public $height   = 100;
       public $size     = 0;
       public $angle    = 0.00;
       public $textX    = 0;
       public $textY    = 0;
   ```

2. Identify the properties and their data type in the __construct() method signature, as follows:

   ```
   const DEFAULT_TX_X = 25;
   const DEFAULT_TX_Y = 75;
   const DEFAULT_TX_SIZE  = 60;
   const DEFAULT_TX_ANGLE = 0;
   public function __construct(
       string $text,
       string $fontFile,
       int $width    = 100,
       int $height   = 100,
       int $size     = self::DEFAULT_TX_SIZE,
       float $angle  = self::DEFAULT_TX_ANGLE,
       int $textX    = self::DEFAULT_TX_X,
       int $textY    = self::DEFAULT_TX_Y)
   ```

3. In the body of the __construct() method, assign values to properties, like this:

```
{   $this->text     = $text;
    $this->fontFile = $fontFile;
    $this->width    = $width;
    $this->height   = $height;
    $this->size     = $size;
    $this->angle    = $angle;
    $this->textX    = $textX;
    $this->textY    = $textY;
    // other code not shown
}
```

As the number of constructor arguments increases, the amount of work you need to do also increases significantly. When constructor property promotion is applied, the amount of code required to do the same as previously shown is reduced to one-third of the original.

Let's now have a look at the same block of code as shown previously, but rewritten using this powerful new PHP 8 feature:

```
// /repo/src/Php8/Image/SingleChar.php
// not all code shown
public function __construct(
    public string $text,
    public string $fontFile,
    public int    $width   = 100,
    public int    $height  = 100,
    public int    $size    = self::DEFAULT_TX_SIZE,
    public float  $angle   = self::DEFAULT_TX_ANGLE,
    public int    $textX   = self::DEFAULT_TX_X,
    public int    $textY   = self::DEFAULT_TX_Y)
    { // other code not shown }
```

Amazingly, what took 24 lines of code in PHP 7 and earlier can be collapsed into eight lines of code using this new PHP 8 feature!

You are completely free to include other code in the constructor. In many cases, however, constructor property promotion takes care of everything normally done in the __construct() method, which means you can literally leave it empty ({ }).

Now, in the next section, you learn about a new feature called attributes.

> **Tip**
> Have a look at the full SingleChar class for PHP 7 here:
> `https://github.com/PacktPublishing/PHP-8-Programming-Tips-Tricks-and-Best-Practices/tree/main/src/Php7/Image`
> Also, the equivalent PHP 8 class is found here:
> `https://github.com/PacktPublishing/PHP-8-Programming-Tips-Tricks-and-Best-Practices/tree/main/src/Php8/Image`
> For more information on this new feature, have a look at the following:
> `https://wiki.php.net/rfc/constructor_promotion`

Working with attributes

Another significant addition to PHP 8 is the addition of a brand-new class and language construct known as **attributes**. Simply put, attributes are replacements for traditional PHP comment blocks that follow a prescribed syntax. When the PHP code is compiled, these attributes are converted internally into `Attribute` class instances.

This new feature is not going to have an immediate impact on your code today. It will start to become more and more influential, however, as the various PHP open source vendors start to incorporate attributes into their code.

The `Attribute` class addresses a potentially significant performance issue we discuss in this section, pertaining to an abuse of the traditional PHP comment block to provide meta-instructions. Before we dive into that issue and how `Attribute` class instances address the problem, we first must review PHP comments.

Overview of PHP comments

The need for this form of language construct arose with the increasing use (and abuse!) of the plain workhorse PHP comment. As you are aware, comments come in many forms, including all of the following:

```
# This is a "bash" shell script style comment
// this can either be inline or on its own line
/* This is the traditional "C" language style */
```

```
/**
 * This is a PHP "DocBlock"
 */
```

The last item, the famous PHP `DocBlock`, is now so widely used it's become a de facto standard. The use of DocBlocks is not a bad thing. On the contrary—it's often the *only way* a developer is able to communicate information about properties, classes, and methods. The problem only arises in how it is treated by the PHP interpretation process.

PHP DocBlock considerations

The original intent of the **PHP DocBlock** has been stretched by a number of extremely important PHP open-source projects. One striking example is the Doctrine **Object-Relational Mapper (ORM)** project. Although not mandatory, many developers choose to define ORM properties using **annotations** nested inside PHP DocBlocks.

Have a look at this partial code example, which defines a class interacting with a database table called `events`:

```
namespace Php7\Entity;
use Doctrine\ORM\Mapping as ORM;
/**
 * @ORM\Table(name="events")
 * @ORM\Entity("Application\Entity\Events")
 */
class Events {
    /**
     * @ORM\Column(name="id",type="integer",nullable=false)
     * @ORM\Id
     * @ORM\GeneratedValue(strategy="IDENTITY")
     */
    private $id;
    /**
     * @ORM\Column(name="event_key", type="string",
     *      length=16, nullable=true, options={"fixed"=true})
     */
    private $eventKey;
    // other code not shown
```

If you were to use this class as part of a Doctrine ORM implementation, Doctrine would open the file and parse the DocBlocks, searching for `@ORM` annotations. Despite some concerns over the time and resources needed to parse DocBlocks, this is an extremely convenient way to define the relationship between object properties and database table columns, and is popular with developers who use Doctrine.

> **Tip**
> Doctrine offers a number of alternatives to this form of ORM, including **Extensible Markup Language** (**XML**) and native PHP arrays. For more information, see `https://www.doctrine-project.org/projects/doctrine-orm/en/latest/reference/annotations-reference.html#annotations-reference`.

Hidden dangers associated with the misuse of DocBlocks

There is yet another danger associated with this abuse of the original purpose of a DocBlock. In the `php.ini` file, there is a setting named `opcache.save_comments`. If disabled, this would cause the OpCode cache engine (**OPcache**) to *ignore* all comments, including DocBlocks. If this setting is in effect, a Doctrine-based application using `@ORM` annotations in DocBlocks would malfunction.

Another problem has to do with how comments are parsed—or, more to the point, how comments are *not* parsed. In order to use the contents of a comment, the PHP application needs to open the file and parse it line by line. This is an expensive process in terms of time and resource utilization.

The Attribute class

In order to address hidden dangers, in PHP 8 a new `Attribute` class is provided. Instead of using DocBlocks with annotations, developers can define the equivalent in the form of attributes. An advantage of using attributes rather than DocBlocks is that they are a *formal part of the language* and are thus tokenized and compiled along with the rest of your code.

> **Important note**
>
> In this chapter, and also in the PHP documentation, reference to *attributes* refers to instances of the `Attribute` class.
>
> Actual performance metrics are not yet available that compare the loading of PHP code containing DocBlocks with the loading of code that contains attributes.

Although the benefits of this approach are not yet seen, as the various open source project vendors start to incorporate attributes into their offerings you will start to see an improvement in speed and performance.

Here is the `Attribute` class definition:

```
class Attribute {
    public const int TARGET_CLASS = 1;
    public const int TARGET_FUNCTION = (1 << 1);
    public const int TARGET_METHOD = (1 << 2);
    public const int TARGET_PROPERTY = (1 << 3);
    public const int TARGET_CLASS_CONSTANT = (1 << 4);
    public const int TARGET_PARAMETER = (1 << 5);
    public const int TARGET_ALL = ((1 << 6) - 1);
    public function __construct(
        int $flags = self::TARGET_ALL) {}
}
```

As you can see from the class definition, the main contribution from this class, used internally by PHP 8, is a set of class constants. The constants represent bit flags that can be combined using bitwise operators.

Attribute syntax

Attributes are enclosed using a special syntax borrowed from the **Rust** programming language. What goes inside the square brackets is pretty much left to the developer. An example can be seen in the following snippet:

```
#[attribute("some text")]
// class, property, method or function (or whatever!)
```

Returning to our example of the `SingleChar` class, here's how it might appear using traditional DocBlocks:

```
// /repo/src/Php7/Image/SingleChar.php
namespace Php7\Image;
/**
 * Creates a single image, by default black on white
 */
class SingleChar {
    /**
     * Allocates a color resource
     *
     * @param array|int $r,
     * @param int $g
     * @param int $b]
     * @return int $color
     */
    public function colorAlloc()
    { /* code not shown */ }
```

Now, have a look at the same thing using attributes:

```
// /repo/src/Php8/Image/SingleChar.php
namespace Php8\Image;
#[description("Creates a single image")]
class SingleChar {
    #[SingleChar\colorAlloc\description("Allocates color")]
    #[SingleChar\colorAlloc\param("r","int|array")]
    #[SingleChar\colorAlloc\param("g","int")]
    #[SingleChar\colorAlloc\param("b","int")]
    #[SingleChar\colorAlloc\returns("int")]
    public function colorAlloc() { /* code not shown */ }
```

As you can see, in addition to providing a more robust compilation and avoiding the hidden dangers mentioned, it's also more efficient in terms of space usage.

> **Tip**
> What goes inside the square brackets does have some restrictions; for example, although `#[returns("int")]` is allowed, this is not: `#[return("int")]`. The reason for this is because `return` is a keyword.
>
> Another example has to do with **union types** (explained in the *Exploring new data types* section). You can use `#[param("int|array test")]` in an attribute, but this is not allowed: `#[int|array("test")]`. Another peculiarity is that class-level attributes must be placed *immediately before* the `class` keyword and after any `use` statements.

Viewing attributes using Reflection

If you need to get attribute information from a PHP 8 class, the `Reflection` extension has been updated to include attribute support. A new `getAttributes()` method that returns an array of `ReflectionAttribute` instances has been added.

In the following block of code, all the attributes from the `Php8\Image\SingleChar::colorAlloc()` method are revealed:

```
<?php
// /repo/ch01/php8_attrib_reflect.php
define('FONT_FILE', __DIR__ . '/../fonts/FreeSansBold.ttf');
require_once __DIR__ . '/../src/Server/Autoload/Loader.php';
$loader = new \Server\Autoload\Loader();
use Php8\Image\SingleChar;
$char    = new SingleChar('A', FONT_FILE);
$reflect = new ReflectionObject($char);
$attribs = $reflect->getAttributes();
echo "Class Attributes\n";
foreach ($attribs as $obj) {
    echo "\n" . $obj->getName() . "\n";
    echo implode("\t", $obj->getArguments());
}
echo "Method Attributes for colorAlloc()\n";
$reflect = new ReflectionMethod($char, 'colorAlloc');
```

```
$attribs = $reflect->getAttributes();
foreach ($attribs as $obj) {
    echo "\n" . $obj->getName() . "\n";
    echo implode("\t", $obj->getArguments());
}
```

Here is the output from the code shown in the preceding snippet:

```
<pre>Class Attributes

Php8\Image\SingleChar
Php8\Image\description
Creates a single image, by default black on whiteMethod
Attributes for colorAlloc()
Php8\Image\SingleChar\colorAlloc\description
Allocates a color resource
Php8\Image\SingleChar\colorAlloc\param
r       int|array
Php8\Image\SingleChar\colorAlloc\param
g       int
Php8\Image\SingleChar\colorAlloc\param
b       int
Php8\Image\SingleChar\colorAlloc\returns
int
```

The preceding output shows that attributes can be detected using the Reflection extension classes. Finally, the actual method is shown in this code example:

```
namespace Php8\Image;use Attribute;
use Php8\Image\Strategy\ {PlainText,PlainFill};
#[SingleChar]
#[description("Creates black on white image")]
class SingleChar {
    // not all code is shown
    #[SingleChar\colorAlloc\description("Allocates color")]
    #[SingleChar\colorAlloc\param("r","int|array")]
    #[SingleChar\colorAlloc\param("g","int")]
```

```
#[SingleChar\colorAlloc\param("b","int")]
#[SingleChar\colorAlloc\returns("int")]
public function colorAlloc(
    int|array $r, int $g = 0, int $b = 0) {
    if (is_array($r))
        [$r, $g, $b] = $r;
    return \imagecolorallocate(
        $this->image, $r, $g, $b);
}
}
```

Now that you have an idea of how attributes can be used, let's continue our coverage of new features by discussing `match` expressions, followed by named arguments.

> **Tip**
>
> For more information on this new feature, have a look at the following web page:
>
> `https://wiki.php.net/rfc/attributes_v2`
>
> Also, see this update:
>
> `https://wiki.php.net/rfc/shorter_attribute_syntax_change`
>
> Information on PHP DocBlocks can be found here:
>
> `https://phpdoc.org/`
>
> For more information about Doctrine ORM, have a look here:
>
> `https://www.doctrine-project.org/projects/orm.html`
>
> Documentation on `php.ini` file settings can be found here:
>
> `https://www.php.net/manual/en/ini.list.php`
>
> Read about PHP Reflection here:
>
> `https://www.php.net/manual/en/language.attributes.reflection.php`
>
> Information about the Rust programming language can be found in this book: `https://www.packtpub.com/product/mastering-rust-second-edition/9781789346572`

Incorporating match expressions into your program code

Among the many incredibly useful features introduced in PHP 8, **match expressions** definitely stand out. `Match` expressions are a more accurate shorthand syntax that can potentially replace the tired old `switch` statement that came directly from the C language. In this section, you will learn how to produce cleaner and more accurate program code by replacing `switch` statements with `match` expressions.

Match expression general syntax

`Match` expression syntax is much like that of an array, where the key is the item to match and the value is an expression. Here is the general syntax for `match`:

```
$result = match(<EXPRESSION>) {
    <ITEM> => <EXPRESSION>,
    [<ITEM> => <EXPRESSION>,]
    default => <DEFAULT EXPRESSION>
};
```

The expression must be a valid PHP expression. Examples of expressions could include any of the following:

- A specific value (for example, `"some text"`)
- An operation (for example, `$a + $b`)
- An anonymous function or class

The only limitation is that the expression has to be defined in a single line of code. Major differences between `match` and `switch` are summarized here:

Switch	Match
Loose type comparisons (for example `$a == $b`)	Strict type comparisons (for example `$a === $b`)
Does not return a value	Returns a value
Requires `break`	Does not require `break`
Multiple commands per case	One command per match

Table 1.1 – Differences between match and switch

Other than the differences noted, `match` and `switch` both allow case aggregation, as well as providing support for a *default* case.

switch and match examples

Here is a simple example that renders a currency symbol using `switch`:

```php
// /repo/ch01/php7_switch.php
function get_symbol($iso) {
    switch ($iso) {
        case 'CNY' :
            $sym = '¥';
            break;
        case 'EUR' :
            $sym = '€';
            break;
        case 'EGP' :
        case 'GBP' :
            $sym = '£';
            break;
        case 'THB' :
            $sym = '฿';
            break;
        default :
            $sym = '$';
    }
    return $sym;
}
$test = ['CNY', 'EGP', 'EUR', 'GBP', 'THB', 'MXD'];
foreach ($test as $iso)
    echo 'The currency symbol for ' . $iso
        . ' is ' . get_symbol($iso) . "\n";
```

When this code is executed, you see the currency symbols for each of the **International Organization for Standardization** (**ISO**) currency codes in the `$test` array. The same result as that shown in the preceding code snippet can be obtained in PHP 8, using the following code:

```
// /repo/ch01/php8_switch.php
function get_symbol($iso) {
    return match ($iso) {
        'EGP','GBP' => '£',
        'CNY'       => '¥',
        'EUR'       => '€',
        'THB'       => '฿',
        default     => '$'
    };
}
$test = ['CNY', 'EGP', 'EUR', 'GBP', 'THB', 'MXD'];
foreach ($test as $iso)
    echo 'The currency symbol for ' . $iso
        . ' is ' . get_symbol($iso) . "\n";
```

Both examples produce an identical output, as illustrated here:

```
The currency symbol for CNY is ¥
The currency symbol for EGP is £
The currency symbol for EUR is €
The currency symbol for GBP is £
The currency symbol for THB is ฿
The currency symbol for MXD is $
```

As mentioned previously, both code examples produce a list of currency symbols for the list of ISO currency codes stored in the `$test` array.

Complex match example

Returning to our CAPTCHA project, assume that we wish to introduce distortion to make the CAPTCHA characters more difficult to read. To accomplish this goal, we introduce a number of **strategy** classes, each producing a different distortion, as summarized in this table:

Php8\Image\Strategy*	Description
`DotFill($num)`	Fills background with `$num` dots
`LineFill($num)`	Fills background with `$num` lines
`RotateText($angle)`	Rotates text by `$angle`
`Shadow($offset, $r, $g, $b)`	Adds a shadow with `$offset` pixels apart, with a color determined by `$r`, `$g` and `$b` (red, green, blue)

Table 1.2 – CAPTCHA distortion strategy classes

After randomizing the list of strategies to be employed, we use a `match` expression to execute the results, as follows:

1. First we define an **autoloader**, import the classes to be used, and list potential strategies to employ, as illustrated in the following code snippet:

```
// /repo/ch01/php8_single_strategies.php
// not all code is shown
require_once __DIR__ . '/../src/Server/Autoload/Loader.php';
$loader = new \Server\Autoload\Loader();
use Php8\Image\SingleChar;
use Php8\Image\Strategy\
    {LineFill,DotFill,Shadow,RotateText};
$strategies = ['rotate', 'line', 'line',
               'dot', 'dot', 'shadow'];
```

2. Next, we generate the CAPTCHA phrase, as follows:

```
$phrase = strtoupper(bin2hex(random_bytes(NUM_BYTES)));
$length = strlen($phrase);
```

3. We then loop through each character in the CAPTCHA phrase and create a `SingleChar` instance. The initial call to `writeFill()` creates the white background canvas. We also need to call `shuffle()` to randomize the list of distortion strategies. The process is illustrated in the following code snippet:

```
$images = [];
for ($x = 0; $x < $length; $x++) {
    $char = new SingleChar($phrase[$x], FONT_FILE);
    $char->writeFill();
    shuffle($strategies);
```

4. We then loop through the strategies and layer distortions upon the original image. This is where the `match` expression comes into play. Notice that one strategy needs additional lines of code. Because `match` can only support a single expression, we simply wrap the multiple lines of code into an **anonymous function**, as follows:

```
foreach ($strategies as $item) {
    $func = match ($item) {
        'rotate' => RotateText::writeText($char),
        'line'   => LineFill::writeFill(
            $char, rand(1, 10)),
        'dot'    => DotFill::writeFill($char, rand(10, 20)),
        'shadow' => function ($char) {
            $num = rand(1, 8);
            $r   = rand(0x70, 0xEF);
            $g   = rand(0x70, 0xEF);
            $b   = rand(0x70, 0xEF);
            return Shadow::writeText(
                $char, $num, $r, $g, $b);},
        'default' => TRUE
    };
    if (is_callable($func)) $func($char);
}
```

5. All that remains to be done is to overlay the image with the actual CAPTCHA phrase by calling `writeText()` with no arguments. After that, we save the distorted image as a **Portable Network Graphics (PNG)** file for display, as illustrated in the following code snippet:

```
    $char->writeText();
    $fn = $x . '_'
        . substr(basename(__FILE__), 0, -4)
        . '.png';
    $char->save(IMG_DIR . '/' . $fn);
    $images[] = $fn;
}
include __DIR__ . '/captcha_simple.phtml';
```

Here is the result, running the preceding example from a browser that points to the Docker container associated with this book:

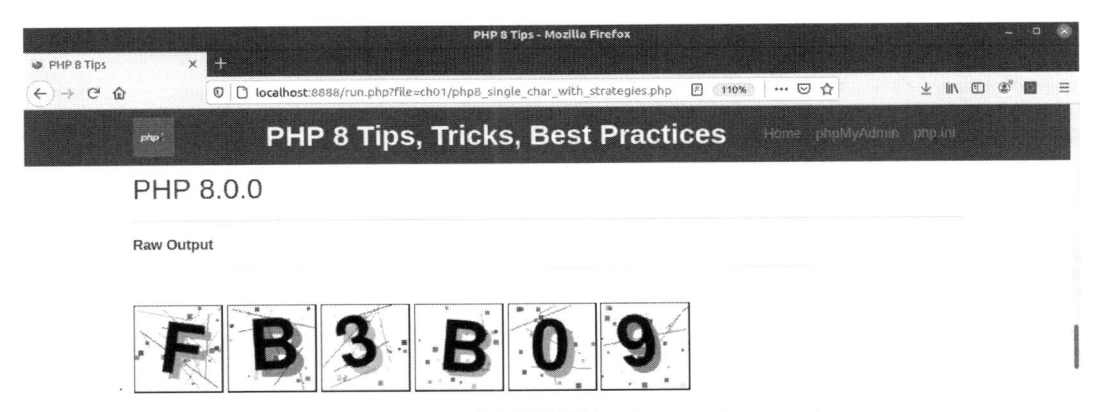

Figure 1.1 – Distorted CAPTCHA using match expression

Next, we'll have a look at another really great feature: named arguments.

> **Tip**
> You can see the original proposal for `match` expressions here:
> `https://wiki.php.net/rfc/match_expression_v2`

Understanding named arguments

Named arguments represent a way to avoid confusion when calling functions or methods with a large number of arguments. This not only helps avoid problems with arguments being supplied in an incorrect order, but also helps you to skip arguments with defaults. In this section, you will learn how to apply named arguments to improve the accuracy of your code, reduce confusion during future maintenance cycles, and make your method and function calls more concise. We start by examining the generic syntax required to use named arguments.

Named argument generic syntax

In order to use named arguments, you need to know the names of the variables used in the function or method signature. You then specify that name, without the dollar sign, followed by a colon and the value to be supplied, as follows:

```
$result = function_name( arg1 : <VALUE>, arg2 : <value>);
```

When the `function_name()` function is invoked, the values are passed to the arguments corresponding to `arg1`, `arg2`, and so on.

Calling core functions using named arguments

One of the most common reasons to use named arguments is when you call a core PHP function that has a large number of parameters. As an example, here's the function signature for `setcookie()`:

```
setcookie ( string $name [, string $value = ""
    [, int $expires = 0 [, string $path = ""
    [, string $domain = "" [, bool $secure = FALSE
    [, bool $httponly = FALSE ]]]]]] ) : bool
```

Let's say that all you really wanted to set were the `name`, `value`, and `httponly` arguments. Before PHP 8, you would have had to look up the default values and supply them, in order, until you got to the one you wished to override. In the following case, we wish to set `httponly` to TRUE:

```
setcookie('test',1,0,0,'','',FALSE,TRUE);
```

Using named arguments, the equivalent in PHP 8 would be as follows:

```
setcookie('test',1,httponly: TRUE);
```

Note that we do not need to name the first two parameters as they are supplied in order.

> **Tip**
> In PHP extensions, named arguments do not always match the names of variables you see in the PHP documentation for function or method signatures. As an example, the function `imagettftext()` shows a variable `$font_filename` in its function signature. If you scroll down a bit further, however, you'll see in the *Parameters* section, that the named parameter is `fontfile`.
>
> If you encounter a fatal Error: `Unknown named parameter $NAMED_PARAM`. Always use the name as listed in the *Parameters* section of the documentation rather than the name of the variable in the function or method signature.

Order independence and documentation

Another use for named arguments is to provide **order independence**. In addition, for certain core PHP functions, the sheer number of parameters presents a documentation nightmare.

As an example, have a look here at the function signature for `imagefttext()` (note that this function is central to the chapter project of producing a secure CAPTCHA image):

```
imagefttext ( object $image , float $size , float $angle ,
    int $x , int $y , int $color , string $fontfile ,
    string $text [, array $extrainfo ] ) : array
```

As you can imagine, trying to remember the names and order of these parameters when reviewing your work 6 months later might be problematic.

> **Important note**
> In PHP 8, the image creation functions (for example, `imagecreate()`) now return a `GdImage` object instance instead of a resource. All image functions in the GD extension have been rewritten to accommodate this change. There's no need to rewrite your code!

Accordingly, using named arguments, the following function call would be acceptable in PHP 8:

```php
// /repo/ch01/php8_named_args.php
// not all code is shown
$rotation = range(40, -40, 10);
foreach ($rotation as $key => $offset) {
    $char->writeFill();
    [$x, $y] = RotateText::calcXYadjust($char, $offset);
    $angle = ($offset > 0) ? $offset : 360 + $offset;
    imagettftext(
        angle         : $angle,
        color         : $char->fgColor,
        font_filename : FONT_FILE,
        image         : $char->image,
        size          : 60,
        x             : $x,
        y             : $y,
        text          : $char->text);
    $fn = IMG_DIR . '/' . $baseFn . '_' . $key . '.png';
    imagepng($char->image, $fn);
    $images[] = basename($fn);
}
```

The code example just shown writes out a string of distorted characters as a set of PNG image files. Each character is rotated 10 degrees clockwise with respect to its neighboring images. Note how named arguments are applied to make arguments to the `imagettftext()` function easier to understand.

Named arguments can also be applied to functions and methods of your own creation. In the next section, we cover new data types.

> **Tip**
> A detailed analysis of named arguments can be found here:
> `https://wiki.php.net/rfc/named_params`

Exploring new data types

One thing any entry-level PHP developer learns is which **data types** PHP has available and how to use them. The basic data types include `int` (integer), `float`, `bool` (Boolean), and `string`. Complex data types include `array` and `object`. In addition, there are other data types such as `NULL` and `resource`. In this section, we discuss a few new data types introduced in PHP 8, including union types and mixed types.

> **Important note**
> It's extremely important not to confuse a **data type** with a **data format**. This section describes data types. A data format, on the other hand, would be a way of *representing* data used as part of a transmission or for storage. Examples of a data format would include XML, **JavaScript Object Notation (JSON)**, and **YAML Ain't Markup Language (YAML)**.

Union types

Unlike other data types such as `int` or `string`, it's important to note that there is no data type explicitly called *union*. Rather, when you see a reference to **union types**, what is meant is that PHP 8 introduces a new syntax that allows you to specify a union of types, instead of just one. Let's now have a look at the generic syntax for union types.

Union type syntax

The generic syntax for union types is as follows:

```
function ( type|type|type $var) {}
```

In place of `type`, you would supply any of the existing data types (for example, `float` or `string`). There are a few restrictions, however, which for the most part make complete sense. This table summarizes the more important restrictions:

Disallowed	Not Allowed Example
`void` cannot be included in a union type	`void|int`
`mixed` cannot be included in a union type (more on that below)	`mixed|int`
Nullable types cannot be included in a union type	`string|?array`
Cannot include both `TRUE` and `FALSE` in a union type.	`TRUE|FALSE`
Redundant types are not allowed	`int|float|int` `array|iterable|Traversable`

Table 1.3 – Disallowed union types

As you can see from this list of exceptions, defining a union type is primarily a matter of common sense.

> **Tip**
>
> **Best practice**: When using union types, **type coercion** (the process whereby PHP converts a data type internally to satisfy the requirements of the function) can be an issue if strict type checking is not enforced. Accordingly, it's a best practice to add the following at the top of any file where union types are used: `declare(strict_types=1);`.
>
> For more information, see the documentation reference here:
>
> `https://www.php.net/manual/en/language.types.declarations.php#language.types.declarations.strict`

Union type example

For a simple illustration, let's return to the `SingleChar` class used as an example in this chapter. One of the methods is `colorAlloc()`. This method allocates a color from an image, leveraging the `imagecolorallocate()` function. It accepts as arguments integer values that represent red, green, and blue.

For the sake of argument, let's say that the first argument could actually be an array representing three values—one each for red, green, and blue. In this case, the argument type for the first value cannot be `int` otherwise, if an array were provided, an error would be thrown if strict type checking were to be turned on.

In earlier versions of PHP, the only solution would be to remove any type check from the first argument and to indicate that multiple types are accepted in the associated DocBlock. Here's how the method might appear in PHP 7:

```
/**
 * Allocates a color resource
 *
 * @param array|int $r
 * @param int $g
 * @param int $b]
 * @return int $color
 */
public function colorAlloc($r, $g = 0, $b = 0) {
    if (is_array($r)) {
        [$r, $g, $b] = $r;
    }
    return \imagecolorallocate($this->image, $r, $g, $b);
}
```

The only indication of the data type for the first parameter, `$r`, is the `@param array|int $r` DocBlock annotation and the fact that there is no data type hint associated with that argument. In PHP 8, taking advantage of union types, notice the difference here:

```
#[description("Allocates a color resource")]
#[param("int|array r")]
#[int("g")]
#[int("b")]
```

```
#[returns("int")]
public function colorAlloc(
    int|array $r, int $g = 0, int $b = 0) {
    if (is_array($r)) {
        [$r, $g, $b] = $r;
    }
    return \imagecolorallocate($this->image, $r, $g, $b);
}
```

In the preceding example, in addition to the presence of `attribute` that indicates the first argument can accept either an `array` or an `int` type, in the method signature itself, the `int|array` union type makes this choice clear.

mixed type

`mixed` is another new type introduced in PHP 8. Unlike a union type, `mixed` is an actual data type that represents the ultimate union of types. It's used to indicate that any and all data types are accepted. In a certain sense, PHP already has this facility: simply omit the data type altogether, and it's an implied `mixed` type!

> **Tip**
> You will see references to a `mixed` type in the PHP documentation. PHP 8 formalizes this representation by making it an actual data type.

Why use a mixed type?

Hold for a second—you might be thinking at this point: why bother using a `mixed` type at all? To put your mind at ease, this is an excellent question, and there is no compelling reason to use this type.

However, by using `mixed` in a function or method signature, you clearly *signal your intention* for the use of this parameter. If you were to simply leave the data type blank, other developers later using or reviewing your code might think that you forgot to add the type. At the very least, they will be uncertain of the nature of the untyped argument.

The effect of a mixed type on inheritance

As a `mixed` type represents the ultimate example of **widening**, it can be used to *widen* the data type definition when one class extends from another. Here is an example using a `mixed` type, illustrating this principle:

1. First, we define the parent class with the more restrictive data type of `object`, as follows:

```php
// /repo/ch01/php8_mixed_type.php
declare(strict_types=1);
class High {
    const LOG_FILE = __DIR__ . '/../data/test.log';
    protected static function logVar(object $var) {
        $item = date('Y-m-d') . ':'
            . var_export($var, TRUE);
        return error_log($item, 3, self::LOG_FILE);
    }
}
```

2. Next, we define a `Low` class that extends `High`, as follows:

```php
class Low extends High {
    public static function logVar(mixed $var) {
        $item = date('Y-m-d') . ':'
            . var_export($var, TRUE);
        return error_log($item, 3, self::LOG_FILE);
    }
}
```

Note in the `Low` class that the data type for the `logVar()` method has been *widened* into `mixed`.

3. Finally, we create an instance of `Low` and execute it with test data. As you can see from the results shown in the following code snippet, everything works fine:

```php
if (file_exists(High::LOG_FILE)) unlink(High::LOG_FILE)
$test = [
    'array' => range('A', 'F'),
    'func'  => function () { return __CLASS__; },
    'anon'  => new class () {
```

```
             public function __invoke() {
                return __CLASS__; } },
];
foreach ($test as $item) Low::logVar($item);
readfile(High::LOG_FILE);
```

Here is the output from the preceding example:

```
2020-10-15:array (
  0 => 'A',
  1 => 'B',
  2 => 'C',
  3 => 'D',
  4 => 'E',
  5 => 'F',
)2020-10-15:Closure::__set_state(array(
))2020-10-15:class@anonymous/repo/ch01/php8_mixed_type.
php:28$1::__set_state(array())
```

The preceding code block logs a variety of different data types and then displays the contents of the log file. In the process, this shows us there are no inheritance issues in PHP 8 when a child class overrides a parent class method and substitutes a data type of `mixed` in place of a more restrictive data type, such as `object`.

Next, we have a look at using typed properties.

> **Tip**
>
> **Best practice**: Assign specific data types to all arguments when defining functions or methods. If a few different data types are acceptable, define a union type. Otherwise, if none of this applies, fall back to a `mixed` type.
>
> For information on union types, see this documentation page:
>
> `https://wiki.php.net/rfc/union_types_v2`
>
> For more information on a `mixed` type, have a look here: `https://wiki.php.net/rfc/mixed_type_v2`.

Improving code using typed properties

In the first section of this chapter, *Using constructor property promotion*, we discussed how data types can be used to control the type of data supplied as arguments to functions or class methods. What this approach fails to do, however, is guarantee that the data type never changes. In this section, you will learn how assigning a data type at the property level provides stricter control over the use of variables in PHP 8.

What are typed properties?

This extremely important feature was introduced in PHP 7.4 and continues in PHP 8. Simply put, a **typed property** is a class property with a data type preassigned. Here is a simple example:

```
// /repo/ch01/php8_prop_type_1.php
declare(strict_types=1)
class Test {
    public int $id = 0;
    public int $token = 0;
    public string $name = '';
}
$test = new Test();
$test->id = 'ABC';
```

In this example, if we attempt to assign a value representing a data type other than `int` to `$test->id`, a `Fatal error` is thrown. Here is the output:

```
Fatal error: Uncaught TypeError: Cannot assign string to
property Test::$id of type int in /repo/ch01/php8_prop_type_1.
php:11 Stack trace: #0 {main} thrown in /repo/ch01/php8_prop_
type_1.php on line 11
```

As you can see from the preceding output, a `Fatal error` is thrown when the wrong data type is assigned to a typed property.

You have already been exposed to one form of property typing: **constructor property promotion**. All properties defined using constructor property promotion are automatically property typed!

Why is property typing important?

Typed properties is part of a general trend in PHP first seen in PHP 7. The trend is toward making language refinements that restrict and tighten the use of your code. This leads to better code, which means fewer bugs.

The following example illustrates the danger of relying solely upon property-type hinting to control the data type of properties:

```php
// /repo/ch01/php7_prop_danger.php
declare(strict_types=1);
class Test {
    protected $id = 0;
    protected $token = 0;
    protected $name = '';
    public function __construct(
        int $id, int $token, string $name) {
        $this->id = $id;
        $this->token = md5((string) $token);
        $this->name = $name;
    }
}
$test = new Test(111, 123456, 'Fred');
var_dump($test);
```

In the preceding example, notice in the `__construct()` method that the `$token` property is accidentally converted to a string. Here is the output:

```
object(Test)#1 (3) {
  ["id":protected]=>  int(111)
  ["token":protected]=>
  string(32) "e10adc3949ba59abbe56e057f20f883e"
  ["name":protected]=>  string(4) "Fred"
}
```

Any subsequent code expecting `$token` to be an integer might either fail or produce unexpected results. Now, have a look at the same thing in PHP 8 using typed properties:

```php
// /repo/ch01/php8_prop_danger.php
declare(strict_types=1);
class Test {
    protected int $id = 0;
    protected int $token = 0;
    protected string $name = '';
    public function __construct(
        int $id, int $token, string $name) {
        $this->id = $id;
        $this->token = md5((string) $token);
        $this->name = $name;
    }
}
$test = new Test(111, 123456, 'Fred');
var_dump($test);
```

Property typing prevents any change to the preassigned data type from occurring, as you can see from the output shown here:

```
Fatal error: Uncaught TypeError: Cannot assign string to property Test::$token of type int in /repo/ch01/php8_prop_danger.php:12
```

As you can see from the preceding output, a `Fatal error` is thrown when the wrong data type is assigned to a typed property. This example demonstrates that not only does assigning a data type to a property prevent misuse when making direct assignments, but it also prevents misuse of the property inside class methods as well!

Property typing can lead to a reduction in code

Another beneficial side effect of introducing property typing to your code is a potential reduction in the amount of code needed. As an example, consider the current practice of marking properties with a visibility of `private` or `protected`, and then creating a series of `get` and `set` methods to control access (also called *getters* and *setters*).

Here is how that might appear:

1. First, we define a `Test` class with protected properties, as follows:

```php
// /repo/ch01/php7_prop_reduce.php
declare(strict_types=1);
class Test {
  protected $id = 0;
  protected $token = 0;
  protected $name = '';o
```

2. Next, we define a series of `get` and `set` methods to control access to the protected properties, as follows:

```php
    public function getId() { return $this->id; }
    public function setId(int $id) { $this->id = $id;
    public function getToken() { return $this->token; }
    public function setToken(int $token) {
        $this->token = $token;
    }
    public function getName() {
        return $this->name;
    }
    public function setName(string $name) {
        $this->name = $name;
    }
}
```

3. We then use the `set` methods to assign values, as follows:

```php
$test = new Test();
$test->setId(111);
$test->setToken(999999);
$test->setName('Fred');
```

4. Finally, we display the results in a table, using the `get` methods to retrieve property values, as follows:

```
$pattern = '<tr><th>%s</th><td>%s</td></tr>';
echo '<table width="50%" border=1>';
printf($pattern, 'ID', $test->getId());
printf($pattern, 'Token', $test->getToken());
printf($pattern, 'Name', $test->getName());
echo '</table>';
```

Here is how that might appear:

ID	111
Token	999999
Name	Fred

Table 1.4 – Output using Get methods

The main purpose achieved by marking properties as `protected` (or `private`) and by defining *getters* and *setters* is to control access. Often, this translates into a desire to prevent the property data type from changing. If this is the case, the entire infrastructure can be replaced by assigning property types.

Simply changing the visibility to `public` alleviates the need for `get` and `set` methods; however, it does not prevent the property data from being changed! Using PHP 8 property types achieves both goals: it eliminates the need for `get` and `set` methods and also prevents the data type from being accidentally changed.

Notice here how much less code is needed to achieve the same results in PHP 8 using property typing:

```
// /repo/ch01/php8_prop_reduce.php
declare(strict_types=1);
class Test {
    public int $id = 0;
    public int $token = 0;
    public string $name = '';
}
// assign values
$test = new Test();
$test->id = 111;
$test->token = 999999;
```

```
$test->name = 'Fred';
// display results
$pattern = '<tr><th>%s</th><td>%s</td></tr>';
echo '<table width="50%" border=1>';
printf($pattern, 'ID', $test->id);
printf($pattern, 'Token', $test->token);
printf($pattern, 'Name', $test->name);
echo '</table>';
```

The preceding code example shown produces exactly the same output as the previous example and also achieves even better control over property data types. Using typed properties, in this example, we achieved a *50% reduction* in the amount of code needed to produce the same result!

> **Tip**
>
> **Best practice**: Use typed properties whenever possible, except in situations where you explicitly want to allow the data type to change.

Summary

In this chapter, you learned how to write better code using the new PHP 8 data types: mixed and union types. You also learned about how using named arguments can not only improve the readability of your code but can also help prevent accidental misuse of class methods and PHP functions, as well as providing a great way to skip over default arguments.

This chapter also taught you how the new `Attribute` class can be used as an eventual replacement for PHP DocBlocks, serving to improve the overall performance of your code while providing a solid means of documenting classes, methods, and functions.

In addition, we looked at how PHP 8 can greatly reduce the amount of code needed by earlier PHP versions by taking advantage of constructor argument promotion and typed properties.

In the next chapter, you will learn about new PHP 8 features at the functional and procedural level.

2
Learning about PHP 8's Functional Additions

This chapter walks you through important additions and enhancements introduced to **PHP 8** at the procedural level. The code examples used show new PHP 8 features and techniques to facilitate procedural programming.

Mastering the use of the new functions and techniques in this chapter will help you to write faster and cleaner applications. Even though this chapter focuses on commands and functions, all of the techniques are also useful when developing class methods as well.

The following topics are covered in this chapter:

- Working with new PHP 8 operators
- Using arrow functions
- Understanding uniform variable syntax
- Learning new array- and string-handling techniques
- Securing SQLite databases with the authorizer

Technical requirements

To examine and run the code examples provided in this chapter, the minimum recommended hardware is listed here:

- x86_64-based desktop PC or laptop
- 1 gigabyte (GB) free disk space
- 4 GB of random-access memory (RAM)
- 500 kilobits per second (Kbps) or faster internet connection
- In addition, you need to install the following software:
- Docker
- Docker Compose

Please refer to the *Technical requirements* section of *Chapter 1, Introducing New PHP 8 OOP Features,* for more information on Docker and Docker Compose installation, as well as how to build the Docker container used to demonstrate code explained in this book. Throughout, we refer to the directory in which you restored the sample code for this book as `/repo`.

The source code for this chapter is located here: `https://github.com/PacktPublishing/PHP-8-Programming-Tips-Tricks-and-Best-Practices`.

We can now begin our discussion by examining new PHP 8 operators.

Working with new PHP 8 operators

A number of new **operators** have been introduced with PHP 8. In addition, PHP 8 generally introduces a uniform and consistent manner in which these operators can be used. In this section, we examine the following operators:

- Variadics operator
- Nullsafe operator
- Concatenate operator
- Ternary operator

Let's start with a discussion of the variadics operator.

Using the variadics operator

The **variadics** operator consists of three leading dots (...) preceding a normal PHP variable (or object property). This operator has actually been with the language since PHP 5.6. It's also referred to as the following:

- Splat operator
- Scatter operator
- Spread operator

Before we dive into the improvements PHP 8 has made using this operator, let's have a quick look at how the operator is normally used.

Unknown number of arguments

One of the most common uses for the variadics operator is in a situation where you define a function with an unknown number of arguments.

In the following code example, the `multiVardump()` function is able to accept any number of variables. It then concatenates the `var_export()` output and returns a string:

```php
// /repo/ch02/php7_variadic_params.php
function multiVardump(...$args) {
    $output = '';
    foreach ($args as $var)
        $output .= var_export($var, TRUE);
    return $output;
}
$a = new ArrayIterator(range('A','F'));
$b = function (string $val) { return str_rot13($val); };
$c = [1,2,3];
$d = 'TEST';
echo multiVardump($a, $b, $c);
echo multiVardump($d);
```

The first time the function is called, we provide three arguments. The second time it's called, we only provide a single argument. Because we used a variadics operator, there's no need to rewrite the function to accommodate more or fewer arguments.

> **Tip**
> There is a `func_get_args()` PHP function that gathers all function arguments into an array. The variadics operator is preferred, however, as it must be stated in the function signature, and thus makes the intentions of the program developer much clearer. For more information, see https://php.net/func_get_args.

Vacuuming up remaining arguments

Another use for the variadics operator is to **vacuum up** any remaining arguments. This technique allows you to mix mandatory parameters with an unknown number of optional parameters.

In this example, a `where()` function produces a WHERE clause to be added to a **Structured Query Language (SQL)** SELECT statement. The first two arguments are mandatory: it's not reasonable to produce a WHERE clause with no arguments! Have a look at the code here:

```php
// ch02/includes/php7_sql_lib.php
// other functions not shown
function where(stdClass $obj, $a, $b = '', $c = '',
    $d = '') {
    $obj->where[] = $a;
    $obj->where[] = $b;
    $obj->where[] = $c;
    $obj->where[] = $d;
}
```

The calling code using this function might look like this:

```php
// /repo/ch02/php7_variadics_sql.php
require_once __DIR__ . '/includes/php7_sql_lib.php';
$start = '2021-01-01';
$end   = '2021-04-01';
$select = new stdClass();
from($select, 'events');
cols($select, ['id', 'event_key',
    'event_name', 'event_date']);
limit($select, 10);
where($select, 'event_date', '>=', "'$start'");
```

```
where($select, 'AND');
where($select, 'event_date', '<', "'$end'");
$sql = render($select);
// remaining code not shown
```

You might have noted that `where()` has to be called multiple times as the number of arguments is limited. This is a perfect candidate for the variadics operator! Here is how the rewritten `where()` function might look:

```
// ch02/includes/php8_sql_lib.php
// other functions not shown
function where(stdClass $obj, ...$args) {
    $obj->where = (empty($obj->where))
                ? $args
                : array_merge($obj->where, $args);
}
```

Because `...$args` is always returned as an array, to ensure any additional calls to the function do not lose clauses we need to perform an `array_merge()` operation. Here is the rewritten calling program:

```
// /repo/ch02/php8_variadics_sql.php
require_once __DIR__ . '/includes/sql_lib2.php';
$start = '2021-01-01';
$end   = '2021-04-01';
$select = new stdClass();
from($select, 'events');
cols($select, ['id', 'event_key',
    'event_name', 'event_date']);
limit($select, 10);
where($select, 'event_date', '>=', "'$start'",
    'AND', 'event_date', '<', "'$end'");
$sql = render($select);
// remaining code not shown
```

The resultant SQL statement is shown here:

```
SELECT id,event_key,event_name,event_date
FROM events
WHERE event_date >= '2021-01-01'
    AND event_date <= '2021-04-01'
LIMIT 10
```

The preceding output shows that our SQL generation logic produces a valid statement.

Using variadics operator as a replacement

So far, none of this is foreign to an experienced PHP developer. What's different in PHP 8 is that the variadics operator can now be used in situations where *widening* might come into play.

To properly describe the difference in how the variadics operator can be used, we'll need to briefly return to **Object-Oriented Programming (OOP)**. If we rewrite the `where()` function described just now into a class method, it might look like this:

```php
// src/Php7/Sql/Where.php
namespace Php7\Sql;
class Where {
    public $where = [];
    public function where($a, $b = '', $c = '', $d = '') {
        $this->where[] = $a;
        $this->where[] = $b;
        $this->where[] = $c;
        $this->where[] = $d;
        return $this;
    }
    // other code not shown
}
```

Now, let's say we have a `Select` class that extends `Where` but redefines the method signature using a variadics operator. This is how it might look:

```php
// src/Php7/Sql/Select.php
namespace Php7\Sql;
class Select extends Where {
    public function where(...$args)     {
        $this->where = (empty($obj->where))
                    ? $args
                    : array_merge($obj->where, $args);
    }
    // other code not shown
}
```

It's reasonable to use a variadics operator, as the number of arguments provided to formulate a WHERE clause is unknown. Here is the rewritten calling program using OOP:

```php
// /repo/ch02/php7_variadics_problem.php
require_once __DIR__ . '/../src/Server/Autoload/Loader.php'
$loader = new \Server\Autoload\Loader();
use Php7\Sql\Select;
$start = "'2021-01-01'";
$end   = "'2021-04-01'";
$select = new Select();
$select->from($select, 'events')
       ->cols($select, ['id', 'event_key',
           'event_name', 'event_date'])
       ->limit($select, 10)
       ->where($select, 'event_date', '>=', "'$start'",
           'AND', 'event_date', '<=', "'$end'");
$sql = $select->render();
// other code not shown
```

However, when you try to run this example under PHP 7, the following warning appears:

```
Warning: Declaration of Php7\Sql\Select::where(...$args) should
be compatible with Php7\Sql\Where::where($a, $b = '', $c = '',
$d = '') in /repo/src/Php7/Sql/Select.php on line 5
```

Note that the code still works; however, the variadics operator is not seen by PHP 7 as a viable replacement. Here's the same code running under PHP 8 (using `/repo/ch02/php8_variadics_no_problem.php`):

PHP 8.0.0

Raw Output

```
SELECT id,event_key,event_name,event_date FROM events WHERE event_date >= '2021-01-01' AND event_date <= '2021-04-01' LIMIT 10
  ID |            Key |                          Title |                Date
---- | -------------- | ------------------------------ | -------------------
 153 | CON-PRO-WQ-145 | Conservation Promotion Symposium | 2021-02-15 00:00:00
 155 | TRE-PRO-DF-540 |          Tree Promotion Meeting | 2021-02-28 00:00:00
 157 | SOL-LOV-KV-312 |            Solar Energy Lovers Summit | 2021-03-22 00:00:00
 158 | TRE-BEN-UC-744 |             Tree Benefit Summit | 2021-03-19 00:00:00
 160 | HOR-IND-QM-995 |    Horticulture Industry Showcase | 2021-02-27 00:00:00
 166 | WIN-BEN-AE-715 |         Wind Power Benefit Meeting | 2021-03-12 00:00:00
 178 | HOR-PRO-QT-891 |    Horticulture Promotion Seminar | 2021-03-06 00:00:00
 182 | DOG-BEN-YQ-576 |              Dog Benefit Summit | 2021-03-16 00:00:00
 186 | CAT-PRO-BM-255 |              Cat Promotion Show | 2021-02-25 00:00:00
 211 | DOG-BEN-GZ-755 |           Dog Benefit Conference | 2021-03-28 00:00:00
```

Figure 2.1 – Variadics operator acceptable in extending class

> **Tip**
> Here are two PHP documentation references that explain the reasoning behind the PHP variadics operator:
> `https://wiki.php.net/rfc/variadics`
> `https://wiki.php.net/rfc/argument_unpacking`

Let's now have a look at the nullsafe operator.

Using the nullsafe operator

The **nullsafe** operator is used in a chain of object property references. If one of the properties in the chain does not exist (in other words, it is considered `NULL`), the operator returns a value of `NULL` safely, without issuing a warning.

As an example, let's assume we have the following **Extended Markup Language** (**XML**) file:

```xml
<?xml version='1.0' standalone='yes'?>
<produce>
    <file>/repo/ch02/includes/produce.xml</file>
    <dept>
        <fruit>
```

```
                <apple>11</apple>
                <banana>22</banana>
                <cherry>33</cherry>
            </fruit>
            <vegetable>
                <artichoke>11</artichoke>
                <beans>22</beans>
                <cabbage>33</cabbage>
            </vegetable>
        </dept>
</produce>
```

Here is a code snippet that scans through the XML document and displays quantities:

```
// /repo/ch02/php7_nullsafe_xml.php
$xml = simplexml_load_file(__DIR__ .
        '/includes/produce.xml');
$produce = [
    'fruit' => ['apple','banana','cherry','pear'],
    'vegetable' => ['artichoke','beans','cabbage','squash']
];
$pattern = "%10s : %d\n";
foreach ($produce as $type => $items) {
    echo ucfirst($type) . ":\n";
    foreach ($items as $item) {
        $qty = getQuantity($xml, $type, $item);
        printf($pattern, $item, $qty);
    }
}
```

We also need to define a `getQuantity()` function that first checks to see if that property is not empty before proceeding to the next level, as follows:

```
function getQuantity(SimpleXMLElement $xml,
        string $type, string $item {
    $qty = 0;
    if (!empty($xml->dept)) {
        if (!empty($xml->dept->$type)) {
```

```
            if (!empty($xml->dept->$type->$item)) {
                $qty = $xml->dept->$type->$item;
            }
        }
    }
    return $qty;
}
```

As you start dealing with deeper nesting levels, the function needed to check for the existence of a property grows in complexity. This is exactly where the nullsafe operator can be employed.

Have a look at the same program code, but without the need for the `getQuantity()` function, as follows:

```
// /repo/ch02/php8_nullsafe_xml.php
$xml = simplexml_load_file(__DIR__ .
        '/includes/produce.xml'
$produce = [
    'fruit' => ['apple','banana','cherry','pear'],
    'vegetable' => ['artichoke','beans','cabbage','squash']
];
$pattern = "%10s : %d\n";
foreach ($produce as $type => $items) {
    echo ucfirst($type) . ":\n";
    foreach ($items as $item) {
        printf($pattern, $item,
            $xml?->dept?->$type?->$item);
    }
}
```

Let's now have a look at another use for the nullsafe operator.

Using the nullsafe operator to short-circuit a chain

The nullsafe operator is also useful when used in a chain of connected operations including references to object properties, array-element method calls, and static references.

By way of illustration, here is a configuration file that returns an anonymous class. It defines different methods of extracting data depending on the type of file:

```php
// ch02/includes/nullsafe_config.php
return new class() {
    const HEADERS = ['Name','Amt','Age','ISO','Company'];
    const PATTERN = "%20s | %16s | %3s | %3s | %s\n";
    public function json($fn) {
        $json = file_get_contents($fn);
        return json_decode($json, TRUE);
    }
    public function csv($fn) {
        $arr = [];
        $fh = new SplFileObject($fn, 'r');
        while ($node = $fh->fgetcsv()) $arr[] = $node;
        return $arr;
    }
    public function txt($fn) {
        $arr = [];
        $fh = new SplFileObject($fn, 'r');
        while ($node = $fh->fgets())
            $arr[] = explode("\t", $node);
        return $arr;
    }
    // all code not shown
};
```

This class also includes a method to display the data, as illustrated in the following code snippet:

```php
    public function display(array $data) {
        $total = 0;
        vprintf(self::PATTERN, self::HEADERS);
        foreach ($data as $row) {
            $total += $row[1];
            $row[1] = number_format($row[1], 0);
            $row[2] = (string) $row[2];
            vprintf(self::PATTERN, $row);
```

```
        }
        echo 'Combined Wealth: '
            . number_format($total, 0) . "\n"
}
```

In the calling program, in order to safely execute the `display()` method we need to add an `is_object()` extra safety check and also `method_exists()` before executing the callback, as illustrated in the following code snippet:

```
// /repo/ch02/php7_nullsafe_short.php
$config  = include __DIR__ .
           '/includes/nullsafe_config.php';
$allowed = ['csv' => 'csv','json' => 'json','txt'
            => 'txt'];
$format  = $_GET['format'] ?? 'txt';
$ext     = $allowed[$format] ?? 'txt';
$fn      = __DIR__ . '/includes/nullsafe_data.' . $ext;
if (file_exists($fn)) {
    if (is_object($config)) {
        if (method_exists($config, 'display')) {
            if (method_exists($config, $ext)) {
                $config->display($config->$ext($fn));
            }
        }
    }
}
```

As with the previous example, the nullsafe operator can be used to confirm the existence of `$config` as an object. By simply using the nullsafe operator in the first object reference, if the object or methods do not exist, the operator *short-circuits* the entire chain and returns NULL.

Here is the rewritten code using the PHP 8 nullsafe operator:

```
// /repo/ch02/php8_nullsafe_short.php
$config  = include __DIR__ .
           '/includes/nullsafe_config.php';
$allowed = ['csv' => 'csv','json' => 'json',
            'txt' => 'txt'];
```

```
$format   = $_GET['format'] ?? $argv[1] ?? 'txt';
$ext      = $allowed[$format] ?? 'txt';
$fn       = __DIR__ . '/includes/nullsafe_data.' . $ext;
if (file_exists($fn)) {
    $config?->display($config->$ext($fn));
}
```

If `$config` comes back as NULL, the entire chain of operations is cancelled, no warning or notice is generated, and the return value (if any) is NULL. The net result is that we saved having to write three additional `if()` statements!

> **Tip**
> For more information on other considerations when using this operator, please have a look here: https://wiki.php.net/rfc/nullsafe_operator.

> **Important note**
> In order to pass the format parameter to the sample code file, you need to run the code from your browser as follows: http://localhost:8888/ch02/php7_nullsafe_short.php?format=json.

Next, we look at changes to the concatenation operator.

The concatenation operator has been demoted

Although the precise usage of the **concatenation** operator (for example, the period (.) has not changed in PHP 8, an extremely important change has been made in its relative position in the **order of precedence**. In earlier versions of PHP, the concatenation operator was considered equal to the lower-order arithmetic operators plus (+) and minus (-) in terms of precedence. Next, let's look at a potential problem with the traditional order of precedence: counter-intuitive results.

Dealing with counter-intuitive results

Unfortunately, this arrangement produces unexpected results. The following code snippet presents a counter-intuitive output when executed using PHP 7:

```
// /repo/ch02/php7_ops_concat_1.php
$a = 11;
$b = 22;
echo "Sum: " . $a + $b;
```

Just looking at the code, you would expect output something along the lines of `"Sum:33"`. That's not the case! Have a look at the following output when running on PHP 7.1:

```
root@php8_tips_php7 [ /repo/ch02 ]# php php7_ops_concat_1.php
PHP Warning:  A non-numeric value encountered in /repo/ch02/php7_ops_concat_1.php on line 5
PHP Stack trace:
PHP   1. {main}() /repo/ch02/php7_ops_concat_1.php:0
Warning: A non-numeric value encountered in /repo/ch02/php7_ops_concat_1.php on line 5
Call Stack:
    0.0001     345896   1. {main}()
22
```

At this point, you're probably wondering, *as the code never lies* where does the sum of `11 + 22` come out to `22`, as we see in the preceding output (last line)?

The answer involves order of precedence: starting with PHP 7, it's consistently left-to-right. So, if we use parentheses to make the order of operations clearer, this is what actually happens:

```
echo ("Sum: " . $a) + $b;
```

`11` gets concatenated to `"Sum: "`, resulting in `"Sum: 11"`. as a string. The string is then type-juggled to an integer, resulting in a `0 + 22` expression, which gives us our result.

If you run the same code in PHP 8, notice the difference here:

```
root@php8_tips_php8 [ /repo/ch02 ]# php php8_ops_concat_1.php
Sum: 33
```

As you can see, the arithmetic operator took precedence over the concatenate operator. Using parentheses, this is effectively how the code was processed in PHP 8:

```
echo "Sum: " . ($a + $b);
```

> **Tip**
> **Best practice**: Use parentheses to avoid complications arising from reliance upon order of precedence. For more information on the reasoning behind demoting the order of precedence of the concatenate operator, have a look here: https://wiki.php.net/rfc/concatenation_precedence.

We now turn our attention to the ternary operator.

Using nested ternary operators

Ternary operators are not new to the PHP language. There is, however, a major difference in how they are interpreted in PHP 8. This change has to do with the traditional **left-associative behavior** of this operator. To illustrate, let's have a look at a simple example, as follows:

1. In this example, let's say that we are using a `RecursiveDirectoryIterator` class in conjunction with a `RecursiveIteratorIterator` class to scan a directory structure. The starting code might look like this:

   ```
   // /repo/ch02/php7_nested_ternary.php
   $path       = realpath(__DIR__ . '/..');
   $searchPath = '/ch';
   $searchExt  = 'php';
   $dirIter    = new RecursiveDirectoryIterator($path);
   $itIter     = new RecursiveIteratorIterator($dirIter);
   ```

2. We then define a function that matches those files containing the `$searchPath` search path and ending with the `$searchExt` extension, as follows:

   ```
   function find_using_if($iter, $searchPath, $searchExt) {
       $matching  = [];
       $non_match = [];
       $discard   = [];
       foreach ($iter as $name => $obj) {
           if (!$obj->isFile()) {
               $discard[] = $name;
   ```

```
            } elseif (!strpos($name, $searchPath)) {
                $discard[] = $name;
            } elseif ($obj->getExtension() !== $searchExt) {
                $non_match[] = $name;
            } else {
                $matching[] = $name;
            }
        }
        show($matching, $non_match);
    }
```

3. Instead of using if / elseif / else, however, some developers might be tempted to refactor this function using nested ternary operators instead. Here is how the same code used in the preceding step might look:

```
    function find_using_tern($iter, $searchPath,
        $searchExt) {
        $matching  = [];
        $non_match = [];
        $discard   = [];
        foreach ($iter as $name => $obj) {
            $match = !$obj->isFile()
                ? $discard[] = $name
                : !strpos($name, $searchPath)
                    ? $discard[] = $name
                    : $obj->getExtension() !== $searchExt
                        ? $non_match[] = $name
                        : $matching[] = $name;
        }
        show($matching, $non_match);
    }
```

The output from both functions produces identical results in PHP 7, as illustrated in the following screenshot:

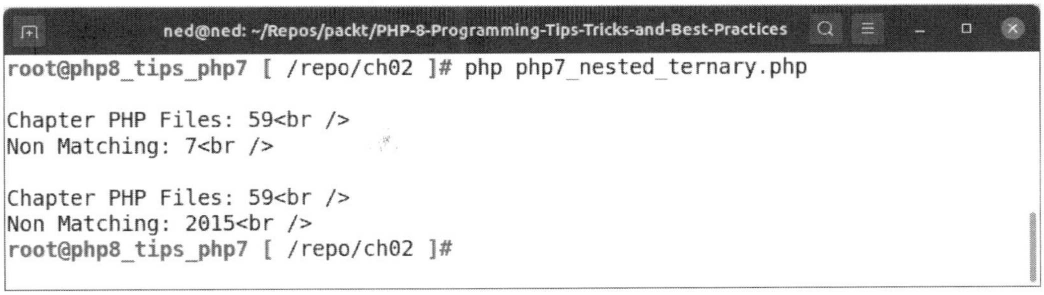

Figure 2.2 – Nested ternary output using PHP 7

In PHP 8, however, the use of nested ternary operations without parentheses is no longer allowed. Here is the output when running the same block of code:

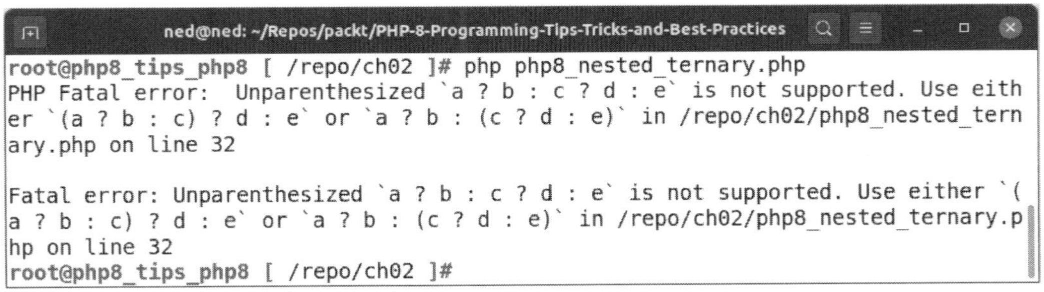

Figure 2.3 – Nested ternary output using PHP 8

> **Tip**
>
> **Best practice**: Use parentheses to avoid issues with nested ternary operations. For more information on the differences in ternary operator nesting, have a look at this article: `https://wiki.php.net/rfc/ternary_associativity`.

You now have an idea of the new nullsafe operator. You have also learned how three existing operators—the variadics, concatenation, and ternary operators—have had their functionality slightly modified. You are now in a good position to avoid potential hazards when upgrading to PHP 8. Let's now have a look at another new feature, *arrow functions*.

Using arrow functions

Arrow functions were actually first introduced in PHP 7.4. However, as many developers do not follow every single release update, it's important to include coverage of this excellent new feature in this book.

In this section, you will learn about arrow functions and their syntax, as well as advantages and disadvantages compared with anonymous functions.

Generic syntax

Simply put, an *arrow function* is a shorthand syntax for the traditional **anonymous function**, much like the ternary operator is a shorthand syntax for if () {} else {}. The generic syntax for an arrow function is shown here:

```
fn(<ARGS>) => <EXPRESSION>
```

`<ARGS>` is optional and include anything seen in any other user-defined PHP function. `<EXPRESSION>` can include any standard PHP expression such as function calls, arithmetic operations, and so forth.

Let's now have a look at the differences between arrow functions and anonymous functions.

Arrow functions versus anonymous functions

In this subsection, you will learn the differences between **arrow functions** and **anonymous functions**. In order to become an effective PHP 8 developer, it's important to gain an understanding of where and when arrow functions might replace anonymous functions and improve code performance.

Before getting into arrow functions, let's look at a simple anonymous function. In the following example, the anonymous function assigned to $addOld produces the sum of the two arguments:

```
// /repo/ch02/php8_arrow_func_1.php
$addOld = function ($a, $b) { return $a + $b; };
```

In PHP 8, you can produce exactly the same result, as follows:

```
$addNew = fn($a, $b) => $a + $b;
```

Although the code is much more readable, there are advantages and disadvantages to this new feature, summarized in this table:

	Anonymous Function	Arrow Function
Less code	No	Yes
Inherits variables	requires `use()`	Yes
Can be nested	Yes	Yes
`$this` automatically bound	Yes	Yes
`$$` indirection supported	Yes	No
Multiple lines of code	Yes	No

Table 2.1 – Anonymous functions versus arrow functions

As you can see from the preceding table, arrow functions are more efficient than anonymous functions. However, the lack of indirection and lack of support for multiple lines means that you still need to use anonymous functions on occasion.

Variable inheritance

Anonymous functions, much like any standard PHP function, only recognize variables outside their scope if you pass the value as a parameter, use a global keyword, or add a `use()` modifier.

Here is an example of where a `DateTime` instance is inherited into an anonymous function by way of `use()`:

```
// /repo/ch02/php8_arrow_func_2.php
// not all code shown

$old = function ($today) use ($format) {
    return $today->format($format);
};
```

Here is exactly the same thing using an arrow function:

```
$new = fn($today) => $today->format($format);
```

As you can see, the syntax is extremely readable and concise. Let's now examine a practical example that incorporates arrow functions.

Practical example: Using arrow functions

Returning to the idea of producing a difficult-to-read CAPTCHA (first presented in *Chapter 1*, *Introducing New PHP 8 OOP Features*), let's have a look at how incorporating arrow functions might improve efficiency and reduce the amount of coding required. We now examine a script that produces a text-based CAPTCHA, as follows:

1. First, we define a function that generates a string consisting of a random selection of letters, numbers, and special characters. Note in the following code snippet the use of the new PHP 8 `match` expression combined with arrow functions (highlighted):

```php
// /repo/ch02/php8_arrow_func_3.php
function genKey(int $size) {
    $alpha1   = range('A','Z');
    $alpha2   = range('a','z');
    $special  = '!@#$%^&*()_+,./[]{}|=-';
    $len      = strlen($special) - 1;
    $numeric  = range(0, 9);
    $text     = '';
    for ($x = 0; $x < $size; $x++) {
        $algo = rand(1,4);
        $func = match ($algo) {
            1 => fn() => $alpha1[array_rand($alpha1)],
            2 => fn() => $alpha2[array_rand($alpha2)],
            3 => fn() => $special[rand(0,$len)],
            4 => fn() =>
                    $numeric[array_rand($numeric)],
            default => fn() => ' '
        };
        $text .= $func();
    }
    return $text;
}
```

2. We then define a `textCaptcha()` function to produce the text CAPTCHA. We first define two arrays representing algorithms and colors. These are then *shuffled* to further the randomization. We also define **HyperText Markup Language (HTML)** `<span>` elements to produce large and small characters, as illustrated in the following code snippet:

```
function textCaptcha(string $text) {
    $algos = ['upper','lower','bold',
             'italics','large','small'];
    $color = ['#EAA8A8','#B0F6B0','#F5F596',
             '#E5E5E5','white','white'];
    $lgSpan = '<span style="font-size:32pt;">';
    $smSpan = '<span style="font-size:8pt;">';
    shuffle($algos);
    shuffle($color);
```

3. Next, we define a series of `InfiniteIterator` instances. This is a useful **Standard PHP Library (SPL)** class that allows you to continue to call `next()` without having to check to see if you're at the end of the iteration. What this iterator class does is automatically move the pointer back to the top of the array, allowing you to iterate infinitely. The code can be seen in the following snippet:

```
    $bkgTmp  = new ArrayIterator($color);
    $bkgIter = new InfiniteIterator($bkgTmp);
    $algoTmp  = new ArrayIterator($algos);
    $algoIter = new InfiniteIterator($algoTmp);
    $len = strlen($text);
```

4. We then build the text CAPTCHA one character at a time, applying the appropriate algorithm and background color, as follows:

```
    $captcha = '';
    for ($x = 0; $x < $len; $x++) {
        $char = $text[$x];
        $bkg  = $bkgIter->current();
        $algo = $algoIter->current();
        $func = match ($algo) {
            'upper' => fn() => strtoupper($char),
            'lower' => fn() => strtolower($char),
```

```
                 'bold'    => fn() => "<b>$char</b>",
                 'italics' => fn() => "<i>$char</i>",
                 'large'   => fn() => $lgSpan
                                    . $char . '</span>',
                 'small'   => fn() => $smSpan
                                    . $char . '</span>',
                 default   => fn() => $char
             };
             $captcha .= '<span style="background-color:'
                       . $bkg . ';">'
                       . $func() . '</span>';
             $algoIter->next();
             $bkgIter->next();
         }
         return $captcha;
}
```

Again, note the mix of `match` and `arrow` functions to achieve the desired result.

The remainder of the script simply calls the two functions, as follows:

```
$text = genKey(8);
echo "Original: $text<br />\n";
echo 'Captcha : ' . textCaptcha($text) . "\n";
```

Here is how the output from `/repo/ch02/php8_arrow_func_3.php` might look from a browser:

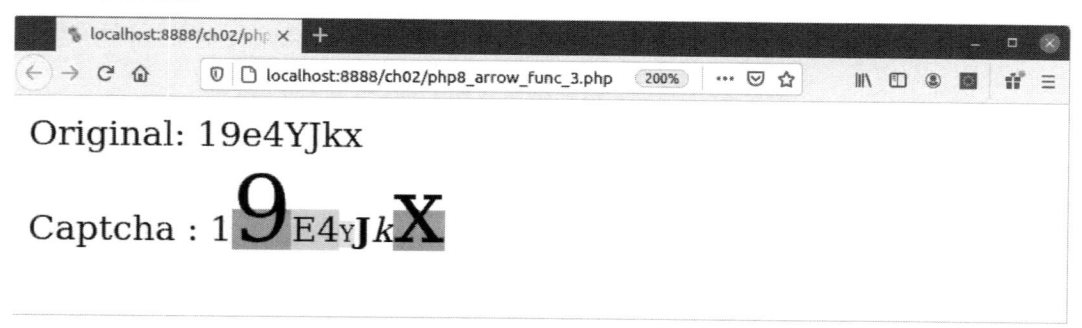

Figure 2.4 – Output from php8_arrow_func_3.php

> **Tip**
> For more background information on arrow functions, have a look here: `https://wiki.php.net/rfc/arrow_functions_v2`.
>
> For information on `InfiniteIterator`, have a look at the PHP documentation here: `https://www.php.net/InfiniteIterator`.

Let's now have a look at *uniform variable syntax*.

Understanding uniform variable syntax

One of the most radical initiatives introduced in PHP 7.0 was an effort at normalizing PHP syntax. The problem with earlier versions of PHP was that in some cases operations were parsed from left to right, whereas in other cases this was done from right to left. This inconsistency was the root cause of any of a number of programming vulnerabilities and difficulties. As a result, an initiative known as **uniform variable syntax** was launched by the PHP core development team. But first, let's define key points that form the uniform variable syntax initiative.

Defining uniform variable syntax

Uniform variable syntax is neither a protocol nor a formal language construct. Rather, it is a guiding principle that strives to ensure all operations are performed in a uniform and consistent manner.

Here are some key points from this initiative:

- Uniformity in the order and referencing of variables
- Uniformity in function calls
- Straightening out problems with array de-referencing
- Providing the ability to mix function calls and array de-referencing in a single command

> **Tip**
> For more information on the original proposal for PHP 7 uniform variable syntax, have a look here: `https://wiki.php.net/rfc/uniform_variable_syntax`.

Let's now examine how the uniform variable syntax initiative affects PHP 8.

How does uniform variable syntax affect PHP 8?

The uniform variable syntax initiative was extremely successful in all versions of PHP 7, and the transition was relatively smooth. There were a few areas not upgraded to this standard, however. Accordingly, a new proposal was introduced to address these holdouts. Uniformity has been introduced to the following in PHP 8:

- De-referencing interpolated strings
- Inconsistent de-referencing of magic constants
- Consistency in class-constant dereferencing
- Enhanced expression support for `new` and `instanceof`

Before getting into examples of each of these areas, we must first define what is meant by *de-referencing*.

Defining de-referencing

De-referencing is the process of extracting the value of an array element or object property. It also refers to the process of obtaining the return value for an object method or function call. Here's a simple example:

```
// /repo/ch02/php7_dereference_1.php
$alpha = range('A','Z');
echo $alpha[15] . $alpha[7] . $alpha[15];
// output: PHP
```

The `$alpha` alpha contains 26 elements representing the letters A through Z. This example de-references the array, extracting the 7th and 15th elements, producing an output of PHP. De-referencing a function or method call simply means executing the function or method and accessing the results.

De-referencing interpolated strings

The next example is a bit crazy, so please follow closely. The following example works in PHP 8, but does not work in PHP 7 or earlier versions:

```php
// /repo/ch02/php8_dereference_2.php
$alpha = 'ABCDEFGHIJKLMNOPQRSTUVWXYZ';
$num   = '0123456789';
$test  = [15, 7, 15, 34];
foreach ($test as $pos)
    echo "$alpha$num"[$pos];
```

In this example, two strings, $alpha and $num, are interpolated using double quotes inside a `foreach()` loop. Here is the output from PHP 7:

```
root@php8_tips_php7 [ /repo/ch02 ]# php php7_dereference_2.php
PHP Parse error:  syntax error, unexpected '[', expecting ','
or ';' in /repo/ch02/php7_dereference_2.php on line 7

Parse error: syntax error, unexpected '[', expecting ',' or ';'
in /repo/ch02/php7_dereference_2.php on line 7
```

The same code in PHP 8 produces the following output:

```
root@php8_tips_php8 [ /repo/ch02 ]# php php8_dereference_2.php
PHP8
```

The conclusion is that PHP 7 is not consistent in how it de-references interpolated strings, whereas PHP 8 demonstrates improved consistency.

Inconsistent de-referencing of magic constants

In PHP 7 and earlier versions, constants can be de-referenced whereas magic constants cannot. Here is a simple example that produces the last three letters of the current file:

```php
// /repo/ch02/php8_dereference_3.php
define('FILENAME', __FILE__);
echo FILENAME[-3] . FILENAME[-2] . FILENAME[-1];
echo __FILE__[-3] . __FILE__[-2] . __FILE__[-1];
```

Here is the result in PHP 7:

```
root@php8_tips_php7 [ /repo/ch02 ]# php php7_dereference_3.php
PHP Parse error:  syntax error, unexpected '[', expecting ','
or ';' in /repo/ch02/php7_dereference_3.php on line 7
Parse error: syntax error, unexpected '[', expecting ',' or ';'
in /repo/ch02/php7_dereference_3.php on line 7
```

And here is the result in PHP 8:

```
root@php8_tips_php8 [ /repo/ch02 ]# php php8_dereference_3.php
phpphp
```

Again, the point here is that de-referencing operations in PHP 8 are applied consistently (which is a good thing!).

Consistency in class-constant de-referencing

A related issue arises when attempting to de-reference class constants. To best illustrate the problem, imagine that we have three classes. The first class, `JsonResponse`, produces the data in **JavaScript Object Notation** (**JSON**) format, as illustrated in the following code snippet:

```
class JsonResponse {
    public static function render($data) {
        return json_encode($data, JSON_PRETTY_PRINT);
    }
}
```

The second class, `SerialResponse`, produces a response using the built-in PHP `serialize()` function, as illustrated in the following code snippet:

```
class SerialResponse {
    public static function render($data) {
        return serialize($data);
    }
}
```

Finally, a `Test` class is able to produce either response, as illustrated in the following code snippet:

```
class Test {
    const JSON = ['JsonResponse'];
    const TEXT = 'SerialResponse';
    public static function getJson($data) {
        echo self::JSON[0]::render($data);
    }
    public static function getText($data) {
        echo self::TEXT::render($data);
    }
}
```

As you've seen in earlier examples in this section, results in earlier versions of PHP are inconsistent. A call to `Test::getJson($data)` works fine. However, a call to `Test::getText($data)` produces this error:

```
root@php8_tips_php7 [ /repo/ch02 ]# php php7_dereference_4.
php PHP Parse error:  syntax error, unexpected '::' (T_
PAAMAYIM_NEKUDOTAYIM), expecting ',' or ';' in /repo/ch02/php7_
dereference_4.php on line 26
Parse error: syntax error, unexpected '::' (T_PAAMAYIM_
NEKUDOTAYIM), expecting ',' or ';' in /repo/ch02/php7_
dereference_4.php on line 26
```

Exactly the same code under PHP 8 produces consistent results for both method calls defined in the class shown previously, as illustrated here:

```
root@php8_tips_php8 [ /repo/ch02 ]# php php8_dereference_4.php
{
    "A": 111,
    "B": 222,
    "C": 333}
a:3:{s:1:"A";i:111;s:1:"B";i:222;s:1:"C";i:333;}
```

To summarize, in PHP 8, class constants are now de-referenced in a uniform manner, allowing you to produce cleaner code. Now, let's have a look at how PHP 8 allows you to use expressions in more places than before.

Enhanced expression support for new and instanceof

One of the joys associated with PHP 7 programming is the ability to use arbitrary PHP expressions just about anywhere. In this simple example, note the use of a `$_GET['page'] ?? 'home'` arbitrary expression inside the square brackets referencing the `$nav` array:

```
// /repo/ch02/php7_arbitrary_exp.php
$nav = [
    'home'     => 'home.html',
    'about'    => 'about.html',
    'services' => 'services/index.html',
    'support'  => 'support/index.html',
];
$html = __DIR__ . '/../includes/'
    . $nav[$_GET['page'] ?? 'home'];
```

In PHP 7 and earlier versions, however, the same thing is not possible if the expression involves the `new` or `instanceof` keyword. As you may have guessed, this inconsistency has been addressed in PHP 8. The following is now possible:

```
// /repo/ch02/php8_arbitrary_exp_new.php
// definition of the JsonRespone and SerialResponse
// classes are shown above
$allowed = [
    'json' => 'JsonResponse',
    'text' => 'SerialResponse'
];
$data = ['A' => 111, 'B' => 222, 'C' => 333];
echo (new $allowed[$_GET['type'] ?? 'json'])
    ->render($data);
```

This code example shows the use of an arbitrary expression inside the array reference, used in conjunction with the `new` keyword.

> **Tip**
>
> For more information on uniform variable syntax updates in PHP 8, see this article: `https://wiki.php.net/rfc/variable_syntax_tweaks`.

Let's now have a look at new techniques available for string and array handling in PHP 8.

Learning new array- and string-handling techniques

There have been a number of improvements in PHP 8 array- and string-handling techniques. Although there is insufficient space in this book to cover every single enhancement, we will examine the more significant improvements in this section.

Working with array_splice()

The `array_splice()` function is a cross between `substr()` and `str_replace()`: it lets you replace a subset of one array with another. Its use gets awkward, however, when all you need to do is replace the last part of the array with something different. A quick look at the syntax reveals where it starts to get inconvenient—the `replacement` parameter is preceded by the `length` parameter, as illustrated here:

```
array_splice(&$input,$offset[,$length[,$replacement]]):array
```

Traditionally, developers first run `count()` on the original array and use that for the `length` argument, as shown here:

```
array_splice($arr, 3, count($arr), $repl);
```

In PHP 8, the third argument can be `NULL`, saving an extra call to `count()`. If you take advantage of the **named arguments** feature of PHP 8, the code becomes even more concise. Here's the same code snippet written for PHP 8:

```
array_splice($arr, 3, replacement: $repl);
```

Here's another example that clearly demonstrates the difference between PHP 7 and PHP 8:

```
// /repo/ch02/php7_array_splice.php
$arr  = ['Person', 'Camera', 'TV', 'Woman', 'Man'];
$repl = ['Female', 'Male'];
$tmp  = $arr;
$out  = array_splice($arr, 3, count($arr), $repl);
var_dump($arr);
$arr  = $tmp;
$out  = array_splice($arr, 3, NULL, $repl);
var_dump($arr);
```

If you run the code in PHP 7, note the result of the last `var_dump()` instance, as illustrated here:

```
repo/ch02/php7_array_splice.php:11:
array(7) {
  [0] => string(6) "Person"
  [1] => string(6) "Camera"
  [2] => string(2) "TV"
  [3] => string(6) "Female"
  [4] => string(4) "Male"
  [5] => string(5) "Woman"
  [6] => string(3) "Man"
}
```

In PHP 7, providing a NULL value to the third argument of `array_splice()` causes the two arrays to be simply merged, which is not the desired result!

Now, have a look here at the output from the last `var_dump()`, but this time running under PHP 8:

```
root@php8_tips_php8 [ /repo/ch02 ]# php php8_array_splice.php
// some output omitted
array(5) {
  [0] => string(6) "Person"
  [1] => string(6) "Camera"
  [2] => string(2) "TV"
  [3] => string(6) "Female"
  [4] => string(4) "Male"
}
```

As you can see, having the third parameter as NULL has the same functionality as providing an array `count()` for the third argument to `array_splice()` when running under PHP 8. You will also note that the total number of array elements is 5 in PHP 8, whereas the total was 7 from the same code running in PHP 7.

Using array_slice()

The `array_slice()` function operates on arrays as much as `substr()` does on strings. The big problem with earlier versions of PHP is that internally, the PHP engine iterated through the *entire array sequentially* until the desired offset was reached. If the offset is large, performance suffers in direct correlation to the size of the array.

In PHP 8, a different algorithm is used that does not require sequential array iteration. As the size of the array increases, performance improvement becomes increasingly evident.

1. In the example shown here, we first build a massive array of approximately 6 million entries:

    ```
    // /repo/ch02/php8_array_slice.php
    ini_set('memory_limit', '1G');
    $start = microtime(TRUE);
    $arr   = [];
    $alpha = range('A', 'Z');
    $beta  = $alpha;
    $loops = 10000;      // size of outer array
    $iters = 500;        // total iterations
    $drip  = 10;         // output every $drip times
    $cols  = 4;
    for ($x = 0; $x < $loops; $x++)
        foreach ($alpha as $left)
            foreach ($beta as $right)
                $arr[] = $left . $right . rand(111,999);
    ```

2. Next, we iterate through the array, taking random offsets all greater than `999,999`. This forces `array_slice()` to work hard, and shows a significant performance difference between PHP 7 and 8, as illustrated in the following code snippet:

    ```
    $max = count($arr);
    for ($x = 0; $x < $iters; $x++ ) {
        $offset = rand(999999, $max);
        $slice  = array_slice($arr, $offset, 4);
        // not all display logic is shown
    }
    $time = (microtime(TRUE) - $start);
    echo "\nElapsed Time: $time seconds\n";
    ```

Here is the output when running the code under PHP 7:

```
ned@ned: ~/Repos/packt/PHP-8-Programming-Tips-Tricks-and-Best-Practices
root@php8_tips_php7 [ /repo/ch02 ]# php php7_array_slice.php

Total Elements : 6,760,000
Iterations     : 500
Output Every   : 10 iterations
   5326286 : DE976  |    1459624 : FK570  |    5124216 : FG922  |    5184985 : CN280  |    6150764 : TW599  |
   2141412 : UA692  |    2476971 : ED454  |    1109151 : TR444  |    1169144 : NC573  |    1725761 : XL182  |
   1074824 : ZK853  |    5675948 : JS935  |    3355797 : FD230  |    4680661 : BL636  |    4277145 : DP343  |
   5009483 : ML173  |    3111089 : FH648  |    4766533 : CF922  |    4202015 : ZZ521  |    4455268 : QM368  |
   3096074 : ZU593  |    1024600 : RS762  |    6117826 : BA156  |    3200822 : YO381  |    6389744 : HK591  |
   1033419 : SX530  |    4749989 : PX343  |    6219269 : CR635  |    6676753 : WF475  |    3013320 : OY233  |
   5378777 : UB448  |    5404284 : NC913  |    3968949 : FX712  |    6230174 : GC870  |    2370442 : OW689  |
   2233334 : TM415  |    4568440 : BG808  |    5290640 : KE433  |    4169243 : NN639  |    5305548 : LO437  |
   3922199 : BV314  |    1185229 : HT610  |    6465057 : SB946  |    1305651 : LJ671  |    4935368 : VW589  |
   6711430 : DY665  |    6704402 : TQ582  |    6713508 : FW328  |    3584164 : AM373  |    2149293 : LD184  |

Elapsed Time: 7.3698909282684 seconds
root@php8_tips_php7 [ /repo/ch02 ]#
```

Figure 2.5 – array_slice() example using PHP 7

Notice here the massive performance difference when running the same code under PHP 8:

```
ned@ned: ~/Repos/packt/PHP-8-Programming-Tips-Tricks-and-Best-Practices
root@php8_tips_php8 [ /repo/ch02 ]# php php8_array_slice.php

Total Elements : 6,760,000
Iterations     : 500
Output Every   : 10 iterations
   5206219 : NF452  |    5956429 : HL705  |    3299989 : QR491  |    3286930 : IK502  |    3614739 : GL977  |
   3403365 : OR683  |    2805489 : DL397  |    1717522 : SO681  |    6574381 : KV685  |    4185913 : ER710  |
   3359339 : LJ954  |    2827506 : SG111  |    4933318 : VA834  |    1382645 : IR257  |    1283102 : CC251  |
   3472077 : FL122  |    3550052 : OM172  |    5868277 : WZ837  |    3107605 : BH361  |    5446581 : BX704  |
   3852741 : IJ137  |    1005786 : WC244  |    1368052 : TK846  |    2713304 : TW438  |    6118334 : UO623  |
   5437126 : CG329  |    1480742 : LQ115  |    3154850 : YK442  |    2334535 : LV415  |    5677366 : MG422  |
   4821130 : WC412  |    1777480 : KQ576  |    1669496 : RK590  |    1220459 : KT984  |    4612669 : MJ195  |
   1573504 : RK681  |    6700611 : DV348  |    5659625 : FX491  |    5663479 : YD647  |    4516488 : FC627  |
   2814690 : TI401  |    1727074 : VY150  |    4000088 : HO301  |    3940046 : MG152  |    1882901 : JH205  |
   1888944 : HS356  |    3371001 : RX971  |    1126950 : CG220  |    3220029 : JH801  |    4033689 : ZX974  |

Elapsed Time: 0.76895713806152 seconds
root@php8_tips_php8 [ /repo/ch02 ]#
```

Figure 2.6 – array_slice() example using PHP 8

> **Important note**
>
> The new algorithm is only effective if the array does not contain elements with a NULL value. If the array contains NULL elements, the old algorithm is triggered, and a sequential iteration occurs.

Let's now turn our attention to some excellent new string functions.

Detecting string beginning, middle, and end

Something PHP developers deal with on a constant basis is having to check for sets of characters that appear at the beginning, middle, or end of a string. The problem with the current set of string functions is that they are *not designed* to deal with the presence or absence of a substring. Rather, the current set of functions is designed to determine the *position* of a substring. This, in turn, can then be interpolated in a Boolean manner to determine the presence or absence of a substring.

The problem with this approach is summarized in a famous quote attributed to Sir Winston Churchill:

> *"Golf is a game whose aim is to hit a very small ball into an ever smaller hole, with weapons singularly ill-designed for the purpose."*
>
> – Winston S. Churchill

Let's now have a look at three incredibly useful new string functions that address this issue.

str_starts_with()

The first function we examine is `str_starts_with()`. To illustrate its use, consider a code example where we're looking for `https` at the beginning and `login` at the end, as illustrated in the following code snippet:

```php
// /repo/ch02/php7_starts_ends_with.php
$start = 'https';
if (substr($url, 0, strlen($start)) !== $start)
    $msg .= "URL does not start with $start\n";
// not all code is shown
```

As we mentioned in the introduction to this section, in order to determine if a string starts with `https`, we need to invoke both `substr()` and `strlen()`. Neither function is designed to give us the desired answer. Further, having to use both functions introduces inefficiency in our code and results in a needless resource utilization increase.

The same code can be written in PHP 8, as follows:

```php
// /repo/ch02/php8_starts_ends_with.php
$start = 'https';
if (!str_starts_with($url, $start))
    $msg .= "URL does not start with $start\n";
// not all code is shown
```

str_ends_with()

In a similar vein to `str_starts_with()`, PHP 8 has introduced a new function, `str_ends_with()`, that can be used to determine if the end of a string matches some value. To illustrate the usefulness of this new function, consider old PHP code using `strrev()` and `strpos()`, which might appear as follows:

```
$end = 'login';
if (strpos(strrev($url), strrev($end)) !== 0)
    $msg .= "URL does not end with $end\n";
```

In an operation, both `$url` and `$end` need to be reversed, a process that can gets progressively more expensive in direct proportion to the length of the string. Also, as mentioned earlier, the purpose of `strpos()` is to return the *position* of a substring, not to determine its presence or absence.

The same functionality is achieved as follows in PHP 8:

```
if (!str_ends_with($url, $end))
    $msg .= "URL does not end with $end\n";
```

str_contains()

The last function in this context is `str_contains()`. As we've discussed, in PHP 7 and earlier there was no specific PHP function that tells you whether or not a substring exists within a string, aside from `preg_match()`.

The problem with using `preg_match()`, as we've all been warned time and again, is performance degradation. In order to process a *regular expression*, `preg_match()` needs to first analyze the pattern. It then has to perform a second pass in order to determine which part of the string matches the pattern. This is an enormously expensive operation in terms of time and resource utilization.

> **Important note**
> When we mention that an operation is *expensive* in terms of time and resources, please bear in mind that if your script only consists of a few dozen lines of code and/or you are not repeating the operation thousands of times in a loop, chances are that you will not see any significant performance gains using the new functions and techniques described in this section.

In the following example, a PHP script uses `preg_match()` to search the *GeoNames* project database of cities greater than 15,000 in population for any listing containing a reference to London:

```php
// /repo/ch02/php7_str_contains.php
$start    = microtime(TRUE);
$target   = '/ London /';
$data_src = __DIR__ . '/../sample_data
                    /cities15000_min.txt';
$fileObj  = new SplFileObject($data_src, 'r');
while ($line = $fileObj->fgetcsv("\t")) {
    $tz     = $line[17] ?? '';
    if ($tz) unset($line[17]);
    $str    = implode(' ', $line);
    $city   = $line[1] ?? 'Unknown';
    $local1 = $line[10] ?? 'Unknown';
    $iso    = $line[8] ?? '??';
    if (preg_match($target, $str))
        printf("%25s : %12s : %4s\n", $city, $local1,
            $iso);
}
echo "Elapsed Time: " . (microtime(TRUE) - $start) . "\n";
```

Here is the output when running in PHP 7:

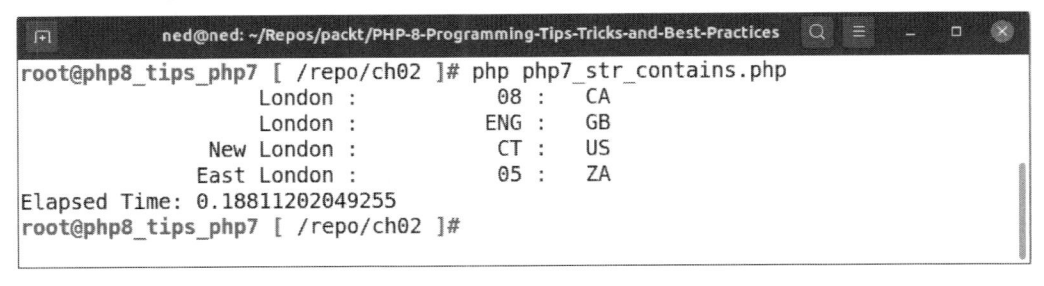

```
root@php8_tips_php7 [ /repo/ch02 ]# php php7_str_contains.php
                   London :       08 :   CA
                   London :      ENG :   GB
               New London :       CT :   US
              East London :       05 :   ZA
Elapsed Time: 0.18811202049255
root@php8_tips_php7 [ /repo/ch02 ]#
```

Figure 2.7 – Scanning GeoNames file using preg_match()

The same output can be achieved in PHP 8 by replacing the `if` statement with the following code:

```
// /repo/ch02/php8_str_contains.php
// not all code is shown
    if (str_contains($str, $target))
        printf("%25s : %12s : %4s\n", $city, $local1,
            $iso);
```

Here is the output from PHP 8:

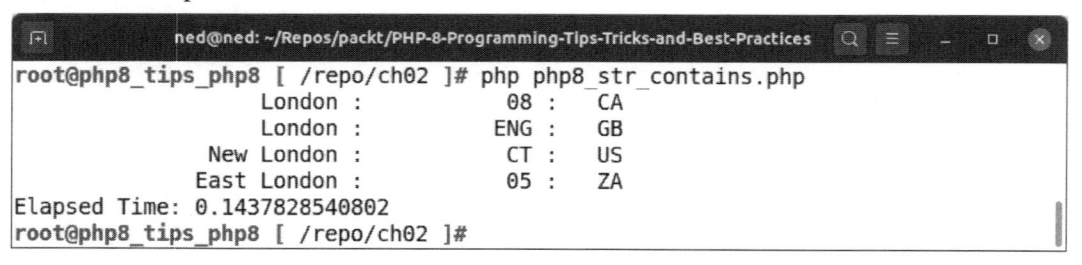

```
root@php8_tips_php8 [ /repo/ch02 ]# php php8_str_contains.php
                   London :           08 :   CA
                   London :          ENG :   GB
               New London :           CT :   US
              East London :           05 :   ZA
Elapsed Time: 0.1437828540802
root@php8_tips_php8 [ /repo/ch02 ]#
```

Figure 2.8 – Scanning GeoNames file using str_contains()

As you can see from the two different output screens, the PHP 8 code runs for approximately `0.14` microseconds compared with `0.19` microseconds in PHP 7. This by itself is not a massive performance gain but, as was mentioned earlier in this section, more data, longer strings, and more iterations magnify any small performance gain you achieve.

> **Tip**
>
> **Best practice**: Small code modifications that achieve small performance gains eventually add up to a large overall performance gain!
>
> For more information on the *GeoNames* open source project, go to their website here: `https://www.geonames.org/`.

You now have an idea how and where to use three new string functions. You are also able to write more efficient code, using functions specifically designed to detect the presence or absence of substrings at the beginning, middle, or end of target strings.

Finally, we end this chapter with a little bit of fun by having a look at the new SQLite3 authorizer.

Securing SQLite databases with the authorizer

Many PHP developers prefer to use **SQLite** as their database engine rather than a separate database server such as PostgreSQL, MySQL, Oracle, or MongoDB. The reasons for using SQLite are many, but often come down to the following:

- **SQLite is a file-based database**: You don't have to install a separate database server.
- **It's easy to distribute**: The only requirement is that the target server needs to have the `SQLite` executable installed.
- **SQLite is lightweight**: Since there's no constantly running server, it takes fewer resources.

That said, the downside is that it's not very scalable. If you have a fairly substantial amount of data to deal with, it's probably better to install a more powerful database server. The other potentially major drawback is that SQLite has no security, covered in the next subsection.

> **Tip**
> For more information about SQLite, please have a look at their main web page: `https://sqlite.org/index.html`.

Wait a minute... no security?

Yes, you heard correctly: by default, by its very design, SQLite has no security. That, of course, is the reason many developers like to use it: having no security makes it super-easy to work with!

Here's a sample block of code that connects to a SQLite database and conducts a simple query of the `geonames` table. It returns a list of cities in India where the population is greater than 2 million:

```
// /repo/ch02/php8_sqlite_query.php
define('DB_FILE', __DIR__ . '/tmp/sqlite.db');
$sqlite = new SQLite3(DB_FILE);
$sql = 'SELECT * FROM geonames '
     . 'WHERE country_code = :cc AND population > :pop';
$stmt = $sqlite->prepare($sql);
$stmt->bindValue(':cc', 'IN');
$stmt->bindValue(':pop', 2000000);
$result = $stmt->execute();
```

```
while ($row = $result->fetchArray(SQLITE3_ASSOC)) {
    printf("%20s : %2s : %16s\n",
        $row['name'], $row['country_code'],
        number_format($row['population']));
} // not all code is shown
```

Most other database extensions require at least a username and password when establishing a connection. As you can see in the preceding code snippet, the `$sqlite` instance is created with absolutely no security involved: no username or password.

What's a SQLite authorization callback?

The SQLite3 engine now allows you to register an **authorization callback** to your SQLite database connection. The callback routine is invoked when sending a **prepared statement** to the database for compilation. Here is the generic syntax to set an authorization callback on a `SQLite3` instance:

`$sqlite3->setAuthorizer(callable $callback);`

The callback is expected to return one of three `SQLite3` class constants, each of which represents an integer value. If the callback returns anything other than one of these three values, `SQLite3::DENY` is assumed and the operation does not proceed. The table shown next lists the three expected return values:

Constant	Description
SQLite3::OK	Success
SQLite3::IGNORE	Statement is allowed to prepare, but is rendered neutral
SQLite3::DENY	Deny access

Table 2.2 – Valid SQLite authorization callback return values

Now that you've got an idea about the callback, let's have a look at how it gets invoked.

What gets sent to the callback?

The callback is invoked when you execute `$sqlite->prepare($sql)`. At that time, the SQLite3 engine passes between one to five parameters to the callback. The first argument is an **action code** that determines the nature of the remaining arguments. Accordingly, the following might be an appropriate generic function signature for the callback that you ultimately define:

```
function NAME (int $actionCode, ...$params)
{ /* callback code */ };
```

The action codes for the most part mirror the SQL statement to be prepared. The following table summarizes a number of more common action codes:

Code (1st Param)	2nd Param	3rd Param	SQL
SQLITE_READ	Table Name	Column Name	SELECT (each result)
SQLITE_SELECT	NULL	NULL	SELECT (first issued)
SQLITE_INSERT	Table Name	NULL	INSERT
SQLITE_UPDATE	Table Name	Column Name	UPDATE
SQLITE_DELETE	Table Name	NULL	DELETE
SQLITE_CREATE_*	Name of item created	Either Table Name or NULL	CREATE TABLE | INDEX | VIEW and so on
SQLITE_DROP_*	Name of item created	Either Table Name or NULL	DROP TABLE | INDEX | VIEW and so on

Table 2.3 – Common action codes sent to callback

It's now time to have a look at a usage example.

Authorizer usage example

In the following example, we're allowed to read from the SQLite `geonames` table, but not to insert, delete, or update:

1. We start by defining an `auth_callback.php` include file in the `/repo/ch02/includes/` directory. In the `include` file, we first define constants that are used in the callback, as illustrated in the following code snippet:

```
// /repo/ch02/includes/auth_callback.php
define('DB_FILE', '/tmp/sqlite.db');
define('PATTERN', '%-8s | %4s | %-28s | %-15s');
define('DEFAULT_TABLE', 'Unknown');
define('DEFAULT_USER', 'guest');
define('ACL' , [
    'admin' => [
        'users' => [SQLite3::READ, SQLite3::SELECT,
            SQLite3::INSERT, SQLite3::UPDATE,
            SQLite3::DELETE],
        'geonames' => [SQLite3::READ, SQLite3::SELECT,
```

```
                SQLite3::INSERT, SQLite3::UPDATE,
                SQLite3::DELETE],
    ],
    'guest' => [
        'geonames' => [SQLite3::READ,
                       SQLite3::SELECT],
    ],
]);
```

The way the **access control list** (**ACL**) works is that the primary outer key is the user (for example, `admin` or `guest`); the secondary key is the table (for example, `users` or `geonames`); and the value is an array of `SQLite3` action codes allowed for this user and table.

In the example shown previously, the `admin` user has all rights to both tables, whereas the `guest` user can only read from the `geonames` table.

2. Next, we define the actual authorization callback function. The first thing in the function we need to do is set the default return value to `SQLite3::DENY`. We also check to see if the action code is `SQLite3::SELECT`, in which case we simply return `OK`. This action code is issued when a `SELECT` statement is first processed and does not provide any information on tables or columns. The code can be seen in the following snippet:

```
function auth_callback(int $code, ...$args) {
    $status = SQLite3::DENY;
    $table  = DEFAULT_TABLE;
    if ($code === SQLite3::SELECT) {
        $status = SQLite3::OK;
```

3. If the action code is anything other than `SQLite3::SELECT`, we need to first determine which table is involved before we can make a decision to allow or deny the action. The table name is reported as the second argument provided to our callback.

4. Here is the perfect time to use a *variadics operator* as we are unsure exactly how many parameters might be passed. However, for the major operations of concern (for example, `INSERT`, `UPDATE`, or `DELETE`), what is placed into the first position in `$args` is the table name. Otherwise, we get the table name from the session.

The code is illustrated in the following snippet:
```
    } else {
        if (!empty($args[0])) {
            $table = $args[0];
        } elseif (!empty($_SESSION['table'])) {
            $table = $_SESSION['table'];
        }
```

5. In a like manner, we retrieve the username from the session, as follows:
```
    $user = $_SESSION['user'] ?? DEFAULT_USER;
```

6. Next, we check to see if the user is defined in the ACL, and after that, if the table is assigned rights for this user. If the action code given is in the array associated with the user and table combination, `SQLite3::OK` is returned.

The code is shown in the following snippet:
```
        if (!empty(ACL[$user])) {
            if (!empty(ACL[$user][$table])) {
                if (in_array($code, ACL[$user][$table])) {
                    $status = SQLite3::OK;
                }
            }
        }
```

7. We then store the table name in the session and return the status code, as illustrated in the following code snippet:
```
    } // end of "if ($code === SQLite3::SELECT)"
    $_SESSION['table'] = $table;
    return $status;
} // end of function definition
```

We now turn our attention to the calling program.

8. After including the PHP file defining the authorization callback, we simulate acquiring the username by accepting a command-line parameter, a **Uniform Resource Locator** (**URL**) parameter, or simply assigning admin, as illustrated in the following code snippet:

```
// /repo/ch02/php8_sqlite_auth_admin.php
include __DIR__ . '/includes/auth_callback.php';
// Here we simulate the user acquisition:
session_start();
$_SESSION['user'] =
    $argv[1] ?? $_GET['usr'] ?? DEFAULT_USER;
```

9. Next, we create two arrays and use shuffle() to make their order random. We build the username, email, and ID values from the randomized arrays, as illustrated in the following code snippet:

```
$name = ['jclayton','mpaulovich','nrousseau',
         'jporter'];
$email = ['unlikelysource.com',
          'lfphpcloud.net','phptraining.net'];
shuffle($name);
shuffle($email);
$user_name = $name[0];
$user_email = $name[0] . '@' . $email[0];
$id = md5($user_email . rand(0,999999));
```

10. We then create the SQLite3 instance and assign the authorization callback, as follows:

```
$sqlite = new SQLite3(DB_FILE);
$sqlite->setAuthorizer('auth_callback');
```

11. The SQL INSERT statement is now defined and sent to SQLite to be prepared. Note that this is when the authorization callback is invoked.

The code is shown in the following snippet:
```
$sql = 'INSERT INTO users '
     . 'VALUES (:id, :name, :email, :pwd);';
$stmt = $sqlite->prepare($sql);
```

12. If the authorization callback denies the action, the statement object is NULL, so it's best to use an `if()` statement to test its presence. If so, we then proceed to bind the value and execute the statement, as illustrated in the following code snippet:
```
if ($stmt) {
    $stmt->bindValue(':id', $id);
    $stmt->bindValue(':name', $user_name);
    $stmt->bindValue(':email', $user_email);
    $stmt->bindValue(':pwd', 'password');
    $result = $stmt->execute();
```

13. To confirm the results, we define a SQL `SELECT` statement to display the contents of the `users` table, as follows:
```
    $sql = 'SELECT * FROM users';
    $result = $sqlite->query($sql);
    while ($row = $result->fetchArray(SQLITE3_ASSOC))
        printf("%-10s : %- 10s\n",
            $row['user_name'], $row['user_email']);
}
```

> **Important note**
> Not all code is shown here. For complete code, please refer to `/repo/ch02/php8_sqlite_auth_admin.php`.

Here is the result if we run the calling program, setting the user to `admin`:

```
root@php8_tips_php8 [ /repo/ch02 ]# php php8_sqlite_auth_admin.php admin
<pre>
TABLE     | CODE | ARGS                     | SESS
users     |  18  | users::main:             | admin
Unknown   |  21  | :::                      | admin:users
users     |  20  | users:id:main:           | admin:Unknown
users     |  20  | users:user_name:main:    | admin:users
users     |  20  | users:user_email:main:   | admin:users
users     |  20  | users:user_pwd:main:     | admin:users
Name      : Email
fred      : fred@caveman.com
wilma     : wilma@gmail.com
barney    : brubble@rock.net
betty     : bettyr@new.clothes.biz
jporter   : jporter@unlikelysource.com
</pre>root@php8_tips_php8 [ /repo/ch02 ]#
```

Figure 2.9 – SQLite3 authorization callback: admin user

The output from the preceding screenshot shows us that the operation is successful as we are running as the `admin` user, with sufficient authorization privileges. Here is the output when the user is set to `guest`:

```
root@php8_tips_php8 [ /repo/ch02 ]# php php8_sqlite_auth_admin.php guest
<pre>
TABLE     | CODE | ARGS                     | SESS
users     |  18  | users::main:             | guest
PHP Warning:  SQLite3::prepare(): Unable to prepare statement: 23, not autho
rized in /repo/ch02/php8_sqlite_auth_admin.php on line 19

Warning: SQLite3::prepare(): Unable to prepare statement: 23, not authorized
 in /repo/ch02/php8_sqlite_auth_admin.php on line 19
</pre>root@php8_tips_php8 [ /repo/ch02 ]#
```

Figure 2.10 – SQLite3 authorization callback: guest user

The output shows us that the attempt to run `prepare()` is unsuccessful as we are running as a user who lacks sufficient authorization.

This concludes our discussion of this long-awaited feature. You now know how to add authorization to an otherwise insecure database technology.

> **Tip**
>
> Original pull request describing the addition of the SQLite authorizer: `https://github.com/php/php-src/pull/4797`
>
> Official SQLite documentation on the authorizer callback: `https://www.sqlite.org/c3ref/set_authorizer.html`
>
> Action codes passed to the callback: `https://www.sqlite.org/c3ref/c_alter_table.html`
>
> Full list of result codes: `https://www.sqlite.org/rescode.html`
>
> Documentation on the `SQLite3` class: `https://www.php.net/sqlite3`

Summary

In this chapter, you learned about a number of changes introduced by PHP 8 at the procedural level. You first learned about the new nullsafe operator, which allows you to considerably shorten any code in which a chain of object references might fail. You also learned how usage of the ternary operator and the variadics operator has been tightened and improved, and that the concatenate operator has been demoted in the order of precedence. This chapter also covered advantages and disadvantages of arrow functions, as well as how they can be used as a clean and concise alternative to anonymous functions.

Later sections in this chapter showed you how PHP 8 continues the trend toward uniform variable syntax first introduced in PHP 7. You learned how remaining inconsistencies have been addressed in PHP 8, including interpolated string and magic constant de-referencing, as well as improvements in array and string handling that promise to make your PHP 8 cleaner, more concise, and more highly performant.

Finally, in the last section, you learned about a new feature that provides support for a SQLite authorization callback, allowing you to finally provide a degree of security when using SQLite as your database.

In the next chapter, you will learn about PHP 8 error-handling enhancements.

3
Taking Advantage of Error-Handling Enhancements

If you've been a PHP developer for any length of time, you will have noticed that as the language continues to mature, more safeguards are put into place that ultimately enforce good coding practices. Along these lines, one of the key improvements in PHP 8 is its advanced error-handling capabilities. In this chapter, you will learn which `Notices` have been upgraded to `Warnings`, and which `Warnings` have been upgraded to `Errors`.

This chapter gives you an excellent understanding of the background and intent of the security enhancements, allowing you to better control the use of your code. In addition, it's critical to be aware of error conditions that formerly only generated `Warnings` but now also generate `Errors`, in order to take measures to prevent your applications from failing following an upgrade to PHP 8.

The following topics are covered in this chapter:

- Understanding PHP 8 error handling
- Dealing with warnings that are now errors
- Understanding notices promoted to warnings
- Handling the @ error control operator

Technical requirements

To examine and run the code examples provided in this chapter, the minimum recommended hardware is listed here:

- x86_64 based desktop PC or laptop
- 1 **gigabyte** (**GB**) free disk space
- 4 GB of **random-access memory** (**RAM**)
- 500 **kilobits per second** (**Kbps**) or faster internet connection

In addition, you will need to install the following software:

- Docker
- Docker Compose

Please refer to the *Technical requirements* section of *Chapter 1, Introducing New PHP 8 OOP Features,* for more information on Docker and Docker Compose installation, as well as how to build the Docker container used to demonstrate the code explained in this book. Throughout this book, we refer to the directory in which you restored the sample code for this book as /repo.

The source code for this chapter is located here:

https://github.com/PacktPublishing/PHP-8-Programming-Tips-Tricks-and-Best-Practices

We can now begin our discussion by examining new PHP 8 operators.

Understanding PHP 8 error handling

Historically, many PHP error conditions were assigned an error level far below their actual severity. This gave developers a false sense of security as seeing *only* a `Notice` led them to believe that their code was not deficient. Many situations only formerly generated a `Notice` or a `Warning` when in fact their seriousness merited greater attention.

In this section, we look at a number of error-handling enhancements in PHP 8 that continue with the overall trend of enforcing good coding practices. The discussion in this chapter will help you to re-examine your code, with an eye toward greater efficiency and fewer maintenance issues down the road.

In the next several subsections, we have a look at changes to certain `Notice` and `Warning` error conditions that could have an impact on your code. Let's first have a look at changes in how PHP 8 handles undefined variables.

Undefined variable handling

One notorious feature of PHP is how it treats **undefined variables**. Have a look at this simple block of code. Note that the $a and $b variables have not been defined:

```
// /repo/ch03/php8_undef_var.php
$c = $a + $b;
var_dump($c);
```

Running under PHP 7, here's the output:

```
PHP Notice:  Undefined variable: a in /repo/ch03/php7_undef_var.php on line 3
PHP Notice:  Undefined variable: b in /repo/ch03/php7_undef_var.php on line 3
int(0)
```

As you can see from the output, PHP 7 emits a Notice, letting us know we are using variables that have not been defined. If we run exactly the same code using PHP 8, you can quickly see that what was previously a Notice has been promoted to a Warning, as illustrated here:

```
PHP Warning:  Undefined variable $a in /repo/ch03/php8_undef_var.php on line 3
PHP Warning:  Undefined variable $b in /repo/ch03/php8_undef_var.php on line 3
int(0)
```

The reasoning behind this error-level promotion in PHP 8 is that the use of undefined variables, thought by many developers to be a harmless practice, is actually **quite dangerous!** *Why?*, you might ask. The answer is that PHP silently, without your explicit direction, assigns a value of NULL to any undefined variable. Effectively, your program is relying upon a default behavior of PHP that could change in future upgrades to the language.

We cover other error-level promotions in the next few sections of this chapter. Please note, however, that situations where Notices are promoted to Warnings *will not affect the functioning of your code*. It might serve to bring more potential problems to your attention, however, and if so, serves the purpose of producing better code. Unlike undefined variables, undefined constants' errors have now been even further promoted, as you'll see in the next subsection.

Undefined constant handling

The treatment of **undefined constants** has changed when running under PHP 8. However, in this case, what was previously a `Warning` is now an `Error` in PHP 8. Have a look at this innocuous-looking block of code:

```
// /repo/ch03/php7_undef_const.php
echo PHP_OS . "\n";
echo UNDEFINED_CONSTANT . "\n";
echo "Program Continues ... \n";
```

The first line echoes a `PHP_OS` **pre-defined constant** that identifies the operating system. In PHP 7, a `Notice` is generated; however, the last line of output is `Program Continues ...`, as shown here:

```
PHP Notice:  Use of undefined constant UNDEFINED_CONSTANT - assumed 'UNDEFINED_CONSTANT' in /repo/ch03/php7_undef_const.php on line 6
Program Continues ...
```

The same code now produces a *fatal error* when running in PHP 8, as shown here:

```
PHP Fatal error:  Uncaught Error: Undefined constant "UNDEFINED_CONSTANT" in /repo/ch03/php8_undef_const.php:6
```

Accordingly, any bad code you have lying around that fails to first define any constants before use will crash and burn in PHP 8! A good habit is to assign a default value to all variables at the start of your application code. If you plan to use constants, it's also a good idea to define them as soon as possible, preferably in one place.

> **Important note**
> One idea is to define all constants in an *included file*. If this is the case, be sure that any program script using such constants has loaded the file containing the constant definition.

> **Tip**
> **Best practice**: Assign default values to all variables at the beginning of your program code before use. Be sure to define any custom constants before they are used. If this is the case, be sure that any program script using such constants has loaded the file containing the constant definition.

Error-level defaults

It's useful to note that the error-level defaults assigned to the `php.ini` file `error_reporting` directive have been updated in PHP 8. In PHP 7, the default `error_reporting` level was as follows:

```
error_reporting=E_ALL & ~E_NOTICE & ~E_STRICT & ~E_DEPRECATED
```

In PHP 8, the new level is much simpler, as you can see here:

```
error_reporting=E_ALL
```

It's also worth noting that the `php.ini` file setting `display_startup_errors` is now enabled by default. This might be an issue for production servers, as your website might start to unintentionally reveal error information upon PHP startup.

The key takeaway from this section is that in the past, PHP has allowed you to *get away with* certain bad practices by only issuing `Notices` or `Warnings`. As you've learned in this section, however, the danger in not addressing the issues behind the `Warning` or `Notice` generation lies in the actions PHP silently takes on your behalf. Not relying upon PHP to make decisions on your behalf leads to fewer hidden logic errors. Following good coding practices, such as that of assigning defaults to all variables before they are used, helps you to avoid such errors. Let's now have a closer look at error situations where `Warnings` have been promoted to `Errors` in PHP 8.

Dealing with warnings that are now errors

In this section, we look at upgraded PHP 8 error handling pertaining to objects, arrays, and strings. We also examine situations where, in the past, PHP issued a `Warning` but where PHP 8 now throws an `Error`. It is critical that you become aware of any of the potential error situations addressed in this section. The reason is simple: if you fail to address the situations described in this section, when your server is upgraded to PHP 8 your code will break.

Developers are often pressed for time. It could be that there's a massive queue of new features or other changes that must be made. In other cases, resources have been pulled away to other projects, meaning fewer developers are available to perform maintenance. `Warnings` are often ignored because the application continues to run, so many developers simply turn off the error display and hope for the best.

Over the years, mountains upon mountains of badly written code have accumulated. Unfortunately, the PHP community is now paying the price, in the form of mysterious runtime errors that take hours to track down. By promoting to `Error` certain dangerous practices previously raising only a `Warning`, bad coding practices quickly become apparent in PHP 8 as `Errors` are fatal and cause the application to stop running.

Let's start by examining error promotion in object error handling.

> **Important note**
> As a general rule, in PHP 8, `Warnings` are promoted to `Errors` when an attempt is made to *write* data. On the other hand, for the same general circumstance (for example, attempting to read/write properties of non-existent objects), a `Notice` is promoted to a `Warning` in PHP 8 when an attempt is made to *read* data. The overall rationale is that write attempts could result in loss or corruption of data, whereas read attempts do not.

Promoted warnings in object error handling

Here is a brief summation of `Warnings` that are now `Errors` pertaining to the treatment of objects. PHP 8 will throw an `Error` if you attempt to do the following:

- Increment/decrement a property of a non-object
- Modify a property of a non-object
- Assign a value to a property of a non-object
- Create a default object from an empty value

Let's have a look at a simple example. In the following code snippet, a value is assigned to a non-existent object, `$a`. This value is then incremented:

```
// /repo/ch03/php8_warn_prop_nobj.php
$a->test = 0;
$a->test++;
var_dump($a);
```

Here is the PHP 7 output:

```
PHP Warning:  Creating default object from empty value in /
repo/ch03/php8_warn_prop_nobj.php on line 4
class stdClass#1 (1) {
  public $test =>
  int(1)
}
```

As you can see, in PHP 7 a `stdClass()` instance is silently created and a `Warning` is issued, but the operation is allowed to continue. If we run the same code under PHP 8, notice here the difference in output:

```
PHP Fatal error:  Uncaught Error: Attempt to assign property
"test" on null in /repo/ch03/php8_warn_prop_nobj.php:4
```

The good news is in PHP 8 the `Error` is **thrown**, which means we could easily catch it by implementing a `try()`/`catch()` block. As an example, here's how the code shown previously might be rewritten:

```
try {
    $a->test = 0;
    $a->test++;
    var_dump($a);
} catch (Error $e) {
    error_log(__FILE__ . ':' . $e->getMessage());
}
```

As you can see, any problems with the three lines are now wrapped safely inside a `try()`/`catch()` block, meaning that recovery is possible. We now turn our attention to array error-handling enhancements.

Promoted warnings in array handling

A number of bad practices regarding arrays, allowed in PHP 7 and earlier versions, now throw an `Error`. As discussed in the previous subsection, PHP 8 array error-handling changes serve to give you a more forceful response to the error situations we describe here. The ultimate goal of these enhancements is to nudge developers toward good coding practices.

Here is brief list of array-handling warnings promoted to errors:

- Cannot add an element to the array as the next element is already occupied
- Cannot unset the offset in a non-array variable
- Only `array` and `Traversable` types can be unpacked
- Illegal offset types

Let's now examine each of the error conditions on this list, one by one.

Next element already occupied

In order to illustrate one possible scenario where the next array element cannot be assigned as it's already occupied, have a look at this simple code example:

```
// ch03/php8_warn_array_occupied.php
$a[PHP_INT_MAX] = 'This is the end!';
$a[] = 'Off the deep end';
```

Assume that, for some reason, an assignment is made to an array element whose numeric key is the largest-sized integer possible (represented by the `PHP_INT_MAX` pre-defined constant). If we subsequently attempt to assign a value to the next element, we have a problem!

Here is the result of running this block of code in PHP 7:

```
PHP Warning:  Cannot add element to the array as the next
element is already occupied in
/repo/ch03/php8_warn_array_occupied.php on line 7
array(1) {
  [9223372036854775807] =>
  string(16) "This is the end!"
}
```

In PHP 8, however, the `Warning` has been promoted to an `Error`, with this output as a result:

```
PHP Fatal error:  Uncaught Error: Cannot add element to the
array as the next element is already occupied in
/repo/ch03/php8_warn_array_occupied.php:7
```

Next, we turn our attention to the use of offsets in non-array variables.

Offsets in non-array variables

Treating a non-array variable as an array can produce unexpected results, with the exception of certain object classes that implement a `Traversable` (`ArrayObject` or `ArrayIterator` as examples). A case in point is using array-style offsets on a string.

Accessing string characters using array syntax can be useful in some cases. One example is checking to see if a **Uniform Resource Locator** (**URL**) ends with a trailing comma or slash. In the following code example, we check to see if a URL ends with a trailing slash. If so, we chop it off using `substr()`:

```
// ch03/php8_string_access_using_array_syntax.php
$url = 'https://unlikelysource.com/';
if ($url[-1] == '/')
    $url = substr($url, 0, -1);
echo $url;
// returns: "https://unlikelysource.com"
```

In the example shown previously, the `$url[-1]` array syntax gives you access to the last character in the string.

> **Tip**
>
> You could also use the new PHP 8 `str_ends_with()` function to do the same thing!

However, strings are definitely **not** arrays and should not be treated as such. In order to avoid bad code potentially leading to unexpected results, minor abuse of the ability to reference string characters using array syntax has been curtailed in PHP 8.

In the following code example, we attempt to use `unset()` on a string:

```
// ch03/php8_warn_array_unset.php
$alpha = 'ABCDEF';
unset($alpha[2]);
var_dump($alpha);
```

The preceding code example will actually generate a fatal error in both PHP 7 and 8. Likewise, do not use a non-array (or non-`Traversable` object) as an argument to a `foreach()` loop. In the example shown next, a string is supplied as an argument to `foreach()`:

```
// ch03/php8_warn_array_foreach.php
$alpha = 'ABCDEF';
foreach ($alpha as $letter) echo $letter;
echo "Continues ... \n";
```

In PHP 7 and earlier versions, a `Warning` is generated but the code continues. Here is the output when running in PHP 7.1:

```
PHP Warning:   Invalid argument supplied for foreach() in /repo/ch03/php8_warn_array_foreach.php on line 6
Continues ...
```

Interestingly, PHP 8 also allows the code to continue, but the `Warning` message is slightly more detailed, as shown here:

```
PHP Warning:   foreach() argument must be of type array|object, string given in /repo/ch03/php8_warn_array_foreach.php on line 6
Continues ...
```

Next, we have a look at situations where in the past you could get away with unpacking non-array/non-`Traversable` types.

Array unpacking

After seeing this sub-section title, you may well ask: *what is array unpacking?* Much like the concept of de-referencing, **unpacking** an array is simply a term for extracting values from an array into discrete variables. As an example, consider the following simple code:

1. We start the example by defining a simple function that adds two numbers, as follows:

    ```
    // ch03/php8_array_unpack.php
    function add($a, $b) { return $a + $b; }
    ```

2. For the sake of the following illustration, assume that the data is in the form of an array of number pairs, each to be added:

```
$vals = [ [18,48], [72,99], [11,37] ];
```

3. In a loop, we use the variadics operator (...) to unpack the array pairs in the call to the add() function, as follows:

```
foreach ($vals as $pair) {
    echo 'The sum of ' . implode(' + ', $pair) .
        ' is ';
    echo add(...$pair);
}
```

The example just shown demonstrates how a developer can force unpacking by using the variadics operator. However, many PHP array functions perform an unpacking operation internally. Consider the following example:

1. First, we define an array whose elements comprise letters of the alphabet. If we echo the return value of array_pop() we see the letter Z as output, as illustrated in the following code snippet:

```
// ch03/php8_warn_array_unpack.php
$alpha = range('A','Z');
echo array_pop($alpha) . "\n";
```

2. We can achieve the same result using implode() to flatten the array into a string, and use string de-referencing to return the last letter, as illustrated in the following code snippet:

```
$alpha = implode('', range('A','Z'));
echo $alpha[-1];
```

3. However, if we attempt to use array_pop() on a string as shown here, in PHP 7 and earlier versions we get a Warning:

```
echo array_pop($alpha);
```

4. Here is the output when running under PHP 7.1:

```
ZZPHP Warning:  array_pop() expects parameter 1 to be
array, string given in /repo/ch03/php8_warn_array_unpack.
php on line 14
```

5. And here is the output from the same code file but when running under PHP 8:

   ```
   ZZPHP Fatal error:  Uncaught TypeError: array_pop():
   Argument #1 ($array) must be of type array, string given
   in /repo/ch03/php8_warn_array_unpack.php:14
   ```

As we have mentioned, here is yet another example of where a situation formerly resulting in a `Warning` now results in `TypeError` in PHP 8. However, both sets of output also illustrate the fact that although you can de-reference a string as you would an array, strings cannot be unpacked in the same manner as arrays.

Next, we examine illegal offset types.

Illegal offset types

According to the PHP documentation (https://www.php.net/manual/en/language.types.array.php), an array is an ordered list of key/value pairs. The array keys, also called **indices** or **offsets**, can be one of two data types: `integer` or `string`. If an array consists only of `integer` keys, it is often referred to as a **numeric array**. An **associative array**, on the other hand, is a term used where `string` indices are used. An **illegal offset** would be where the array key is of a data type other than `integer` or `string`.

> **Important note**
>
> Interestingly, the following code snippet does not generate a `Warning` or an Error: `$x = (float) 22/7; $arr[$x] = 'Value of Pi';`. The value of `$x` is first converted to an `integer`, truncating any decimal component, before the array assignment is made.

As an example, have a look at this code fragment. Note that the index key for the last array element is an object:

```
// ch03/php8_warn_array_offset.php
$obj = new stdClass();
$b = ['A' => 1, 'B' => 2, $obj => 3];
var_dump($b);
```

The output running under PHP 7 produces the `var_dump()` output with a `Warning`, as illustrated here:

```
PHP Warning:  Illegal offset type in /repo/ch03/php8_warn_
array_offset.php on line 6
```

```
array(2) {
  'A' => int(1)
  'B' => int(2)
}
```

In PHP 8, however, `var_dump()` is never executed as a `TypeError` is thrown, as shown here:

```
PHP Fatal error: Uncaught TypeError: Illegal offset type in /
repo/ch03/php8_warn_array_offset.php:6
```

The same principle regarding illegal array offsets is present when using `unset()`, as illustrated in this code example:

```
// ch03/php8_warn_array_offset.php
$obj = new stdClass();
$b = ['A' => 1, 'B' => 2, 'C' => 3];
unset($b[$obj]);
var_dump($b);
```

The stricter control of array index keys is also seen when using illegal offsets in `empty()` or `isset()`, as shown in this code fragment:

```
// ch03/php8_warn_array_empty.php
$obj = new stdClass();
$obj->c = 'C';
$b = ['A' => 1, 'B' => 2, 'C' => 3];
$message = (empty($b[$obj])) ? 'NOT FOUND' : 'FOUND';
echo "$message\n";
```

In both of the previous code examples, in PHP 7 and earlier the code example completes with a `Warning`, whereas in PHP 8 an `Error` is thrown. Unless the `Error` is caught, the code example will not complete.

> **Tip**
> **Best practice**: When initializing an array, be sure that the array index data type is either an `integer` or a `string`.

Next, we have a look at error promotions in string handling.

Promoted warnings in string handling

The same discussion about promoted warnings pertaining to objects and arrays also applies to PHP 8 string error handling. In this subsection, we examine two string-handling `Warnings` promoted to `Errors`, outlined here:

- Offset not contained in the string
- Empty string offset
- Let's start by examining offsets not contained in a string.

Offset not contained in the string.

As an example of the first situation, have a look at the following code sample. Here, we start with a string assigned all letters of the alphabet. We then use `strpos()` to return the position of the letter `Z`, starting at offset `0`. On the next line, we do the same thing; however, the offset of `27` is off the end of the string:

```
// /repo/ch03/php8_error_str_pos.php
$str = 'ABCDEFGHIJKLMNOPQRSTUVWXYZ';
echo $str[strpos($str, 'Z', 0)];
echo $str[strpos($str, 'Z', 27)];
```

In PHP 7, as expected, an output of `Z` is returned, with a `Warning` from `strpos()` and a `Notice` that an offset cast (more on that in the next section) occurred. Here is the PHP 7 output:

```
Z
PHP Warning:  strpos(): Offset not contained in string in /repo/ch03/php8_error_str_pos.php on line 7
PHP Notice:  String offset cast occurred in /repo/ch03/php8_error_str_pos.php on line 7
```

In PHP 8, however, a fatal `ValueError` is thrown, as seen here:

```
Z
PHP Fatal error:  Uncaught ValueError: strpos(): Argument #3 ($offset) must be contained in argument #1 ($haystack) in /repo/ch03/php8_error_str_pos.php:7
```

The key point we need to convey in this situation is that allowing such bad coding to remain was marginally acceptable in the past. Following a PHP 8 upgrade, however, as you can clearly see from the output, your code will fail. Now, let's have a look at empty string offsets.

Empty string offset error handling

Believe it or not, in versions of PHP prior to PHP 7, developers were allowed to remove characters from a string by assigning an empty value to the target offset. As an example, have a look at this block of code:

```
// /repo/ch03/php8_error_str_empty.php
$str = 'ABCDEFGHIJKLMNOPQRSTUVWXYZ';
$str[5] = '';
echo $str . "\n";
```

The intent of this code example is to remove the letter F from the string represented by `$str`. Amazingly, in PHP 5.6, you can see from this screenshot that the attempt is entirely successful:

```
root@d11f85970fce [ /tmp ]# php --version
PHP 5.6.40 (cli) (built: May 16 2020 12:23:14)
Copyright (c) 1997-2016 The PHP Group
Zend Engine v2.6.0, Copyright (c) 1998-2016 Zend Technologies
    with Xdebug v2.5.5, Copyright (c) 2002-2017, by Derick Rethans
root@d11f85970fce [ /tmp ]# cat test.php
<?php
// /repo/ch03/php8_error_str_empty.php

$str = 'ABCDEFGHIJKLMNOPQRSTUVWXYZ';
$str[5] = '';
echo $str . "\n";

root@d11f85970fce [ /tmp ]# php test.php
ABCDEGHIJKLMNOPQRSTUVWXYZ
root@d11f85970fce [ /tmp ]#
```

Figure 3.1 – PHP 5.6 output showing successful character removal

Please note that the virtual environments we use to demonstrate code in this book allow access to both PHP 7.1 and PHP 8. In order to properly demonstrate how PHP 5 behaved, we mounted a PHP 5.6 Docker image and took a screenshot of the result.

In PHP 7, however, this practice is prohibited and a `Warning` is issued, as seen here:

```
PHP Warning:  Cannot assign an empty string to a string offset in /repo/ch03/php8_error_str_empty.php on line 5
ABCDEFGHIJKLMNOPQRSTUVWXYZ
```

As you can see from the preceding output, the script is allowed to execute; however, the attempt to remove the letter F is unsuccessful. In PHP 8, as we have discussed, the `Warning` is promoted to an `Error` and the entire script aborts, as shown here:

```
PHP Fatal error:  Uncaught Error: Cannot assign an empty string to a string offset in /repo/ch03/php8_error_str_empty.php:5
```

We next examine situations where former `Notices` are promoted to `Warnings` in PHP 8.

Understanding notices promoted to warnings

There are a number of situations that are considered less critical to the stability of the PHP engine during runtime that were underrated in versions of PHP prior to PHP 7. Unfortunately, it was customary for new (or perhaps lazy!) PHP developers to simply ignore `Notices` in their rush to get their code into production.

PHP standards have dramatically tightened over the years, leading the PHP core team to upgrade certain error conditions from `Notice` to `Warning`. Neither error reporting level will cause the code to stop working. However, it is felt by the PHP core team that the *Notice-to-Warning* promotion will make bad programming practices keenly visible. `Warnings` are much less likely to be ignored, ultimately leading to better code.

Here is a brief list of error conditions leading to a `Notice` being issued in earlier versions of PHP, where the same condition now generates a `Warning` in PHP 8:

- Non-existent object property access attempts
- Non-existent static property access attempts
- Attempt to access an array element using a non-existent key
- Misusing a resource as an array offset
- Ambiguous string offset cast
- Non-existent or uninitialized string offset

Let's first have a look at `Notice` promotions in cases involving objects.

Non-existent object property access handling

In earlier versions of PHP, a `Notice` was issued when attempting to access non-existent properties. The only exception is when it's a custom class where you defined the magic `__get()` and/or `__set()` methods.

In the following code example, we define a `Test` class with two properties, one being marked `static`:

```
// /repo/ch03/php8_warn_undef_prop.php
class Test {
    public static $stat = 'STATIC';
    public $exists = 'NORMAL';
}
$obj = new Test();
```

We then attempt to `echo` existing and non-existent properties, as follows:

```
echo $obj->exists;
echo $obj->does_not_exist;
```

Unsurprisingly, the output in PHP 7 returns a `Notice` when the non-existent property `echo` attempt is made, as shown here:

```
NORMAL
PHP Notice:  Undefined property: Test::$does_not_exist in /repo/ch03/php8_warn_undef_prop.php on line 14
```

The same code file, in PHP 8, now returns a `Warning`, as seen here:

```
NORMAL
PHP Warning:  Undefined property: Test::$does_not_exist in /repo/ch03/php8_warn_undef_prop.php on line 14
```

> **Important note**
> The `Test::$does_not_exist` error message does not mean we attempted static access. It simply means that a `$does_not_exist` property is associated with a `Test` class.

We now add lines of code attempting to access a non-existent static property, as follows:

```
try {
    echo Test::$stat;
    echo Test::$does_not_exist;
} catch (Error $e) {
    echo __LINE__ . ':' . $e;
}
```

Interestingly, both PHP 7 and PHP 8 now issue a fatal error, as seen here:

```
STATIC
22:Error: Access to undeclared static property Test::$does_not_exist in /repo/ch03/php8_warn_undef_prop.php:20
```

Anytime a block of code that previously issued a `Warning` now issues an `Error` is cause for concern. If possible, scan your code for static references to static class properties and make sure they are defined. Otherwise, after a PHP 8 upgrade, your code will fail.

Let's now have a look at non-existent offset handling.

Non-existent offset handling

As mentioned in the previous section, in general, `Notices` have been promoted to `Warnings` where data is read, whereas `Warnings` have been promoted to `Errors` where data is written (and could conceivably result in *lost* data). The handling of non-existent offsets follows this logic.

In the following example, an array key is drawn from a string. In both cases, the offset doesn't exist:

```
// /repo/ch03/php8_warn_undef_array_key.php
$key  = 'ABCDEF';
$vals = ['A' => 111, 'B' => 222, 'C' => 333];
echo $vals[$key[6]];
```

In PHP 7, the result is a `Notice`, as seen here:

```
PHP Notice:  Uninitialized string offset: 6 in /repo/ch03/php8_warn_undef_array_key.php on line 6
PHP Notice:  Undefined index:  in /repo/ch03/php8_warn_undef_array_key.php on line 6
```

In PHP 8, the result is a `Warning`, as shown here:

```
PHP Warning:  Uninitialized string offset 6 in /repo/ch03/php8_
warn_undef_array_key.php on line 6
PHP Warning:  Undefined array key "" in /repo/ch03/php8_warn_
undef_array_key.php on line 6
```

This example further illustrates the general rationale behind PHP 8 error handling enhancements: if your code *writes* data to a non-existent offset, what was previously a `Warning` is an `Error` in PHP 8. The preceding output shows where an attempt made to *read* data from a non-existent offset in PHP 8, a `Warning` is now issued. The next `Notice` promotion to examine deals with misuse of resource IDs.

Misusing resource IDs as array offsets

A **resource** is generated when creating a connection to a service external to your application code. A classic example of this data type would be a file handle. In the following code example, we open a file handle (thus creating `resource`) to a `gettysburg.txt` file:

```
// /repo/ch03/php8_warn_resource_offset.php
$fn = __DIR__ . '/../sample_data/gettysburg.txt';
$fh = fopen($fn, 'r');
echo $fh . "\n";
```

Note that we echo the `resource` directly in the last line. This reveals the resource ID number. If we now try to use the resource ID as an array offset, however, PHP 7 generates a `Notice`, as shown here:

```
Resource id #5
PHP Notice:  Resource ID#5 used as offset, casting to integer
(5) in /repo/ch03/php8_warn_resource_offset.php on line 9
```

PHP 8, as expected, generates a `Warning`, as shown here:

```
Resource id #5
PHP Warning:  Resource ID#5 used as offset, casting to integer
(5) in /repo/ch03/php8_warn_resource_offset.php on line 9
```

Note that in PHP 8, many functions that formerly produced a `resource` now produce an object instead. This topic is covered in *Chapter 7, Avoiding Traps When Using PHP 8 Extensions*.

> **Tip**
> **Best practice**: Do not use resource IDs as array offsets!

We now turn our attention to string-related `Notices` promoted to `Warnings` in the case of ambiguous string offsets.

Ambiguous string offset cast

Turning our attention to string handling, we once again revisit the idea of identifying a single character in a string using array syntax. An **ambiguous string offset cast** might occur if PHP has to perform an internal type cast in order to evaluate a string offset, but where in that type-cast is not clear.

In this very simple example, we define a string that contains all the letters of the alphabet. We then define an array of keys with these values: `NULL`; a Boolean, `TRUE`; and a float, `22/7` (the approximate value of *Pi*). We then loop through the keys and attempt to use the key as a string offset, as illustrated here:

```
// /repo/ch03/php8_warn_amb_offset.php
$str = 'ABCDEFGHIJKLMNOPQRSTUVWXYZ';
$ptr = [ NULL, TRUE, 22/7 ];
foreach ($ptr as $key) {
    var_dump($key);
    echo $str[$key];
}
```

As you might have anticipated, the output running in PHP 7 produces the output A, B, and D, along with a series of `Notices`, shown here:

```
NULL
PHP Notice:  String offset cast occurred in /repo/ch03/php8_warn_amb_offset.php on line 8
A
/repo/ch03/php8_warn_amb_offset.php:7:
bool(true)
PHP Notice:  String offset cast occurred in /repo/ch03/php8_
```

```
warn_amb_offset.php on line 8
B
/repo/ch03/php8_warn_amb_offset.php:7:
double(3.1428571428571)
PHP Notice:  String offset cast occurred in /repo/ch03/php8_warn_amb_offset.php on line 8
D
```

PHP 8 consistently produces the same results, but here, a `Warning` has taken the place of the `Notice`:

```
NULL
PHP Warning:  String offset cast occurred in /repo/ch03/php8_warn_amb_offset.php on line 8
A
bool(true)
PHP Warning:  String offset cast occurred in /repo/ch03/php8_warn_amb_offset.php on line 8
B
float(3.142857142857143)
PHP Warning:  String offset cast occurred in /repo/ch03/php8_warn_amb_offset.php on line 8
D
```

Let's now have a look at non-existent offset handling.

Uninitialized or non-existent string offsets

This type of error is designed to trap access to strings using offsets, where the offset is out of bounds. Here's a very simple code example that illustrates this situation:

```
// /repo/ch03/php8_warn_un_init_offset.php
$str = 'ABCDEFGHIJKLMNOPQRSTUVWXYZ';
echo $str[27];
```

Running this code in PHP 7 results in a `Notice`. Here's the output from PHP 7:

```
PHP Notice:  Uninitialized string offset: 27 in /repo/ch03/php8_warn_un_init_offset.php on line 5
```

Predictably, the output from PHP 8 produces a `Warning`, as seen here:

```
PHP Warning:  Uninitialized string offset 27 in /repo/ch03/
php8_warn_un_init_offset.php on line 5
```

All of the examples in this section confirm the general trend in PHP 8 toward enforcing best coding practices.

> **Tip**
>
> For more information on promoted `Notices` and `Warnings`, have a look at this article: https://wiki.php.net/rfc/engine_warnings.

Now, we turn our attention to the (infamous) @ warning suppressor.

Handling the @ error control operator

For years and years, many PHP developers have used the @ **error control operator** to mask errors. This was especially true when using unreliable PHP libraries with badly written code. Unfortunately, the net effect of this usage only serves to propagate bad code!

Many PHP developers are exercising *wishful thinking*, believing that when they use the @ operator to prevent errors from being displayed, this makes it *seem* as if the problem has magically gone away! Trust me when I say this: *it hasn't!* In this section, we first examine traditional use of the @ operator, after which we examine @ operator changes in PHP 8.

> **Tip**
>
> For more information on traditional @ operator syntax and usage, have a look at this documentation reference page: https://www.php.net/manual/en/language.operators.errorcontrol.php.

@ operator usage

Before presenting a code example, once again it's extremely important to emphasize that we are **not** promoting the usage of this mechanism! On the contrary—you should avoid this usage in every case. If an error message appears, the best solution is to *fix the error*, not to silence it!

In the following code example, two functions are defined. The `bad()` function deliberately triggers an error. The `worse()` function includes a file in which there is a parse error. Note that when the functions are called, the @ symbol precedes the function name, causing the error output to be suppressed:

```
// /repo/ch03/php8_at_silencer.php
function bad() {
    trigger_error(__FUNCTION__, E_USER_ERROR);
}
function worse() {
    return include __DIR__ . '/includes/
                              causes_parse_error.php';
}
echo @bad();
echo @worse();
echo "\nLast Line\n";
```

In PHP 7, there's simply no output at all, as shown here:

```
root@php8_tips_php7 [ /repo/ch03 ]# php php8_at_silencer.php
root@php8_tips_php7 [ /repo/ch03 ]#
```

What's interesting to note is that the program is actually not allowed to continue in PHP 7: we never saw the `Last Line` output. This is because, although masked, a fatal error was nonetheless generated, causing the program to fail. In PHP 8, however, the fatal error is not masked, as seen here:

```
root@php8_tips_php8 [ /repo/ch03 ]# php8 php8_at_silencer.php
PHP Fatal error:  bad in /repo/ch03/php8_at_silencer.php on line 5
```

Let's now have a look at another difference in PHP 8 regarding the @ operator.

@ operator and error_reporting()

The `error_reporting()` function is normally used to override the `error_reporting` directive set in the `php.ini` file. Another use of this function, however, is to return the latest error code. However, an odd exception was present in versions of PHP prior to PHP 8, in that `error_reporting()` returned a value of 0 if the @ operator was used.

In the following code example, we define an error handler that reports on the received error number and string when it's invoked. In addition, we also display the value returned by `error_reporting()`:

```php
// /repo/ch03/php8_at_silencer_err_rep.php
function handler(int $errno , string $errstr) {
    $report = error_reporting();
    echo 'Error Reporting : ' . $report . "\n";
    echo 'Error Number    : ' . $errno  . "\n";
    echo 'Error String    : ' . $errstr . "\n";
    if (error_reporting() == 0) {
        echo "IF statement works!\n";
    }
}
```

As before, we define a `bad()` function that deliberately triggers an error, and then call the function using the `@` operator, as follows:

```php
function bad() {
    trigger_error('We Be Bad', E_USER_ERROR);
}
set_error_handler('handler');
echo @bad();
```

In PHP 7, you'll note that `error_reporting()` returns 0, thus causing `IF statement works!` to appear in the output, as illustrated here:

```
root@root@php8_tips_php7 [ /repo/ch03 ] #
php php8_at_silencer_err_rep.php
Error Reporting : 0
Error Number    : 256
Error String    : We Be Bad
IF statement works!
```

Running in PHP 8, on the other hand, `error_reporting()` returns the value of the last error—in this case, `4437`. Also, of course, the `if()` expression fails, causing no additional output. Here is the result of the same code running in PHP 8:

```
root@php8_tips_php8 [ /repo/ch03 ] #
php php8_at_silencer_err_rep.php
Error Reporting : 4437
Error Number    : 256
Error String    : We Be Bad
```

This concludes consideration of the differences in @ operator usage in PHP 8.

> **Tip**
> **Best practice**: Do not use the @ error control operator! The intent of the @ operator is to suppress the display of an error message, but you need to consider why this error message is appearing in the first place. By using the @ operator, you are only avoiding providing a solution to a problem!

Summary

In this chapter, you received an overview of major changes in error handling in PHP 8. You were also given examples of situations where error conditions might arise, and now have an idea of how to properly manage errors in PHP 8. You now have a solid path toward refactoring code that under PHP 8 now produces errors. If your code could potentially lead to any of the conditions described where former `Warnings` are now `Errors`, you risk having your code break.

In a like manner, although the second set of error conditions described only produced `Notices` in the past, these same conditions now cause a `Warning`. The new set of `Warnings` gives you a chance to adjust faulty code and prevent having your application devolve into a seriously unstable condition.

Finally, you learned how use of the @ operator is strongly discouraged. In PHP 8, this syntax will no longer mask fatal errors. In the next chapter, you will learn how to create C-language structures and make direct calls to C-language functions in PHP 8.

4
Making Direct C-Language Calls

This chapter introduces the **Foreign Function Interface** (**FFI**). In this chapter, you will learn what FFI is all about, what it's good for, and how to use it. This information in this chapter is important for developers interested in rapid custom prototyping using direct C-language calls.

In this chapter, not only do you learn about the background behind introducing FFI into the PHP language, but you also learn how to incorporate C-language structures and functions directly into your code. Although—as you will learn—this should not be done to achieve greater speed, it does give you the ability to incorporate any C-language libraries directly into your PHP application. This ability opens the doors to an entire world of functionality hitherto unavailable to PHP.

Topics covered in this chapter include the following:

- Understanding FFI
- Learning where to use FFI
- Examining the FFI class
- Using FFI in an application
- Working with PHP callbacks

Technical requirements

To examine and run the code examples provided in this chapter, the minimum recommended hardware is listed here:

- X86_64-based desktop PC or laptop
- 1 **gigabyte** (**GB**) free disk space
- 4 GB of **random-access memory** (**RAM**)
- 500 **kilobits per second** (**Kbps**) or faster internet connection

In addition, you will need to install the following software:

- Docker
- Docker Compose

Please refer to the *Technical requirements* section of *Chapter 1, Introducing New PHP 8 OOP Features,* for more information on Docker and Docker Compose installation, as well as how to build the Docker container used to demonstrate code explained in this book. In this book, we refer to the directory in which you restored the sample code as `/repo`.

The source code for this chapter is located here:

https://github.com/PacktPublishing/PHP-8-Programming-Tips-Tricks-and-Best-Practices

We can now begin our discussion by gaining an understanding of FFI.

Understanding FFI

The main purpose of a FFI is to allow any given programming language the ability to incorporate code and function calls from external libraries written in other languages. An early example of this was the ability of 1980s microcomputers to incorporate assembler language into otherwise sluggish **Beginners' All-purpose Symbolic Instruction Code** (**BASIC**) programming language scripts using the `PEEK` and `POKE` commands. Unlike many other languages, PHP did not have this capability prior to PHP 7.4, although it had been under discussion since 2004.

In order to gain a full understanding of FFI in PHP 8, it's necessary to digress and have a look at why it took so long for FFI to be fully adopted into the PHP language. It's also necessary to take a quick look at PHP extensions in general, and the ability to work with C-language code. We first examine the relationship between PHP and the C language.

Relationship between PHP and the C language

The **C language** was developed at Bell Labs by Dennis Ritchie in late 1972. Since that time, despite the introduction of its object-oriented cousin C++, this language continues to dominate the programming language landscape. PHP itself is written in C; accordingly, the ability to directly load C-shared libraries, and to gain direct access to C functions and data structures, is an incredibly important addition to the PHP language.

The introduction of the FFI extension into the PHP language gives PHP the ability to load and directly work with both C structures and C functions. In order to make intelligent decisions about where and when you might want to use the FFI extension, let's look at PHP extensions in general.

Understanding PHP extensions

PHP extensions, as the title implies, *extend* the PHP language. Each extension can add **object-oriented programming** (**OOP**) classes as well as procedural-level functions. Each extension serves a distinct logical purpose—for example, the GD extension handles graphic image manipulation, while the PDO extension handles database access.

As an analogy, consider a hospital. In the hospital, you have departments such as Emergency, Surgery, Pediatrics, Orthopedics, Cardiac, X-Ray, and so forth. Each department is self-contained and serves a distinct purpose. Collectively the departments form the hospital. In a like manner, PHP is like the hospital, and its extensions are like the various departments.

Not all extensions are equal. Some extensions, referred to as **core extensions**, are always available when PHP is installed. Other extensions must be downloaded, compiled, and enabled manually. Let's now have a look at core extensions.

Accessing PHP core extensions

PHP core extensions are directly included in the main PHP source code repository located here: `https://github.com/php/php-src/tree/master/ext`. If you go to this web page, you'll see a list of subdirectories, as shown in the following screenshot. Each subdirectory contains C-language code comprising the particular extension:

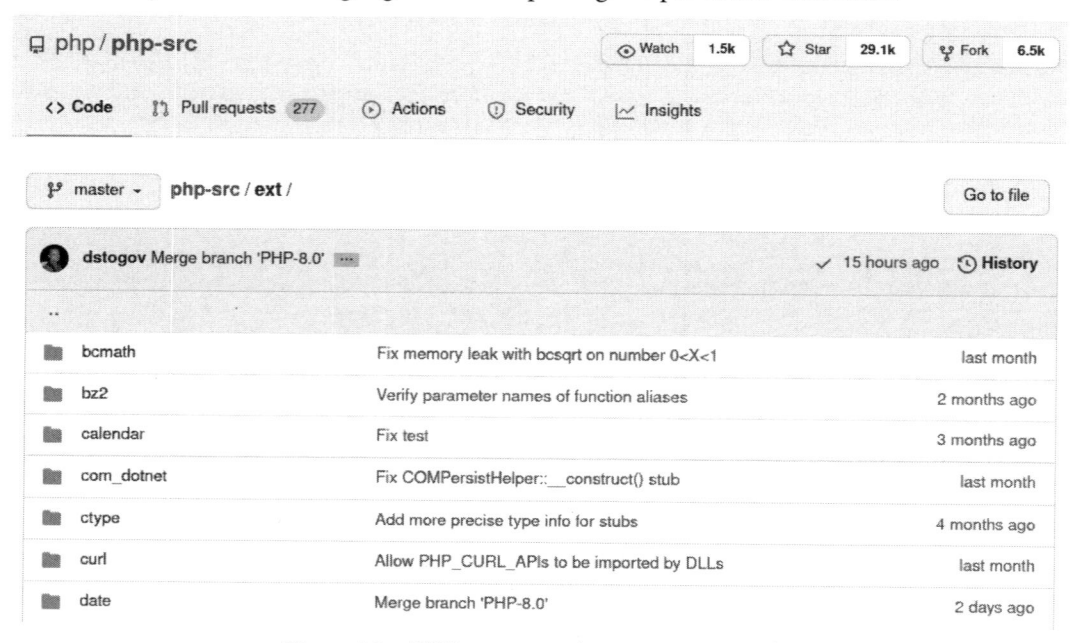

Figure 4.1 – PHP core extensions seen on GitHub

Thus, when PHP is installed on a server, all of the core extensions are compiled and installed as well. We will now have a brief look at extensions that are not part of the core.

Examining non-core PHP extensions

PHP extensions that are not part of the core are usually maintained by a specific vendor (**Microsoft** is an example). Very typically, non-core extensions are considered optional and are not widely used.

Once a non-core extension starts getting used more and more frequently, it's quite possible that it will eventually be migrated into the core. Examples of this are numerous. The most recent is the `JSON` extension: it's now not only part of the core, but in PHP 8 this extension can no longer be disabled.

It's also possible for a core extension to be removed. An example of this is the `mcrypt` extension. This was deprecated in PHP 7.1 as the underlying library upon which this extension relied had been *abandoned* for over 9 years. In PHP 7.2, it was formally removed from the core. We now consider where to find non-core extensions.

Finding non-core extensions

A logical question you might ask at this point is: *Where do you get non-core extensions?* In general, non-core extensions are available directly from the vendor, from `github.com`, or from this website: `http://pecl.php.net/`. There have been complaints over the years that `pecl.php.net` contains outdated and unmaintained code. Although this is partially true, it is also true that up-to-date, actively maintained code does exist on this website.

As an example, if you have a look at the PHP extension for MongoDB, you'll see that the last release was at the end of November 2020. The following screenshot shows the **PHP Extension Community Library** (**PECL**) website page for this extension:

Available Releases				
Version	State	Release Date	Downloads	
1.9.0	stable	2020-11-25	mongodb-1.9.0.tgz (1269.9kB) DLL	[Changelog]

Figure 4.2 – pecl.php.net page for the PHP MongoDB extension

In many cases, the vendor prefers to retain full control over the extension. This means you need to go to their website to obtain the PHP extension. An example of this is the PHP extension for Microsoft SQL Server, found at this **Uniform Resource Locator** (**URL**): `https://docs.microsoft.com/en-us/sql/connect/php/download-drivers-php-sql-server?view=sql-server-ver15`.

The key takeaway from this subsection is that the PHP language is enhanced through its extensions. The extensions are written in the C language. Accordingly, the ability to model the logic of a prototype extension directly inside a PHP script is extremely important. Let's now turn our attention to where you should use FFI.

Learning where to use FFI

The potential for importing C libraries directly into PHP is truly staggering. One of the PHP core developers actually used the FFI extension to bind PHP to the C-language **TensorFlow** machine learning platform!

> **Tip**
>
> For information on the TensorFlow machine learning platform, head over to this web page: `https://www.tensorflow.org/`. To see how PHP can be bound to this library, have a look here: `https://github.com/dstogov/php-tensorflow`.

As we show you in this section, the FFI extension is not a magic solution for all of your needs. This section discusses the main strengths and weaknesses of the FFI extension, as well as giving you guidelines for its use. A myth we debunk in this section is that making direct C-language calls using the FFI extension speeds up PHP 8 program execution. First, let's have a look at what took so long to get the FFI extension into PHP.

Adopting FFI into PHP

The first FFI extension was actually introduced for PHP 5 on the PECL website (`https://pecl.php.net/`) in January 2004 by PHP core developers **Wez Furlong** and **Ilia Alshanetsky**. The project never passed its Alpha stage, however, and development was dropped within a month.

As PHP developed and matured over the next 14 years, it became apparent that PHP would benefit from the ability to rapidly prototype potential extensions directly within a PHP script. Without this capability, PHP was in danger of falling behind other languages such as Python and Ruby.

In the past, lacking a fast-prototyping capability, extension developers were forced to compile their full extension and install it using `pecl`, before being able to test it in a PHP script. In some cases, developers had to *recompile PHP itself* just to test their new extension! In contrast, the FFI extension allows a developer to *directly place* C function calls inside the PHP script for immediate testing.

Starting with PHP 7.4 and carried on into PHP 8, an improved version of the FFI extension was proposed by core developer Dmitry Stogov. After a compelling proof of concept (see the preceding *Tip* box regarding PHP binding to the TensorFlow machine learning platform), this FFI extension version was incorporated into the PHP language.

> **Tip**
>
> The original FFI PHP extension can be found here: `http://pecl.php.net/package/ffi`. For more information on the revised FFI proposal, see the following article: `https://wiki.php.net/rfc/ffi`.

Let's now examine why FFI should not be used to gain speed.

Do not use FFI for speed

Because the FFI extension allows PHP direct access to C-language libraries, there is a temptation to believe that your PHP applications will suddenly operate blindingly fast, at machine-language speeds. Unfortunately, this is not the case. The FFI extension needs to first open the given C library and then parse and pseudo-compile a `FFI` instance before execution. The FFI extension then acts as a bridge between the C-library code and the PHP script.

It might be of relief to some readers that relatively sluggish FFI extension performance is not limited to PHP 8. Other languages suffer the same throttling effect when using their own FFI implementations. There's an excellent performance comparison, based upon the *Ary 3 benchmark*, available here: `https://wiki.php.net/rfc/ffi#php_ffi_performance`.

If you have a look at the table shown on the web page just referenced, you'll see that the Python FFI implementation performed the benchmark in 0.343 seconds, whereas running the same benchmark using only native Python code executed in 0.212 seconds.

Looking at the same table, the PHP 7.4 FFI extension ran the benchmark in 0.093 seconds (30 times faster than Python!), whereas the same benchmark running with just native PHP code executed in 0.040 seconds.

The next logical question is: *Why should you use the FFI extension at all?* This is covered in the next section.

Why use the FFI extension?

The answer to the preceding question is simple: this extension is primarily designed for rapid **PHP extension prototyping**. PHP extensions are the lifeblood of the language. Without extensions, PHP is *just another programming language*.

When senior-level developers first embark upon a programming project, they need to determine the best language for the project. One key factor is how many extensions are available and how actively these are maintained. There is generally a direct correlation between the number of actively maintained extensions and the long-term success potential of a project using that language.

So, if there's a way to speed up extension development, the long-term viability of the PHP language itself is improved. The value the FFI extension brings to the PHP language is its ability to test an extension prototype directly in a PHP script without having to go through the entire compile-link-load-test cycle.

Another use case for the FFI extension, outside of rapid prototyping, is a way to allow PHP direct access to obscure or proprietary C code. An example of this would be the custom C code written to control factory machines. In order to have PHP run the factory, the FFI extension can be used to bind PHP directly to the C libraries controlling the various machines.

Finally, another use case for this extension is to use it to *preload* C libraries, potentially reducing memory consumption. Before we show usage examples, let's have a look at the `FFI` class and its methods.

Examining the FFI class

As you learned in this chapter, not every developer has a need to use the FFI extension. Having direct experience with the FFI extension deepens your understanding of the internals of the PHP language, and this deepened understanding can have a beneficial impact on your career as a PHP developer: it's quite possible that at some point in the future, you will be employed by a company that has developed a custom PHP extension. Knowing how to operate the FFI extension in this situation allows you to develop new features for a custom PHP extension, as well as helping you to troubleshoot extension problems.

The `FFI` class consists of 20 methods that fall into four broad categories, outlined as follows:

- **Creational**: Methods in this category create instances of classes available from the FFI extension **application programming interface (API)**.
- **Comparison**: Comparison methods are designed to compare C data values.
- **Informational**: This set of methods gives you metadata on C data values, including size and *alignment*.
- **Infrastructural**: Infrastructural methods are used to carry out logistical operations such as copying, populating, and releasing memory.

> **Tip**
> The complete FFI class is documented here: `https://www.php.net/manual/en/class.ffi.php`.

Interestingly, all `FFI` class methods can be called in a static manner. It's now time to take a dive into the details and usage of the class associated with FFI, starting with the *creational* methods.

Working with FFI creational methods

The `FFI` methods that fall into the *creational* category are designed to produce either `FFI` instances directly or instances of classes provided by the FFI extension. When working with C functions made available through the FFI extension, it's important to recognize that you cannot directly pass native PHP variables into the function and expect it to work. The data must first be either created as a `FFI` data type or imported into a `FFI` data type, before the `FFI` data type can be passed into the C function. In order to create a `FFI` data type, use one of the functions summarized in *Table 4.1*, shown here:

FFI Method	Returns	Notes
`arrayType()`	`FFI\CType`	Produces a C array. The first argument is the data type produced by a call to `FFI::type()`. The second argument is an array representing the dimensions of the array.
`cdef()`	`FFI`	As an argument you must provide a C language code block. The FFI instance returned provides a bridge between the PHP program and the C language library.
`new()`	`FFI\CData`	Produces a native C data structure. If the first argument is a string, it must be a valid C type. Otherwise, supply an `FFI\CType` object as the first argument.
`scope()`	`FFI`	Creates an FFI instance based upon *pre-loaded* C declarations.
`string()`	`string`	Returns a native PHP string from an `FFI\CData` instance consisting of given number of bytes.
`type()`	`FFI\CType`	Creates an `FFI\CType` object that can be used with other FFI extension classes.

Table 4.1 – Summary of FFI class creational methods

Both the `cdef()` and `scope()` methods produce a direct `FFI` instance, while the other methods produce object instances that can be used to create a `FFI` instance. `string()` is used to extract a given number of byes from a native C variable. Let's have a look at creating and using `FFI\CType` instances.

Creating and using FFI\CType instances

It's extremely important to note that once the `FFI\CType` instance has been created, *do not* simply assign a value to it as if it were a native PHP variable. Doing so would simply overwrite the `FFI\CType` instance due to the fact that PHP is loosely typed. Instead, to assign a scalar value to a `FFI\CType` instance, use its `cdata` property.

The following example creates a `$arr` C array. The native C array is then populated with values up to its maximum size, after which we use a simple `var_dump()` to view its contents. We will proceed as follows:

1. First, we create the array using `FFI::arrayType()`. As arguments, we supply a `FFI::type()` method and dimensions. We then use `FFI::new()` to create the `FFI\Ctype` instance. The code is illustrated in the following snippet:

```php
// /repo/ch04/php8_ffi_array.php
$type = FFI::arrayType(FFI::type("char"), [3, 3]);
$arr  = FFI::new($type);
```

2. Alternatively, we could also combine the operations into a single statement, as shown here:

```php
$arr  = FFI::new(FFI::type("char[3][3]"));
```

3. We then initialize three variables that provide test data, as shown in the following code snippet. Note that the native PHP `count()` function works on `FFI\CData` array types:

```php
$pos   = 0;
$val   = 'ABCDEFGHIJKLMNOPQRSTUVWXYZ';
$y_max = count($arr);
```

4. We can now populate it with values, much as with a PHP array, except that we need to use the `cdata` property in order to retain the element as a `FFI\CType` instance. The code is shown in the following snippet:

```php
for ($y = 0; $y < $y_max; $y++) {
    $x_max = count($arr[$y]);
    for ($x = 0; $x < $x_max; $x++) {
        $arr[$y][$x]->cdata = $val[$pos++];
    }
}
var_dump($arr)
```

In the preceding example, we use nested `for()` loops to populate the two-dimensional 3 x 3 array with letters of the alphabet. If we now execute a simple `var_dump()`, we get the following result:

```
root@php8_tips_php8 [ /repo/ch04 ]# php
        php8_ffi_array.php
```

```
object(FFI\CData:char[3][3])#2 (3) {
    [0]=> object(FFI\CData:char[3])#3 (3) {
        [0]=> string(1) "A"
        [1]=> string(1) "B"
        [2]=> string(1) "C"
    }
    [1]=> object(FFI\CData:char[3])#1 (3) {
        [0]=> string(1) "D"
        [1]=> string(1) "E"
        [2]=> string(1) "F"
    }
    [2]=> object(FFI\CData:char[3])#4 (3) {
        [0]=> string(1) "G"
        [1]=> string(1) "H"
        [2]=> string(1) "I"
    }
}
```

The first important thing to note from the output is that the indices are all integers. The second takeaway from the output is that this is clearly not a native PHP array. `var_dump()` shows us that each array element is a `FFI\CData` instance. Also, note that C-language strings are treated like an array.

Because the array is of type `char`, we can use `FFI::string()` to display one of the rows. Here is a command that produces an *ABC* response:

```
echo FFI::string($arr[0], 3);
```

Any attempt to supply the `FFI\CData` instance to a PHP function that takes an array as an argument is doomed to failure, even if it is defined as an array type. In the following code snippet, note the output if we add this command to the preceding code block:

```
echo implode(',', $arr);
```

As you can see from the output shown next, because the data type is not `array`, `implode()` issues a fatal error. Here is the resulting output:

```
PHP Fatal error:  Uncaught TypeError: implode(): Argument #2
($array) must be of type ?array, FFI\CData given in /repo/ch04/
php8_ffi_array.php:25
```

You know now how to create and use `FFI\CType` instances. Let's now turn our attention to creating `FFI` instances.

Creating and using FFI instances

As mentioned in the chapter introduction, the FFI extension facilitates rapid prototyping. Accordingly, using the FFI extension, you can develop the C functions designed to go into your new extension one at a time, and test them right away inside a PHP application.

> **Important note**
> The FFI extension does not compile C code. In order to use a C function with the FFI extension, you must first compile the C code into a shared library using a C compiler. You will learn how to do this in the last section in this chapter, *Using FFI in an application*.

In order to bridge between PHP and a native C-library function call, you need to create a FFI instance. The FFI extension needs you to supply a C definition that defines the C function signature and the C library that you plan to use. Both FFI::cdef() and FFI::scope() can be used to directly create FFI instances.

The following example uses FFI::cdef() to bind two native C-library functions. This is what happens:

1. The first native method, srand(), is used to seed a randomization sequence. rand(), the other native C function, calls the next number in the sequence. The $key variable holds the final product of the randomization. $size represents the number of random numbers to call. The code is illustrated in the following snippet:

```
// /repo/ch04/php8_ffi_cdef.php
$key  = '';
$size = 4;
```

2. We then create the FFI instance by invoking cdef() and identifying the native C functions in a string $code, taken out of the libc.so.6 native C library, as follows:

```
$code = <<<EOT
    void srand (unsigned int seed);
    int rand (void);
EOT;
$ffi = FFI::cdef($code, 'libc.so.6');
```

3. We then seed the randomization by calling `srand()`. Then, in a loop, we invoke the `rand()` native C library function to produce a random number. We use the `sprintf()` native PHP function to convert the resulting integer to hex, the output of which is appended to `$key`, which is echoed. The code can be seen here:

```
$ffi->srand(random_int(0, 999));
for ($x = 0; $x < $size; $x++)
    $key .= sprintf('%x', $ffi->rand());
echo $key
```

And here is the output of the preceding code snippet. Note that the resulting value could be used as a random key:

```
root@php8_tips_php8 [ /repo/ch04 ]# php php8_ffi_cdef.php
23f306d51227432e7d8d921763b7eedf
```

In the output, you see a string of concatenated random integers converted to hexadecimal. Note that the resulting value changes each time the script is invoked.

> **Tip**
> For true randomization, it might be better to just use the `random_int()` native PHP function. There are also excellent key-generation functions that form part of the `openssl` extension. The example shown here is primarily designed to familiarize you with FFI extension usage.

> **Important note**
> The FFI extension also includes two additional creational methods: `FFI::load()` and `FFI::scope()`. `FFI::load()` is used to directly load C-function definitions from a C header (`*.h`) file during the **preloading** process. `FFI::scope()` makes the preloaded C functions available for use via the FFI extension. For more information on preloading, have a look at a complete preloading example in the FFI documentation here: https://www.php.net/manual/en/ffi.examples-complete.php.

Let's now have a look at FFI extension functions used for comparison between native C data types.

Comparing data using FFI

It's important to keep in mind that when you create a C-language data structure using the FFI extension, it exists outside of your PHP application. As you saw in the preceding example (see the *Creating and using FFI\CType instances* section), PHP can interact with the C data to a certain extent. However, for comparison purposes, it's best to use `FFI::memcmp()`, as native PHP functions might return inconsistent results.

The two comparison functions available in the FFI extension are summarized here in *Table 4.2*:

FFI Method	Returns	Notes
isNull()	bool	Returns TRUE if the FFI\CData instance is a null pointer.
memcmp()	int	Operates in much the same manner as the PHP `strcmp()` function, or the `<=>` operator. Returns a value less than 0 if the first FFI\CData instance is less than the second. Returns 0 if both are equal, and returns a value greater than 0 if the second agrument's value is greater than the first.

Table 4.2 – Summary of FFI class comparison methods

`FFI::isNull()` can be used to determine whether or not the `FFI\CData` instance is NULL. What is more interest is `FFI::memcmp()`. Although this function operates in the same manner as the **spaceship operator** (`<=>`), it accepts a *third argument* that represents how many bytes you wish to include in the comparison. The following example illustrates this usage:

1. We first define a set of four variables representing `FFI\CData` instances that can contain up to six characters and populate the instances with sample data, as follows:

```
// /repo/ch04/php8_ffi_memcmp.php
$a = FFI::new("char[6]");
$b = FFI::new("char[6]");
$c = FFI::new("char[6]");
$d = FFI::new("char[6]");
```

2. Recall that the C language treats character data as an array, so we can't just directly assign a string, even if using the cdata property. Accordingly, we need to define an anonymous function that populates the instances with letters of the alphabet. We use the following code to do this:

```
$populate = function ($cdata, $start, $offset, $num) {
    for ($x = 0; $x < $num; $x++)
        $cdata[$x + $offset] = chr($x + $offset +
                                   $start);
    return $cdata;
};
```

3. Next, we use the function to populate the four FFI\CData instances with differing sets of letters, as follows:

```
$a = $populate($a, 65, 0, 6);
$b = $populate($b, 65, 0, 3);
$b = $populate($b, 85, 3, 3);
$c = $populate($c, 71, 0, 6);
$d = $populate($d, 71, 0, 6);
```

4. We can now use the FFI::string() method to display the contents thus far, as follows:

```
$patt = "%2s : %6s\n";
printf($patt, '$a', FFI::string($a, 6));
printf($patt, '$b', FFI::string($b, 6));
printf($patt, '$c', FFI::string($c, 6));
printf($patt, '$d', FFI::string($d, 6));
```

5. Here is the output from the printf() statements:

```
$a : ABCDEF
$b : ABCXYZ
$c : GHIJKL
$d : GHIJKL
```

6. As you can see from the output, the values of $c and $d are the same. The first three characters for $a and $b are the same, but the last three are different.

7. At this point, if we were to try to use the spaceship operator (<=>) for comparison, the result would be the following:

```
PHP Fatal error:  Uncaught FFI\Exception: Comparison of
incompatible C types
```

8. Likewise, an attempt to use strcmp(), even though the data is a character type, the result would be as follows:

```
PHP Warning:  strcmp() expects parameter 1 to be string,
object given
```

9. Accordingly, our only alternative is to use FFI::memcmp(). In the set of comparisons shown here, note that the third argument is 6, indicating PHP should compare up to six characters:

```
$p = "%20s : %2d\n";
printf($p, 'memcmp($a, $b, 6)', FFI::memcmp($a,
       $b, 6));
printf($p, 'memcmp($c, $a, 6)', FFI::memcmp($c,
       $a, 6));
printf($p, 'memcmp($c, $d, 6)', FFI::memcmp($c,
       $d, 6));
```

10. As expected, the output is the same as using the spaceship operator on native PHP strings, as shown here:

```
   memcmp($a, $b, 6) : -1
   memcmp($c, $a, 6) :  1
   memcmp($c, $d, 6) :  0
```

11. Note what happens if we restrict the comparison to only three characters. Here is another FFI::memcmp() comparison added to the code block, setting the third argument to 3:

```
echo "\nUsing FFI::memcmp() but not full length\n";
printf($p, 'memcmp($a, $b, 3)', FFI::memcmp($a,
       $b, 3));
```

12. As you can see from the output shown here, by restricting `memcmp()` to only three characters, `$a` and `$b` are considered equal because they both start with the same three characters, a, b, and c:

```
Using FFI::memcmp() but not full length
    memcmp($a, $b, 3) :  0
```

The most important thing to take away from this illustration is that you need to find a balance between the number of characters to compare and the nature of the data you are comparing. The fewer characters compared, the faster the overall operation. However, if the nature of the data is such that erroneous results are possible, you must increase the character count and suffer a slight loss in performance.

Let's now have a look at gathering information from FFI extension data.

Extracting information from FFI extension data

When you are using `FFI` instances and native C data structures, native PHP informational methods such as `strlen()` and `ctype_digit()` do not yield useful information. Accordingly, the FFI extension includes three methods designed to produce information about FFI extension data. These three methods are summarized here in *Table 4.3*:

FFI Method	Returns	Notes
`alignof()`	int	Returns the *alignment* of an `FFI\CType` or `FFI\CData` instance. A great way to visualize the return value would be the *block size* in memory.
`sizeof()`	int	Returns the amount of memory used by an `FFI\CType` or `FFI\CData` instance.
`typeof()`	`FFI\CType`	Returns the data type of an `FFI\CData` object. The data type returned is not a PHP native data type. Instead what's returned is an `FFI\CType` instance that identifies the C data type.

Table 4.3 – Summary of FFI class informational methods

We first look at `FFI::typeof()`, after which we dive into the other two methods.

Determining the nature of FFI data using FFI::typeof()

Here is an example that illustrates the use of `FFI::typeof()`. The example also demonstrates that native PHP informational functions do not yield useful results when dealing with FFI data. This is what we do:

1. First, we define a `$char` C string and populate it with the first six letters of the alphabet, as follows:

   ```
   // /repo/ch04/php8_ffi_typeof.php
   $char = FFI::new("char[6]");
   for ($x = 0; $x < 6; $x++)
       $char[$x] = chr(65 + $x);
   ```

2. We then attempt to use `strlen()` to get the length of the string. In the following code snippet, note the use of `$t::class`: this is the equivalent of `get_class($t)`. This usage is only available in PHP 8 and above:

   ```
   try {
       echo 'Length of $char is ' . strlen($char);
   } catch (Throwable $t) {
       echo $t::class . ':' . $t->getMessage();
   }
   ```

3. The result in PHP 7.4 is a `Warning` message. However, in PHP 8, if you pass anything other than a string to `strlen()`, a fatal `Error` message is thrown. Here is the PHP 8 output at this point:

   ```
   TypeError:strlen(): Argument #1 ($str) must be of type string, FFI\CData given
   ```

4. In a similar manner, an effort to use `ctype_alnum()` is made, as follows:

   ```
   echo '$char is ' .
       ((ctype_alnum($char)) ? 'alpha' : 'non-alpha');
   ```

5. Here is the output from the `echo` command shown in *Step 4*:

   ```
   $char is non-alpha
   ```

6. As you can clearly see, we are not getting any useful information about the FFI data using native PHP functions! However, using `FFI::typeof()`, as shown here, returns better results:

```
$type = FFI::typeOf($char);
var_dump($type);
```

7. Here is the output from `var_dump()`:

```
object(FFI\CType:char[6])#3 (0) {}
```

As you can see from the final output, we now have useful information! Let's now have a look at the other two FFI informational methods.

Making use of FFI::alignof() and FFI::sizeof()

Before getting into a practical example showing the use of these two methods, it's important to understand what exactly is meant by **alignment**. In order to understand alignment, you need to have a basic understanding of how memory is organized in most computers.

RAM is still the fastest way to temporarily store information used during a program run cycle. Your computer's **central processing unit** (**CPU**) moves information in and out of memory as the program executes. Memory is organized in parallel arrays. The alignment value returned by `alignof()` would be how many bytes can be obtained at once from parallel slices of the aligned memory arrays. In older computers, a value of 4 was typical. For most modern microcomputers, values of 8 or 16 (or greater) are common.

Let's now have a look at an example that illustrates how these two FFI extension informational methods are used, and how that information can produce a performance improvement. This is how we'll proceed:

1. First, we create a FFI instance, `$ffi`, in which we define two C structures labeled `Good` and `Bad`. Notice in the following code snippet that both structures have the same properties; however, the properties are arranged in a different order:

```
$struct = 'struct Bad { char c; double d; int i; }; '
        . 'struct Good { double d; int i; char c; };'
        ;
$ffi = FFI::cdef($struct);
```

2. We then extract the two structures from $ffi, as follows:

```
$bad = $ffi->new("struct Bad");
$good = $ffi->new("struct Good");
var_dump($bad, $good);
```

3. The `var_dump()` output is shown here:

```
object(FFI\CData:struct Bad)#2 (3) {
  ["c"]=> string(1) ""
  ["d"]=> float(0)
  ["i"]=> int(0)
}
object(FFI\CData:struct Good)#3 (3) {
  ["d"]=> float(0)
  ["i"]=> int(0)
  ["c"]=> string(1) ""
}
```

4. We then use the two informational methods to report on the two data structures, as follows:

```
echo "\nBad Alignment:\t" . FFI::alignof($bad);
echo "\nBad Size:\t" . FFI::sizeof($bad);
echo "\nGood Alignment:\t" . FFI::alignof($good);
echo "\nGood Size:\t" . FFI::sizeof($good);
```

The last four lines of output from this code example are shown here:

```
Bad Alignment:   8
Bad Size:        24
Good Alignment:  8
Good Size:       16
```

As you can see from the output, the return from `FFI::alignof()` tells us that the alignment blocks are 8 bytes wide. However, you can also see that the size in bytes taken up by the Bad structure is 50% larger than the size required for the Good structure. Since the two data structures have exactly the same properties, any developer in their right mind would choose the Good structure.

From this example, you can see that the FFI extension informational methods are able to give us an idea on how best to structure our C data in order to produce the most efficient results.

> **Tip**
> For an excellent discussion on the difference between `sizeof()` and `alignof()` in the C language, see this article: https://stackoverflow.com/questions/11386946/whats-the-difference-between-sizeof-and-alignof.

You now have an understanding of what the FFI extension informational methods are and have seen some examples of their use. Let's now have a look at the FFI extension methods pertaining to infrastructure.

Using FFI infrastructural methods

FFI extension infrastructural category methods can be thought of as *behind-the-scenes* components that support the infrastructure needed for C function binding to work properly. As we have stressed throughout this chapter, the FFI extension is needed if you wish to directly access C data structures from within a PHP application. Thus, if you need to do the equivalent of a PHP `unset()` statement to release memory, or a PHP `include()` statement to include external program code, the FFI extension infrastructural methods provide the bridge between native C data and PHP.

Table 4.4, shown here, summarizes methods in this category:

FFI Method	Returns	Notes
`addr()`	`FFI\CData`	Creates pointer to C data
`cast()`	`FFI\CData`	Performs a C language type cast
`free()`	`void`	Releases an FFI pointer. There is no direct equivalent in PHP
`memcpy()`	`void`	Copies specified bytes from one `FFI\CData` instance to another.
`memset()`	`void`	Populates a `FFI\CData` instance with `$size` bytes consisting of `$value`.

Table 4.4 – FFI class infrastructural methods

Let's first have a look at `FFI::addr()`, `free()`, `memset()`, and `memcpy()`.

Working with FFI::addr(), free(), memset(), and memcpy()

PHP developers often assign a value to a variable by **reference**. This allows a change in one variable to be automatically reflected in another. The use of references is especially useful when passing parameters to a function or method where you need to return more than a single value. Passing by reference allows the function or method to return an unlimited number of values.

The `FFI::addr()` method creates a C pointer to an existing `FFI\CData` instance. Just as with a PHP reference, any changes made to the data associated with the pointer will likewise be changed.

In the process of building an example using the `FFI::addr()` method, we also introduce you to `FFI::memset()`. This function is much like the `str_repeat()` PHP function, in that it (`FFI::memset()`) populates a specified number of bytes with a specific value. In this example, we use `FFI::memset()` to populate a C character string with letters of the alphabet.

In this subsection, we also have a look at `FFI::memcpy()`. This function is used to copy data from one `FFI\CData` instance to another. Unlike the `FFI::addr()` method, `FFI::memcpy()` creates a clone that has no connection to the source of the copied data. In addition, we introduce `FFI::free()`, a method used to release a pointer created using `FFI::addr()`.

Let's have a look at how these FFI extension methods can be used, as follows:

1. First, a `FFI\CData` instance, `$arr`, is created, consisting of a C string of six characters. Note in the following code snippet the use of `FFI::memset()`, another infrastructural method, to populate the string with **American Standard Code for Information Interchange** (**ASCII**) code 65: the letter A:

    ```
    // /repo/ch04/php8_ffi_addr_free_memset_memcpy.php
    $size = 6;
    $arr  = FFI::new(FFI::type("char[$size]"));
    FFI::memset($arr, 65, $size);
    echo FFI::string($arr, $size);
    ```

2. The `echo` result using the `FFI::string()` method is shown here:

    ```
    AAAAAA
    ```

3. As you can see from the output, six instances of ASCII code 65 (the letter A) appears. We then create another `FFI\CData` instance, `$arr2`, and use `FFI::memcpy()` to copy six characters from one instance to the other, as follows:

```php
$arr2 = FFI::new(FFI::type("char[$size]"));
FFI::memcpy($arr2, $arr, $size);
echo FFI::string($arr2, $size);
```

4. Unsurprisingly, the output is identical to the output in *Step 2*, as we can see here:

AAAAAA

5. Next, we create a C pointer to `$arr`. Note that when pointers are assigned, they appear to the native PHP `var_dump()` function as array elements. We can then change the value of array element 0, and use `FFI::memset()` to populate it with the letter B. The code is shown in the following snippet:

```php
$ref = FFI::addr($arr);
FFI::memset($ref[0], 66, 6);
echo FFI::string($arr, $size);
var_dump($ref, $arr, $arr2);
```

6. Here is the output associated with the remaining code shown in *Step 5*:

```
BBBBBB
object(FFI\CData:char(*)[6])#2 (1) {
    [0]=>  object(FFI\CData:char[6])#4 (6) {
        [0]=>  string(1) "B"
        [1]=>  string(1) "B"
        [2]=>  string(1) "B"
        [3]=>  string(1) "B"
        [4]=>  string(1) "B"
        [5]=>  string(1) "B"
    }
}
object(FFI\CData:char[6])#3 (6) {
    [0]=>  string(1) "B"
    [1]=>  string(1) "B"
    [2]=>  string(1) "B"
    [3]=>  string(1) "B"
```

```
      [4] => string(1) "B"
      [5] => string(1) "B"
}
object(FFI\CData:char[6])#4 (6) {
      [0] => string(1) "A"
      [1] => string(1) "A"
      [2] => string(1) "A"
      [3] => string(1) "A"
      [4] => string(1) "A"
      [5] => string(1) "A"
}
```

As you can see from the output, we first have a BBBBBB string. You can see that the pointer is in the form of a PHP array. The original FFI\CData instance, $arr, has now changed to letter B. However, the preceding output also clearly shows that the copy, $arr2, is not affected by changes made to $arr or its $ref[0] pointer.

7. Finally, in order to release the pointer created using FFI::addr(), we use FFI::free(). This method is much like the native PHP unset() function but is designed to work with C pointers. Here is the last line of code added to our example:

```
FFI::free($ref);
```

Now that you have an idea about how to work with C pointers and about populating C data with information, let's have a look at how to do type casting with a FFI\CData instance.

Learning about FFI::cast()

In PHP, the process of **type casting** occurs quite frequently. It's used when PHP is asked to perform operations involving dissimilar data types. A classic example of this is shown in the following block of code:

```
$a = 123;
$b = "456";
echo $a + $b;
```

In this trivial example, $a is assigned a data type of int (integer) and $b is assigned a type of string. The echo statement requires PHP to first typecast $b to int, perform the addition, and then typecast the result to string.

Native PHP also allows the developer to force the data type by prepending the desired data type in parentheses in front of the variable or expression. The rewritten example from the previous code snippet might appear as follows:

```
$a = 123;
$b = "456";
echo (string) ($a + (int) $b);
```

Forced type casting makes your intention extremely clear to other developers who make use of your code. It also guarantees results in that forcing the type cast exerts greater control over the flow of your code, and does not rely upon PHP default behavior.

The FFI extension has a similar capability in the form of the `FFI::cast()` method. As you have seen throughout this chapter, FFI extension data is isolated from PHP and is immune to PHP type casting. In order to force the data type, you can use `FFI::cast()` to return a parallel `FFI\CData` type as required. Let's see how to do that in the following steps:

1. In this example, we create a `FFI\CData` instance, `$int1`, of type `int`. We use its cdata property to assign a value `123`, as follows:

    ```
    // /repo/ch04/php8_ffi_cast.php
    // not all lines are shown
    $patt = "%2d : %16s\n";
    $int1 = FFI::new("int");
    $int1->cdata = 123;
    $bool = FFI::cast(FFI::type("bool"), $int1);
    printf($patt, __LINE__, (string) $int1->cdata);
    printf($patt, __LINE__, (string) $bool->cdata);
    ```

2. As you can see from the output shown here, the integer value of `123`, when typecast to `bool` (Boolean), shows up in the output as `1`:

    ```
     8 :              123
     9 :                1
    ```

3. Next we create a `FFI\CData` instance, `$int2`, of type `int` and assign a value `123`. We then typecast it to `float` and back again to `int`, as illustrated in the following code snippet:

    ```
    $int2 = FFI::new("int");
    $int2->cdata = 123;
    ```

```
$float1 = FFI::cast(FFI::type("float"), $int2);
$int3   = FFI::cast(FFI::type("int"), $float1);
printf($patt, __LINE__, (string) $int2->cdata);
printf($patt, __LINE__, (string) $float1->cdata);
printf($patt, __LINE__, (string) $int3->cdata);
```

4. The output from the last three lines is quite gratifying. We see that our original value `123` is represented as `1.7235971111195E-43`. When typecast back to `int`, our original value is restored. Here is the output from the last three lines:

```
15 :                    123
16 : 1.7235971111195E-43
17 :                    123
```

5. The FFI extension, as with the C language in general, does not allow all types to be converted. As an example, in the last block of code, we attempt to typecast a `FFI\CData` instance, `$float2`, of type `float` to type `char`, as follows:

```
try {
    $float2 = FFI::new("float");
    $float2->cdata = 22/7;
    $char1  = FFI::cast(FFI::type("char[20]"),
        $float2);
    printf($patt, __LINE__, (string) $float2->cdata);
    printf($patt, __LINE__, (string) $char1->cdata);
} catch (Throwable $t) {
    echo get_class($t) . ':' . $t->getMessage();
}
```

6. The results are disastrous! As you can see from the output shown here, a `FFI\Exception` is thrown:

```
FFI\Exception:attempt to cast to larger type
```

In this section, we addressed a series of FFI extension methods that create FFI extension object instances, compare values, gather information, and work with the C data infrastructure created. You learned there are FFI extension methods that mirror these same capabilities in the native PHP language. In the next section, we review a practical example that incorporates a C-function library into a PHP script using the FFI extension.

Using FFI in an application

Any shared C library (generally with a *.so extension) can be included in a PHP application using the FFI extension. If you plan to work with any of the core PHP libraries or libraries produced when PHP extensions are installed, it's important to note that you have the ability to modify the behavior of the PHP language itself.

Before we examine how that works, let's first have a look at incorporating an external C library into a PHP script using the FFI extension.

Integrating an external C library into a PHP script

For the purposes of illustration, we use a simple function that might have originated from a **Computer Science 101** (**CS101**) class: the famous **bubble sort**. This algorithm is widely used in beginner's computer science classes because it's easy to follow.

> **Important note**
>
> The **bubble sort** is an extremely inefficient sort algorithm and has long been superseded by faster sorting algorithms such as the **shell sort**, **quick sort**, or **merge sort** algorithms. Although there is no authoritative reference for the bubble-sort algorithm, you can read a good general discussion of it here: https://en.wikipedia.org/wiki/Bubble_sort.

In this subsection, we do not go through details of the algorithm. Rather, the purpose of this subsection is to demonstrate how to take an existing C library and incorporate one of its functions into a PHP script. We now show you the original C source code, how to convert it into a shared library, and—finally—how to incorporate the library into PHP using FFI. Here's what we'll do:

1. The first step, of course, is to compile the C code into object code. Here is the bubble-sort C code used for this example:

```c
#include <stdio.h>
void bubble_sort(int [], int);
void bubble_sort(int list[], int n) {
    int c, d, t, p;
    for (c = 0 ; c < n - 1; c++) {
        p = 0;
        for (d = 0 ; d < n - c - 1; d++) {
            if (list[d] > list[d+1]) {
                t = list[d];
```

```
                    list[d] = list[d+1];
                    list[d+1] = t;
                    p++;
                }
            }
            if (p == 0) break;
        }
}
```

2. We then compile the C code into object code using the GNU C compiler (included in the Docker image used for this course), as follows:

   ```
   gcc -c -Wall -Werror -fpic bubble.c
   ```

3. Next, we incorporate the object code into a shared library. This step is necessary as the FFI extension is only able to access shared libraries. We run the following code to do this:

   ```
   gcc -shared -o libbubble.so bubble.o
   ```

4. We are now ready to define the PHP script that uses our new shared library. We begin by defining a function that shows output from a `FFI\CData` array, as follows:

   ```
   // /repo/ch04/php8_ffi_using_func_from_lib.php
   function show($label, $arr, $max)
   {
       $output = $label . "\n";
       for ($x = 0; $x < $max; $x++)
           $output .= $arr[$x] . ',';
       return substr($output, 0, -1) . "\n";
   }
   ```

5. The critical part is next: defining the FFI instance. We use `FFI::cdef()` to accomplish this and supply two arguments. The first argument is the function signature, and the second argument is a path to our newly created shared library. Both arguments can be seen in the following code snippet:

   ```
   $bubble = FFI::cdef(
       "void bubble_sort(int [], int);",
       "./libbubble.so");
   ```

6. We then create a FFI\CData element as an integer array with 16 values populated with random integers, using the rand() function. The code is shown in the following snippet:

```
$max     = 16;
$arr_b = FFI::new('int[' . $max . ']');
for ($i = 0; $i < $max; $i++)
    $arr_b[$i]->cdata = rand(0,9999);
```

7. Finally, we display the contents of the array before the sort, perform the sort, and display the contents after. Note in the following code snippet that we execute the sort using a call to bubble_sort() from the FFI instance:

```
echo show('Before Sort', $arr_b, $max);
$bubble->bubble_sort($arr_b, $max);
echo show('After Sort', $arr_b, $max);
```

8. The output, as you might expect, shows an array of random integers before the sort. After the sort, the values are in order. Here is the output from the code shown in *Step 7*:

```
Before Sort
245,8405,8580,7586,9416,3524,8577,4713,
9591,1248,798,6656,9064,9846,2803,304
After Sort
245,304,798,1248,2803,3524,4713,6656,7586,
8405,8577,8580,9064,9416,9591,9846
```

Now that you have an idea how to integrate an external C library into a PHP application using the FFI extension, we turn to our last topic: PHP callbacks.

Working with PHP callbacks

As we mentioned at the beginning of this section, it's possible to use the FFI extension to incorporate shared C libraries that are part of the actual PHP language (or its extensions). This integration is important as it allows you to read and write native PHP data in your C library by accessing the C data structures defined in the PHP shared C libraries.

The purpose of this subsection, however, is not to show you how to create a PHP extension. Rather, in this subsection, we introduce you to the FFI extension's ability to override native PHP language functionality. This ability is referred to as a **PHP callback**. Before we get into the implementation details, we must first examine potential dangers associated with this ability.

Understanding the dangers inherent to PHP callbacks

It's important to understand that the C functions defined in the various PHP shared libraries are often used by multiple PHP functions. Accordingly, if you override one of the low-level functions at the C level, you might experience unexpected behavior in your PHP application.

Another known issue is that overriding native PHP C functions has a high probability of producing **memory leaks**. Over time, a long-running application that uses such overrides can fail, and can potentially crash the server!

A final consideration is that the PHP callback capability is not supported on all FFI platforms. Accordingly, although the code might work on a Linux server, it might not work (or might not work the same) on a Windows server.

> **Tip**
> Rather than using a FFI PHP callback to override native PHP C library functionality, it might be easier, faster, and safer to just define your own PHP function!

Now that you have an idea of the dangers involved using PHP callbacks, let's have a look at a sample implementation.

Implementing a PHP callback

In the following example, the `zend_write` internal PHP shared library C function is overridden using a callback that adds a **line feed** (**LF**) to the end of the output. Note that this override affects any native PHP function dependent upon it, including `echo`, `print`, `printf`: in other words, any PHP function that produces direct output. To implement a PHP callback, follow these steps:

1. First, we define a FFI instance using `FFI::cdef()`. The first argument is the function signature of `zend_write`. The code is shown in the following snippet:

    ```
    // /repo/ch04/php8_php_callbacks.php
    $zend = FFI::cdef("
    ```

```
        typedef int (*zend_write_func_t) (
            const char *str,size_t str_length);
        extern zend_write_func_t zend_write;
");
```

2. We then add code to confirm that, unmodified, echo does not add an extra LF at the end. You can see the code here:

```
echo "Original echo command does not output LF:\n";
echo 'A','B','C';
echo 'Next line';
```

3. Unsurprisingly, the output produces ABCNext line. There are no carriage returns or LFs present in the output, which is shown here:

```
Original echo command does not output LF:
ABCNext line
```

4. We then clone the pointer to zend_write into the $orig_zend_write variable. If we didn't do this, we would be unable to use the original function! The code is shown here:

```
$orig_zend_write = clone $zend->zend_write;
```

5. Next, we produce a PHP callback in the form of an anonymous function that overrides the original zend_write function. In the function, we invoke the original zend_write function and append a LF to its output, as follows:

```
$zend->zend_write = function($str, $len) {
    global $orig_zend_write;
    $ret = $orig_zend_write($str, $len);
    $orig_zend_write("\n", 1);
    return $ret;
};
```

6. The remaining code reruns the echo command shown in the preceding step, as we can see here:

```
echo 'Revised echo command adds LF:';
echo 'A','B','C';
```

7. The following output demonstrates that the PHP `echo` command now produces a LF at the end of each command:

```
Revised echo command adds LF:
A
B
C
```

It's also important to note that modifying the PHP library C-language `zend_write` function has an impact on all PHP native functions using this C-language function. This includes `print()`, `printf()` (and its variants), and so forth.

This concludes our discussion of using the FFI extension in a PHP application. You now know how to incorporate native C functions from an external shared library. You also know how to substitute a PHP callback for a native PHP core or extension shared library, giving you the potential to alter the behavior of the PHP language itself.

Summary

In this chapter, you learned about the FFI, its history, and how it can be used to facilitate rapid PHP extension prototyping. You also learned that although the FFI extension should not be used to improve speed, it also serves the purpose of allowing your PHP application to directly call native C functions from an external C library. The power of this ability was demonstrated through an example that called a bubble-sort function from an external C library. This same capability can be extended to encompass any of the thousands of C libraries available, including machine learning, optical character recognition, communications, encryption; *ad infinitum*.

In this chapter, you acquired a deeper understanding of how PHP itself operates at the C- language level. You learned how to create and directly use C-language data structures, giving you the ability to interact, and even override, the PHP language itself. In addition, you now have an idea how to incorporate the functionality of any C-language library directly into a PHP application. A further benefit of this knowledge is that it serves to enhance your career prospects if you find a job with a company that either plans to develop, or has already developed, its own custom PHP extension.

The next chapter marks the beginning of a new section of the book, *PHP 8 Tricks*. In the next section, you will learn about backward-compatibility issues when upgrading to PHP 8. The next chapter specifically addresses backward-compatibility issues with respect to OOP.

Section 2: PHP 8 Tricks

In this part, you are taken into the dark corners of PHP 8: the places where backward-compatibility breaks exist. This part guides you through the critical process of migrating an existing application to PHP 8.

The following chapters are included in this section:

- *Chapter 5, Discovering Potential OOP Backward-Compatibility Breaks*
- *Chapter 6, Understanding PHP 8 Functional Differences*
- *Chapter 7, Avoiding Traps When Using PHP 8 Extensions*
- *Chapter 8, Learning about PHP 8's Deprecated or Removed Functionality*

5
Discovering Potential OOP Backward-Compatibility Breaks

This chapter marks the beginning of Part 2 of the book, *PHP 8 Tricks*. In this part, you'll discover the dark corners of PHP 8: the place where **backward-compatibility breaks** exist. This part gives you insight into how to avoid problems before migrating an existing application to PHP 8. You will learn what to look for in your existing code that could cause it to stop working after a PHP 8 upgrade. Once you master the topics presented in this part of the book, you will be well equipped to modify existing code in such a manner that it continues to function normally following a PHP 8 upgrade.

In this chapter, you will be introduced to new PHP 8 features specific to **object-oriented programming (OOP)**. The chapter provides you with plenty of short code examples that clearly illustrate the new features and concepts. This chapter is critical in helping you quickly take advantage of the power of PHP 8 as you adapt the code examples for your own practice. The focus of this chapter is on situations where object-oriented code might break after a PHP 8 migration.

Topics covered in this chapter include the following:

- Discovering core OOP coding differences
- Navigating changes in magic methods
- Taking control of serialization
- Understanding expanded PHP 8 variance support
- Handling **Standard PHP Library** (**SPL**) changes

Technical requirements

To examine and run the code examples provided in this chapter, the minimum recommended hardware is the following:

- x86_64 based desktop PC or laptop
- 1 gigabyte (GB) of free disk space
- 4 GB of RAM
- A 500 kilobits per second (Kbps) or faster internet connection

In addition, you will need to install the following software:

- Docker
- Docker Compose

Please refer to the *Technical requirements* section of *Chapter 1*, *Introducing New PHP 8 OOP Features*, for more information on Docker and Docker Compose installation, as well as how to build the Docker container used to demonstrate code explained in this book. In this book, we refer to the directory in which you restored the sample code for this book as `/repo`.

The source code for this chapter is located here: `https://github.com/PacktPublishing/PHP-8-Programming-Tips-Tricks-and-Best-Practices`.

We can now begin our discussion by examining core OOP coding differences.

Discovering core OOP coding differences

There are a number of significant changes to how you are able to write OOP code in PHP 8. In this section, we focus on three key areas that might present you with potential backward-compatibility breaks. The areas we address in this section are common bad practices associated with making static method calls, handling object properties, and PHP autoloading.

After reading this section, and working your way through the examples, you are in in a better position to spot OOP bad practices and to learn how PHP 8 has placed restrictions on such usage. In this chapter, you learn good coding practices, which will ultimately make you a better programmer. You will also be able to address changes in PHP autoloading that can potentially cause failure in an application migrated to PHP 8.

Let's first look at how PHP 8 has tightened up on making static calls.

Handling static calls in PHP 8

Surprisingly, PHP versions 7 and below allowed developers to make a static call to a class method not declared `static`. At first glance, any future developer reviewing your code immediately assumes that the method has been defined as `static`. This can lead to unexpected behavior as the future developer, operating under a false assumption, starts to misuse your code.

In this simple example, we define a `Test` class with a `nonStatic()` method. In the procedural code that follows the class definition, we echo the return value of this method, however, in doing so we make a static call:

```
// /repo/ch05/php8_oop_diff_static.php
class Test {
    public function notStatic() {
        return __CLASS__ . PHP_EOL;
    }
}
echo Test::notStatic();
```

When we run this code in PHP 7, here is the result:

```
root@php8_tips_php7 [ /repo/ch05 ]#
php php8_oop_diff_static.php
```

```
PHP Deprecated:  Non-static method Test::notStatic() should not
be called statically in /repo/ch05/php8_oop_diff_static.php on
line 11
Test
```

As you can see from the output, PHP 7 issues a deprecation notice, but allows the call to be made! In PHP 8, however, the result is a fatal `Error`, as shown here:

```
root@php8_tips_php8 [ /repo/ch05 ]#
php php8_oop_diff_static.php
PHP Fatal error:  Uncaught Error: Non-static method
Test::notStatic() cannot be called statically in /repo/ch05/
php8_oop_diff_static.php:11
```

Calling a non-static method using static method call syntax is a bad practice in the sense that well-written code makes the intention of the code developer crystal clear. If you do not define a method as static, but later call it in a static sense, a developer assigned to maintain your code in the future might become confused and could make wrong assumptions about the original intent of the code. The end result will be even more bad code!

In PHP 8, you can no longer call a non-static method using a static method call. Let's now have a look at another bad practice involving treating object properties as keys.

Dealing with object property handling changes

Arrays have been a central feature in PHP all the way back to the earliest versions. OOP, on the other hand, was not introduced until PHP 4. In the early days of OOP, array functions were often expanded to accommodate object properties. This led to a blurring of the distinction between an object and an array, which in turn spawned a number of bad practices.

In order to maintain a clear separation between array handling and object handling, PHP 8 now restricts the `array_key_exists()` function to only accept an array as an argument. To illustrate this, consider the following example:

1. First, we define a simple anonymous class with a single property:

    ```
    // /repo/ch05/php8_oop_diff_array_key_exists.php
    $obj = new class () { public $var = 'OK.'; };
    ```

2. We then run three tests that each check for the existence of $var, using isset(), property_exists(), and array_key_exists():

```
// not all code is shown
$default = 'DEFAULT';
echo (isset($obj->var))
    ? $obj->var : $default;
echo (property_exists($obj,'var'))
    ? $obj->var : $default;
echo (array_key_exists('var',$obj))
    ? $obj->var : $default;
```

When we run this code in PHP 7, all tests succeed, as shown here:

```
root@php8_tips_php7 [ /repo/ch05 ]#
php php8_oop_diff_array_key_exists.php
OK.OK.OK.
```

In PHP 8, however, a fatal TypeError occurs, as array_key_exists() now only accepts an array as an argument. The PHP 8 output is shown here:

```
root@php8_tips_php8 [ /repo/ch05 ]#
php php8_oop_diff_array_key_exists.php
OK.OK.PHP Fatal error:  Uncaught TypeError: array_key_exists():
Argument #2 ($array) must be of type array, class@anonymous
given in /repo/ch05/php8_oop_diff_array_key_exists.php:10
```

The best practice is to use either property_exists() or isset(). We now turn our attention to changes in PHP autoloading.

Working with PHP 8 autoloading

The basic **autoloading** class mechanism first introduced in PHP 5.1 works the same in PHP 8. The main difference is that the support for the global function __autoload(), deprecated in PHP 7.2, has been completely removed in PHP 8. Starting with PHP 7.2, developers were encouraged to register their autoloading logic using spl_autoload_register(), available for that purpose since PHP 5.1. Another major difference is how spl_autoload_register() reacts if unable to register an autoloader.

An understanding of how the autoloading process works when using `spl_autoload_register()` is critical to your work as a developer. Failure to grasp how PHP automatically locates and loads classes will limit your ability to grow as a developer and could have a detrimental impact on your career path.

Before getting into `spl_autoload_register()`, let's first have a look at the `__autoload()` function.

Understanding the __autoload() function

The `__autoload()` function was used by many developers as the primary source of autoloading logic. This function behaves much as a *magic method* does and that's why it's called automatically depending on the context. Circumstances that would trigger an automatic call to the `__autoload()` function include the moment when a new class instance is created, but where the class definition has not yet been loaded. Further, if the class extends another class, the autoload logic is also invoked in order to load the super class prior to the creation of the subclass that extends it.

The advantage of using the `__autoload()` function was that it was quite easy to define, and was often defined in a website's initial `index.php` file. The disadvantages included the following:

- `__autoload()` was a PHP procedural function; not defined nor controlled using OOP principles. This can become an issue when defining unit tests for an application, for example.

- If your application uses namespaces, the `__autoload()` function must be defined in the global namespace; otherwise, classes outside of the namespace in which the `__autoload()` function is defined will fail to load.

- The `__autoload()` function doesn't work well with `spl_autoload_register()`. If you define autoloading logic using both the `__autoload()` function and `spl_autoload_register()`, the `__autoload()` function logic is entirely ignored.

To illustrate potential problems, we'll define an `OopBreakScan` class, discussed in more detail in *Chapter 11, Migrating Existing PHP Apps to PHP 8*:

1. First, we define and then add a method to the `OopBreakScan` class that scans the file contents for the `__autoload()` function. Note that the error message is a class constant defined in the `Base` class that simply warns of the presence of the `__autoload()` function:

```
namespace Migration;
class OopBreakScan extends Base {
    public static function scanMagicAutoloadFunction(
        string $contents, array &$message) : bool {
        $found = 0;
        $found += (stripos($contents,
            'function __autoload(') !== FALSE);
        $message[] = ($found)
                   ? Base::ERR_MAGIC_AUTOLOAD
                   : sprintf(Base::OK_PASSED,
                       __FUNCTION__);
        return (bool) $found;
    }
    // remaining methods not shown
```

This class extends a `Migration\Base` class (not shown). This is significant as any autoloading logic needs to find not only the subclass but its super class as well.

2. Next, we define a calling program in which a magic `__autoload()` function is defined:

```
// /repo/ch05/php7_autoload_function.php
function __autoLoad($class) {
    $fn = __DIR__ . '/../src/'
        . str_replace('\\', '/', $class)
        . '.php';
    require_once $fn;
}
```

3. We then make use of the class by having the calling program scan itself:

```
use Migration\OopBreakScan;
$contents = file_get_contents(__FILE__);
$message = [];
OopBreakScan::
    scanMagicAutoloadFunction($contents, $message);
var_dump($message);
```

Here is the output running in PHP 7:

```
root@php8_tips_php7 [ /repo/ch05 ]#
php php7_autoload_function.php
/repo/ch05/php7_autoload_function.php:23:
array(1) {
  [0] => string(96) "WARNING: the "__autoload()" function is removed in PHP 8: replace with "spl_autoload_register()""
}
```

As you can see from the output, the `Migration\OopBreakScan` class was autoloaded. We know this because the `scanMagicAutoloadFunction` method was invoked, and we have its results. Furthermore, we know that the `Migration\Base` class was also autoloaded. The reason we know this is because the error message that appears in the output is a constant of the super class.

However, the same code running in PHP 8 produces this result:

```
root@php8_tips_php8 [ /repo/ch05 ]#
php php7_autoload_function.php
PHP Fatal error:  __autoload() is no longer supported, use spl_autoload_register() instead in /repo/ch05/php7_autoload_function.php on line 4
```

This result is not surprising as support for the magic `__autoload()` function was removed in PHP 8. In PHP 8, you must use `spl_autoload_register()` instead. We now turn our attention to `spl_autoload_register()`.

Learning to use spl_autoload_register()

The primary advantage of the `spl_autoload_register()` function is that it allows you to register more than one autoloader. Although this might seem like overkill, imagine the nightmare scenario where you are using a number of different open source PHP libraries... and where they all have their *own autoloaders* defined! As long as all such libraries use `spl_autoload_register()`, having multiple autoloader callbacks poses no problem.

Each autoloader registered using `spl_autoload_register()` must be callable. Any of the following are considered `callable`:

- A PHP procedural function
- An anonymous function
- A class method that can be called in a static manner
- Any class instance that defines the `__invoke()` magic method
- An array in this form: `[$instance, 'method']`

> **Tip**
>
> *Composer* maintains its own autoloader, which in turn relies upon `spl_autoload_register()`. If you are using Composer to manage your open source PHP packages, you can simply include `/path/to/project/vendor/autoload.php` at the start of your application code to use the Composer autoloader. To have Composer autoload your application source code files, add one or more entries into the `composer.json` file under the `autoload : psr-4` key. For more information, see https://getcomposer.org/doc/04-schema.md#psr-4.

A quite typical autoloader class might appear as follows. Note that this is the class we use for many of the OOP examples shown in this book:

1. In the `__construct()` method, we assign the source directory. Following that, we call `spl_auto_register()` using the array callable syntax noted above:

```
// /repo/src/Server/Autoload/Loader.php
namespace Server\Autoload;
class Loader {
    const DEFAULT_SRC = __DIR__ . '/../..';
    public $src_dir = '';
    public function __construct($src_dir = NULL) {
```

```
            $this->src_dir = $src_dir
                ?? realpath(self::DEFAULT_SRC);
            spl_autoload_register([$this, 'autoload']);
    }
```

2. The actual autoloading code is similar to that shown in our `__autoload()` function example above. Here is the method that does the actual autoloading:

```
    public function autoload($class) {
        $fn = str_replace('\\', '/', $class);
        $fn = $this->src_dir . '/' . $fn . '.php';
        $fn = str_replace('//', '/', $fn);
        require_once($fn);
    }
}
```

Now that you have an idea of how to use the `spl_auto_register()` function, we must examine a potential code break when running PHP 8.

A potential spl_auto_register() code break in PHP 8

The second argument to the `spl_auto_register()` function is an optional Boolean value that defaults to `FALSE`. If the second argument is set to `TRUE`, the `spl_auto_register()` function throws an `Exception` in PHP 7 and below versions if an autoloader fails to register. In PHP 8, however, if the data type of the second argument is anything other than `callable`, a fatal `TypeError` is thrown instead, regardless of the value of the second argument!

The simple program example shown next illustrates this danger. In this example, we use the `spl_auto_register()` function to register a PHP function that does not exist. We set the second argument to `TRUE`:

```
// /repo/ch05/php7_spl_spl_autoload_register.php
try {
    spl_autoload_register('does_not_exist', TRUE);
    $data = ['A' => [1,2,3],'B' => [4,5,6],'C' => [7,8,9]];
    $response = new \Application\Strategy\JsonResponse($data);
    echo $response->render();
} catch (Exception $e) {
```

```
        echo "A program error has occurred\n";
}
```

If we then run this block of code in PHP 7, here is the result:

```
root@php8_tips_php7 [ /repo/ch05 ]#
php php7_spl_spl_autoload_register.php
A program error has occurred
```

As you can determine from the output, an `Exception` is thrown. The `catch` block is invoked, and the message **A program error has occurred** appears. When we run the same program in PHP 8, however, a fatal `Error` is thrown:

```
root@php8_tips_php8 [ /repo/ch05 ]#
php php7_spl_spl_autoload_register.php
PHP Fatal error:  Uncaught TypeError: spl_autoload_register():
Argument #1 ($callback) must be a valid callback, no array or
string given in /repo/ch05/php7_spl_spl_autoload_register.
php:12
```

Obviously, the `catch` block was bypassed as it was designed to catch an `Exception`, not an `Error`. The simple solution is to have the `catch` block catch `Throwable` instead of `Exception`. This allows the same code to run in either PHP 7 or PHP 8.

Here is how the rewritten code might appear. The output is not shown as it's identical to the same example running in PHP 7:

```
// /repo/ch05/php8_spl_spl_autoload_register.php
try {
    spl_autoload_register('does_not_exist', TRUE);
    $data = ['A' => [1,2,3],'B' => [4,5,6],'C' => [7,8,9]];
    $response = new \Application\Strategy\JsonResponse($data);
    echo $response->render();
} catch (Throwable $e) {
    echo "A program error has occurred\n";
}
```

You now have a better understanding of PHP 8 autoloading, and how to spot and correct potential autoloading backward-compatibility breaks. Let's now have a look at changes in PHP 8 pertaining to magic methods.

Navigating changes in magic methods

PHP **magic methods** are predefined hooks that interrupt the normal flow of an OOP application. Each magic method, if defined, alters the behavior of the application from the minute the object instance is created, up until the point where the instance goes **out of scope**.

> **Important note**
>
> An object instance goes *out of scope* when it's unset or overwritten. Object instances also go out of scope when defined in a function or class method, and the execution of that function or class method ends. Ultimately, if for no other reason, an object instance goes out of scope when the PHP program ends.

This section will give you a solid understanding of important changes to magic method usage and behavior introduced in PHP 8. Once you understand the situations described in this section, you will be in a position to make the appropriate code modifications to prevent your application code from failing should you migrate to PHP 8.

Let's first have a look at changes to the object construct method.

Dealing with constructor changes

Ideally, the **class constructor** is a method that's called automatically when the object instance is created and is used to perform some sort of object initialization. This initialization most typically involves populating object properties with values supplied as arguments to this method. The initialization could also perform any necessary tasks such as opening file handles, establishing a database connection, and so forth.

In PHP 8, a number of changes in how the class constructor is invoked have been made. This means there's a potential for a backwards compatibility break when you migrate your application to PHP 8. The first change we'll examine has to do with deprecated usage of a method with the same name as the class being used as the class constructor.

Handling changes in a method and class of the same name

In the first PHP OOP implementation, introduced in PHP version 4, it was determined that a method with the same name as the class would assume the role of class constructor, and would be automatically called when a new object instance was created.

It's a little known fact that, even in PHP 8, functions, methods, and even class names, are *case-insensitive*. Thus `$a = new ArrayObject();` is equivalent to `$b = new arrayobject();`. Variable names, on the other hand, are case-sensitive.

Starting with PHP 5, along with a new and much more robust OOP implementation, magic methods were introduced. One of these methods is `__construct()`, specifically reserved for class construction, designed to replace the older usage. Using a method with the same name as the class as a constructor was supported through the remaining versions of PHP 5, and all the way through all versions of PHP 7 as well.

In PHP 8, support for a class constructor method with the same name as the class itself has been removed. If a `__construct()` method is also defined, you will have no problem: `__construct()` takes precedence as a class constructor. If there is no `__construct()` method, and you detect a method with the same name as the `class()`, you have the potential for failure. Please bear in mind that both method and class names are case-insensitive!

Have a look at the following example. It works in PHP 7 but not in PHP 8:

1. First, we define a `Text` class with a class constructor method of the same name. The constructor method creates an `SplFileObject` instance based upon the supplied filename:

```php
// /repo/ch05/php8_oop_bc_break_construct.php
class Text {
    public $fh = '';
    public const ERROR_FN = 'ERROR: file not found';
    public function text(string $fn) {
        if (!file_exists($fn))
            throw new Exception(self::ERROR_FN);
        $this->fh = new SplFileObject($fn, 'r');
    }
    public function getText() {
        return $this->fh->fpassthru();
    }
}
```

2. We then add three lines of procedural code to exercise the class, supplying the filename of a file containing the Gettysburg Address:

```php
$fn    = __DIR__ . '/../sample_data/gettysburg.txt';
$text  = new Text($fn);
echo $text->getText();
```

3. Running the program in PHP 7 first produces a deprecation notice, followed by the expected text. Only the first few lines of the output are shown here:

```
root@php8_tips_php7 [ /repo/ch05 ]#
php php8_bc_break_construct.php
PHP Deprecated:  Methods with the same name as their
class will not be constructors in a future version of
PHP; Text has a deprecated constructor in /repo/ch05/
php8_bc_break_construct.php on line 4

Fourscore and seven years ago our fathers brought forth
on this continent a new nation, conceived in liberty and
dedicated to the proposition that all men are created
equal. ... <remaining text not shown>
```

4. Running the same program in PHP 8, however, a fatal `Error` is thrown instead, as you can see from this output:

```
root@php8_tips_php8 [ /repo/ch05 ]# php php8_bc_break_
construct.php
PHP Fatal error:  Uncaught Error: Call to a member
function fpassthru() on string in /repo/ch05/php8_bc_
break_construct.php:16
```

It's important to note that the error shown in PHP 8 does not tell you the real reason why the program failed. Hence, it's extremely important that you scan your PHP applications, especially older applications, to see if there's a method with the same name as the class. Accordingly, the **best practice** is to simply rename the method having the same name as the class to `__construct()`.

Now let's have a look at how inconsistencies in handling `Exception` and `exit` in the class constructor have been addressed in PHP 8.

Addressing inconsistencies in the class constructor

Another issue addressed in PHP 8 has to do with a situation where the class construct method either throws an `Exception`, or executes `exit()`. In PHP versions prior to PHP 8, if an `Exception` is thrown in the class constructor, the `__destruct()` method, if defined, is *not called*. On the other hand, if either `exit()` or `die()` (both PHP functions are equivalent to each other) is used in the constructor, the `__destruct()` method *is* called. In PHP 8, this inconsistency is addressed. Now, in either case, the `__destruct()` method *is not* called.

You may be wondering why this is of concern. The reason why you need to be aware of this important change is that you might have logic residing in the __destruct() method that was called in a situation where you also might call either exit() or die(). In PHP 8, you can no longer rely upon this code, which may cause a backwards compatibility break.

In this example, we have two connection classes. ConnectPdo uses the PDO extension to provide query results, whereas ConnectMysqli uses the MySQLi extension:

1. We begin by defining an interface specifying a query method. This method requires a SQL string as an argument and is expected to return an array as a result:

    ```php
    // /repo/src/Php7/Connector/ConnectInterface.php
    namespace Php7\Connector;
    interface ConnectInterface {
        public function query(string $sql) : array;
    }
    ```

2. Next, we define a base class in which there is a __destruct() magic method defined. Because this class implements ConnectInterface but doesn't define query(), it's marked abstract:

    ```php
    // /repo/src/Php7/Connector/Base.php
    namespace Php7\Connector;
    abstract class Base implements ConnectInterface {
        const CONN_TERMINATED = 'Connection Terminated';
        public $conn = NULL;
        public function __destruct() {
            $message = get_class($this)
                . ':' . self::CONN_TERMINATED;
            error_log($message);
        }
    }
    ```

3. Next, we define the ConnectPdo class. It extends Base, and its query() method uses PDO syntax to produce a result. The __construct() method throws a PDOException if there is a problem creating the connection:

    ```php
    // /repo/src/Php7/Connector/ConnectPdo.php
    namespace Php7\Connector;
    use PDO;
    ```

```php
class ConnectPdo extends Base {
    public function __construct(
        string $dsn, string $usr, string $pwd) {
        $this->conn = new PDO($dsn, $usr, $pwd);
    }
    public function query(string $sql) : array {
        $stmt = $this->conn->query($sql);
        return $stmt->fetchAll(PDO::FETCH_ASSOC);
    }
}
```

4. In a similar manner, we define the `ConnectMysqli` class. It extends `Base`, and its `query()` method uses MySQLi syntax to produce a result. The `__construct()` method executes `die()` if there is a problem creating the connection:

```php
// /repo/src/Php7/Connector/ConnectMysqli.php
namespace Php7\Connector;
class ConnectMysqli extends Base {
    public function __construct(
        string $db, string $usr, string $pwd) {
        $this->conn = mysqli_connect('localhost',
            $usr, $pwd, $db)
            or die("Unable to Connect\n");
    }
    public function query(string $sql) : array {
        $result = mysqli_query($this->conn, $sql);
        return mysqli_fetch_all($result, MYSQLI_ASSOC);
    }
}
```

5. Finally, we define a calling program that uses the two connection classes described previously, and defines invalid values for the connection string, username, and password:

```php
// /repo/ch05/php8_bc_break_destruct.php
include __DIR__ . '/../vendor/autoload.php';
use Php7\Connector\ {ConnectPdo, ConnectMysqli};
$db = 'test';
```

```
$usr = 'fake';
$pwd = 'xyz';
$dsn = 'mysql:host=localhost;dbname=' . $db;
$sql = 'SELECT event_name, event_date FROM events';
```

6. Next, in the calling program, we call both classes and attempt to execute a query. The connection deliberately fails as we supply the wrong username and password:

```
$ptn = "%2d : %s : %s\n";
try {
    $conn = new ConnectPdo($dsn, $usr, $pwd);
    var_dump($conn->query($sql));
} catch (Throwable $t) {
    printf($ptn, __LINE__, get_class($t),
        $t->getMessage());
}
$conn = new ConnectMysqli($db, $usr, $pwd);
var_dump($conn->query($sql));
```

7. As you now know from our discussion above, the output running in PHP 7 shows the `PDOException` being thrown from the class constructor when the `ConnectPdo` instance is created. On the other hand, when the `ConnectMysqli` instance fails, `die()` is called, with the message **Unable to Connect**. You also see, on the very last line of the output, the error log information originating from the `__destruct()` method. Here is that output:

```
root@php8_tips_php7 [ /repo/ch05 ]#
php php8_bc_break_destruct.php
15 : PDOException : SQLSTATE[28000] [1045] Access denied
for user 'fake'@'localhost' (using password: YES)
PHP Warning:  mysqli_connect(): (HY000/1045): Access
denied for user 'fake'@'localhost' (using password: YES)
in /repo/src/Php7/Connector/ConnectMysqli.php on line 8
Unable to Connect
Php7\Connector\ConnectMysqli:Connection Terminated
```

8. In PHP 8, the __destruct() method is not called in either case, resulting in the output shown here. As you can see in the output, the PDOException is caught, and the die() command is issued. There is no output from the __destruct() method. The PHP 8 output is shown here:

```
root@php8_tips_php8 [ /repo/ch05 ]#
php php8_bc_break_destruct.php
15 : PDOException : SQLSTATE[28000] [1045] Access denied
for user 'fake'@'localhost' (using password: YES)
PHP Warning:  mysqli_connect(): (HY000/1045): Access
denied for user 'fake'@'localhost' (using password: YES)
in /repo/src/Php7/Connector/ConnectMysqli.php on line 8
Unable to Connect
```

Now that you have an idea how to spot a potential code break with regards to the __destruct() method along with a call to either die() or exit(), let's turn our attention to changes to the __toString() method.

Working with changes to __toString()

The __toString() magic method is invoked when an object is used as a string. A classic example is when you simply echo an object. The echo command expects a string as an argument. When non-string data is provided, PHP performs type juggling to convert the data to string. As an object cannot be readily converted to string, the PHP engine then looks to see if __toString() is defined, and if so, returns its value.

The major change in this magic method is the introduction of Stringable, a brand new interface. The new interface is defined as follows:

```
interface Stringable {
    public function __toString(): string;
}
```

Any class running in PHP 8 that defines the __toString() magic method silently implements the Stringable interface. This new behavior doesn't present any serious potential for a code break. However, since the class now implements the Stringable interface, you are no longer allowed to modify the __toString() method signature.

Here is a short example that reveals the new association with the `Stringable` interface:

1. In this example, we define a `Test` class that defines `__toString()`:

    ```php
    // /repo/ch05/php8_bc_break_magic_to_string.php
    class Test {
        public $fname = 'Fred';
        public $lname = 'Flintstone';
        public function __toString() : string {
            return $this->fname . ' ' . $this->lname;
        }
    }
    ```

2. We then create an instance of the class, followed by a `ReflectionObject` instance:

    ```php
    $test = new Test;
    $reflect = new ReflectionObject($test);
    echo $reflect;
    ```

The first few lines of output running in PHP 7 (shown here) simply reveal that it's an instance of the `Test` class:

```
root@php8_tips_php7 [ /repo/ch05 ]#
php php8_bc_break_magic_to_string.php
Object of class [ <user> class Test ] {
  @@ /repo/ch05/php8_bc_break_magic_to_string.php 3-12
```

Running the same code example in PHP 8, however, reveals the silent association with the `Stringable` interface:

```
root@php8_tips_php8 [ /repo/ch05 ]#
php php8_bc_break_magic_to_string.php
Object of class [ <user> class Test implements Stringable ] {
  @@ /repo/ch05/php8_bc_break_magic_to_string.php 3-12
```

The output shows that even though you did not explicitly implement the `Stringable` interface, the association was created at runtime, and is revealed by the `ReflectionObject` instance.

> **Tip**
> For more information on magic methods, have a look at this documentation page: `https://www.php.net/manual/en/language.oop5.magic.php`.

Now that you have an understanding of the situations where PHP 8 code involving magic methods could cause a code break, let's have a look at changes in the serialization process.

Taking control of serialization

There are many times when native PHP data needs to be stored in a file, or in a database table. The problem with current technology is that direct storage of complex PHP data such as objects or arrays is simply not possible, with some exceptions.

One way to overcome this limitation is to convert the object or array into a string. **JSON (JavaScript Object Notation)** is often chosen for this reason. Once the data has been converted into a string, it can easily be stored in any file or database. However, there is a problem with formatting objects with JSON. Although JSON is able to represent object properties well enough, it's incapable of directly restoring the original object's class and methods.

To address this deficiency, the PHP language includes two native functions, `serialize()` and `unserialize()`, that can easily convert objects or arrays into a string and restore them back to their original state. As wonderful as this sounds, there are a number of issues associated with native PHP serialization.

Before we can properly discuss the problem with the existing PHP serialization architecture, we need to have a closer look at how native PHP serialization works.

Understanding PHP serialization

When a PHP object or array needs to be saved to a non-OOP environment such as a flat file or relational database table, `serialize()` can be used to *flatten* an object or array into a string, suitable for storage. Conversely, `unserialize()` restores the original object or array.

Here is a simple example that demonstrates this concept:

1. First, we define a class with three properties:

   ```php
   // /repo/ch05/php8_serialization.php
   class Test {
       public $name = 'Doug';
       private $key = 12345;
       protected $status = ['A','B','C'];
   }
   ```

2. We then create an instance, serialize the instance, and display the resulting string:

   ```php
   $test = new Test();
   $str = serialize($test);
   echo $str . "\n";
   ```

3. Here is how the serialized object appears:

   ```
   O:4:"Test":3:{s:4:"name";s:4:"Doug";s:9:"Testkey";
   i:12345;
   s:9:"*status";a:3:{i:0;s:1:"A";i:1;s:1:"B";i:2;s:1:"C";}}
   ```

   As you can see from the serialized string, the letter O designates *Object*, a is for *array*, s is for *string* and i is for *integer*.

4. We then unserialize the object into a new variable and use `var_dump()` to examine the two:

   ```php
   $obj = unserialize($str);
   var_dump($test, $obj);
   ```

5. Placing the `var_dump()` outputs side by side, you can clearly see that the restored object is identical to the original:

```
object(Test)#1 (3) {                    object(Test)#2 (3) {
  ["name"]=> string(4)                    ["name"]=> string(4)
"Doug"                                  "Doug"
  ["key":"Test":private]=>                ["key":"Test":private]=>
int(12345)                              int(12345)
  ["status":protected]=>                  ["status":protected]=>
  array(3) {                              array(3) {
    [0]=> string(1)                         [0]=> string(1)
"A"                                     "A"
    [1]=> string(1)                         [1]=> string(1)
"B"                                     "B"
    [2]=> string(1)                         [2]=> string(1)
"C"                                     "C"
  }                                       }
}                                       }
```

Let's now have a look at the magic methods that supply legacy PHP serialization support: `__sleep()` and `__wakeup()`.

Understanding the __sleep() magic method

The purpose of the `__sleep()` magic method is to provide a filter used to prevent certain properties from appearing in the serialized string. To use a user object as an example, you may wish to exclude sensitive properties such as a national identification number, credit card number, or password from the serialization.

Here is an example using the `__sleep()` magic method to exclude a password:

1. First, we define a `Test` class with three properties:

```
// /repo/ch05/php8_serialization_sleep.php
class Test {
    public $name = 'Doug';
    protected $key = 12345;
    protected $password = '$2y$10$ux07vQNSA0ctbzZcZNA'
        . 'lx0a8hi6kchJrJZzqWcxpw/XQUjSNqacx.';
```

2. We then define a __sleep() method that excludes the $password property:

```
    public function __sleep() {
        return ['name','key'];
    }
}
```

3. We then create an instance of this class and serialize it. The last line echoes the state of the serialized string:

```
$test = new Test();
$str = serialize($test)
echo $str . "\n";
```

4. In the output, you can clearly see that the $password property is not present. Here is the output:

```
O:4:"Test":2:{s:4:"name";s:4:"Doug";s:6:"*key";i:12345;}
```

This is important in that, in most cases, the reason you need to serialize an object is you wish to store it somewhere, whether that be in a session file or in a database. If the filesystem or database is subsequently compromised, you have one less security vulnerability to worry about!

Understanding a potential code break in the __sleep() method

There is a potential code break involving the __sleep() magic method. In versions prior to PHP 8, if __sleep() returns an array with non-existent properties, they are still serialized and assigned a value of NULL. The problem with this approach is that when the object is subsequently unserialized, an extra property now appears, one that is not there by design!

In PHP 8, non-existent properties in the __sleep() magic method return are silently ignored. If your legacy code anticipates the old behavior and takes steps to *delete* the unwanted property, or even worse, if your code assumes the unwanted property exists, you will ultimately have an error. Such assumptions are extremely dangerous as they can lead to unexpected code behavior.

To illustrate the issue, have a look at the following code example:

1. First, we define a `Test` class that defines `__sleep()` to return a variable that doesn't exist:

   ```
   class Test {
       public $name = 'Doug';
       public function __sleep() {
           return ['name', 'missing'];
       }
   }
   ```

2. Next, we create an instance of `Test` and serialize it:

   ```
   echo "Test instance before serialization:\n";
   $test = new Test();
   var_dump($test);
   ```

3. We then unserialize the string into a new instance, `$restored`:

   ```
   echo "Test instance after serialization:\n";
   $stored = serialize($test);
   $restored = unserialize($stored);
   var_dump($restored);
   ```

4. In theory, the two object instances `$test` and `$restored` should be the same. However, have a look at the output running in PHP 7:

   ```
   root@php8_tips_php7 [ /repo/ch05 ]#
   php php8_bc_break_sleep.php
   Test instance before serialization:
   /repo/ch05/php8_bc_break_sleep.php:13:
   class Test#1 (1) {
     public $name => string(4) "Doug"
   }
   Test instance after serialization:
   PHP Notice:  serialize(): "missing" returned as member variable from __sleep() but does not exist in /repo/ch05/php8_bc_break_sleep.php on line 16
   class Test#2 (2) {
     public $name => string(4) "Doug"
   ```

```
    public $missing =>   NULL
}
```

5. As you can see from the output, the two objects are clearly *not* the same! However, in PHP 8, the non-existent property is ignored. Have a look at the same script running in PHP 8:

```
root@php8_tips_php8 [ /repo/ch05 ]# php php8_bc_break_
sleep.php
Test instance before serialization:
object(Test)#1 (1) {
   ["name"]=> string(4) "Doug"
}
Test instance after serialization:
PHP Warning:  serialize(): "missing" returned as member
variable from __sleep() but does not exist in /repo/ch05/
php8_bc_break_sleep.php on line 16
object(Test)#2 (1) {
   ["name"]=> string(4) "Doug"
}
```

You might also observe that in PHP 7, a `Notice` is issued, whereas in PHP 8, the same situation produces a `Warning`. A pre-migration check for a potential code break in this case is difficult because you would need to determine, if the magic method __sleep() is defined, whether or not a non-existent property is being included in the list.

Let's now have a look at the counterpart method, __wakeup().

Learning about __wakeup()

The purpose of the __wakeup() magic method is mainly to perform additional initialization on the unserialized object. Examples would be to restore a database connection or reinstate a file handle. Here's a very simple example that uses __wakeup() magic to re-open a file handle:

1. First, we define a class that opens a file handle upon instantiation. We also define a method that returns the contents of the file:

```
// /repo/ch05/php8_serialization_wakeup.php
class Gettysburg {
    public $fn = __DIR__ . '/gettysburg.txt';
```

```
public $obj = NULL;
public function __construct() {
    $this->obj = new SplFileObject($this->fn, 'r');
}
public function getText() {
    $this->obj->rewind();
    return $this->obj->fpassthru();
}
}
```

2. To use the class, create an instance, and run `getText()`. (This assumes that the file referenced by `$this->fn` exists!)

```
$old = new Gettysburg();
echo $old->getText();
```

3. The output (not shown) is the Gettysburg Address.
4. If we now attempt to serialize this object, a problem arises. Here's an example of code that would serialize the object:

```
$str = serialize($old);
```

5. At this point, running the code in place so far, here is the output:

```
PHP Fatal error:  Uncaught Exception: Serialization
of 'SplFileObject' is not allowed in /repo/ch05/php8_
serialization_wakeup.php:19
```

6. In order to fix this problem, we return to the class and add a `__sleep()` method that prevents the `SplFileObject` instance from being serialized:

```
public function __sleep() {
    return ['fn'];
}
```

7. If we then rerun the code to serialize the object, all is well. Here is the code to unserialize and call `getText()`:

```
$str = serialize($old);
$new = unserialize($str);
echo $new->getText();
```

8. However, if we then attempt to unserialize the object, another error occurs:

```
PHP Fatal error:  Uncaught Error: Call to a member
function rewind() on null in /repo/ch05/php8_
serialization_wakeup.php:13
```

The problem, of course, is that the file handle was lost during serialization. When the object was unserialized, the __construct() method was not called.

9. This is exactly why the __wakeup() magic method exists. To resolve the error, we define a __wakeup() method that calls the __construct() method:

```
public function __wakeup() {
    self::__construct();
}
```

10. If we rerun the code, we now see the Gettysburg Address twice (not shown).

Now you have an idea of how PHP native serialization works, and also know a bit about the __sleep() and __wakeup() magic methods, as well as potential code breaks. Let's now have a look at an interface that was designed to facilitate the custom serialization of objects.

Introducing the Serializable interface

In order to facilitate the serialization of objects, the `Serializable` interface was added to the language beginning with PHP 5.1. The idea behind this interface was to provide a way of identifying objects that had the ability to serialize themselves. In addition, the methods specified by this interface were designed to provide some degree of control over object serialization.

As long as a class implements this interface, developers are assured that two methods are defined: `serialize()` and `unserialize()`. Here is the interface definition:

```
interface Serializable {
    public serialize () : string|null
    public unserialize (string $serialized) : void
}
```

Any class that implements this interface has its custom `serialize()` and `unserialize()` methods automatically invoked during native serialization or unserialization. To illustrate this technique, consider the following example:

1. First, we define a class that implements the `Serializable` interface. The class defines three properties – two of type string, the other representing date and time:

```
// /repo/ch05/php8_bc_break_serializable.php
class A implements Serializable {
    private $a = 'A';
    private $b = 'B';
    private $u = NULL;
```

2. We then define a custom `serialize()` method that initializes the date and time before serializing the object's properties. The `unserialize()` method restores values to all properties:

```
    public function serialize() {
        $this->u = new DateTime();
        return serialize(get_object_vars($this));
    }
    public function unserialize($payload) {
        $vars = unserialize($payload);
        foreach ($vars as $key => $val)
            $this->$key = $val;
    }
}
```

3. We then create an instance and examine its contents using `var_dump()`:

```
$a1 = new A();
var_dump($a1);
```

4. The output from `var_dump()` shows us that the u property is not yet initialized:

```
object(A)#1 (3) {
    ["a":"A":private]=> string(1) "A"
    ["b":"A":private]=> string(1) "B"
    ["u":"A":private]=> NULL
}
```

5. We then serialize it, and restore it to a variable, $a2:

```
$str = serialize($a1);
$a2 = unserialize($str);
var_dump($a2);
```

6. From the `var_dump()` output below, you can see that the object has been fully restored. In addition, we know that the custom `serialize()` method was invoked because the u property is initialized with a date and time value. Here is the output:

```
object(A)#3 (3) {
  ["a":"A":private]=> string(1) "A"
  ["b":"A":private]=> string(1) "B"
  ["u":"A":private]=> object(DateTime)#4 (3) {
    ["date"]=> string(26) "2021-02-12 05:35:10.835999"
    ["timezone_type"]=> int(3)
    ["timezone"]=> string(3) "UTC"
  }
}
```

Let's now have a look at issues with the serialization process for objects that implement the `Serializable` interface.

Examining PHP serializable interface issues

There is an overall problem with the earlier approach to serialization. If a class to be serialized has defined a `__wakeup()` magic method, it's not invoked immediately upon unserialization. Rather, any defined `__wakeup()` magic methods are first queued up, the entire chain of objects is unserialized, and only then are methods in the queue executed. This can result in a mismatch between what is seen by an object's `unserialize()` method compared to what is seen by its queued `__wakeup()` method.

This architectural flaw can result in inconsistent behavior and ambiguous results when dealing with objects that implement the `Serializable` interface. Many developers consider the `Serializable` interface to be severely broken due to the need to create back references when the serialization of nested objects occurs. This need arises in situations where **nested serialization calls** occur.

Such nested calls might occur, for example, when a class defines a method that in turn calls the PHP `serialize()` function. The order in which back references are created is preset in PHP serialization prior to PHP 8, potentially causing an avalanche of cascading failures.

The solution is to use two new magic methods to give you complete control over serialization and unserialization sequencing, described next.

New magic methods to control PHP serialization

A new way of controlling serialization was first introduced in PHP 7.4 and carried over into PHP 8. In order to take advantage of this new technology, all you need to do is to implement two magic methods: `__serialize()` and `__unserialize()`. If implemented, PHP turns control over serialization entirely to the `__serialize()` method. Likewise, unserialization is entirely controlled by the `__unserialize()` magic method. The `__sleep()` and `__wakeup()` methods, if defined, are ignored.

As a further benefit, PHP 8 provides full support for the two new magic methods in the following SPL classes:

- `ArrayObject`
- `ArrayIterator`
- `SplDoublyLinkedList`
- `SplObjectStorage`

> **Best practice**
>
> To gain full control over serialization, implement the new `__serialize()` and `__unserialize()` magic methods. You no longer need to implement the `Serializable` interface, nor do you need to define `__sleep()` and `__wakeup()`. For more information on the eventual discontinuation of the `Serializable` interface, see this RFC: https://wiki.php.net/rfc/phase_out_serializable.

As an example of the new PHP serialization usage, consider the following code example:

1. In the example, a `Test` class is initialized with a random key upon instantiation:

```php
// /repo/ch05/php8_bc_break_serialization.php
class Test extends ArrayObject {
    protected $id = 12345;
    public $name = 'Doug';
```

```php
        private $key = '';
        public function __construct() {
            $this->key = bin2hex(random_bytes(8));
        }
```

2. We add a `getKey()` method that reveals the current key value:

```php
        public function getKey() {
            return $this->key;
        }
```

3. When serialized, the key is filtered out of the resulting string:

```php
        public function __serialize() {
            return ['id' => $this->id,
                    'name' => $this->name];
        }
```

4. Upon unserialization, a new key is generated:

```php
        public function __unserialize($data) {
            $this->id = $data['id'];
            $this->name = $data['name'];
            $this->__construct();
        }
    }
```

5. We now create an instance, and reveal the key:

```php
$test = new Test();
echo "\nOld Key: " . $test->getKey() . "\n";
```

Here is how the key might appear:

```
Old Key: mXq78DhplByDWuPtzk820g==
```

6. We add code to serialize the object and display the string:

```php
$str = serialize($test);
echo $str . "\n";
```

Here is how the serialized string might appear:

```
O:4:"Test":2:{s:2:"id";i:12345;s:4:"name";s:4:"Doug";}
```

Note from the output that the secret does not appear in the serialized string. This is important because if the storage location of the serialized string is compromised, a security vulnerability might be exposed, giving an attacker a way to break into your system.

7. We then add code to unserialize the string and reveal the key:

```
$obj = unserialize($str);
echo "New Key: " . $obj->getKey() . "\n";
```

Here is the last bit of output. Notice that a new key has been generated:

```
New Key: kDgU7FGfJn5qlOKcHEbyqQ==
```

As you can see, using the new PHP serialization feature is not complicated. Any timing issues are now fully in your control because the new magic methods are executed in the order in which the objects are serialized and unserialized.

> **Important note**
> PHP 7.4 and above *understands* serialized strings from older versions of PHP, however, strings serialized by PHP 7.4 or 8.x might not be properly unserialized by older versions of PHP.

> **Tip**
> For a full discussion, please see the RFC on custom serialization:
> https://wiki.php.net/rfc/custom_object_serialization

You now have a full understanding of PHP serialization and the improved support provided by the two new magic methods. It's now time to shift gears and examine how PHP 8 expands variance support.

Understanding PHP 8 expanded variance support

The concept of variance is at the heart of OOP. **Variance** is an umbrella term that covers how the various **subtypes** interrelate. Some 20 years ago, a pair of early computer scientists, Wing and Liskov, devised an important theorem that is at the heart of OOP subtypes, now known as **the Liskov Substitution Principle**.

Without going into the precise mathematics, this principle can be paraphrased as follows:

Class X can be considered a subtype of class Y if you are able to substitute an instance of X in place of an instance of Y, and the application's behavior does not change in any way.

> **Tip**
> The actual paper that first described and provided the precise mathematical formulaic definition of the Liskov Substitution Principle can be found here: *A behavioral notion of subtyping*, ACM Transactions on Programming Languages and Systems, by B. Liskov and J. Wing, November 1994 (`https://dl.acm.org/doi/10.1145/197320.197383`).

In this section, we examine how PHP 8 provides enhanced variance support in the form of **covariant returns** and **contraviariant parameters**. An understanding of covariance and contravariance will increase your ability to write good solid code. Without this understanding, your code might produce inconsistent results and become the source of many bugs.

Let's start by covering covariant returns.

Understanding covariant returns

Covariance support in PHP is designed to preserve the ordering of types from the most specific to the most general. A classic example of this is seen in how `try / catch` blocks are formulated:

1. In this example, a `PDO` instance is created inside the `try` block. The following two `catch` blocks look first for a `PDOException`. Following this is a second `catch` block that catches any class that implements `Throwable`. Because both the PHP `Exception` and `Error` classes implement `Throwable`, the second `catch` block ends up as a fallback for any error other than a `PDOException`:

```
try {
    $pdo = new PDO($dsn, $usr, $pwd, $opts);
```

```
        } catch (PDOException $p) {
            error_log('Database Error: ' . $p->getMessage());
        } catch (Throwable $t) {
            error_log('Unknown Error: ' . $t->getMessage());
        }
```

2. In this example, if a PDO instance fails due to invalid parameters, the error log would have the entry **Database Error** followed by a message gleaned from the PDOException.

3. On the other hand, if some other general error occurred, the error log would have the entry **Unknown Error** followed by the message coming from some other Exception or Error class.

4. In this example, however, the order of the catch blocks is reversed:

```
try {
    $pdo = new PDO($dsn, $usr, $pwd, $opts);
} catch (Throwable $t) {
    error_log('Unknown Error: ' . $t->getMessage());
} catch (PDOException $p) {
    error_log('Database Error: ' . $p->getMessage());
}
```

5. Due to the way PHP covariance support works, the second catch block would never be invoked. Instead, all error log entries originating from this block of code would have an entry starting with **Unknown Error**.

Let's now have a look at how PHP covariance support applies to object method return data types:

1. First, we define an interface, FactoryIterface, that identifies a method, make(). This method accepts an array as an argument and is expected to return an object of type ArrayObject:

```
interface FactoryInterface {
    public function make(array $arr) : ArrayObject;
}
```

2. Next, we define an `ArrTest` class that extends `ArrayObject`:

```
class ArrTest extends ArrayObject {
    const DEFAULT_TEST = 'This is a test';
}
```

3. The `ArrFactory` class implements `FactoryInterface` and fully defines the `make()` method. Note, however, that this method returns the `ArrTest` data type and not `ArrayObject`:

```
class ArrFactory implements FactoryInterface {
    protected array $data;
    public function make(array $data) : ArrTest {
        $this->data = $data;
        return new ArrTest($this->data);
    }
}
```

4. In the block of procedural calling code, we create an instance of `ArrFactory`, and run its `make()` method twice, theoretically producing two `ArrTest` instances. We then use `var_dump()` to reveal the current state of the two objects produced:

```
$factory = new ArrFactory();
$obj1 = $factory->make([1,2,3]);
$obj2 = $factory->make(['A','B','C']);
var_dump($obj1, $obj2);
```

5. In PHP 7.1, as it does not support covariant return data types, a fatal `Error` is thrown. The output, shown here, tells us that the method return type declaration doesn't match what's been defined in `FactoryInterface`:

```
root@php8_tips_php7 [ /repo/ch05 ]#
php php8_variance_covariant.php
PHP Fatal error:  Declaration of ArrFactory::make(array
$data): ArrTest must be compatible with
FactoryInterface::make(array $arr): ArrayObject in /repo/
ch05/php8_variance_covariant.php on line 9
```

6. When we run the same code in PHP 8, you can see that covariance support is provided for return types. Execution proceeds unhindered, as shown here:

```
root@php8_tips_php8 [ /repo/ch05 ]#
php php8_variance_covariant.php
object(ArrTest)#2 (1) {
  ["storage":"ArrayObject":private]=>
  array(3) {
    [0]=>    int(1)
    [1]=>    int(2)
    [2]=>    int(3)
  }
}
object(ArrTest)#3 (1) {
  ["storage":"ArrayObject":private]=>
  array(3) {
    [0]=>    string(1) "A"
    [1]=>    string(1) "B"
    [2]=>    string(1) "C"
  }
}
```

`ArrTest` extends `ArrayObject` and is a suitable subtype that clearly meets the criteria defined by the Liskov Substitution Principle. As you can see from the last output, PHP 8 more fully embraces true OOP principles than the earlier versions of PHP. The end result is that your code and application architecture can be much more intuitive and logically reasonable when using PHP 8.

Let's now have a look at contravariant parameters.

Using contravariant parameters

Whereas covariance concerns the ordering of subtypes from general to specific, **contravariance** concerns the reverse: from specific to general. In PHP 7 and earlier, full support for contravariance was not available. Accordingly, implementing an interface or extending an abstract class, in PHP 7, parameter type hints are **invariant**.

In PHP 8, on the other hand, due to support for contravariant parameters, you are free to be specific in top-level super classes and interfaces. As long as the subtype is compatible, you can then modify the type hint in the extending or implementing class to be more general.

This gives you much more freedom in defining an overall architecture where you define interfaces or abstract classes. Developers using your interfaces or super classes are given a great deal more flexibility in PHP 8 when it comes to implementing descendent class logic.

Let's have a look at how PHP 8 support for contravariant parameters works:

1. In this example, we first define a `IterObj` class that extends the built-in `ArrayIterator` PHP class:

   ```
   // /repo/ch05/php8_variance_contravariant.php
   class IterObj extends ArrayIterator {}
   ```

2. We then define an abstract `Base` class that mandates a method, `stringify()`. Note that the data type for its only argument is `IterObj`:

   ```
   abstract class Base {
       public abstract function stringify(IterObj $it);
   }
   ```

3. Next, we define a `IterTest` class that extends `Base` and provides an implementation for the `stringify()` method. Of particular interest is that we override the data type, changing it to `iterable`:

   ```
   class IterTest extends Base {
       public function stringify(iterable $it) {
           return implode(',',
               iterator_to_array($it)) . "\n";
       }
   }
   class IterObj extends ArrayIterator {}
   ```

4. The next few lines of code create instances of `IterTest`, `IterObj`, and `ArrayIterator`. We then invoke the `stringify()` method twice, supplying each of the latter objects as an argument:

```
$test  = new IterTest();
$objIt = new IterObj([1,2,3]);
$arrIt = new ArrayIterator(['A','B','C']);
echo $test->stringify($objIt);
echo $test->stringify($arrIt);
```

5. Running this code example in PHP 7.1 produces the expected fatal `Error` as shown here:

```
root@php8_tips_php7 [ /repo/ch05 ]#
php php8_variance_contravariant.php
PHP Fatal error:  Declaration of
IterTest::stringify(iterable $it) must be compatible with
Base::stringify(IterObj $it) in /repo/ch05/php8_variance_
contravariant.php on line 11
```

Because PHP 7.1 does not provide support for contravariant parameters, it treats the data type for its parameters as invariant, and simply displays a message indicating that the data type of the child class is incompatible with the data type specified in the parent class.

6. PHP 8, on the other hand, provides support for contravariant parameters. Accordingly, it recognizes that `IterObj`, the data type specified in the `Base` class, is a subtype compatible with `iterable`. Further, both arguments provided are compatible with `iterable` as well, allowing program execution to proceed. Here is the PHP 8 output:

```
root@php8_tips_php8 [ /repo/ch05 ]# php php8_variance_
contravariant.php
1,2,3
A,B,C
```

The main advantage you derive from PHP 8 support for covariant returns and contravariant parameters is the ability to override not only method logic but the **method signature** as well. You will find that although PHP 8 is much stricter in its enforcement of good coding practices, the enhanced variance support gives you greater freedom in designing your inheritance structure. In a certain sense, at least with regards to parameter and return value data types, PHP 8 is, if anything, *less* restrictive!

> **Tip**
> For a full explanation of how variance support is applied in PHP 7.4 and PHP 8, have a look here: `https://wiki.php.net/rfc/covariant-returns-and-contravariant-parameters`.

We'll now have a look at changes to the SPL and how those changes can have an impact on application performance after migrating to PHP 8.

Handling Standard PHP Library (SPL) changes

The **SPL** is an extension that contains key classes that implement basic data structures and enhance OOP functionality. It was first introduced in PHP 5 and is now included by default in all PHP installations. Covering the entire SPL is beyond the scope of this book. Instead, in this section, we discuss where significant changes have occurred in the SPL when running PHP 8. In addition, we give you tips and guidance on SPL changes that have the potential to cause your existing applications to stop working.

We start by examining changes to the `SplFileObject` class.

Understanding changes to SplFileObject

`SplFileObject` is an excellent class that incorporates most of the standalone `f*()` functions, such as `fgets()`, `fread()`, `fwrite()`, and so forth, into a single class. `SplFileObject::__construct()` method arguments mirror the arguments provided to the `fopen()` function.

The main difference in PHP 8 is that a relatively obscure method, `fgetss()`, has been removed from the `SplFileObject` class. The `SplFileObject::fgetss()` method, available in PHP 7 and below, mirrors the standalone `fgetss()` function in that it combines `fgets()` with `strip_tags()`.

For the sake of illustration, let's assume you have created a website that allows users to upload text files. Before displaying content from the text file, you wish to remove any markup tags. Here is an example that uses the `fgetss()` method to accomplish this:

1. We first define a block of code that acquires the filename:

```
// /repo/ch05/php7_spl_splfileobject.php
$fn = $_GET['fn'] ?? '';
if (!$fn || !file_exists($fn))
    exit('Unable to locate file');
```

2. We then create the `SplFileObject` instance, and read the file line by line using the `fgetss()` method. At the end, we echo the safe contents:

```
$obj = new SplFileObject($fn, 'r');
$safe = '';
while ($line = $obj->fgetss()) $safe .= $line;
echo '<h1>Contents</h1><hr>' . $safe;
```

3. Let's say that the file to be read is this:

```
<h1>This File is Infected</h1>
<script>alert('You Been Hacked');</script>
<img src="http://very.bad.site/hacked.php" />
```

4. Here is the output running in PHP 7.1 using this URL:

`http://localhost:7777/ch05/php7_spl_splfileobject.php?fn=includes/you_been_hacked.html`

As you can see from the output shown next, all HTML markup tags have been removed:

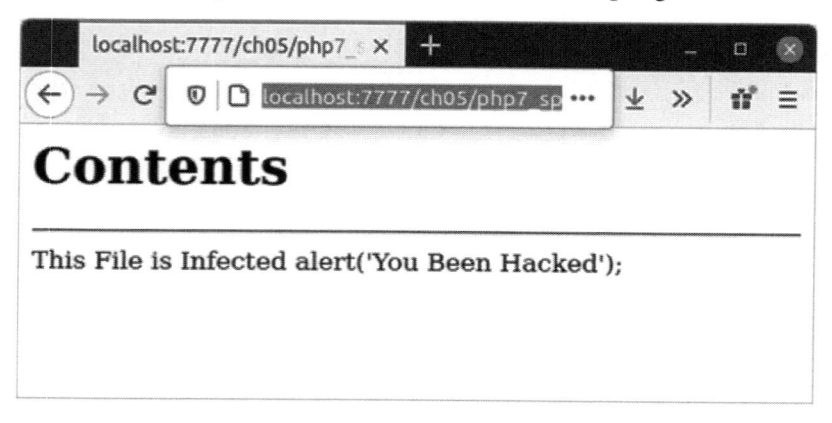

Figure 5.1 – Result after reading a file using SplFileObject::fgetss()

To accomplish the same thing in PHP 8, the code shown previously would need to be modified by replacing `fgetss()` with `fgets()`. We would also need to use `strip_tags()` on the line concatenated to `$safe`. Here is how the modified code might appear:

```
// /repo/ch05/php8_spl_splfileobject.php
$fn = $_GET['fn'] ?? '';
if (!$fn || !file_exists($fn))
    exit('Unable to locate file');
```

```
$obj = new SplFileObject($fn, 'r');
$safe = '';
while ($line = $obj->fgets())
    $safe .= strip_tags($line);
echo '<h1>Contents</h1><hr>' . $safe;
```

The output from the modified code is identical to that shown in *Figure 5.1*. We'll now turn our attention to changes in another SPL class: `SplHeap`.

Examining changes to SplHeap

`SplHeap` is a foundational class used to represent data structured as a **binary tree**. Two additional classes are also available that build upon `SplHeap`. `SplMinHeap` organizes the tree with the minimum value at the top. `SplMaxHeap` does the reverse, placing the maximum value at the top.

A heap structure is especially useful in situations where data arrives out of order. Once inserted into the heap, the item is automatically placed in its proper order. Thus, at any given moment, you can display the heap safe in the knowledge that all items will be in order without having to run one of the PHP sort functions.

The key to maintaining the automatic sort order is to define an abstract method, `compare()`. As this method is abstract, `SplHeap` cannot be instantiated directly. Instead, you need to extend the class and implement `compare()`.

There is the potential for a backward-compatible code break when using `SplHeap` in PHP 8 as the method signature for `compare()` must be exactly as follows: `SplHeap::compare($value1, $value2)`.

Let's now have a look at a code example that uses `SplHeap` to build a list of billionaires organized by last name:

1. First, we define a file with data on billionaires. In this example, we simply copied and pasted data from this source: `https://www.bloomberg.com/billionaires/`.
2. We then define a `BillionaireTracker` class that extracts information from the pasted text into an array of ordered pairs. The full source code (not shown here) for the class can be found in the source code repository here:`/repo/src/Services/BillionaireTracker.php`.

Here is how the data produced by the class appears:

```
array(20) {
  [0] => array(1) {
    [177000000000] =>      string(10) "Bezos,Jeff"
  }
  [1] => array(1) {
    [157000000000] =>      string(9) "Musk,Elon"
  }
  [2] => array(1) {
    [136000000000] =>      string(10) "Gates,Bill"
  }
... remaining data not shown
```

As you can see, the data is presented in descending order where the key represents net worth. In contrast, in our sample program, we plan to produce data in ascending order by last name.

3. We then define a constant that identifies the billionaire data source file, and set up an autoloader:

```
// /repo/ch05/php7_spl_splheap.php
define('SRC_FILE', __DIR__
    . '/../sample_data/billionaires.txt');
require_once __DIR__
    . '/../src/Server/Autoload/Loader.php';
$loader = new \Server\Autoload\Loader();
```

4. Next, we create an instance of the `BillionaireTracker` class and assign the results to `$list`:

```
use Services\BillionaireTracker;
$tracker = new BillionaireTracker();
$list = $tracker->extract(SRC_FILE);
```

5. Now comes the part of most interest: creating the heap. To accomplish this, we define an anonymous class that extends SplHeap. We then define a compare() method that performs the necessary logic to place inserted elements in their proper place. PHP 7 allows you to change the method signature. In this example, we provide arguments in the form of an array:

```
$heap = new class () extends SplHeap {
    public function compare(
        array $arr1, array $arr2) : int {
        $cmp1 = array_values($arr2)[0];
        $cmp2 = array_values($arr1)[0];
        return $cmp1 <=> $cmp2;
    }
};
```

You might also note that the value for $cmp1 is assigned from the second array, and the value for $cmp2 is from the first array. The reason for this switch is because we wish to produce results in ascending order.

6. We then use SplHeap::insert() to add elements to the heap:

```
foreach ($list as $item)
    $heap->insert($item);
```

7. Finally, we define a BillionaireTracker::view() method (not shown) to run through the heap and display results:

```
$patt = "%20s\t%32s\n";
$line = str_repeat('-', 56) . "\n";
echo $tracker->view($heap, $patt, $line);
```

8. Here is the output produced by our little program running in PHP 7.1:

```
root@php8_tips_php7 [ /repo/ch05 ]#
php php7_spl_splheap.php
--------------------------------------------------------
            Net Worth                               Name
--------------------------------------------------------
        84,000,000,000                     Ambani,Mukesh
       115,000,000,000                   Arnault,Bernard
        83,600,000,000                      Ballmer,Steve
```

```
       ... some lines were omitted to save space ...
    58,200,000,000                                Walton,Rob
   100,000,000,000                                Zuckerberg,Mark
------------------------------------------------------------
                                               1,795,100,000,000
------------------------------------------------------------
```

You will note, however, that when we attempt to run the same program in PHP 8, an error is thrown. Here is the output of the same program running in PHP 8:

```
root@php8_tips_php8 [ /repo/ch05 ]# php php7_spl_splheap.php
PHP Fatal error:  Declaration of SplHeap@
anonymous::compare(array $arr1, array $arr2): int must be
compatible with SplHeap::compare(mixed $value1, mixed $value2)
in /repo/ch05/php7_spl_splheap.php on line 16
```

Accordingly, to get this working properly, we must redefine the anonymous class that extends `SplHeap`. Here is a modified version of that portion of the code:

```
$heap = new class () extends SplHeap {
    public function compare($arr1, $arr2) : int {
        $cmp1 = array_values($arr2)[0];
        $cmp2 = array_values($arr1)[0];
        return $cmp1 <=> $cmp2;
    }
};
```

The only change is in the `compare()` method signature. When executed, the results (not shown) are identical. The full code for PHP 8 can be viewed at `/repo/ch05/php8_spl_splheap.php`.

This concludes our discussion of changes to the `SplHeap` class. Please note that the same change also applies to `SplMinHeap` and `SplMaxHeap`. Let's now have a look at a potentially significant change in the `SplDoublyLinkedList` class.

Handling changes in SplDoublyLinkedList

The `SplDoublyLinkedList` class is an iterator that's able to display information in either **FIFO (First-In, First-Out)** or **LIFO (Last-In, First-Out)** order. It's more common, however, to say that you can iterate through the list in either forward or reverse order.

This is a very powerful addition to any developer's library. To do the same thing with `ArrayIterator`, for example, would require at least a dozen lines of code! Accordingly, PHP developers like to use this class for situations where they need to navigate a list in either direction at will.

Unfortunately, there is a potential code break due to a difference in the return value of the `push()` and `unshift()` methods. The `push()` method is used to add a value at the *end* of the list. The `unshift()` method, on the other hand, adds value to the *beginning* of the list.

In PHP 7 and below, these methods, if successful, returned Boolean `TRUE`. If the method failed, it returned Boolean `FALSE`. In PHP 8, however, neither method returns a value. If you look at the method signature in the current documentation, you will see a return data type of `void`. The potential code break can arise where you check to return a value of either `push()` or `unshift()` before continuing.

Let's have a look at a simple example that populates a doubly linked list with a simple list of five values, and displays them in both FIFO and LIFO order:

1. First, we define an anonymous class that extends `SplDoublyLinkedList`. We also add a `show()` method that displays the contents of the list:

    ```php
    // /repo/ch05/php7_spl_spldoublylinkedlist.php
    $double = new class() extends SplDoublyLinkedList {
        public function show(int $mode) {
            $this->setIteratorMode($mode);
            $this->rewind();
            while ($item = $this->current()) {
                echo $item . ' . ';
                $this->next();
            }
        }
    };
    ```

2. Next, we define an array of sample data, and use `push()` to insert the value into the linked list. Note that an `if()` statement is used to determine whether the operation succeeds or fails. If the operation fails, an `Exception` is thrown:

```php
$item = ['Person', 'Woman', 'Man', 'Camera', 'TV'];
foreach ($item as $key => $value)
    if (!$double->push($value))
        throw new Exception('ERROR');
```

This is the block of code where the potential code break exists. In PHP 7 and below, `push()` returns `TRUE` or `FALSE`. In PHP 8, there is no return value.

3. We then use the `SplDoublyLinkedList` class constants to set the mode to FIFO (forward), and display the list:

```php
echo "*************** Foward ******************\n";
$forward = SplDoublyLinkedList::IT_MODE_FIFO
         | SplDoublyLinkedList::IT_MODE_KEEP;
$double->show($forward);
```

4. Next, we use the `SplDoublyLinkedList` class constants to set the mode to LIFO (reverse), and display the list:

```php
echo "\n\n************ Reverse ****************\n";
$reverse = SplDoublyLinkedList::IT_MODE_LIFO
         | SplDoublyLinkedList::IT_MODE_KEEP;
$double->show($reverse);
```

Here is the output running in PHP 7.1:

```
root@php8_tips_php7 [ /repo/ch05 ]#
php php7_spl_spldoublylinkedlist.php
*************** Foward ******************
Person. Woman. Man. Camera. TV.
*************** Reverse ******************
TV. Camera. Man. Woman. Person.
```

5. If we run the same code in PHP 8, this is the result:

```
root@php8_tips_php8 [ /home/ch05 ]#
php php7_spl_spldoublylinkedlist.php
PHP Fatal error:  Uncaught Exception: ERROR in /home/
ch05/php7_spl_spldoublylinkedlist.php:23
```

If no value is returned by push(), inside the if() statement PHP assumes NULL, which in turn is interpolated as Boolean FALSE! Accordingly, after the first push() command, the if() block causes an Exception to be thrown. Because the Exception is not caught, a fatal Error is generated.

To rewrite this block of code to work in PHP 8, all you need to do is to remove the if() statement, and not throw an Exception. Here's how the rewritten code block (shown in *Step 2*) might appear:

```
$item = ['Person', 'Woman', 'Man', 'Camera', 'TV'];
foreach ($item as $key => $value)
    $double->push($value);
```

Now, if we execute the rewritten code, the results are seen here:

```
root@php8_tips_php7 [ /home/ch05 ]#
php php8_spl_spldoublylinkedlist.php
*************** Foward ********************
Person. Woman. Man. Camera. TV.
*************** Reverse *******************
TV. Camera. Man. Woman. Person.
```

Now you have an idea of how to use SplDoublyLinkedList, and also know about the potential code break relating to push() or unshift(). You also have an idea about potential code breaks when using various SPL classes and functions in PHP 8. This concludes our discussion for this chapter.

Summary

In this chapter, you learned about potential problems in OOP code when migrating to PHP 8. In the first section, you learned how a number of bad practices were allowed in PHP 7 and earlier versions, but now represent a potential code break in PHP 8. With this knowledge, you are a better developer and can deliver high-quality code to benefit your company.

In the next section, you learned good habits when using magic methods. Potential code breaks can occur because PHP 8 now enforces a degree of consistency not seen in earlier versions of PHP. These inconsistencies involve class constructor usage and certain aspects of magic method usage. The following section taught you about PHP serialization and how changes made in PHP 8 can make your code more resilient and less vulnerable to errors or attacks during the serialize and unserialize process.

In this chapter, you also learned about enhanced PHP 8 support for covariant return types and contravariant parameters. Having knowledge of variance, and how support has improved in PHP 8, allows you to be more creative and flexible when developing class inheritance structures in PHP 8. You now know how to write code that was simply not possible in earlier versions of PHP.

The last section covered a number of key classes in the SPL. You learned a great deal about how basic data structures such as heap and linked lists can be implemented in PHP 8. The information in that section was critical in helping you to avoid problems with code involving the SPL.

The next chapter continues the discussion on potential code breaks. The emphasis in the next chapter, however, is on *procedural* rather than object code.

6
Understanding PHP 8 Functional Differences

In this chapter, you will learn about potential backward-compatible breaks at the PHP 8 command, or functional, level. This chapter presents important information that highlights potential pitfalls when migrating existing code to PHP 8. The information presented in this chapter is critical to know so that you can produce reliable PHP code. After working through the concepts in this chapter, you'll be in a better position to write code that produces precise results and avoids inconsistencies.

Topics covered in this chapter include the following:

- Learning key advanced string handling differences
- Understanding PHP 8 string-to-numeric comparison improvements
- Handling differences in arithmetic, bitwise, and concatenation operations
- Taking advantage of locale independence
- Handling arrays in PHP 8
- Mastering changes in security functions and settings

Technical requirements

To examine and run the code examples provided in this chapter, the minimum recommended hardware is the following:

- An x86_64-based desktop PC or laptop
- 1 gigabyte (GB) of free disk space
- 4 GB of RAM
- A 500 kilobits per second (Kbps) or faster internet connection

In addition, you will need to install the following software:

- Docker
- Docker Compose

Please refer to the *Technical requirements* section in *Chapter 1, Introducing New PHP 8 OOP Features,* for more information on Docker and Docker Compose installation, as well as how to build the Docker container used to demonstrate the code explained in this book. In this book, we refer to the directory in which you restored the sample code for this book as `/repo`.

The source code for this chapter is located here:

`https://github.com/PacktPublishing/PHP-8-Programming-Tips-Tricks-and-Best-Practices.`

We can now begin our discussion by examining the differences in string handling introduced in PHP 8.

Learning key advanced string handling differences

String functions in general have been tightened and normalized in PHP 8. You will find that usage is more heavily restricted in PHP 8, which ultimately forces you to produce better code. We can say that the nature and order of string function arguments is much more uniform in PHP 8, which is why we say that the PHP core team has normalized usage.

These improvements are especially evident when dealing with numeric strings. Other changes in PHP 8 string handling involve minor changes to arguments. In this section, we introduce you to the key changes in how PHP 8 handles strings.

It's important to understand not only the handling improvements introduced in PHP 8 but also to understand the deficiencies in string handling prior to PHP 8.

Let's first have a look at an aspect of PHP 8 string handling in functions that search for embedded strings.

Handling changes to the needle argument

A number of PHP string functions search for the presence of a substring within a larger string. These functions include `strpos()`, `strrpos()`, `stripos()`, `strripos()`, `strstr()`, `strchr()`, `strrchr()`, and `stristr()`. All of these functions have these two parameters in common: the **needle** and the **haystack**.

Differentiating between the needle and the haystack

To illustrate the difference between the needle and the haystack, have a look at the function signature for `strpos()`:

```
strpos(string $haystack,string $needle,int $pos=0) :
int|false
```

`$haystack` is the target of the search. `$needle` is the substring to be sought. The `strpos()` function returns the position of the substring within the search target. If the substring is not found, the Boolean `FALSE` is returned. The other `str*()` functions produce different types of output that we will not detail here.

Two key changes in how PHP 8 handles the needle argument have the potential to break an application migrated to PHP 8. These changes apply to situations where the needle argument is not a string or where the needle argument is empty. Let's have a look at non-string needle argument handling first.

Dealing with non-string needle arguments

Your PHP application might not be taking the proper precautions to ensure that the needle argument to the `str*()` functions mentioned here is always a string. If that is the case, in PHP 8, the needle argument will now *always be interpreted* as a string rather than an ASCII code point.

If you need to supply an ASCII value, you must use the `chr()` function to convert it to a string. In the following example, the ASCII value for LF (`"\n"`) is used instead of a string. In PHP 7 or below, `strpos()` performs an internal conversion before running the search. In PHP 8, the number is simply typecast into a string, yielding unexpected results.

Here is a code example that searches for the presence of LF within a string. However, note that instead of providing a string as an argument, an integer with a value of 10 is provided:

```php
// /repo/ch06/php8_num_str_needle.php
function search($needle, $haystack) {
    $found = (strpos($haystack, $needle))
            ? 'contains' : 'DOES NOT contain';
    return "This string $found LF characters\n";
}
$haystack = "We're looking\nFor linefeeds\nIn this
            string\n";
$needle = 10;          // ASCII code for LF
echo search($needle, $haystack);
```

Here are the results of the code sample running in PHP 7:

```
root@php8_tips_php7 [ /repo/ch06 ]#
php php8_num_str_needle.php
This string contains LF characters
```

And here are the results of the same code block running in PHP 8:

```
root@php8_tips_php8 [ /repo/ch06 ]#
php php8_num_str_needle.php
This string DOES NOT contain LF characters
```

As you can see, comparing the output in PHP 7 with the output in PHP 8, the same code block yields radically different results. This is an extremely difficult potential code break to spot as no `Warnings` or `Errors` are generated.

The best practice is to apply a `string` type hint to the needle argument of any function or method that incorporates one of the PHP `str*()` functions. If we rewrite the previous example, the output is consistent in both PHP 7 and PHP 8. Here is the same example rewritten using a type hint:

```php
// /repo/ch06/php8_num_str_needle_type_hint.php
declare(strict_types=1);
function search(string $needle, string $haystack) {
    $found = (strpos($haystack, $needle))
            ? 'contains' : 'DOES NOT contain';
```

```
    return "This string $found LF characters\n";
}
$haystack = "We're looking\nFor linefeeds\nIn this
            string\n";
$needle   = 10;              // ASCII code for LF
echo search($needle, $haystack);
```

Now, in either version of PHP, this is the output:

```
PHP Fatal error:  Uncaught TypeError: search(): Argument #1
($needle) must be of type string, int given, called in /repo/
ch06/php8_num_str_needle_type_hint.php on line 14 and defined
in /repo/ch06/php8_num_str_needle_type_hint.php:4
```

By declaring `strict_types=1`, and by adding a type hint of `string` before the `$needle` argument, any developer who misuses your code receives a clear indication that this practice is not acceptable.

Let's now have a look at what happens in PHP 8 when the needle argument is missing.

Handling empty needle arguments

Another major change in the `str*()` function is that the needle argument can now be empty (for example, anything that would make the `empty()` function return `TRUE`). This presents *significant* potential for backward compatibility breaks. In PHP 7, if the needle argument is empty, the return value from `strpos()` would be the Boolean `FALSE`, whereas, in PHP 8, the empty value is first converted to a string, thereby producing entirely different results.

It's extremely important to be aware of this potential code break if you plan to update your PHP version to 8. An empty needle argument is difficult to spot when reviewing code manually. This is a situation where a solid set of unit tests is needed to ensure a smooth PHP migration.

To illustrate the potential problem, consider the following example. Assume that the needle argument is empty. In this situation, a traditional `if()` check to see whether the `strpos()` result is not identical to `FALSE` produces different results between PHP 7 and 8. Here is the code example:

1. First, we define a function that reports whether or not the needle value is found in the haystack using `strpos()`. Note the strict type check against the Boolean `FALSE`:

```php
// php7_num_str_empty_needle.php
function test($haystack, $search) {
    $pattern = '%15s | %15s | %10s' . "\n";
    $result  = (strpos($haystack, $search) !== FALSE)
             ? 'FOUND' : 'NOT FOUND';
    return sprintf($pattern,
        var_export($search, TRUE),
        var_export(strpos($haystack, $search),
            TRUE),
        $result);
};
```

2. We then define the haystack as a string with letters and numbers. The needle argument is provided in the form of an array of values that are all considered empty:

```php
$haystack = 'Something Anything 0123456789';
$needles = ['', NULL, FALSE, 0];
foreach ($needles as $search)
    echo test($haystack, $search);
```

The output in PHP 7 appears as follows:

```
root@php8_tips_php7 [ /repo/ch06 ]#
php php7_num_str_empty_needle.php
PHP Warning:  strpos(): Empty needle in /repo/ch06/php7_num_str_empty_needle.php on line 5
// not all Warnings are shown ...
             '' |           false |  NOT FOUND
           NULL |           false |  NOT FOUND
          false |           false |  NOT FOUND
              0 |           false |  NOT FOUND
```

After a set of `Warnings`, the final output appears. As you can see from the output, the return value from `strpos($haystack, $search)` is consistently the Boolean `FALSE` in PHP 7.

The output running the same code in PHP 8, however, is radically different. Here is the output from PHP 8:

```
root@php8_tips_php8 [ /repo/ch06 ]#
php php7_num_str_empty_needle.php
             ''  |         0  |       FOUND
           NULL  |         0  |       FOUND
          false  |         0  |       FOUND
              0  |        19  |       FOUND
```

In PHP 8, the empty needle argument is first silently converted to a string. None of the needle values return the Boolean `FALSE`. This causes the function to report that the needle has been found. This is certainly not the desired result. In the case of the number `0`, however, it is contained in the haystack, resulting in a value of `19` being returned.

Let's have a look at how this problem might be addressed.

Solving the problem using str_contains()

The intent of the code block shown in the previous section is to determine whether or not the haystack contains the needle. `strpos()` is not the right tool to accomplish this task! Have a look at the same function using `str_contains()` instead:

```
// /repo/ch06/php8_num_str_empty_needle.php
function test($haystack, $search) {
    $pattern = '%15s | %15s | %10s' . "\n";
    $result  = (str_contains($search, $haystack) !==
            FALSE)
                ? 'FOUND' : 'NOT FOUND';
    return sprintf($pattern,
            var_export($search, TRUE),
            var_export(str_contains($search, $haystack),
            TRUE),
            $result);
};
```

If we then run the modified code in PHP 8, we get results similar to those received from PHP 7:

```
root@php8_tips_php8 [ /repo/ch06 ]#
php php8_num_str_empty_needle.php
            ''   |   false   |   NOT FOUND
          NULL   |   false   |   NOT FOUND
         false   |   false   |   NOT FOUND
             0   |   false   |   NOT FOUND
```

You might ask why is it that the number 0 is not found in the string? The answer is that `str_contains()` does a stricter search. Integer 0 is not the same as the string `"0"`! Let's now have a look at the `v*printf()` family; another family of string functions that exerts stricter control over its arguments in PHP 8.

Dealing with v*printf() changes

The `v*printf()` family of functions is a subset of the `printf()` family of functions that include `vprintf()`, `vfprintf()`, and `vsprintf()`. The difference between this subset and the main family is that the `v*printf()` functions are designed to accept an array as an argument rather than an unlimited series of arguments. Here is a simple example that illustrates the difference:

1. First, we define a set of arguments that will be inserted into a pattern, `$patt`:

    ```
    // /repo/ch06/php8_printf_vs_vprintf.php
    $ord   = 'third';
    $day   = 'Thursday';
    $pos   = 'next';
    $date  = new DateTime("$ord $day of $pos month");
    $patt  = "The %s %s of %s month is: %s\n";
    ```

2. We then execute a `printf()` statement using a series of arguments:

    ```
    printf($patt, $ord, $day, $pos,
           $date->format('l, d M Y'));
    ```

3. We then define the arguments as an array, `$arr`, and use `vprintf()` to produce the same result:

```
$arr  = [$ord, $day, $pos, $date->format('l, d M
        Y')];vprintf($patt, $arr);
```

Here is the output of the program running in PHP 8. The output is the same running in PHP 7 (not shown):

```
root@php8_tips_php8 [ /repo/ch06 ]#
php php8_printf_vs_vprintf.php
The third Thursday of next month is: Thursday, 15 Apr
2021
The third Thursday of next month is: Thursday, 15 Apr
2021
```

As you can see, the output of both functions is identical. The only usage difference is that `vprintf()` accepts the parameters in the form of an array.

Prior versions of PHP allowed a developer to play *fast and loose* with arguments presented to the `v*printf()` family of functions. In PHP 8, the data type of the arguments is now strictly enforced. This only presents a problem where code controls do not exist to ensure that an array is presented. Another even more important difference is that PHP 7 will allow `ArrayObject` with `v*printf()`, whereas PHP 8 will not.

In the example shown here, PHP 7 issues a `Warning`, whereas PHP 8 throws an `Error`:

1. First, we define the pattern and the source array:

```
// /repo/ch06/php7_vprintf_bc_break.php
$patt = "\t%s. %s. %s. %s. %s.";
$arr  = ['Person', 'Woman', 'Man', 'Camera', 'TV'];
```

2. We then define a test data array in order to test which arguments are accepted by `vsprintf()`:

```
$args = [
    'Array' => $arr,
    'Int'   => 999,
    'Bool'  => TRUE,
    'Obj'   => new ArrayObject($arr)
];
```

3. We then define a `foreach()` loop that goes through the test data and exercises `vsprintf()`:

```
foreach ($args as $key => $value) {
    try {
        echo $key . ': ' . vsprintf($patt, $value);
    } catch (Throwable $t) {
        echo $key . ': ' . get_class($t)
            . ':' . $t->getMessage();
    }
}
```

Here is the output running in PHP 7:

```
root@php8_tips_php7 [ /repo/ch06 ]#
php php7_vprintf_bc_break.php
Array:     Person. Woman. Man. Camera. TV.
PHP Warning:  vsprintf(): Too few arguments in /repo/ch06/php8_vprintf_bc_break.php on line 14
Int:
PHP Warning:  vsprintf(): Too few arguments in /repo/ch06/php8_vprintf_bc_break.php on line 14
Bool:
Obj:       Person. Woman. Man. Camera. TV.
```

As you can see from the output, both the array and `ArrayObject` arguments are accepted in PHP 7. Here is the same code example running in PHP 8:

```
root@php8_tips_php8 [ /repo/ch06 ]#
php php7_vprintf_bc_break.php
Array:     Person. Woman. Man. Camera. TV.
Int: TypeError:vsprintf(): Argument #2 ($values) must be of type array, int given
Bool: TypeError:vsprintf(): Argument #2 ($values) must be of type array, bool given
Obj: TypeError:vsprintf(): Argument #2 ($values) must be of type array, ArrayObject given
```

As expected, the PHP 8 output is much more consistent. In PHP 8, the `v*printf()` functions are strictly typed to accept only an array as an argument. Unfortunately, there's a real possibility you may have been using `ArrayObject`. This is easily addressed by simply using the `getArrayCopy()` method on the `ArrayObject` instance, which returns an array.

Here is the rewritten code that works in both PHP 7 and PHP 8:

```
if ($value instanceof ArrayObject)
    $value = $value->getArrayCopy();
echo $key . ': ' . vsprintf($patt, $value);
```

Now that you have an idea where to look for a potential code break when using the `v*printf()` functions, let's turn our attention to differences in how string functions with a null length argument work in PHP 8.

Working with null length arguments in PHP 8

In PHP 7 and earlier, a `NULL` length argument resulted in an empty string. In PHP 8, a `NULL` length argument is now treated the same as if the length argument is omitted. Functions affected include the following:

- `substr()`
- `substr_count()`
- `substr_compare()`
- `iconv_substr()`

In the example shown next, PHP 7 returns an empty string whereas PHP 8 returns the remainder of the string. This has a high potential for a code break if the result of the operation is used to confirm or deny the existence of the substring:

1. First, we define a haystack and needle. We then run `strpos()` to get the position of the needle in the haystack:

    ```
    // /repo/ch06/php8_null_length_arg.php
    $str = 'The quick brown fox jumped over the fence';
    $var = 'fox';
    $pos = strpos($str, $var);
    ```

2. Next, we pull out the substring, deliberately leaving the length argument undefined:

```
$res = substr($str, $pos, $len);
$fnd = ($res) ? '' : ' NOT';
echo "$var is$fnd found in the string\n";
```

Here is the output running in PHP 7:

```
root@php8_tips_php7 [ /repo/ch06 ]#
php php8_null_length_arg.php
PHP Notice:  Undefined variable: len in /repo/ch06/php8_null_length_arg.php on line 8
Result    : fox is NOT found in the string
Remainder :
```

As expected, PHP 7 issues a `Notice`. However, as an empty string is returned due to the `NULL` length argument, the search result is incorrect. Here is the same code running in PHP 8:

```
root@php8_tips_php8 [ /repo/ch06 ]#
php php8_null_length_arg.php
PHP Warning:  Undefined variable $len in /repo/ch06/php8_null_length_arg.php on line 8
Result    : fox is found in the string
Remainder : fox jumped over the fence
```

PHP 8 issues a `Warning` and returns the remainder of the string. This is consistent with the behavior where the length argument is entirely omitted. If your code relies upon an empty string being returned, a potential code break exists after a PHP 8 update.

Let's now have a look at another situation where PHP 8 has made string handling more uniform in the `implode()` function.

Examining changes to implode()

Two widely used PHP functions perform array to string conversion and the reverse: `explode()` converts a string to an array, and `implode()` converts an array to a string. However, there lurks a deep dark secret with the `implode()` function: its two parameters can be expressed in any order!

Please bear in mind that when PHP was first introduced in 1994, the initial goal was to make it as easy to use as possible. This approach succeeded, to the point where PHP is the language of choice on over 78% of all web servers today according to a recent survey of server-side programming languages conducted by w3techs. (https://w3techs.com/technologies/overview/programming_language)

However, in the interests of consistency, it makes sense to align the parameters of the `implode()` function with its mirror twin, `explode()`. Accordingly, arguments supplied to `implode()` must now be in this order:

```
implode(<GLUE STRING>, <ARRAY>);
```

Here is the code example that calls the `implode()` function with arguments in either order:

```
// /repo/ch06/php7_implode_args.php
$arr = ['Person', 'Woman', 'Man', 'Camera', 'TV'];
echo __LINE__ . ':' . implode(' ', $arr) . "\n";
echo __LINE__ . ':' . implode($arr, ' ') . "\n";
```

As you can see from the PHP 7 output below, both echo statements produce results:

```
root@php8_tips_php7 [ /repo/ch06 ]# php php7_implode_args.php
5:Person Woman Man Camera TV
6:Person Woman Man Camera TV
```

In PHP 8, only the first statement succeeds, as shown here:

```
root@php8_tips_php8 [ /repo/ch06 ]#
php php7_implode_args.php
5:Person Woman Man Camera TV
PHP Fatal error:  Uncaught TypeError: implode(): Argument #2 ($array) must be of type ?array, string given in /repo/ch06/php7_implode_args.php:6
```

It will be extremely difficult to spot where `implode()` is receiving parameters in the wrong order. The best way to be forewarned prior to a PHP 8 migration would be to make a note of all classes of PHP files that use `implode()`. Another suggestion would be to take advantage of the PHP 8 *named arguments* feature (covered in *Chapter 1, Introducing New PHP 8 OOP Features*).

Learning about constants usage in PHP 8

One of the truly outrageous capabilities of PHP prior to version 8 was the ability to define *case-insensitive* constants. In the beginning, when PHP was first introduced, many developers were writing lots of PHP code with a notable absence of any sort of coding standard. The objective at the time was just to *make it work*.

In line with the general trend toward enforcing good coding standards, this ability was deprecated in PHP 7.3 and removed in PHP 8. A backward-compatible break might appear if you are using `define()` with the third parameter set to `TRUE`.

The example shown here works in PHP 7, but not entirely in PHP 8:

```
// /repo/ch06/php7_constants.php
define('THIS_WORKS', 'This works');
define('Mixed_Case', 'Mixed Case Works');
define('DOES_THIS_WORK', 'Does this work?', TRUE);
echo __LINE__ . ':' . THIS_WORKS . "\n";
echo __LINE__ . ':' . Mixed_Case . "\n";
echo __LINE__ . ':' . DOES_THIS_WORK . "\n";
echo __LINE__ . ':' . Does_This_Work . "\n";
```

In PHP 7, all lines of code work as written. Here is the output:

```
root@php8_tips_php7 [ /repo/ch06 ]# php php7_constants.php
7:This works
8:Mixed Case Works
9:Does this work?
10:Does this work?
```

Please note that the third argument of `define()` was deprecated in PHP 7.3. Accordingly, if you run this code example in PHP 7.3 or 7.4, the output is identical with the addition of a `Deprecation` notice.

In PHP 8, however, quite a different result is produced, as shown here:

```
root@php8_tips_php8 [ /repo/ch06 ]# php php7_constants.php
PHP Warning:  define(): Argument #3 ($case_insensitive) is ignored since declaration of case-insensitive constants is no longer supported in /repo/ch06/php7_constants.php on line 6
7:This works
8:Mixed Case Works
```

```
9:Does this work?
PHP Fatal error:  Uncaught Error: Undefined constant "Does_
This_Work" in /repo/ch06/php7_constants.php:10
```

As you might expect, lines 7, 8, and 9 produce the expected result. The last line, however, throws a fatal `Error`, because constants in PHP 8 are now case-sensitive. Also, a `Warning` is issued for the third `define()` statement as the third parameter is ignored in PHP 8.

You now have an idea about key string handling differences introduced in PHP 8. We next turn our attention to changes in how numeric strings are compared with numbers.

Understanding PHP 8 string-to-numeric comparison improvements

Comparing two numeric values has never been an issue in PHP. A comparison between two strings is also not an issue. A problem arises in non-strict comparisons between strings and numeric data (hardcoded numbers, or variables containing data of the `float` or `int` type). In such cases, PHP will *always* convert the string to a numeric value if a non-strict comparison is executed.

The *only* time a string-to-numeric conversion is 100% successful is when the string only contains numbers (or numeric values such as plus, minus, or the decimal separator). In this section, you learn how to protect against inaccurate non-strict comparisons involving strings and numeric data. Mastering the concepts presented in this chapter is critical if you wish to produce code with consistent and predictable behavior.

Before we get into the details of string-to-numeric comparisons, we need to first gain an understanding of what is meant by a non-strict comparison.

Learning about strict and non-strict comparisons

The concept of **type juggling** is an essential part of the PHP language. This capability was built into the language literally from its first day. Type juggling involves performing an internal data type conversion before performing an operation. This ability is critical to the success of the language.

PHP was originally devised to perform in a web environment and needed a way to handle data transmitted as part of an HTTP packet. HTTP headers and bodies are transmitted as text and are received by PHP as strings stored in a set of **super-globals**, including `$_SERVER`, `$_GET`, `$_POST`, and so forth. Accordingly, the PHP language needs a quick way to deal with string values when performing operations that involve numbers. This is the job of the type-juggling process.

A **strict comparison** is one that first checks the data type. If the data types match, the comparison proceeds. Operators that invoke a strict comparison include `===` and `!==`, among others. Certain functions have an option to enforce a strict data type. One example is `in_array()`. If the third argument is set to `TRUE`, a strict-type search ensues. Here is the method signature for `in_array()`:

`in_array(mixed $needle, array $haystack, bool $strict = false)`

A **non-strict comparison** is where no data type check is made prior to comparison. Operators that perform non-strict comparisons include `==`, `!=`, `<`, and `>`, among others. It's worth noting that the `switch {}` language construct performs non-strict comparisons in its `case` statements. Type juggling is performed if a non-strict comparison is made that involves operands of different data types.

Let's now have a detailed look at numeric strings.

Examining numeric strings

A **numeric string** is a string that contains only numbers or numeric characters, such as the plus sign (+), minus sign (-), and decimal separator.

> **Important note**
> It should be noted that PHP 8 internally uses the period character (.) as the decimal separator. If you need to render numbers in locales that do not use the period as a decimal separator (for example, in France, the comma (,) is used as the decimal separator), use the `number_format()` function (see `https://www.php.net/number_format`). Please have a look at the *Taking advantage of locale independence* section in this chapter for more information.

Numeric strings can also be composed using **engineering notation** (also called **scientific notation**). A **non-well-formed** numeric string is a numeric string containing values other than digits, the plus sign, minus sign, or decimal separator. A **leading-numeric** string starts with a numeric string but is followed by non-numeric characters. Any string that is neither *numeric* nor *leading-numeric* is considered **non-numeric** by the PHP engine.

In previous versions of PHP, type juggling inconsistently parsed strings containing numbers. In PHP 8, only numeric strings can be cleanly converted to a number: no leading or trailing whitespace or other non-numeric characters can be present.

As an example, have a look at the difference in how PHP 7 and 8 handle numeric strings in this code sample:

```php
// /repo/ch06/php8_num_str_handling.php
$test = [
    0 => '111',
    1 => '   111',
    2 => '111   ',
    3 => '111xyz'
];
$patt = "%d : %3d : '%-s'\n";
foreach ($test as $key => $val) {
    $num = 111 + $val;
    printf($patt, $key, $num, $val);
}
```

Here is the output running in PHP 7:

```
root@php8_tips_php7 [ /repo/ch06 ]#
php php8_num_str_handling.php
0 : 222 : '111'
1 : 222 : '   111'
PHP Notice:  A non well formed numeric value encountered in /repo/ch06/php8_num_str_handling.php on line 11
2 : 222 : '111   '
PHP Notice:  A non well formed numeric value encountered in /repo/ch06/php8_num_str_handling.php on line 11
3 : 222 : '111xyz'
```

As you can see from the output, PHP 7 considers a string with a trailing space to be non-well-formed. However, a string with a *leading* space is considered well-formed and passes through without generating a Notice. A string with non-whitespace characters is still processed but merits a Notice.

Here is the same code example running in PHP 8:

```
root@php8_tips_php8 [ /repo/ch06 ]#
php php8_num_str_handling.php
0 : 222 : '111'
1 : 222 : '   111'
2 : 222 : '111   '
PHP Warning:  A non-numeric value encountered in /repo/ch06/
php8_num_str_handling.php on line 11
3 : 222 : '111xyz'
```

PHP 8 is much more consistent in that numeric strings that contain either leading or trailing spaces are treated equally, and no `Notices` or `Warnings` are generated. However, the last string, formerly a `Notice` in PHP 7, now generates a `Warning`.

> **Tip**
>
> You can read about numeric strings in the PHP documentation here:
>
> https://www.php.net/manual/en/language.types.numeric-strings.php
>
> For more information on type juggling, have a look at the following URL:
>
> https://www.php.net/manual/en/language.types.type-juggling.php

Now that you have an idea of what is considered a well-formed and non-well-formed numeric string, let's turn our attention to the more serious issue of potential backward-compatible breaks when dealing with numeric strings in PHP 8.

Detecting backward-compatible breaks involving numeric strings

You must understand where there is potential for your code to break following a PHP 8 upgrade. In this subsection, we show you a number of extremely subtle differences that can have large consequences.

Potential code breaks could surface any time a non-well-formed numeric string is used:

- With `is_numeric()`
- In a string offset (for example, `$str['4x']`)

- With bitwise operators
- When incrementing or decrementing a variable whose value is a non-well-formed numeric string

Here are some suggestions to fix your code:

- Consider using `trim()` on numeric strings that might include leading or trailing white space (for example, numeric strings embedded within posted form data).
- If your code relies upon strings that start with a number, use an explicit typecast to ensure that the number is correctly interpolated.
- Do not rely upon an empty string (for example, `$str = ' '`) to cleanly convert to 0.

In this following code example, a non-well-formed string with a trailing space is assigned to $age:

```php
// /repo/ch06/php8_num_str_is_numeric.php
$age = '77 ';
echo (is_numeric($age))
    ? "Age must be a number\n"
    : "Age is $age\n";
```

When we run this code in PHP 7, `is_numeric()` returns TRUE. Here is the PHP 7 output:

```
root@php8_tips_php7 [ /repo/ch06 ]#
php php8_num_str_is_numeric.php
Age is 77
```

On the other hand, when we run this code in PHP 8, `is_numeric()` returns FALSE as the string is not considered numeric. Here is the PHP 8 output:

```
root@php8_tips_php8 [ /repo/ch06 ]#
php php8_num_str_is_numeric.php
Age must be a number
```

As you can see, string handling differences between PHP 7 and PHP 8 can cause applications to behave differently, with potentially disastrous results. Let's now have a look at inconsistent results involving well-formed strings.

Dealing with inconsistent string-to-numeric comparison results

To complete a non-strict comparison involving string and numeric data, the PHP engine first performs a type-juggling operation that internally converts the string to a number before performing the comparison. Even a well-formed numeric string, however, can yield results that would be viewed as nonsensical from a human perspective.

As an example, have a look at this code sample:

1. First we perform a non-strict comparison between a variable, $zero, with a value of zero and a variable, $string, with a value of ABC:

```
$zero    = 0;
$string  = 'ABC';
$result  = ($zero == $string) ? 'is' : 'is not';
echo "The value $zero $result the same as $string\n"2
```

2. The following non-strict comparison uses in_array() to locate a value of zero in the $array array:

```
$array  = [1 => 'A', 2 => 'B', 3 => 'C'];
$result = (in_array($zero, $array))
        ? 'is in' : 'is not in';
echo "The value $zero $result\n"
      . var_export($array, TRUE)3
```

3. Finally, we perform a non-strict comparison between a leading-numeric string, 42abc88, and a hardcoded number, 42:

```
$mixed  = '42abc88';
$result = ($mixed == 42) ? 'is' : 'is not';
echo "\nThe value $mixed $result the same as 42\n";
```

The results running in PHP 7 defy human comprehension! Here are the PHP 7 results:

```
root@php8_tips_php7 [ /repo/ch06 ]#
php php7_compare_num_str.php
The value 0 is the same as ABC
The value 0 is in
array (1 => 'A', 2 => 'B', 3 => 'C')
The value 42abc88 is the same as 42
```

From a human perspective, none of these results make any sense! From the computer's perspective, on the other hand, it makes perfect sense. The string ABC, when converted to a number, ends up with a value of zero. Likewise, when the array search is made, each array element, having only a string value, ends up being interpolated as zero.

The case of the leading-numeric string is a bit trickier. In PHP 7, the interpolation algorithm converts numeric characters until the first non-numeric character is encountered. Once that happens, the interpolation stops. Accordingly, the string 42abc88 becomes an integer, 42, for comparison purposes. Now let's have a look at how PHP 8 handles string-to-numeric comparisons.

Understanding comparison changes made in PHP 8

In PHP 8, if a string is compared with a number, only numeric strings are considered valid for comparison. Strings in exponential notation are also considered valid for comparison, as well as numeric strings with leading or trailing whitespace. It's extremely important to note that PHP 8 makes this determination *before* converting the string.

Have a look at the output of the same code example described in the previous subsection (*Dealing with inconsistent string-to-numeric comparison results*), running in PHP 8:

```
root@php8_tips_php8 [ /repo/ch06 ]#
php php7_compare_num_str.php
The value 0 is not the same as ABC
The value 0 is not in
array (1 => 'A', 2 => 'B', 3 => 'C')
The value 42abc88 is not the same as 42
```

So, as you can see from the output, there is a massive potential for your application to change its behavior following a PHP 8 upgrade. As a final note in PHP 8 string handling, let's look at how you can avoid upgrade issues.

Avoiding problems during a PHP 8 upgrade

The main issue you face is the difference in how PHP 8 handles non-strict comparisons that involve operands with different data types. If one operand is either `int` or `float`, and the other operand is `string`, you have a potential problem post-upgrade. If the string is a valid numeric string, the non-strict comparison will proceed without any issues.

The following operators are affected: `<=>`, `==`, `!=`, `>`, `>=`, `<`, and `<=`. The following functions are affected if the option flags are set to default:

- `in_array()`
- `array_search()`
- `array_keys()`
- `sort()`
- `rsort()`
- `asort()`
- `arsort()`
- `array_multisort()`

> **Tip**
> For more information on improved numeric string handling in PHP 8, refer to the following link: `https://wiki.php.net/rfc/saner-numeric-strings`. A related PHP 8 change is documented here: `https://wiki.php.net/rfc/string_to_number_comparison`.

The best practice is to minimize PHP type juggling by providing type hints for functions or methods. You can also force the data type before the comparison. Finally, consider making use of strict comparisons, although this might not be suitable in all situations.

Now that you have an understanding of how to properly handle comparisons involving numeric strings in PHP 8, let's now have a look at PHP 8 changes involving arithmetic, bitwise, and concatenation operations.

Handling differences in arithmetic, bitwise, and concatenation operations

Arithmetic, bitwise, and concatenation operations are at the heart of any PHP application. In this section, you learn about hidden dangers that might arise in these simple operations following a PHP 8 migration. You must learn about the changes made in PHP 8 so that you can avoid a potential code break in your application. Because these operations are so ordinary, without this knowledge, you will be hard pressed to discover post-migration errors.

Let's first have a look at how PHP handles non-scalar data types in arithmetic and bitwise operations.

Handling non-scalar data types in arithmetic and bitwise operations

Historically, the PHP engine has been very *forgiving* about using mixed data types in an arithmetic or bitwise operation. We've already had a look at comparison operations that involve *numeric*, *leading-numeric*, and *non-numeric* strings and numbers. As you learned, when a non-strict comparison is used, PHP invokes type juggling to convert the string to a number before performing the comparison. A similar action takes place when PHP performs an arithmetic operation that involves numbers and strings.

Prior to PHP 8, **non-scalar data types** (data types other than `string`, `int`, `float`, or `boolean`) were allowed in an arithmetic operation. PHP 8 has clamped down on this bad practice, and no longer allows operands of the `array`, `resource`, or `object` type. PHP 8 consistently throws a `TypeError` when the non-scalar operands are used in an arithmetic operation. The only exception to this general change is that you can still perform arithmetic operations where all operands are of the `array` type.

> **Tip**
> For further information on the vital change in arithmetic and bitwise operations, have a look here: https://wiki.php.net/rfc/arithmetic_operator_type_checks.

Here is a code example to illustrate arithmetic operator handling differences in PHP 8:

1. First, we define sample non-scalar data to test in an arithmetic operation:

   ```
   // /repo/ch06/php8_arith_non_scalar_ops.php
   $fn  = __DIR__ . '/../sample_data/gettysburg.txt';
   $fh  = fopen($fn, 'r');
   $obj = new class() { public $val = 99; };
   $arr = [1,2,3];
   ```

2. We then attempt to add the integer `99` to a resource, object, and to perform a modulus operation on an array:

   ```
   echo "Adding 99 to a resource\n";
   try { var_dump($fh + 99); }
   catch (Error $e) { echo $e . "\n"; }
   ```

```
echo "\nAdding 99 to an object\n";
try { var_dump($obj + 99); }
catch (Error $e) { echo $e . "\n"; }
echo "\nPerforming array % 99\n";
try { var_dump($arr % 99); }
catch (Error $e) { echo $e . "\n"; }
```

3. Finally, we add two arrays together:

```
echo "\nAdding two arrays\n";
try { var_dump($arr + [99]); }
catch (Error $e) { echo $e . "\n"; }
```

When we run the code example, note how PHP 7 performs silent conversions and allows the operations to continue:

```
root@php8_tips_php7 [ /repo/ch06 ]#
php php8_arith_non_scalar_ops.php
Adding 99 to a resource
/repo/ch06/php8_arith_non_scalar_ops.php:10:
int(104)
Adding 99 to an object
PHP Notice:  Object of class class@anonymous could not be converted to int in /repo/ch06/php8_arith_non_scalar_ops.php on line 13
/repo/ch06/php8_arith_non_scalar_ops.php:13:
int(100)
Performing array % 99
/repo/ch06/php8_arith_non_scalar_ops.php:16:
int(1)
Adding two arrays
/repo/ch06/php8_arith_non_scalar_ops.php:19:
array(3) {
  [0] => int(1)
  [1] => int(2)
  [2] => int(3)
}
```

What is particularly astonishing is how we can perform a modulus operation against an array! When adding a value to an object, a `Notice` is generated in PHP 7. However, PHP type juggles the object to an integer with a value of 1, giving a result of 100 to the arithmetic operation.

The output running the same code sample in PHP 8 is quite different:

```
root@php8_tips_php8 [ /repo/ch06 ]#
php php8_arith_non_scalar_ops.php
Adding 99 to a resource
TypeError: Unsupported operand types: resource + int in /repo/ch06/php8_arith_non_scalar_ops.php:10
Adding 99 to an object
TypeError: Unsupported operand types: class@anonymous + int in /repo/ch06/php8_arith_non_scalar_ops.php:13
Performing array % 99
TypeError: Unsupported operand types: array % int in /repo/ch06/php8_arith_non_scalar_ops.php:16
Adding two arrays
array(3) {
  [0]=> int(1)
  [1]=> int(2)
  [2]=> int(3)
}
```

As you can see from the output, PHP 8 consistently throws a `TypeError`, except when adding two arrays. In both outputs, you may observe that when adding two arrays, the second operand is ignored. If the objective is to combine the two arrays, you must use `array_merge()` instead.

Let's now turn our attention to a potentially significant change in PHP 8 string handling pertaining to the order of precedence.

Examining changes in the order of precedence

The **order of precedence**, also known as the *order of operations*, or *operator precedence*, is a mathematical concept established in the late 18th and early 19th centuries. PHP also adopted the mathematical operator precedence rules, with a unique addition: the concatenate operator. An assumption was made by the founders of the PHP language that the concatenate operator had equal precedence over the arithmetic operators. This assumption was never challenged until the arrival of PHP 8.

In PHP 8, arithmetic operations are given precedence over concatenation. The concatenate operator demotion now places it below the bit shift operators (<< and >>). There is a potential backward-compatible break in any place where you don't use parentheses to clearly define mixed arithmetic and concatenate operations.

This change, in itself, will not throw an `Error` or generate `Warnings` or `Notices`, and thereby presents the potential for a hidden code break.

> **Tip**
> For more information on the reasoning for this change, refer to the following link:
> `https://wiki.php.net/rfc/concatenation_precedence`

The following example most clearly shows the effect of this change:

```
echo 'The sum of 2 + 2 is: ' . 2 + 2;
```

Here is the output of this simple statement in PHP 7:

```
root@php8_tips_php7 [ /repo/ch06 ]#
php -r "echo 'The sum of 2 + 2 is: ' . 2 + 2;"
PHP Warning:  A non-numeric value encountered in Command line code on line 1
2
```

In PHP 7, because the concatenate operator has equal precedence over the addition operator, the string `The sum of 2 + 2 is:` is first concatenated with the integer value 2. The new string is then type juggled to an integer, generating a `Warning`. The value of the new string is evaluated at 0, which is then added to integer 2, producing the output of 2.

In PHP 8, however, the addition takes place first, after which the result is concatenated with the initial string. Here is the result running in PHP 8:

```
root@php8_tips_php8 [ /repo/ch06 ]#
php -r "echo 'The sum of 2 + 2 is: ' . 2 + 2;"
The sum of 2 + 2 is: 4
```

As you can see from the output, the result is much closer to human expectations!

One more illustration should drive home the differences demoting the concatenate operator can make. Have a look at this line of code:

```
echo '1' . '11' + 222;
```

Here is the result running in PHP 7:

```
root@php8_tips_php7 [ /repo/ch06 ]#
php -r "echo '1' . '11' + 222;"
333
```

PHP 7 performs the concatenation first, producing a string, `111`. This is type juggled and added to integer `222`, resulting in a final value integer, `333`. Here is the result running in PHP 8:

```
root@php8_tips_php8 [ /repo/ch06 ]#
php -r "echo '1' . '11' + 222;"
1233
```

In PHP 8, the second string, `11`, is type juggled and added to integer `222`, producing an interim value, `233`. This is type juggled to a string and prepended with `1`, resulting in a final string value of `1233`.

Now that you are aware of changes to arithmetic, bitwise, and concatenation operations in PHP 8, let's have a look at a new trend introduced in PHP 8: locale independence.

Taking advantage of locale independence

In versions of PHP prior to PHP 8, several string functions and operations were tied to the **locale**. The net effect was that numbers were internally stored differently depending on the locale. This practice introduced subtle inconsistencies that were extremely difficult to detect. After reviewing the material presented in this chapter, you will be in a better position to detect potential application code changes following a PHP 8 upgrade, thereby avoiding application failure.

Understanding the problems associated with locale dependence

The unfortunate side effect of locale dependence in earlier PHP versions was inconsistent results when typecasting from `float` to `string` and then back again. Inconsistencies were also seen when a `float` value was concatenated to a `string`. Certain optimizing operations performed by *OpCache* resulted in the concatenation operation occurring before the locale had been set, yet another way in which inconsistent results might be produced.

In PHP 8, vulnerable operations and functions are now locale-independent. What this means is that all float values are now stored using a period as the decimal separator. The default locale is no longer inherited from the environment by default. If you need the default locale to be set, you must now explicitly call `setlocale()`.

Reviewing functions and operations affected by locale independence

Most PHP functions are not affected by the switch to locale independence for the simple reason that locale is irrelevant to that function or extension. Furthermore, most PHP functions and extensions are already locale-independent. Examples include the `PDO` extension, along with functions such as `var_export()` and `json_encode()`, and the `printf()` family.

Functions and operations affected by locale independence include the following:

- `(string) $float`
- `strval($float)`
- `print_r($float)`
- `var_dump($float)`
- `debug_zval_dump($float)`
- `settype($float, "string")`
- `implode([$float])`
- `xmlrpc_encode($float)`

Here is a code example that illustrates handling differences due to locale independence:

1. First, we define an array of locales to test. The locales chosen use different ways to represent the decimal portion of a number:

```php
// /repo/ch06/php8_locale_independent.php
$list = ['en_GB', 'fr_FR', 'de_DE'];
$patt = "%15s | %15s \n";
```

2. We then loop through the locales, set the locale, and perform a float-to-string followed by a string-to-float conversion, echoing the results at each step:

```php
foreach ($list as $locale) {
    setlocale(LC_ALL, $locale);
    echo "Locale          : $locale\n";
    $f = 123456.789;
    echo "Original        : $f\n";
    $s = (string) $f;
    echo "Float to String : $s\n";
    $r = (float) $s;
    echo "String to Float : $r\n";
}
```

If we run this example in PHP 7, note the result:

```
root@php8_tips_php7 [ /repo/ch06 ]#
php php8_locale_independent.php
Locale          : en_GB
Original        : 123456.789
Float to String : 123456.789
String to Float : 123456.789
Locale          : fr_FR
Original        : 123456,789
Float to String : 123456,789
String to Float : 123456
Locale          : de_DE
Original        : 123456,789
Float to String : 123456,789
String to Float : 123456
```

As you can see from the output, the number is stored internally using a period for a decimal separator for en_GB, whereas the comma is used for locales fr_FR and de_DE. However, when the string is converted back to a number, the string is treated as a leading-numeric string if the decimal separator is not a period. In two of the locales, the presence of the comma stops the conversion process. The net effect is that the decimal portion is dropped and precision is lost.

The results when running the same code sample in PHP 8 are shown here:

```
root@php8_tips_php8 [ /repo/ch06 ]#
php php8_locale_independent.php
Locale            : en_GB
Original          : 123456.789
Float to String   : 123456.789
String to Float   : 123456.789
Locale            : fr_FR
Original          : 123456.789
Float to String   : 123456.789
String to Float   : 123456.789
Locale            : de_DE
Original          : 123456.789
Float to String   : 123456.789
String to Float   : 123456.789
```

In PHP 8, no precision is lost and the number is consistently represented using a period for the decimal separator, regardless of the locale.

Please note that you can still represent a number according to its locale by using the `number_format()` function, or by using the `NumberFormatter` class (from the `Intl` extension). It's interesting to note that the `NumberFormatter` class stores numbers internally in a locale-independent manner!

> **Tip**
>
> For more information, have a look at this article: https://wiki.php.net/rfc/locale_independent_float_to_string.
>
> For more information on international number formatting, refer to the following link: https://www.php.net/manual/en/class.numberformatter.php

Now that you are aware of the locale-independent aspects present in PHP 8, we need to have a look at changes in array handling.

Handling arrays in PHP 8

Aside from improvements in performance, the two main changes in PHP 8 array handling pertain to the handling of negative offsets and curly brace ({ }) usage. Since both of these changes could result in application code breaks following a PHP 8 migration, it's important to cover them here. Awareness of the issues presented here gives you a better chance to get broken code working again in short order.

Let's have a look at negative array offset handling first.

Dealing with negative offsets

When assigning a value to an array in PHP, if you do not specify an index, PHP will automatically assign one for you. The index chosen in this manner is an integer that represents a value one higher than the highest currently assigned integer key. If no integer index key has yet been assigned, the automatic index assignment algorithm starts at zero.

In PHP 7 and below, however, this algorithm is not applied consistently in the case of a negative integer index. If a numeric array started with a negative number for its index, auto-indexing jumps to zero (0) regardless of what the next number would ordinarily be. In PHP 8, on the other hand, automatic indexing consistently increments by a value of +1 regardless of whether the index is a negative or positive integer.

A possible backward-compatible code break is present if your code relies upon auto-indexing, and any of the starting indices are negative numbers. Detection of this issue is difficult as auto-indexing occurs silently, without any `Warnings` or `Notices`.

The following code example illustrates the difference in behavior between PHP 7 and PHP 8:

1. First, we define an array with only negative integers as indexes. We use `var_dump()` to reveal this array:

```
// /repo/ch06/php8_array_negative_index.php
$a = [-3 => 'CCC', -2 => 'BBB', -1 => 'AAA'];
var_dump($a);
```

2. We then define a second array and initialize the first index to -3. We then add additional array elements, but without specifying an index. This causes auto-indexing to occur:

```
$b[-3] = 'CCC';
$b[]   = 'BBB';
$b[]   = 'AAA';
var_dump($b);
```

3. If we then run the program in PHP 7, note that the first array is rendered correctly. It's entirely possible to have negative array indexes in PHP 7 and earlier as long as they're directly assigned. Here is the output:

```
root@php8_tips_php7 [ /repo/ch06 ]#
php php8_array_negative_index.php
/repo/ch06/php8_array_negative_index.php:6:
array(3) {
  [-3] => string(3) "CCC"
  [-2] => string(3) "BBB"
  [-1] => string(3) "AAA"
}
/repo/ch06/php8_array_negative_index.php:12:
array(3) {
  [-3] => string(3) "CCC"
  [0]  => string(3) "BBB"
  [1]  => string(3) "AAA"
}
```

4. However, as you can see from the second `var_dump()` output, automatic array indexing skips to zero regardless of the previous high value.

5. In PHP 8, on the other hand, you can see that the output is consistent. Here's the PHP 8 output:

```
root@php8_tips_php8 [ /repo/ch06 ]#
php php8_array_negative_index.php
array(3) {
  [-3]=> string(3) "CCC"
  [-2]=> string(3) "BBB"
  [-1]=> string(3) "AAA"
```

```
}
array(3) {
  [-3]=>
  string(3) "CCC"
  [-2]=>
  string(3) "BBB"
  [-1]=>
  string(3) "AAA"
}
```

6. As you can see from the output, the array indexes are automatically assigned, incremented by a value of 1, making the two arrays identical.

> **Tip**
> For more information on this enhancement, have a look at this article: `https://wiki.php.net/rfc/negative_array_index`.

Now that you are aware of the potential code break regarding auto-assignment of indexes involving negative values, let's turn our attention to the other area of interest: the use of curly braces.

Handling curly brace usage changes

Curly braces (`{ }`) are a familiar sight for any developer creating PHP code. The PHP language, written in C, makes extensive use of C syntax, including curly braces. It is well known that curly braces are used to delineate blocks of code in control structures (for example, `if { }`), in loops (for example, `for () { }`), in functions (for example, `function xyz() { }`), and classes.

In this subsection, however, we will restrict our examination of curly brace usage to that associated with variables. One potentially significant change in PHP 8 is the use of curly braces to identify an array element. The use of curly braces to designate array offsets is now deprecated as of PHP 8.

The old usage has been highly contentious given the following:

- Its use can easily be confused with the use of curly braces inside doubly quoted strings.
- Curly braces cannot be used to make array assignments.

  Accordingly, the PHP core team needed to either make the use of curly braces consistent with square brackets (`[ ]`) ... or just get rid of this curly brace usage. The final decision was to remove support for curly braces with arrays.

> **Tip**
> For more information on the background behind the change, refer to the following link: https://wiki.php.net/rfc/deprecate_curly_braces_array_access.

Here is a code example that illustrates the point:

1. First, we define an array of callbacks that illustrate removed or illegal curly brace usage:

```
// /repo/ch06/php7_curly_brace_usage.php
$func = [
    1 => function () {
        $a = ['A' => 111, 'B' => 222, 'C' => 333];
        echo 'WORKS: ' . $a{'C'} . "\n";},
    2 => function () {
        eval('$a = {"A","B","C"};');
    },
    3 => function () {
        eval('$a = ["A","B"]; $a{} = "C";');
    }
];
```

2. We then loop through the callbacks using a `try/catch` block to capture errors that are thrown:

```
foreach ($func as $example => $callback) {
    try {
        echo "\nTesting Example $example\n";
        $callback();
    } catch (Throwable $t) {
        echo $t->getMessage() . "\n";
    }
}
```

If we run the example in PHP 7, the first callback works. The second and third cause a `ParseError` to be thrown:

```
root@php8_tips_php7 [ /repo/ch06 ]#
php php7_curly_brace_usage.php
Testing Example 1
WORKS: 333
Testing Example 2
syntax error, unexpected '{'
Testing Example 3
syntax error, unexpected '}'
```

When we run the same example in PHP 8, however, none of the examples work. Here is the PHP 8 output:

```
root@php8_tips_php8 [ /repo/ch06 ]#
php php7_curly_brace_usage.php
PHP Fatal error:  Array and string offset access syntax with curly braces is no longer supported in /repo/ch06/php7_curly_brace_usage.php on line 8
```

This potential code break is easy to detect. However, because your code has many curly braces, you might have to wait for the fatal `Error` to be thrown to capture the code break.

Now that you have an idea of changes in array handling in PHP 8, let's have a look at changes in security-related functions.

Mastering changes in security functions and settings

Any changes to PHP security features are worth noting. Unfortunately, given the state of the world today, attacks on any web-facing code are a given. Accordingly, in this section, we address several changes to security-related PHP functions in PHP 8. The changed functions affected include the following:

- `assert()`
- `password_hash()`
- `crypt()`

In addition, there was a change in how PHP 8 treats any functions defined in the `php.ini` file using the `disable_functions` directive. Let's have a look at this directive to begin with.

Understanding changes in disabled functions handling

Web hosting companies often offer heavily discounted **shared hosting** packages. Once a customer signs up, the IT staff at the hosting company creates an account on the shared server, assigns a disk quota to control disk space usage, and creates a **virtual host** definition on the web service. The problem such hosting companies face, however, is that allowing unrestricted access to PHP poses a security risk to both the shared hosting company as well as other users on the same server.

To address this issue, IT staff often assign a comma-separated list of functions to the `php.ini` directive, **disable_functions**. In so doing, any function on this list cannot be used in PHP code running on that server. Functions that typically end up on this list are those that allow operating system access, such as `system()` or `shell_exec()`.

Only internal PHP functions can end up on this list. Internal functions are those included in the PHP core as well as functions provided via extensions. User-defined functions are not affected by this directive.

Examining disabled functions' handling differences

In PHP 7 and earlier, disabled functions could not be re-defined. In PHP 8, disabled functions are treated as if they never existed, which means re-definition is possible.

> **Important note**
> Just because you can redefine the disabled function in PHP 8 *does not* mean that the original functionality has been restored!

To illustrate this concept, we first add this line to the `php.ini` file: `disable_functions=system`.

Note that we need to add this to *both* Docker containers (both PHP 7 and PHP 8) in order to complete the illustration. The commands to update the `php.ini` files are shown here:

```
root@php8_tips_php7 [ /repo/ch06 ]#
echo "disable_functions=system">>/etc/php.ini
root@php8_tips_php8 [ /repo/ch06 ]#
echo "disable_functions=system">>/etc/php.ini
```

If we then attempt to use the `system()` function, the attempt fails in both PHP 7 and PHP 8. Here, we show the output from PHP 8:

```
root@php8_tips_php8 [ /repo/ch06 ]#
php -r "system('ls -l');"
PHP Fatal error:  Uncaught Error: Call to undefined function system() in Command line code:1
```

We then define some program code that redefines the banned function:

```php
// /repo/ch06/php8_disabled_funcs_redefine.php
function system(string $cmd, string $path = NULL) {
    $output = '';
    $path = $path ?? __DIR__;
    if ($cmd === 'ls -l') {
        $iter = new RecursiveDirectoryIterator($path);
        foreach ($iter as $fn => $obj)
            $output .= $fn . "\n";
    }
    return $output;
}
echo system('ls -l');
```

As you can see from the code example, we've created a function that mimics the behavior of an `ls -l` Linux system call, but only uses safe PHP functions and classes. If we try to run this in PHP 7, however, a fatal `Error` is thrown. Here is the PHP 7 output:

```
root@php8_tips_php7 [ /repo/ch06 ]#
php php8_disabled_funcs_redefine.php
PHP Fatal error:  Cannot redeclare system() in /repo/ch06/php8_disabled_funcs_redefine.php on line 17
```

In PHP 8, however, our function redefinition succeeds, as shown here:

```
root@php8_tips_php8 [ /repo/ch06 ]#
php php8_disabled_funcs_redefine.php
/repo/ch06/php8_printf_vs_vprintf.php
/repo/ch06/php8_num_str_non_wf_extracted.php
/repo/ch06/php8_vprintf_bc_break.php
/repo/ch06/php7_vprintf_bc_break.php
```

```
... not all output is shown ...
/repo/ch06/php7_curly_brace_usage.php
/repo/ch06/php7_compare_num_str_valid.php
/repo/ch06/php8_compare_num_str.php
/repo/ch06/php8_disabled_funcs_redefine.php
```

You now have an idea of how to work with disabled functions. Next, let's have a look at changes to the vital `crypt()` function.

Learning about changes to the crypt() function

The **crypt()** function has been a staple of PHP hash generation since PHP version 4. One of the reasons for its resilience is because it has so many options. If your code uses `crypt()` directly, you'll be pleased to note that if an unusable **salt** value is provided, Defense Encryption Standard (**DES**), long considered broken, is *no longer* the fallback in PHP 8! The salt is also sometimes referred to as the **initialization vector** (**IV**).

Another important change involves the **rounds** value. A *round* is like shuffling a deck of cards: the more times you shuffle, the higher the degree of randomization (unless you're dealing with a Las Vegas card shark!). In cryptography, blocks are analogous to cards. During each round, a cryptographic function is applied to each block. If the cryptographic function is simple, the hash can be generated more quickly; however, a larger number of rounds are required to fully randomize the blocks.

The **SHA-1** (**Secure Hash Algorithm**) family uses a fast but simple algorithm, and thus requires more rounds. The SHA-2 family, on the other hand, uses a more complex hashing function, which takes more resources, but fewer rounds.

When using the PHP `crypt()` function in conjunction with `CRYPT_SHA256`, (SHA-2 family), PHP 8 will no longer silently resolve the `rounds` parameter to the closest limit. Instead, `crypt()` will fail with a `*0` return, matching `glibc` behavior. In addition, in PHP 8, the second argument (the salt), is now mandatory.

The following example illustrates the differences between PHP 7 and PHP 8 when using the `crypt()` function:

1. First, we define variables representing an unusable salt value, and an illegal number of rounds:

    ```
    // /repo/ch06/php8_crypt_sha256.php
    $password = 'password';
    $salt     = str_repeat('+x=', CRYPT_SALT_LENGTH + 1);
    $rounds   = 1;
    ```

2. We then create two hashes using the `crypt()` function. In the first usage, `$default` is the result after supplying an invalid salt argument. The second usage, `$sha256`, provides a valid salt value, but an invalid number of rounds:

```
$default = crypt($password, $salt);
$sha256  = crypt($password,
    '$5$rounds=' . $rounds . '$' . $salt . '$');
echo "Default : $default\n";
echo "SHA-256 : $sha256\n";
```

Here is the output of the code example running in PHP 7:

```
root@php8_tips_php7 [ /repo/ch06 ]#
php php8_crypt_sha256.php
PHP Deprecated: crypt(): Supplied salt is not valid for DES. Possible bug in provided salt format. in /repo/ch06/php8_crypt_sha256.php on line 7
Default : +xj31ZMTZzkVA
SHA-256 : $5$rounds=1000$+x=+x=+x=+x=+x=+$3Si/vFn6/xmdTdyleJl7Rb9Heg6DWgkRVKS9T0ZZy/B
```

Notice how PHP 7 silently modifies the original request. In the first case, `crypt()` falls back to DES (!). In the second case, PHP 7 silently alters the `rounds` value from `1` to the nearest limit of `1000`.

The same code running in PHP 8, on the other hand, fails and returns `*0`, as shown here:

```
root@php8_tips_php8 [ /repo/ch06 ]#
php php8_crypt_sha256.php
Default : *0
SHA-256 : *0
```

As we have stressed repeatedly in this book, when PHP makes assumptions for you, ultimately you end up with bad code that produces inconsistent results. In the code example just shown, the best practice would be to define a class method or function that exerts greater control over its parameters. In this manner, you can validate the parameters and avoid having to rely upon PHP assumptions.

Next, we take a look at changes to the `password_hash()` function.

Dealing with changes to password_hash()

Over the years, so many developers had misused `crypt()` that the PHP core team decided to add a wrapper function, `password_hash()`. This proved to be a smashing success and is now one of the most widely used security functions. Here is the function signature for `password_hash()`:

```
password_hash(string $password, mixed $algo, array $options=?)
```

Algorithms currently supported include **bcrypt**, **Argon2i**, and **Argon2id**. It's recommended that you use the predefined constants for algorithms: `PASSWORD_BCRYPT`, `PASSWORD_ARGON2I`, and `PASSWORD_ARGON2ID`. The `PASSWORD_DEFAULT` algorithm is currently set to `bcrypt`. Options vary according to the algorithm. If you use either `PASSWORD_BCRYPT` or the `PASSWORD_DEFAULT` algorithms, the options include `cost` and `salt`.

Conventional wisdom suggests that it's better to use the randomly generated `salt` created by the `password_hash()` function. In PHP 7, the `salt` option was deprecated and is now ignored in PHP 8. This won't cause a backward-compatible break unless you're relying on `salt` for some other reason.

In this code example, a non-random salt value is used:

```
// /repo/ch06/php8_password_hash.php
$salt = 'xxxxxxxxxxxxxxxxxxxxxx';
$password = 'password';
$hash = password_hash(
    $password, PASSWORD_DEFAULT, ['salt' => $salt]);
echo $hash . "\n";
var_dump(password_get_info($hash));
```

In the PHP 7 output, a deprecation `Notice` is issued:

```
root@php8_tips_php7 [ /repo/ch06 ]# php php8_password_hash.php
PHP Deprecated:  password_hash(): Use of the 'salt' option to password_hash is deprecated in /repo/ch06/php8_password_hash.php on line 6
$2y$10$xxxxxxxxxxxxxxxxxxxxxuOd9YtxiLKHM/198x//sqUV1V2XTZEZ.
/repo/ch06/php8_password_hash.php:8:
array(3) {
  'algo' => int(1)
```

```
    'algoName' =>   string(6) "bcrypt"
    'options'  =>   array(1) { 'cost' => int(10) }
}
```

You'll also note from the PHP 7 output that the non-random `salt` value is clearly visible. One other thing to note is that when `password_get_info()` is executed, the `algo` key shows an integer value that corresponds to one of the predefined algorithm constants.

The PHP 8 output is somewhat different, as seen here:

```
root@php8_tips_php8 [ /repo/ch06 ]# php php8_password_hash.
php PHP Warning:  password_hash(): The "salt" option has been
ignored, since providing a custom salt is no longer supported
in /repo/ch06/php8_password_hash.php on line 6
$2y$10$HQNRjL.kCkXaR1ZAOFI3TuBJd11k4YCRWmtrI1B7ZDaX1Jngh9UNW
array(3) {
  ["algo"]=> string(2) "2y"
  ["algoName"]=> string(6) "bcrypt"
  ["options"]=> array(1) { ["cost"]=> int(10) }
}
```

You can see that the `salt` value was ignored, and a random `salt` used instead. Instead of a `Notice`, PHP 8 issues a `Warning` regarding the use of the `salt` option. Another point to note from the output is that when `password_get_info()` is called, the `algorithm` key returns a string rather than an integer in PHP 8. This is because the predefined algorithm constants are now string values that correspond to their signature when used in the `crypt()` function.

The last function we will examine, in the next subsection, is `assert()`.

Learning about changes to assert()

The `assert()` function is normally associated with testing and diagnostics. We include it in this subsection, as it often has security implications. Developers sometimes use this function when attempting to trace potential security vulnerabilities.

To use the `assert()` function, you must first enable it by adding a `php.ini` file setting `zend.assertions=1`. Once enabled, you can place one or more `assert()` function calls at any place within your application code.

Understanding changes to assert() usage

As of PHP 8, it's no longer possible to present `assert()` with string arguments to be evaluated: instead, you must provide an expression. This presents a potential code break because in PHP 8, the string is treated as an expression, and therefore always resolves to the Boolean `TRUE`. Also, both the `assert.quiet_eval` `php.ini` directive, and the `ASSERT_QUIET_EVAL` pre-defined constant used with `assert_options()`, have been removed in PHP 8 as they now have no effect.

To illustrate the potential problem, we first activate assertions by setting the `php.ini` directive, `zend.assertions=1`. We then define an example program as follows:

1. We use `ini_set()` to cause `assert()` to throw an exception. We also define a variable, `$pi`:

```
// /repo/ch06/php8_assert.php
ini_set('assert.exception', 1);
$pi = 22/7;
echo 'Value of 22/7: ' . $pi . "\n";
echo 'Value of M_PI: ' . M_PI . "\n";
```

2. We then attempt an assertion as an expression, `$pi === M_PI`:

```
try {
    $line    = __LINE__ + 2;
    $message = "Assertion expression failed ${line}\n";
    $result  = assert($pi === M_PI,
        new AssertionError($message));
    echo ($result) ? "Everything's OK\n"
                   : "We have a problem\n";
} catch (Throwable $t) {
    echo $t->getMessage() . "\n";
}
```

3. In the last `try/catch` block, we attempt an assertion as a string:

```
try {
    $line    = __LINE__ + 2;
    $message = "Assertion string failed ${line}\n";
    $result  = assert('$pi === M_PI',
        new AssertionError($message));
```

```
        echo ($result) ? "Everything's OK\n"
                       : "We have a problem\n";
    } catch (Throwable $t) {
        echo $t->getMessage() . "\n";
    }
```

4. When we run the program in PHP 7, everything works as expected:

```
root@php8_tips_php7 [ /repo/ch06 ]# php php8_assert.php
Value of 22/7: 3.1428571428571
Value of M_PI: 3.1415926535898
Assertion as expression failed on line 18
Assertion as a string failed on line 28
```

5. The value of M_PI comes from the math extension, and is far more accurate than simply dividing 22 by 7! Accordingly, both assertions throw an exception. In PHP 8, however, the output is significantly different:

```
root@php8_tips_php8 [ /repo/ch06 ]# php php8_assert.php
Value of 22/7: 3.1428571428571
Value of M_PI: 3.1415926535898
Assertion as expression failed on line 18
Everything's OK
```

The assertion as a string is interpreted as an expression. Because the string is not empty, the Boolean result is TRUE, returning a false positive. If your code relies upon the result of an assertion as a string, it is bound to fail. As you can see from the PHP 8 output, however, an assertion as an expression works the same in PHP 8 as in PHP 7.

> **Tip**
> Best practice: Do not use assert() in production code. If you do use assert(), always provide an expression, not a string.

Now that you have an idea of changes to security-related functions, we bring this chapter to a close.

Summary

In this chapter, you learned about differences in string handling between PHP 8 and earlier versions, and how to develop workarounds that address differences in string handling. As you learned, PHP 8 exerts greater control over the data types of string function arguments, as well as introducing consistency in what happens if an argument is missing or null. As you learned, a big problem with earlier versions of PHP is that several assumptions were silently made on your behalf, resulting in a huge potential for unexpected results.

In this chapter, we also highlighted issues involving comparisons between numeric strings and numeric data. You learned not only about numeric strings, type-juggling, and non-strict comparisons, but also how PHP 8 corrects flaws inherent in numeric string handling that were present in earlier versions. Another topic covered in this chapter demonstrated potential issues having to do with how several operators behave differently in PHP 8. You learned how to spot potential problems and were given best practices to improve the resilience of your code.

This chapter also addressed how a number of PHP functions retained dependence upon the locale setting, and how this problem has been addressed in PHP 8. You learned that in PHP 8, floating-point representations are now uniform and no longer dependent upon the locale. You also learned about changes in how PHP 8 addresses array elements as well as changes in several security-related functions.

The tips, tricks, and techniques covered in this chapter raise awareness of inconsistent behavior in earlier versions of PHP. With this new awareness, you are in a better position to gain greater control over the use of PHP code. You are also now in a better position to detect situations that could lead to potential code breaks following a PHP 8 migration, giving you an advantage over other developers, and ultimately leading you to write PHP code that performs reliably and consistently.

The next chapter shows you how to avoid potential code breaks involving changes to PHP extensions.

7
Avoiding Traps When Using PHP 8 Extensions

One of the main strengths of the **PHP: Hypertext Preprocessor** (**PHP**) language is its extensions. Changes to the PHP language introduced in PHP 8 also require extension development teams to update their extensions at the same time. In this chapter, you will learn which major changes to extensions have been made and how to avoid traps when updating an existing application to PHP 8.

Once you have finished reviewing the sample code and topics presented in this chapter, you will be able to prepare any existing PHP code for migration to PHP 8. In addition to learning about the changes to the various extensions, you will also gain deep insight into their operation. This ability will allow you to make informed decisions when using extensions in PHP 8.

Topics covered in this chapter include the following:

- Understanding the shift from resources to objects
- Learning about changes to **Extensible Markup Language** (**XML**) extensions
- Avoiding problems with the updated `mbstring` extension
- Dealing with changes to the `gd` extension
- Discovering changes to the `Reflection` extension
- Working with other extension gotchas

Technical requirements

To examine and run the code examples provided in this chapter, the minimum recommended hardware is outlined here:

- x86_64-based desktop PC or laptop
- 1 **gigabyte** (**GB**) free disk space
- 4 GB of **random-access memory** (**RAM**)
- 500 **kilobits per second** (**Kbps**) or faster internet connection

In addition, you will need to install the following software:

- Docker
- Docker Compose

Please refer to the *Technical requirements* section of *Chapter 1, Introducing New PHP 8 OOP Features,* for more information on Docker and Docker Compose installation, as well as how to build a Docker container like the one used to demonstrate the code used in this book. In this book, we refer to the directory in which you restored the sample code for this book as `/repo`.

The source code for this chapter is located here:

https://github.com/PacktPublishing/PHP-8-Programming-Tips-Tricks-and-Best-Practices/tree/main/ch07

We can now begin our discussion by examining the overall trend in PHP 8 toward objects rather than resources.

Understanding the shift from resources to objects

The PHP language has always had an uneasy relationship with **resources**. Resources represent a connection to an external system such as a file handle or a connection to a remote web service using the **client URL (cURL)** extension. One big problem with resources, however, is that they defy attempts at data typing. There's no way to distinguish a file handle from a `cURL` connection—they're both identified as resources.

In PHP 8, a major effort has taken place to move away from resources and to replace them with objects. One of the earliest examples of this trend prior to PHP 8 is the `PDO` class. When you create a `PDO` instance, it automatically creates a database connection. Starting with PHP 8, many functions that previously produced a resource now produce an object instance instead. Let's start our discussion by having a look at extension functions that now produce objects rather than resources.

PHP 8 extension resource-to-object migration

It's important for you to be aware of which functions in PHP 8 now produce objects instead of resources. The good news is that the extension functions have also been rewritten to accommodate an object as an argument rather than a resource. The bad news is that there is a potential backward-compatible code break where you initialize the resource (now object) and test for success using the `is_resource()` function.

The following table summarizes the functions that formerly returned resources but now return object instances:

Extension	Function	Returns
Core	socket_create() socket_create_listen() socket_accept() socket_import_stream() socket_addrinfo_connect() socket_addrinfo_bind() socket_wsaprotocol_info_import() socket_addrinfo_lookup()	Socket Socket Socket Socket Socket Socket Socket array of AddressInfo
cURL	curl_init() curl_multi_init() curl_share_init()	CurlHandle CurlMultiHandle CurlShareHandle
Enchant	enchant_broker_init() enchant_broker_request_dict() enchant_broker_request_pwl_dict()	EnchantBroker EnchantDictionary EnchantDictionary
GD	imagecreate*()	GdImage
OpenSSL	openssl_x509_read() openssl_csr_sign() openssl_csr_new() openssl_pkey_new()	OpenSSLCertificate OpenSSLCertificate OpenSSLCertificateSigningRequest OpenSSLAsymmetricKey
Semaphore	msg_get_queue() sem_get() shm_attach()	SysvMessageQueue SysvSemaphore SysvSharedMemory
Shared Memory	shmop_open()	Shmop
XML Parser	xml_parser_create() xml_parser_create_ns()	XMLParser XMLParser
Zlib	inflate_init() deflate_init()	InflateContext DeflateContext

Table 7.1 – PHP 8 resource-to-object migration

Table 7.1 serves as a valuable guide to functions that now produce objects rather than resources. Consult this table before you migrate any existing applications to PHP 8. The next section gives you a detailed look at a potential backward-compatible code break and guidelines on how to adjust problematic code, before moving on to the benefits.

Potential code break involving is_resource()

A problem you might face is that code written prior to PHP 8 assumes the functions listed in *Table 7.1* return a *resource*. Accordingly, clever developers were in the habit of using is_resource() as a test to see if a connection was successfully established.

Although this was an extremely sensible way to check, this technique now introduces a backward-compatible code break after a PHP 8 upgrade. The following example demonstrates this issue.

In this code example, a cURL connection is initialized for an external website. The next few lines test for success using the `is_resource()` function:

```
// //repo/ch07/php7_ext_is_resource.php
$url = 'https://unlikelysource.com/';
$ch  = curl_init($url);
if (is_resource($ch))
    echo "Connection Established\n"
else
    throw new Exception('Unable to establish connection');
```

The following output from PHP 7 shows success:

```
root@php8_tips_php7 [ /repo/ch07 ]#
php php7_ext_is_resource.php
Connection Established
```

The output of the same code running in PHP 8 is not successful, as we can see here:

```
root@php8_tips_php8 [ /repo/ch07 ]#
php php7_ext_is_resource.php
PHP Fatal error:  Uncaught Exception: Unable to establish connection in /repo/ch07/php7_ext_is_resource.php:9
```

The output from PHP 8 is deceptive in that a connection *has* been established! Because the program code is checking to see if the cURL handle is a resource, however, the code throws an `Exception` error. The reason for the failure is because a `CurlHandle` instance is returned rather than a resource.

In this situation, you can avoid a code break and have the code run successfully in both PHP 8 and any earlier PHP version by substituting `!empty()` (not empty) in place of `is_resource()`, as shown here:

```
// //repo/ch07/php8_ext_is_resource.php
$url = 'https://unlikelysource.com/';
$ch  = curl_init($url);
if (!empty($ch))
    echo "Connection Established\n";
else
    throw new Exception('Unable to establish connection');
var_dump($ch);
```

Here is the output of the code example running in PHP 7:

```
root@php8_tips_php7 [ /repo/ch07 ]#
php php8_ext_is_resource.php
Connection Established
/repo/ch07/php8_ext_is_resource.php:11:
resource(4) of type (curl)
```

Here is the same code example running in PHP 8:

```
root@php8_tips_php8 [ /repo/ch07 ]#
php php8_ext_is_resource.php
Connection Established
object(CurlHandle)#1 (0) {}
```

As you can see from both outputs, the code runs successfully: in PHP 7, $ch is a *resource*. In PHP 8, $ch is a `CurlHandle` instance. Now that you understand the potential issue regarding `is_resource()`, let's have a look at the advantages that stem from this change.

Advantages of objects over resources

Prior to PHP 8, there was no way to provide a data type when passing a resource into or returning a resource out of a function or method. A clear advantage in producing objects rather than resources is that you can take advantage of object type hints.

To illustrate this advantage, imagine a set of **HyperText Transfer Protocol** (**HTTP**) client classes that implement a **strategy software design pattern**. One strategy involves using the cURL extension to send a message. Another strategy uses PHP streams, as follows:

1. We start by defining an `Http/Request` class. The class constructor parses the given URL into its component parts, as illustrated in the following code snippet:

    ```
    // /repo/src/Http/Request.php
    namespace Http;
    class Request {
        public $url      = '';
        public $method   = 'GET';
        // not all properties shown
        public $query    = '';
        public function __construct(string $url) {
    ```

```
        $result  = [];
        $parsed  = parse_url($url);
        $vars    = array_keys(get_object_vars($this));
        foreach ($vars as $name)
            $this->$name = $parsed[$name] ?? '';
        if (!empty($this->query))
            parse_str($this->query, $result);
        $this->query = $result;
        $this->url   = $url;
    }
}
```

2. Next, we define a `CurlStrategy` class that uses the cURL extension to send a message. Note that the `__construct()` method uses constructor-argument promotion. You might also note that we provide a `CurlHandle` data type for the `$handle` argument. This is a tremendous advantage only available in PHP 8, and it ensures that any program creating an instance of this strategy class must provide the correct resource data type. The code is illustrated in the following snippet:

```
// /repo/src/Http/Client/CurlStrategy.php
namespace Http\Client;
use CurlHandle;
use Http\Request;
class CurlStrategy {
    public function __construct(
        public CurlHandle $handle) {}
```

3. We then define the actual logic used to send the message, as follows:

```
    public function send(Request $request) {
        // not all code is shown
        curl_setopt($this->handle,
            CURLOPT_URL, $request->url);
        if (strtolower($request->method) === 'post') {
            $opts = [CURLOPT_POST => 1,
                CURLOPT_POSTFIELDS =>
                    http_build_query($request->query)];
            curl_setopt_array($this->handle, $opts);
```

```
            }
            return curl_exec($this->handle);
        }
}
```

4. We can then do the same thing with a `StreamsStrategy` class. Again, note in the following code snippet how we can use a class as a constructor-argument type hint to ensure proper usage of the strategy:

```
// /repo/src/Http/Client/StreamsStrategy.php
namespace Http\Client;
use SplFileObject;
use Exception;
use Http\Request;
class StreamsStrategy {
    public function __construct(
        public ?SplFileObject $obj) {}
    // remaining code not shown
```

5. We then define a calling program that invokes both strategies and delivers the results. After setting up autoloading, we create a new `Http\Request` instance, supplying an arbitrary URL as an argument, as follows:

```
// //repo/ch07/php8_objs_returned.php
require_once __DIR__
    . '/../src/Server/Autoload/Loader.php';
$autoload = new \Server\Autoload\Loader();
use Http\Request;
use Http\Client\{CurlStrategy,StreamsStrategy};
$url = 'https://api.unlikelysource.com/api
    ?city=Livonia&country=US';
$request = new Request($url);
```

6. Next, we define a `StreamsStrategy` instance and send the request, as follows:

```
$streams  = new StreamsStrategy();
$response = $streams->send($request);
echo $response;
```

7. We then define a `CurlStrategy` instance and send the same request, as illustrated in the following code snippet:

```
$curl     = new CurlStrategy(curl_init());
$response = $curl->send($request);
echo $response;
```

The output from both strategies is identical. Partial output is shown here (note that this example can only be used in PHP 8!):

```
root@php8_tips_php8 [ /repo/ch07 ]#
php php8_objs_returned.php
CurlStrategy Results:
{"data":[{"id":"1227826","country":"US","postcode":"14487",
"city":"Livonia","state_prov_name":"New York","state_prov_code"
:"NY","locality_name":"Livingston","locality_code":"051",
"region_name":"","region_code":"","latitude":"42.8135",
"longitude":"-77.6635","accuracy":"4"},{"id":"1227827",
"country":"US","postcode":"14488","city":"Livonia Center",
"state_prov_name":"New York","state_prov_code":"NY","locality_
name":"Livingston","locality_code":"051","region_name":"",
"region_code":"","latitude":"42.8215","longitude":"-77.6386",
"accuracy":"4"}]}
```

Let's now have a look at another aspect of resource-to-object migration: its effect on iteration.

Traversable to IteratorAggregate migration

The **Traversable** interface was first introduced in PHP 5. It has no methods and was mainly created to allow objects to iterate using a simple `foreach()` loop. As PHP development continues to evolve, a need often arises to obtain the inner iterator. Accordingly, in PHP 8, many classes that formerly implemented `Traversable` now implement `IteratorAggregate` instead.

This doesn't mean that the enhanced classes no longer support the abilities inherent in the `Traversable` interface. Quite the contrary: `IteratorAggregate` extends `Traversable`! This enhancement means that you can now call `getIterator()` on an instance of any of the affected classes. This is potentially of immense benefit as prior to PHP 8, there was no way to access the inner iterator used in the various extensions. The following table summarizes the extensions and classes affected by this enhancement:

Extension	Implements IteratorAggregate
Date	`DatePeriod`
DOM	`DOMNamedNodeMap` and `DOMNodeList`
Intl	`IntlBreakIterator` and `ResourceBundle`
MySQLi	`mysqli_result`
PDO_MySQL	`PDOStatement`
SPL	`SplFixedArray`

Table 7.2 – Classes that now implement IteratorAggregate instead of Traversable

In this section, you were introduced to a significant change introduced in PHP 8: the trend toward using objects rather than resources. One of the advantages you learned is that objects allow you greater control as compared to resources. Another advantage covered in this section is that the movement in PHP 8 toward `IteratorAggregate` allows access to built-in iterators that were previously inaccessible.

We now turn our attention to changes to XML-based extensions.

Learning about changes to XML extensions

XML version 1.0 was introduced as a **World Wide Web Consortium** (**W3C**) specification in 1998. XML bears some resemblance to **HyperText Markup Language** (**HTML**); however, the main purpose of XML is to provide a way to format data that's readable to both machines and humans. One of the reasons why XML is still widely used is because it's easily understandable and does a stellar job at representing tree-structured data.

PHP provides a number of extensions that allow you to both consume and produce XML documents. There have been a few changes introduced to many of these extensions in PHP 8. For the most part, these changes are minor; however, it's important to be aware of these changes if you wish to be a well-rounded and informed PHP developer.

Let's first have a look at changes to the `XMLWriter` extension.

Examining XMLWriter extension differences

All `XMLWriter` extension procedural functions now accept and return `XMLWriter` objects instead of resources. If you have a look at the official PHP documentation for the `XMLWriter` extension, however, you'll see no references to the procedural functions. The reason for this is twofold: first, the PHP language is slowly moving away from discrete procedural functions in favor of **object-oriented programming** (**OOP**).

The second reason is that `XMLWriter` procedural functions are in reality just wrappers for `XMLWriter` OOP methods! As an example, `xmlwriter_open_memory()` is a wrapper for `XMLWriter::openMemory()`, `xmlwriter_text()` is a wrapper for `XMLWriter::text()`, and so forth.

If you are really set on using the `XMLWriter` extension using procedural programming techniques, `xmlwriter_open_memory()` creates an `XMLWriter` instance in PHP 8 rather than a resource. Likewise, all `XMLWriter` extension procedural functions work with `XMLWriter` instances rather than resources.

As with any of the extensions mentioned in this chapter that now produce object instances rather than resources, a potential backward-compatible break is possible. An example of such a break would be where you are using `XMLWriter` procedural functions and `is_resource()` to check to see if a resource has been created. We do not show you an example here, as the problem and the solution are the same as described in the previous section: use `!empty()` instead of `is_resource()`.

It is a *best practice* to use the `XMLWriter` extension OOP **application programming interface** (**API**) instead of the procedural API. Fortunately, the OOP API has been available since PHP 5.1. Here is a sample XML file to be used in the next example:

```
<?xml version="1.0" encoding="UTF-8"?>
<fruit>
    <item>Apple</item>
    <item>Banana</item>
</fruit>
```

The example shown here works in both PHP 7 and 8. The purpose of this example is to use the `XMLWriter` extension to build the XML document shown previously. Here are the steps to accomplish this:

1. We start by creating an `XMLWriter` instance. We then open a connection to shared memory and initialize the XML document type, as follows:

    ```
    // //repo/ch07/php8_xml_writer.php
    $xml = new XMLWriter();
    ```

```
$xml->openMemory();
$xml->startDocument('1.0', 'UTF-8');
```

2. Following this, we use `startElement()` to initialize the `fruit` root node, and add a child node item that has a value of `Apple`, as follows:

```
$xml->startElement('fruit');
$xml->startElement('item');
$xml->text('Apple');
$xml->endElement();
```

3. Next, we add another child node item that has a value of `Banana`, as follows:

```
$xml->startElement('item');
$xml->text('Banana');
$xml->endElement();
```

4. Finally, we close the `fruit` root node and end the XML document. The last command in the following code snippet displays the current XML document:

```
$xml->endElement();
$xml->endDocument();
echo $xml->outputMemory();
```

Here is the output of the example program running in PHP 7:

```
root@php8_tips_php7 [ /repo/ch07 ]# php php8_xml_writer.php
<?xml version="1.0" encoding="UTF-8"?>
<fruit><item>Apple</item><item>Banana</item></fruit>
```

As you can see, the desired XML document is produced. If we run the same program in PHP 8, the results are identical (not shown).

We now turn our attention to changes to the `SimpleXML` extension.

Working with changes to the SimpleXML extension

The `SimpleXML` extension is object-oriented and is widely used. Accordingly, it's vital that you learn about a couple of significant changes made to this extension in PHP 8. The good news is that you won't have to rewrite any code! The even better news is that the changes substantially improve `SimpleXML` extension functionality.

As of PHP 8, the `SimpleXMLElement` class now implements the **Standard PHP Library** (**SPL**) `RecursiveIterator` interface and includes the functionality of the `SimpleXMLIterator` class. In PHP 8, `SimpleXMLIterator` is now an empty extension of `SimpleXMLElement`. This seemingly simple update assumes major significance when you consider that XML is often used to represent complex tree-structured data.

As an example, have a look at a partial view of a family tree for the *House of Windsor*, shown here:

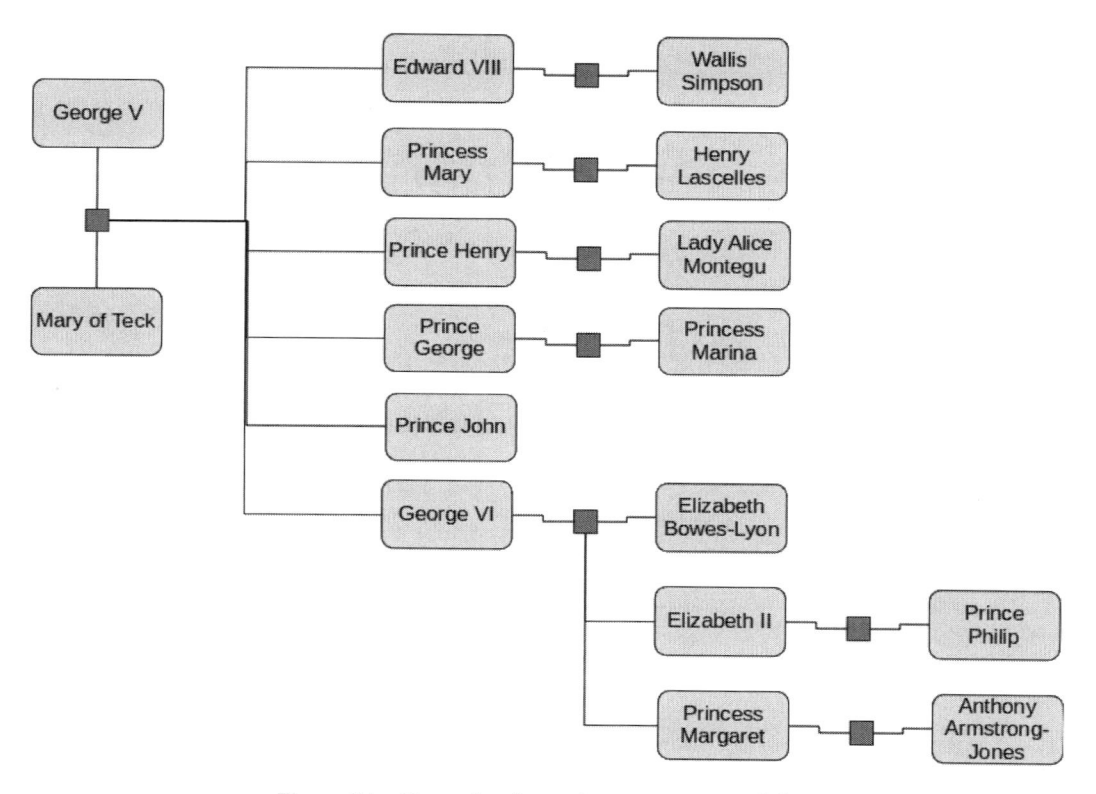

Figure 7.1 – Example of complex tree-structured data

If we were to model this using XML, the document might look like this:

```xml
<?xml version="1.0" encoding="UTF-8"?>
<!-- /repo/ch07/tree.xml -->
<family>
  <branch name="Windsor">
    <descendent gender="M">George V</descendent>
```

```
            <spouse gender="F">Mary of Treck</spouse>
            <branch name="George V">
                <descendent gender="M">George VI</descendent>
                <spouse gender="F">Elizabeth Bowes-Lyon</spouse>
                <branch name="George VI">
                    <descendent gender="F">Elizabeth II</descendent>
                    <spouse gender="M">Prince Philip</spouse>
                    <branch name="Elizabeth II">
                        <descendent gender="M">Prince Charles</descendent>
                        <spouse gender="F">Diana Spencer</spouse>
                        <spouse gender="F">Camilla Parker Bowles</spouse>
                        <branch name="Prince Charles">
                            <descendent gender="M">William</descendent>
                            <spouse gender="F">Kate Middleton</spouse>
                        </branch>
                        <!-- not all nodes are shown -->
                    </branch>
                </branch>
            </branch>
        </branch>
</family>
```

We then develop code to parse the tree. In versions of PHP before PHP 8, however, we need to define a recursive function in order to parse the entire tree. To do so, we'll follow these next steps:

1. We start by defining a recursive function that displays the descendant's name and spouse (if any), as illustrated in the following code snippet. This function also identifies the descendant's gender and checks to see if there are any children. If the latter is `true`, the function then calls itself:

```
function recurse($branch) {
    foreach ($branch as $node) {
        echo $node->descendent;
        echo ($node->descendent['gender'] == 'F')
            ? ', daughter of '
            : ', son of ';
        echo $node['name'];
```

```
            if (empty($node->spouse)) echo "\n";
            else echo ", married to {$node->spouse}\n";
            if (!empty($node->branch))
                recurse($node->branch);
        }
    }
```

2. We then create a `SimpleXMLElement` instance from the external XML file and call the recursive function, as follows:

```
// //repo/ch07/php7_simple_xml.php
$fn = __DIR__ . '/includes/tree.xml';
$xml = simplexml_load_file($fn);
recurse($xml);
```

This code block works in both PHP 7 and PHP 8. Here is the output running in PHP 7:

```
root@php8_tips_php7 [ /repo/ch07 ]#
php php7_simple_xml.php
George V, son of Windsor, married to Mary of Treck
George VI, son of George V, married to Elizabeth Bowes-
Lyon
Elizabeth II, daughter of George VI, married to Philip
Prince Charles, son of Elizabeth II, married to Diana
Spencer
William, son of Prince Charles, married to Kate Middleton
Harry, son of Prince Charles, married to Meghan Markle
Princess Anne, daughter of Elizabeth II, married to
M.Phillips
Princess Margaret, daughter of George VI, married to
A.Jones
Edward VIII, son of George V, married to Wallis Simpson
Princess Mary, daughter of George V, married to
H.Lascelles
Prince Henry, son of George V, married to Lady Alice
Montegu
Prince George, son of George V, married to Princess
Marina
Prince John, son of George V
```

In PHP 8, however, because `SimpleXMLElement` now implements `RecursiveIterator`, the code to produce the same results is simpler.

3. As with the example shown earlier, we define a `SimpleXMLElement` instance from an external file. There is no need to define a recursive function, however—all we need to do is define a `RecursiveIteratorIterator` instance, as follows:

```
// //repo/ch07/php8_simple_xml.php
$fn = __DIR__ . '/includes/tree.xml';
$xml = simplexml_load_file($fn);
$iter = new RecursiveIteratorIterator($xml,
    RecursiveIteratorIterator::SELF_FIRST);
```

4. After that, all we need is a simple `foreach()` loop, with the same internal logic as in the preceding example. There's no need to check to see if a branch node exists, nor is there a need for recursion—that's taken care of by the `RecursiveIteratorIterator` instance! The code you'll need is illustrated here:

```
foreach ($iter as $branch) {
    if (!empty($branch->descendent)) {
        echo $branch->descendent;
        echo ($branch->descendent['gender'] == 'F')
            ? ', daughter of '
            : ', son of ';
        echo $branch['name'];
        if (empty($branch->spouse)) echo "\n";
        else echo ", married to {$branch->spouse}\n";
    }
}
```

The output from this code example running in PHP 8 is shown here. As you can see, the output is exactly the same:

```
root@php8_tips_php8 [ /repo/ch07 ]# php php8_simple_xml.php
George V, son of Windsor, married to Mary of Treck
George VI, son of George V, married to Elizabeth Bowes-Lyon
Elizabeth II, daughter of George VI, married to Philip
Prince Charles, son of Elizabeth II, married to Diana Spencer
William, son of Prince Charles, married to Kate Middleton
```

```
Harry, son of Prince Charles, married to Meghan Markle
Princess Anne, daughter of Elizabeth II, married to M.Phillips
Princess Margaret, daughter of George VI, married to A.Jones
Edward VIII, son of George V, married to Wallis Simpson
Princess Mary, daughter of George V, married to H.Lascelles
Prince Henry, son of George V, married to Lady Alice Montegu
Prince George, son of George V, married to Princess Marina
Prince John, son of George V
```

> **Important note**
> Please note as you run these examples using the Docker containers that the output shown here has been slightly modified to fit the page width.

Let's now have a look at other XML extension changes.

Understanding other XML extension changes

There have been a number of changes to other PHP 8 XML extensions. For the most part, the changes are minor and do not present a significant potential for a backward-compatible code break. However, we would be remiss if we did not address these additional changes. We recommend that you go through the remaining changes present in this subsection so that your awareness is raised. Using these XML extensions will empower you to troubleshoot application code that is behaving inconsistently after a PHP 8 update.

Changes to the libxml extension

The **libxml** extension leverages the **Expat C library**, providing XML parsing functions used by the various PHP XML extensions (https://libexpat.github.io/).

There is a new requirement for the version of `libxml` installed on your server. The minimum version when running PHP 8 must be 2.9.0 (or above). One of the major benefits of this updated requirement is to increase protection against **XML external entity** (**XXE**) processing attacks.

The recommended minimum version of `libxml` disables the ability of PHP XML extensions that rely upon the `libxml` extension to load external XML entities by default. This, in turn, reduces the need for costly and time-consuming extra steps to protect against XXE attacks.

> **Tip**
> For more information on XXE attacks, consult the **Open Web Application Security Project** (**OWASP**) using this link: https://owasp.org/www-community/vulnerabilities/XML_External_Entity_(XXE)_Processing.

Changes to the XMLReader extension

The `XMLReader` extension complements the `XMLWriter` extension. Where the `XMLWriter` extension is designed to produce an XML document, the `XMLReader` extension is designed to read.

Two methods, `XMLReader::open()` and `XMLReader::xml()`, are now defined as **static methods**. You can still create `XMLReader` instances, but if you extend `XMLReader` and override either of these methods, be sure to declare them as static.

Changes to the XMLParser extension

The `XMLParser` extension is one of the oldest PHP XML extensions. Accordingly, it almost entirely consists of procedural functions rather than classes and methods. In PHP 8, however, this extension follows a trend toward producing objects rather than resources. Thus, when you run `xml_parser_create()` or `xml_parser_create_ns()`, an `XMLParser` instance is created rather than a resource.

As mentioned in the *Potential code break involving is_resource()* section, all you need to do is to replace any checks using `is_resource()` with `!empty()` instead. Another side effect of resource-to-object migration is to make redundant the `xml_parser_free()` function. To deactivate the parser, simply use the `XmlParser` object.

Now that you have an understanding of the changes associated with XML extensions, this will help you to more efficiently parse and otherwise manage XML data. By taking advantage of the new features mentioned in this section, you can produce code that's much more efficient and that offers better performance than was possible prior to PHP 8. Let's now have a look at the `mbstring` extension.

Avoiding problems with the updated mbstring extension

The `mbstring` extension was first introduced in PHP 4 and has been an active part of the language ever since. The original purpose of this extension was to provide support for the various Japanese character-encoding systems. Since that time, support for a wide variety of other encodings has been added—most notably, support for encodings based upon **Universal Coded Character Set 2 (UCS-2), UCS-4, Unicode Transformation Format 8 (UTF-8), UTF-16, UTF-32, Shift Japanese Industrial Standards (SJIS)**, and **International Organization for Standardization 8859 (ISO-8859)**, among others.

If you aren't sure which encodings are supported on your server, just run the `mb_list_encodings()` command, as follows (partial output shown):

```
root@php8_tips_php7 [ /repo/ch07 ]#
php -r "var_dump(mb_list_encodings());"
Command line code:1:
array(87) {
   ... only selected output is shown ...
   [14] => string(7) "UCS-4BE"
   [16] => string(5) "UCS-2"
   [19] => string(6) "UTF-32"
   [22] => string(6) "UTF-16"
   [25] => string(5) "UTF-8"
   [26] => string(5) "UTF-7"
   [27] => string(9) "UTF7-IMAP"
   [28] => string(5) "ASCII"
   [29] => string(6) "EUC-JP"
   [30] => string(4) "SJIS"
   [31] => string(9) "eucJP-win"
   [32] => string(11) "EUC-JP-2004"
   [76] => string(6) "KOI8-R"
   [78] => string(9) "ArmSCII-8"
   [79] => string(5) "CP850"
   [80] => string(6) "JIS-ms"
   [81] => string(16) "ISO-2022-JP-2004"
   [86] => string(7) "CP50222"
}
```

As you can see from the preceding output, in the PHP 7.1 Docker container we use for the book, 87 encodings are supported. In the PHP 8.0 Docker container (output not shown), 80 encodings are supported. Let's now have a look at the changes introduced in PHP 8, starting with the `mb_str*()` functions.

Discovering needle-argument differences in mb_str*() functions

In *Chapter 6, Understanding PHP 8 Functional Differences*, you learned how PHP 8 introduced changes to **needle-argument handling** in the core `str*pos()`, `str*str()`, and `str*chr()` functions. The two primary needle-argument differences are the ability to accept an empty needle argument and strict type checking to ensure the needle argument is a string only. In order to maintain consistency, PHP 8 introduces the same changes in the corresponding `mb_str*()` functions.

Let's have a look at empty needle-argument handling first.

mb_str*() function empty needle-argument handling

To keep the `mbstring` extension in line with this change to the core string functions, the following `mbstring` extension functions now allow an empty needle argument. It's important to note that this doesn't mean the argument can be omitted or is optional! What is meant by this change is that any value supplied as the needle argument can now also include what is considered *empty*. A good, quick way to learn what PHP considers to be empty can be found in the documentation for the `empty()` function (https://www.php.net/empty). Here is a list of `mbstring` functions that now allow an empty needle-argument value:

- `mb_strpos()`
- `mb_strrpos()`
- `mb_stripos()`
- `mb_strripos()`
- `mb_strstr()`
- `mb_stristr()`
- `mb_strrchr()`
- `mb_strrichr()`

> **Tip**
> Each of the eight `mbstring` extension functions mentioned here exactly parallels its core PHP counterpart function. For more information on these functions, have a look at this reference documentation: https://www.php.net/manual/en/ref.mbstring.php.

The short code example that follows illustrates empty needle handling in the eight aforementioned functions. Here are the steps leading to this:

1. First, we initialize a multi-byte text string. In the following example, this is a Thai language translation of *The quick brown fox jumped over the fence*. The needle argument is set to `NULL`, and an array of functions to test is initialized:

```
// /repo/ch07/php8_mb_string_empty_needle.php
$text    = 'สุนัขจิ้งจอกสีน้ำตาลกระโดดข้ามรั้วอย่างรวดเร็ว';
$needle  = NULL;
$funcs   = ['mb_strpos',    'mb_strrpos',  'mb_stripos',
            'mb_strripos',  'mb_strstr',   'mb_stristr',
            'mb_strrchr',   'mb_strrichr'];
```

2. We then define a `printf()` pattern, and loop through the functions to be tested. For each function call, we supply the text followed by an empty needle argument, as follows:

```
$patt = "Testing: %12s : %s\n";
foreach ($funcs as $str)
    printf($patt, $str, $str($text, $needle));
```

The output from PHP 7 is shown here:

```
root@php8_tips_php7 [ /repo/ch07 ]#
php php8_mb_string_empty_needle.php
PHP Warning:  mb_strpos(): Empty delimiter in /repo/ch07/php8_mb_string_empty_needle.php on line 12
Testing:      mb_strpos :
Testing:     mb_strrpos :
PHP Warning:  mb_stripos(): Empty delimiter in /repo/ch07/php8_mb_string_empty_needle.php on line 12
Testing:     mb_stripos :
Testing:    mb_strripos :
```

```
PHP Warning:  mb_strstr(): Empty delimiter in /repo/ch07/php8_
mb_string_empty_needle.php on line 12
Testing:    mb_strstr :
PHP Warning:  mb_stristr(): Empty delimiter in /repo/ch07/php8_
mb_string_empty_needle.php on line 12
Testing:    mb_stristr :
Testing:    mb_strrchr :
Testing:    mb_strrichr :
```

As you can see, the output is blank, and, in some cases, a `Warning` message is issued. The output running in PHP 8 is radically different, as expected, as we can see here:

```
root@php8_tips_php8 [ /repo/ch07 ]#
php php8_mb_string_empty_needle.php
Testing:      mb_strpos   : 0
Testing:      mb_strrpos  : 46
Testing:      mb_stripos  : 0
Testing:      mb_strripos : 46
Testing:      mb_strstr   : สุนัขจึงจอกสีน้ำตาลกระโดดข้ามรั้วอย่างรวดเร็ว
Testing:      mb_stristr  : สุนัขจึงจอกสีน้ำตาลกระโดดข้ามรั้วอย่างรวดเร็ว
Testing:      mb_strrchr  :
Testing:      mb_strrichr :
```

It's interesting to note that when this code runs in PHP 8, an empty needle argument returns a value of integer `0` for `mb_strpos()` and `mb_stripos()`, and integer `46` for `mb_strrpos()` and `mb_strripos()`. In PHP 8, an empty needle argument is interpreted as either the beginning or end of the string in this case. The result for both `mb_strstr()` and `mb_stristr()` is the entire string.

mb_str*() function data type checking

To maintain alignment with the core `str*()` functions, the needle argument must be of type string in the corresponding `mb_str*()` functions. If you supply an **American Standard Code for Information Interchange** (**ASCII**) value instead of a string, the affected functions will now throw an `ArgumentTypeError` error. No example is shown in this subsection, as *Chapter 6, Understanding PHP 8 Functional Differences*, already provides an example of this difference in the core `str*()` functions.

Differences in mb_strrpos()

In earlier versions of PHP, you were allowed to pass a character encoding as a third argument to `mb_strrpos()` instead of an offset. This bad practice is no longer supported in PHP 8. Instead, you can either supply 0 as a third argument or consider using PHP 8 *named arguments* (discussed in *Chapter 1, Introducing New PHP 8 OOP Features*, in the *Understanding named arguments* section) to avoid having to supply a value as an optional parameter.

Let's now look at a code example that demonstrates the differences in handling between PHP 7 and PHP 8. Proceed as follows:

1. We first define a constant to represent the character encoding we wish to use. A text string representing a Thai language translation for *The quick brown fox jumped over the fence* is assigned. We then use `mb_convert_encoding()` to ensure the correct encoding is used. The code is illustrated in the following snippet:

```
// /repo/ch07/php7_mb_string_strpos.php
define('ENCODING', 'UTF-8');
$text    = 'สุนัขจิ้งจอกสีน้ำตาลกระโดดข้ามรั้วอย่างรวดเร็ว';
$encoded = mb_convert_encoding($text, ENCODING);
```

2. We then assign the Thai language translation of *fence* to `$needle` and echo the length of the string and the position of `$needle` in the text. We then invoke `mb_strrpos()` to find the last occurrence of `$needle`. Note in the following code snippet that we deliberately follow the bad practice of using the encoding as a third argument rather than an offset:

```
$needle = 'รั้ว';
echo 'String Length: '
    . mb_strlen($encoded, ENCODING) . "\n";
echo 'Substring Pos: '
    . mb_strrpos($encoded, $needle, ENCODING) . "\n";
```

The output of this code example works perfectly in PHP 7, as we can see here:

```
root@php8_tips_php7 [ /repo/ch07 ]#
php php7_mb_string_strpos.php
String Length: 46
Substring Pos: 30
```

As you can see from the preceding output, the length of the multi-byte string is `46`, and the position of the needle is `30`. In PHP 8, on the other hand, we end up with a fatal `Uncaught TypeError` message, as seen here:

```
root@php8_tips_php8 [ /repo/ch07 ]#
php php7_mb_string_strpos.php
String Length: 46
PHP Fatal error:  Uncaught TypeError: mb_strrpos(): Argument #3 ($offset) must be of type int, string given in /repo/ch07/php7_mb_string_strpos.php:14
```

As you can see from the PHP 8 output, the third argument for `mb_strrpos()` must be an offset value in the form of an integer. A simple way to rewrite this example would be to take advantage of PHP 8 *named arguments*. Here is the rewritten line of code:

```
echo 'Substring Pos: '
    . mb_strrpos($encoded, $needle, encoding:ENCODING) . "\n";
```

The output is identical to the PHP 7 example and is not shown here. Let's now turn our attention to `mbstring` extension's **regular expression** (**regex**)-handling differences.

Examining changes to mb_ereg*() functions

The `mb_ereg*()` family of functions allows **regex** processing of strings encoded using multi-byte character sets. In contrast, the core PHP language provides the **Perl Compatible Regular Expressions** (**PCRE**) family of functions, with modern and more up-to-date functionality.

If you add a `u` (lowercase letter *U*) modifier to a regex pattern when using the PCRE functions, any **UTF-8** encoded multi-byte character string is accepted. However, UTF-8 is the *only* multi-byte character encoding accepted. If you are dealing with other character encodings and wish to perform regex functionality, you will need to either convert to UTF-8 or use the `mb_ereg*()` family of functions. Let's now have a look at a number of changes to the `mb_ereg*()` family of functions.

Oniguruma library required in PHP 8

One change to this family of functions is in how your PHP installation is compiled. In PHP 8, your operating system must provide the `libonig` library. This library provides **Oniguruma** functionality. (See `https://github.com/kkos/oniguruma` for more information.) The older `--with-onig` PHP source-compile-configure option has been removed in favor of using `pkg-config` to detect `libonig`.

Changes to mb_ereg_replace()

Formerly, you were able to supply an integer as an argument to `mb_ereg_replace()`. This argument was interpreted as an **ASCII code point**. In PHP 8, such an argument is now typecast as `string`. If you need an ASCII code point, you need to use `mb_chr()` instead. As the typecast to `string` is done silently, there is a potential backward-compatible code break, in that you won't see any `Notice` or `Warning` messages.

The following program code example illustrates the differences between PHP 7 and PHP 8. We'll follow these next steps:

1. First, we define the encoding to be used and assign the Thai translation of *Two quick brown foxes jumped over the fence* as a multi-byte string to `$text`. Next, we use `mb_convert_encoding()` to ensure that the proper encoding is used. We then set `mb_ereg*` to the chosen encoding, using `mb_regex_encoding()`. The code is illustrated in the following snippet:

```
// /repo/ch07/php7_mb_string_strpos.php
define('ENCODING', 'UTF-8');
$text = 'สุนัขจิ้งจอกสีน้ำตาล 2 ตัวกระโดดข้ามรั้ว';
$str  = mb_convert_encoding($text, ENCODING);
mb_regex_encoding(ENCODING);
```

2. We then call `mb_ereg_replace()` and supply as a first argument an integer value `50`, and replace it with the string `"3"`. Both the original and modified strings are echoed. You can view the code here:

```
$mod1 = mb_ereg_replace(50, '3', $str);
echo "Original: $str\n";
echo "Modified: $mod1\n";
```

Note that the first argument for `mb_ereg_replace()` should be a string, but we supply an integer instead. In versions of the `mbstring` extension prior to PHP 8, if an integer is supplied as the first argument, it's treated as an ASCII code point.

If we run this code example in PHP 7, the number `50` is interpreted as the ASCII code point value for `"2"`, as expected, as we can see here:

```
root@php8_tips_php7 [ /repo/ch07 ]#
php php7_mb_string_ereg_replace.php
Original: สุนัขจิ้งจอกสีน้ำตาล 2 ตัวกระโดดข้ามรั้ว
Modified: สุนัขจิ้งจอกสีน้ำตาล 3 ตัวกระโดดข้ามรั้ว
```

As you can see from the preceding output, the number 2 is replaced by the number 3. In PHP 8, however, the number 50 is typecast into a string. As this source string doesn't contain the number 50, no replacements are made, as we can see here:

```
root@php8_tips_php8 [ /repo/ch07 ]#
php php7_mb_string_ereg_replace.php
Original: สุนัขจึงจอกสีน้ำตาล 2 ตัวกระโดดข้ามรัว
Modified: สุนัขจึงจอกสีน้ำตาล 2 ตัวกระโดดข้ามรัว
```

The danger here is that if your code relies upon this silent interpretation process, your application might either fail or exhibit inconsistent behavior. You'll also note a lack of `Notice` or `Warning` messages. PHP 8 relies upon the developer to supply the correct arguments!

The *best practice*, if you do actually need to use an ASCII code point, is to use `mb_chr()` to produce the desired search string. The modified code example might look like this:

```
$mod1 = mb_ereg_replace(mb_chr(50), '3', $str);
```

You now have an idea about what changed in the `mbstring` extension. Without this information, you could easily end up writing faulty code. Developers who are unaware of this information might end up making mistakes in PHP 8, such as assuming the `mbstring` aliases are still in place. Such mistaken understanding can easily cause hours of lost time tracking down errors in program code following a PHP 8 migration.

It's now time to have a look at another extension with major changes: the GD extension.

Dealing with changes to the GD extension

The **GD extension** is an image-manipulation extension that leverages the GD library. GD originally stood for **GIF Draw**. Oddly, the GD library had to withdraw support for the **Graphics Interchange Format** (**GIF**) after Unisys revoked the open source license for the compression technology used when generating GIFs. After 2004, however, the Unisys patent on this technology expired and GIF support was restored. As it stands today, the PHP GD extension offers support for the **Joint Photographic Experts Group** (**JPEG** or **JPG**), **Portable Network Graphic** (**PNG**), GIF, **X BitMap** (**XBM**), **X PixMap** (**XPM**), **Wireless Bitmap** (**WBMP**), **WebP**, and **Bitmap** (**BMP**) formats.

> **Tip**
> For more information on the GD library, see `https://libgd.github.io/`.

Let's now have a look at the impact of resource-to-object migration on the GD extension.

GD extension resource-to-object migration

As with other PHP extensions that previously used *resources*, the GD extension has also primarily migrated from `resource` to `object`. As mentioned in the *PHP 8 extension resource-to-object migration* section, all of the `imagecreate*()` functions now produce `GdImage` objects rather than resources.

For an example of how this might present a code break after a PHP 8 migration, run these examples in two different browser tabs (on your local computer) and compare the difference. First, we run the PHP 7 example using this URL: `http://172.16.0.77/ch07/php7_gd_is_resource.php`. Here is the result:

Figure 7.2 – PHP 7 GD image resource

As you can see from the preceding output, a `resource` extension is identified, but there's no descriptive information. Now, let's run the PHP 8 example using this URL: http://172.16.0.88/ch07/php8_gd_is_resource.php. Here is the result:

Figure 7.3 – PHP 8 GD image object instance

The output from PHP 8 not only identifies the return type as a `GdImage` instance but also displays descriptive information below the image.

We now turn our attention to other `GD` extension changes.

GD extension compile flag changes

The `GD` extension not only leverages the GD library but a number of supporting libraries as well. These libraries are needed to provide support for the various graphics formats. Previously, when compiling a custom version of PHP from the source code, you needed to specify the location of the libraries for *JPEG*, *PNG*, *XPM*, and *VPX* formats. In addition, as compression is an important aspect in reducing the overall final file size, the location of `ZLIB` was needed as well.

When compiling PHP 8 from source, there are a number of significant configuration flag changes that were first introduced in PHP 7.4 and subsequently carried into PHP 8. The primary change is that you no longer need to specify the directory where libraries are located. PHP 8 now locates libraries using the `pkg-config` operating system equivalent.

The following table summarizes compile flag changes. These flags are used with the `configure` utility just prior to the actual compile process itself:

Old Compile Flag	New Compile Flag
`--with-gd`	`--enable-gd`
`--with-jpeg-dir=DIR`	`--with-jpeg`
`--with-xpm-dir=DIR`	`--with-xpm`
`--with-vpx-dir=DIR`	`--with-webp`
`--with-png-dir=DIR`	removed: `libpng` is required
`--with-zlib-dir`	removed: `zlib` is required

Table 7.3 – GD compile option changes

You will note from the table that for the most part, most `--with-*-dir` options are replaced with `--with-*`. Also, *PNG* and *ZLIB* support is now automatic; however, you must have `libpng` and `zlib` installed on your operating system.

We will now have a look at other minor changes to the GD extension.

Other GD extension changes

Aside from the major changes described in the previous section, a number of other minor changes have taken place, in the form of function signature changes and a new function. Let's start this discussion by having a look at the `imagecropauto()` function.

Here is the old function signature for `imagecropauto()`:

```
imagecropauto(resource $image , int $mode = -1,
              float $threshold = .5 , int $color = -1 )
```

In PHP 8, the `$image` parameter is now of type `GdImage`. The `$mode` parameter now defaults to an `IMG_CROP_DEFAULT` predefined constant.

Another change affects the `imagepolygon()`, `imageopenpolygon()`, and `imagefilledpolygon()` functions. Here is the old function signature for `imagepolygon()`:

```
imagepolygon(resource $image, array $points,
             int $num_points, int $color)
```

In PHP 8, the `$num_points` parameter is now optional. If omitted, the number of points is calculated as follows: `count($points)/2`. However, this means that the number of elements in the `$points` array must be an even number!

The last significant change is the addition of a new function, `imagegetinterpolation()`. Here is its function signature:

`imagegetinterpolation(GdImage $image) : int`

The return value is an integer that, in and of itself, isn't very useful. However, if you examine the documentation for the `imagesetinterpolation()` function (https://www.php.net/manual/en/function.imagesetinterpolation.php), you will see a list of interpolation method code along with an explanation.

You now have an idea of which changes were introduced in the GD extension. We next examine changes to the `Reflection` extension.

Discovering changes to the Reflection extension

The **Reflection extension** is used to perform *introspection* on objects, classes, methods, and functions, among other things. `ReflectionClass` and `ReflectionObject` produce information on a class or an object instance respectively. `ReflectionFunction` provides information on procedural-level functions. In addition, the `Reflection` extension has a set of secondary classes produced by the main classes mentioned just now. These secondary classes include `ReflectionMethod`, produced by `ReflectionClass::getMethod()`, `ReflectionProperty`, produced by `ReflectionClass::getProperty()`, and so forth.

You might wonder: *Who uses this extension?* The answer is: any application that needs to perform analysis on an external set of classes. This might include software that performs automated **code generation**, **testing**, or **documentation generation**. Classes that perform **hydration** (populating objects from arrays) also benefit from the `Reflection` extension.

> **Tip**
>
> We do not have enough room in the book to cover every single `Reflection` extension class and method. If you wish to get more information, please have a look at the documentation reference here: https://www.php.net/manual/en/book.reflection.php.

Let's now have a look at a `Reflection` extension usage example.

Reflection extension usage

We will now show a code example that demonstrates how the `Reflection` extension might be used to generate **docblocks** (a `docblock` is a PHP comment that uses a special syntax to denote the purpose of a method, its incoming parameters, and return value). Here are the steps leading to this:

1. We first define a `__construct()` method that creates a `ReflectionClass` instance of the target class, as follows:

```php
// /repo/src/Services/DocBlockChecker.php
namespace Services;
use ReflectionClass;
class DocBlockChecker {
    public $target = '';       // class to check
    public $reflect = NULL;    // ReflectionClass instance
    public function __construct(string $target) {
        $this->target = $target;
        $this->reflect = new ReflectionClass($target);
    }
```

2. We then define a `check()` method that grabs all the class methods, returning an array of `ReflectionMethod` instances, as follows:

```php
public function check() {
    $methods = [];
    $list = $this->reflect->getMethods();
```

3. We then loop through all the methods and use `getDocComment()` to check to see if a `docblock` already exists, as follows:

```php
foreach ($list as $refMeth) {
    $docBlock = $refMeth->getDocComment();
```

4. If a `docblock` does not already exist, we start a new one and then call `getParameters()`, which returns an array of `ReflectionParameter` instances, as illustrated in the following code snippet:

```php
if (!$docBlock) {
    $docBlock = "/**\n * "
```

```php
                . $refMeth->getName() . "\n";
            $params = $refMeth->getParameters();
```

5. If we do have parameters, we gather information for display, as follows:

```php
            if ($params) {
                foreach ($params as $refParm) {
                    $type = $refParm->getType()
                        ?? 'mixed';
                    $type = (string) $type;
                    $name = $refParm->getName();
                    $default = '';
                    if (!$refParm->isVariadic()
                        && $refParm->isOptional()) {
                            $default=$refParm->getDefaultValue(); }
                    if ($default === '') {
                        $default = "(empty string)"; }
                    $docBlock .= " * @param $type "
                        . "\${$name} : $default\n";
                }
            }
```

6. We then set the return type and assign the `docblock` to a `$methods` array that is then returned, as follows:

```php
            if ($refMeth->isConstructor())
                $return = 'void';
            else
                $return = $refMeth->getReturnType()
                    ?? 'mixed';
            $docBlock .= " * @return $return\n";
            $docBlock .= " */\n";
        }
        $methods[$refMeth->getName()] = $docBlock;
    }
    return $methods;
}
```

7. Now the new `docblock` checking class is complete, we define a calling program, as shown in the following code snippet. The calling program targets a `/repo/src/Php7/Reflection/Test.php` class (not shown here). This class has a mixture of methods with parameters and return values:

```php
// //repo/ch07/php7_reflection_usage.php
$target = 'Php7\Reflection\Test';
require_once __DIR__
    . '/../src/Server/Autoload/Loader.php';
use Server\Autoload\Loader;
use Services\DocBlockChecker;
$autoload = new Loader();
$checker = new DocBlockChecker($target);
var_dump($checker->check());
```

The output of the calling program is shown here:

```
root@php8_tips_php7 [ /repo/ch07 ]#
php php7_reflection_usage.php
/repo/ch07/php7_reflection_usage.php:10:
array(4) {
  '__construct' =>  string(75)
"/**
 * __construct
 * @param PDO $pdo : (empty string)
 * @return void
 */"
  'fetchAll' =>  string(41)
"/**
 * fetchAll
 * @return Generator
 */"
  'fetchByName' =>  string(80)
"/**
 * fetchByName
 * @param string $name : (empty string)
 * @return array
 */"
```

```
    'fetchLastId' =>   string(38)
"/**
 * fetchLastId
 * @return int
 */"
}
```

As you can see, this class forms the basis of potentially automatic documentation or a code-generation application.

Let's now have a look at `Reflection` extension improvements.

Learning about Reflection extension improvements

There have also been a number of improvements to the `Reflection` extension that might be important for you to know about. Please bear in mind that, although there are a limited number of developers who use the `Reflection` extension, you might one day find yourself in a situation where you are working with code that uses this extension. If you notice odd behavior after a PHP 8 upgrade, the material covered in this section gives you a head start in the troubleshooting process.

ReflectionType modifications

The `ReflectionType` class is now abstract in PHP 8. When you use the `ReflectionProperty::getType()` or `ReflectionFunction::getReturnType()` methods, you might note that a `ReflectionNamedType` instance is returned. This change does not affect the normal functioning of your program code, unless you are relying upon a `ReflectionType` instance being returned. However, `ReflectionNamedType` extends `ReflectionType`, so any `instanceof` operations will not be affected.

It's also worth noting that the `isBuiltIn()` method has been moved from `ReflectionType` to `ReflectionNamedType`. Again, since `ReflectionNamedType` extends `ReflectionType`, this should not present any backward-compatible break in your current code.

ReflectionParameter::*DefaultValue* methods enhanced

In earlier versions of PHP, `ReflectionParameter` methods pertaining to default values were unable to reflect internal PHP functions. This has changed in PHP 8. The following `ReflectionParameter` methods are now also able to return default value information from internal functions:

- `getDefaultValue()`
- `getDefaultValueConstantName()`
- `isDefaultValueAvailable()`
- `isDefaultValueConstant()`

As you can see from the list, the method names are self-explanatory. We'll now show a code example that makes use of these enhancements. Here are the steps leading to this:

1. First, we define a function that accepts a `ReflectionParameter` instance and returns an array with the parameter name and default value, as follows:

```php
// /repo/ch07/php8_reflection_parms_defaults.php
$func = function (ReflectionParameter $parm) {
    $name = $parm->getName();
    $opts = NULL;
    if ($parm->isDefaultValueAvailable())
        $opts = $parm->getDefaultValue();
```

2. Next, we define a `switch()` statement to sanitize the options, as follows:

```php
    switch (TRUE) {
        case (is_array($opts)) :
            $tmp = '';
            foreach ($opts as $key => $val)
                $tmp .= $key . ':' . $val . ',';
            $opts = substr($tmp, 0, -1);
            break;
        case (is_bool($opts)) :
            $opts = ($opts) ? 'TRUE' : 'FALSE';
            break;
        case ($opts === '') :
            $opts = "''";
            break;
```

```
            default :
                $opts = 'No Default';
    }
    return [$name, $opts];
};
```

3. We then determine which function to reflect and pull its parameters. In the following example, we reflect `setcookie()`:

```
$test = 'setcookie';
$ref = new ReflectionFunction($test);
$parms = $ref->getParameters();
```

4. We then loop through the array of `ReflectionParameter` instances and produce an output, as follows:

```
$patt = "%18s : %s\n";
foreach ($parms as $obj)
    vprintf($patt, $func($obj));
```

Here is the output running in PHP 7:

```
root@php8_tips_php7 [ /repo/ch07 ]#
php php8_reflection_parms_defaults.php
Reflecting on setcookie
         Parameter : Default(s)
        ---------- : ------------
              name : No Default
             value : No Default
           expires : No Default
              path : No Default
            domain : No Default
            secure : No Default
          httponly : No Default
```

The result is always No Default because, in PHP 7 and earlier, the Reflection extension is unable to read defaults for internal PHP functions. The PHP 8 output, on the other hand, is much more accurate, as we can see here:

```
root@php8_tips_php8 [ /repo/ch07 ]#
php php8_reflection_parms_defaults.php
Reflecting on setcookie
           Parameter : Default(s)
           --------- : ----------
                name : No Default
               value : ''
   expires_or_options : No Default
                path : ''
              domain : ''
              secure : FALSE
            httponly : FALSE
```

As you can see from the output, the Reflection extension in PHP 8 is able to accurately report on internal function default values!

Let's now have a look at other Reflection extension changes.

Other Reflection extension changes

In PHP versions prior to PHP 8, ReflectionMethod::isConstructor() and ReflectionMethod::isDestructor() were unable to reflect magic methods defined in interfaces. In PHP 8, these two methods now return TRUE for the corresponding magic methods defined in interfaces.

When using the ReflectionClass::getConstants() or ReflectionClass::getReflectionConstants() methods, a new $filter parameter has now been added. The parameter allows you to filter the results by visibility level. Accordingly, the new parameter can accept any of the following newly added predefined constants:

- ReflectionClassConstant::IS_PUBLIC
- ReflectionClassConstant::IS_PROTECTED
- ReflectionClassConstant::IS_PRIVATE

You now have an idea of how to use the `Reflection` extension and what to expect after a PHP 8 migration. It's time to have a look at a number of other extensions that saw changes in PHP 8.

Working with other extension gotchas

PHP 8 introduced a number of other noteworthy changes to several PHP extensions other than the ones already discussed in this chapter. As we have stressed time and again in this book, it's extremely important for your future career as a PHP developer to be aware of these changes.

Let's first have a look at changes to database extensions.

New database extension operating system library requirements

Any developer using **MySQL**, **MariaDB**, **PostgreSQL**, or **PHP Data Objects (PDO)** needs to be aware of new requirements for supporting operating system libraries. The following table summarizes the new minimum versions required in PHP 8:

Extension	Library	Minimum Vers
PgSQL	libpq	9.1
PDO_PGSQL	libpq	9.1
MySQLi	libmysqlclient	5.1
PDO_MySQL	libmysqlclient	5.1

Table 7.4 – PHP 8 database library requirements

As you can see from the preceding table, there are two main library changes. `libpq` affects both the `PostgreSQL` extension and the driver for the `PDO` extension. `libmysqlclient` is the library used by both the **MySQL Improved** (**MySQLi**) extension and as the MySQL driver for the `PDO` extension. It should also be noted that if you are using MariaDB, a popular open source version of MySQL, the new minimum `MySQL` library requirement applies to you as well.

Now that you are aware of database extension changes, we next turn our attention to the ZIP extension.

Reviewing changes to the ZIP extension

The ZIP **extension** is used to programmatically create and manage compressed archive files, leveraging the `libzip` operating system library. Other compression extensions exist, such as **Zlib**, **bzip2**, **LZF**, **PHP Archive Format** (**phar**), and **Roshal Archive Compressed** (**RAR**); however, none of the other extensions offers the rich range of functionality offered by the `ZIP` extension. Also, for the most part, the other extensions are special-purpose and are generally unsuitable for generic ZIP file management.

Let's first have a look at the most notable change to this extension.

Dealing with ZIP extension OOP migration

The biggest change to the ZIP extension is one that presents a potentially massive backward-compatible code break down the road. As of PHP 8, the procedural API (all procedural functions) has been deprecated! Although this does not affect any code at present, all ZIP extension functions will eventually be removed from the language.

The *best practice* is to migrate any `ZIP` extension procedural code over to the OOP API using the `ZipArchive` class. The following code example illustrates how to migrate from procedural code to object code, opening a `test.zip` file and producing a list of entries:

```
// /repo/ch07/php7_zip_functions.php
$fn  = __DIR__ . '/includes/test.zip';
$zip = zip_open($fn);
$cnt = 0;
if (!is_resource($zip)) exit('Unable to open zip file');
while ($entry = zip_read($zip)) {
    echo zip_entry_name($entry) . "\n";
    $cnt++;
}
echo "Total Entries: $cnt\n";
```

Here is the output running in PHP 7:

```
root@php8_tips_php7 [ /repo/ch07 ]#
php php7_zip_functions.php
ch07/includes/
ch07/includes/test.zip
ch07/includes/tree.xml
ch07/includes/test.png
```

```
ch07/includes/kitten.jpg
ch07/includes/reflection.html
ch07/php7_ext_is_resource.php
ch07/php7_gd_is_resource.php
... not all entries shown ...
ch07/php8_simple_xml.php
ch07/php8_xml_writer.php
ch07/php8_zip_oop.php
Total Entries: 27
```

As you can see from the preceding output, a total of 27 entries are found. (Also, note that not all ZIP file entries are shown.) If we try the same code example in PHP 8, however, we get a very different result, as we can see here:

```
root@php8_tips_php8 [ /repo/ch07 ]#
php php7_zip_functions.php
PHP Deprecated:  Function zip_open() is deprecated in /repo/ch07/php7_zip_functions.php on line 5
PHP Deprecated:  Function zip_read() is deprecated in /repo/ch07/php7_zip_functions.php on line 8
PHP Deprecated:  Function zip_entry_name() is deprecated in /repo/ch07/php7_zip_functions.php on line 9
ch07/includes/
Deprecated: Function zip_entry_name() is deprecated in /repo/ch07/php7_zip_functions.php on line 9
... not all entries shown ...
ch07/php8_zip_oop.php
PHP Deprecated:  Function zip_read() is deprecated in /repo/ch07/php7_zip_functions.php on line 8
Total Entries: 27
```

As you can see from the preceding PHP 8 output, the code example works, but a series of deprecation `Notice` messages are issued.

Here is how you need to write the same code example in PHP 8:

```
// /repo/ch07/php8_zip_oop.php
$fn  = __DIR__ . '/includes/test.zip';
$obj = new ZipArchive();
$res = $obj->open($fn);
```

```
if ($res !== TRUE) exit('Unable to open zip file');
for ($i = 0; $entry = $obj->statIndex($i); $i++) {
    echo $entry['name'] . "\n";
}
echo "Total Entries: $i\n";
```

The output (not shown) is exactly the same as for the previous example. Interestingly, the rewritten example also works in PHP 7! It's also worth noting that in PHP 8, you can get a count of the total number of entries (per directory) using `ZipArchive::count()`. You may also have noticed that to check to see if the ZIP archive is opened properly, in PHP 8 you can no longer use `is_resource()`.

New ZipArchive class methods

In addition to resource-to-object migration, a number of improvements have been made to the `ZipArchive` class. One such improvement is that the following new methods have been added:

- `setMtimeName()`
- `setMtimeIndex()`
- `registerProgressCallback()`
- `registerCancelCallback()`
- `replaceFile()`
- `isCompressionMethodSupported()`
- `isEncryptionMethodSupported()`

The method names are self-explanatory. `Mtime` refers to **modification time**.

New options for addGlob() and addPattern()

The `ZipArchive::addGlob()` and `ZipArchive::addPattern()` methods have a new set of options. These two methods are similar in that both are used to add files to the archive. The difference is that `addGlob()` uses the same file pattern as the core PHP `glob()` command, whereas `addPattern()` filters files using a regex. The new set of options is summarized here:

- `flags`: Lets you combine the appropriate class constants using *bitwise operators*
- `comp_method`: Specifies the compression method using any of the `ZipArchive::CM_*` constants as an argument

- `comp_flags`: Specifies compression flags using the desired `ZipArchive::FL_*` constant(s)
- `enc_method`: Lets you specify the desired character encoding (using any of the `ZipArchive::FL_ENC_*` flags)
- `enc_password`: Lets you specify the encryption password if it is set for this ZIP archive

It's also worth mentioning here that the `remove_path` option prior to PHP 8 had to be a valid directory path. As of PHP 8, this option is a simple string that represents characters to be removed. This allows you to remove filename prefixes as well as undesired directory paths.

While we are still examining options, it's worth noting that two new encoding method class constants have been added: `ZipArchive::EM_UNKNOWN` and `ZipArchive::EM_TRAD_PKWARE`. Also, a new `lastId` property has been added so that you are able to determine the index value of the last ZIP archive entry.

Other ZipArchive method changes

In addition to the changes mentioned earlier, a few other `ZipArchive` methods have changed in PHP 8. In this section, we summarize other `ZipArchive` method changes, as follows:

- `ZipArchive::extractTo()` previously used the current date and time for the modification time. As of PHP 8, this method restores the original file modification time.
- `ZipArchive::getStatusString()` returns results even after `ZipArchive::close()` has been invoked.
- `ZipArchive::addEmptyDir()`, `ZipArchive::addFile()`, and `ZipArchive::addFromString()` methods all have a new `flags` argument. You can use any of the appropriate `ZipArchive::FL_*` class constants, combined using bitwise operators.
- `ZipArchive::open()` can now open an empty (zero-byte) file.

Now you have an idea of the changes and improvements that have been introduced to the `ZIP` extension, let's examine changes in the area of regular expressions.

Examining PCRE extension changes

The **PCRE** extension contains a number of functions designed to perform pattern matching using *regular expressions*. The term *regular expression* is commonly shortened to *regex*. A **regex** is a string that describes another string. Here are some changes to note in the `PCRE` extension.

Invalid escape sequences in patterns are no longer interpreted as literals. In the past, you could use an X modifier; however, that modifier is now ignored in PHP 8. Happily, to assist you with internal PCRE pattern-analysis errors, a new `preg_last_error_msg()` function has been added that returns a human-readable message when PCRE errors are encountered.

The `preg_last_error()` function allows you to determine whether or not an internal PCRE error occurred during pattern analysis. This function only returns an integer, however. Prior to PHP 8, it was up to the developer to look up the code and to figure out the actual error.

> **Tip**
> A list of error codes returned by `preg_last_error()` can be found here:
> https://www.php.net/manual/en/function.preg-last-error.php#refsect1-function.preg-last-error-returnvalues

A brief code example follows that illustrates the aforementioned issues. Here are the steps leading to this:

1. First, we define a function that performs a match and checks to see if any errors have occurred, as follows:

```
$pregTest = function ($pattern, $string) {
    $result  = preg_match($pattern, $string);
    $lastErr = preg_last_error();
    if ($lastErr == PREG_NO_ERROR) {
        $msg = 'RESULT: ';
        $msg .= ($result) ? 'MATCH' : 'NO MATCH';
    } else {
        $msg = 'ERROR : ';
        if (function_exists('preg_last_error_msg'))
            $msg .= preg_last_error_msg();
        else
```

```
                    $msg .= $lastErr;
            }
            return "$msg\n";
    };
```

2. We then create a pattern that deliberately contains a \8+ invalid escape sequence, as follows:

```
$pattern = '/\8+/';
$string  = 'test 8';
echo $pregTest($pattern, $string);
```

3. Next, we define a pattern that deliberately causes PCRE to exceed its backtrace limit, as follows:

```
$pattern = '/(?:\D+|<\d+>)*[!?]/';
$string  = 'test ';
echo $pregTest($pattern, $string);
```

Here is the output in PHP 7.1:

```
root@php8_tips_php7 [ /repo/ch07 ]# php php7_pcre.php
RESULT: MATCH
ERROR : 2
```

As you can see from the preceding output, the invalid pattern is treated as a literal value 8. Because 8 exists in the string, a match is considered found. As for the second pattern, the backtrace limit is exceeded; however, PHP 7.1 is unable to report the problem, forcing you to look it up.

The output in PHP 8 is quite different, as seen here:

```
root@php8_tips_php8 [ /repo/ch07 ]# php php7_pcre.php
PHP Warning:  preg_match(): Compilation failed: reference to
non-existent subpattern at offset 1 in /repo/ch07/php7_pcre.php
on line 5
ERROR : Internal error
ERROR : Backtrack limit exhausted
```

As you can see from the preceding output, PHP 8 produces a Warning message. You can also see that preg_last_error_msg() produces a useful message. Let's now have a look at the **Internationalization (Intl)** extension.

Working with Intl extension changes

The **Intl extension** consists of several classes that handle a number of application aspects that might change depending on the locale. The various classes handle such tasks as internationalized number and currency formatting, text parsing, calendar generation, time and date formatting, and character-set conversion, among other things.

The main change introduced to the Intl extension in PHP 8 is the following new date formats:

- `IntlDateFormatter::RELATIVE_FULL`
- `IntlDateFormatter::RELATIVE_LONG`
- `IntlDateFormatter::RELATIVE_MEDIUM`
- `IntlDateFormatter::RELATIVE_SHORT`

A code example follows, showing the new formats. Here are the steps leading to this:

1. First, we define a `DateTime` instance and an array containing the new format codes, as follows:

   ```
   $dt = new DateTime('tomorrow');
   $pt = [IntlDateFormatter::RELATIVE_FULL,
          IntlDateFormatter::RELATIVE_LONG,
          IntlDateFormatter::RELATIVE_MEDIUM,
          IntlDateFormatter::RELATIVE_SHORT
   ];
   ```

2. We then loop through the formats and echo the output, as follows:

   ```
   foreach ($pt as $fmt)
       echo IntlDateFormatter::formatObject($dt, $fmt)."\n";
   ```

This example doesn't work in PHP 7. Here is the output from PHP 8:

```
root@php8_tips_php8 [ /repo/ch07 ]#
php php8_intl_date_fmt.php
tomorrow at 12:00:00 AM Coordinated Universal Time
tomorrow at 12:00:00 AM UTC
tomorrow, 12:00:00 AM
tomorrow, 12:00 AM
```

As you can see, the new relative date formats work quite well! We now briefly return to the cURL extension.

Understanding cURL extension changes

The cURL extension leverages libcurl (http://curl.haxx.se/) to provide powerful and highly efficient HTTP client capabilities. In PHP 8, you must have libcurl version 7.29 (or above) installed on your server's operating system.

Another difference in PHP 8 is that this extension now uses objects rather than resources. This change was described earlier in this chapter, in *Table 7.1, PHP 8 resource-to-object migration*. An example was shown in the *Potential code break involving is_resource()* section. A side effect of this change is that any of the curl*close() functions are redundant, as the connection is closed when the object is unset or otherwise goes out of scope.

Let's now have a look at changes to the COM extension.

Reviewing COM extension changes

Component Object Model (COM) is a Windows-only extension that enables programming code written in one language to call and interoperate with code written in any other COM-aware programming language. This information is important for any PHP developers who plan to develop PHP applications that run on Windows servers.

The most significant change to the COM extension is that case sensitivity is now automatically enforced. Accordingly, you can no longer import from type libraries any constants that are case-insensitive. In addition, you can no longer specify $case_insensitive, the second argument to the com_load_typelib() function, as FALSE.

Along these lines, COM extension php.ini settings that deal with case sensitivity have been altered. These include the following:

- com.autoregister_casesensitive: Permanently enabled in PHP 8.
- com.typelib_file: Any type libraries whose names end with either #cis or #case_insensitive no longer cause the constants to be treated as case-insensitive.

One change is a new php.ini setting, com.dotnet_version. This setting sets the **.NET** version to use for dotnet objects. We now examine other extension changes of note.

Examining other extension changes

There are a few other changes to other PHP extensions that deserve a mention. *Table 7.5*, shown next, summarizes these changes:

Extension	Functions	Notes
Date	`mktime()` `gmmktime()`	The first argument (`$hour`) is now mandatory

Enchant	`enchant_broker_list_dicts()`
	`enchant_broker_describe()`
	`enchant_dict_suggest()`
		If no results, these three functions now return an empty array instead of `NULL`

Tidy	`tidy_repair_string()`	The `$use_include_path` parameter is no longer supported.

Table 7.5 – PHP 8 database library requirements

You now have an idea about changes to extensions in PHP 8. This wraps up the chapter. Now, it's time for a recap!

Summary

One of the most important concepts you learned in this chapter is a general trend away from resources and toward objects. You learned where this trend is noticeable in the various PHP extensions covered in this chapter, and how to develop workarounds to avoid problems in code that relies upon resources. You also learned how to detect and develop code to address changes in XML extensions, especially in the `SimpleXML` and `XMLWriter` extensions.

Another important extension with significant changes covered in this chapter is the `mbstring` extension. You learned to detect code that relies upon changed `mbstring` functionality. As you learned, changes to the `mbstring` extension for the most part mirror changes made to the equivalent core PHP string functions.

You also learned about major changes to the `GD`, `Reflection`, and `ZIP` extensions. In this chapter, you also learned about changes to a number of database extensions, as well as a medley of additional extension changes to note. All in all, with the awareness you will have gained by reading this chapter and by studying the examples, you are now in a better position to prevent your applications from failing after you have performed a PHP 8 upgrade.

In the next chapter, you will learn about functionality that has been deprecated or removed in PHP 8.

8
Learning about PHP 8's Deprecated or Removed Functionality

This chapter walks you through functionality that has been deprecated or removed in **PHP Hypertext Preprocessor 8** (**PHP 8**). This information is extremely important for any developer to know. Any code that uses removed functionality must be rewritten before an upgrade to PHP 8. Likewise, any deprecation is a clear signal to you that you must rewrite any code that depends upon such functionality, or risk problems in the future.

After you have read the material in this chapter and followed the example application code, you can detect and rewrite code that has been deprecated. You can also develop workarounds for functionality that has been removed and learn how to refactor code that uses removed functionality involving extensions. Another important skill you will learn from this chapter is how to improve application security by rewriting code depending on removed functions.

Topics covered in this chapter include the following:

- Discovering what has been removed from the core
- Examining core deprecations
- Working with removed functionality in PHP 8 extensions
- Dealing with deprecated or removed security-related functionality

Technical requirements

To examine and run the code examples provided in this chapter, the minimum recommended hardware is outlined here:

- x86_64-based desktop PC or laptop
- 1 gigabyte (GB) free disk space
- 4 GB of random-access memory (RAM)
- 500 kilobits per second (Kbps) or faster internet connection

In addition, you will need to install the following software:

- Docker
- Docker Compose

Please refer to the *Technical requirements* section of *Chapter 1, Introducing New PHP 8 OOP Features*, for more information on Docker and Docker Compose installation, as well as how to build the Docker container used to demonstrate the code explained in this book. In this book, we refer to the directory in which you restored the sample code for the book as `/repo`.

The source code for this chapter is located here:

`https://github.com/PacktPublishing/PHP-8-Programming-Tips-Tricks-and-Best-Practices`

We can now begin our discussion by examining the core functionality removed in PHP 8.

Discovering what has been removed from the core

In this section, we consider not only functions and classes that have been removed from PHP 8, but we will also have a look at usage that has been removed as well. We will then have a look at class methods and functions that still exist but no longer serve any useful purpose due to other changes in PHP 8. Knowing which functions have been removed is extremely important in order to protect against a potential code break following a PHP 8 migration.

Let's start by examining functions removed in PHP 8.

Examining functions removed in PHP 8

There are a number of functions in the PHP language that have only been retained thus far in order to maintain backward compatibility. However, maintenance of such functions drains resources away from core language development. Further, for the most part, such functions have been superseded by better programming constructs. Accordingly, there has been a slow process whereby such commands have been slowly dropped from the language as evidence has mounted that they are no longer being used.

> **Tip**
> The PHP core team occasionally runs statistical analysis on PHP repositories based on GitHub. In this way, they are able to determine the frequency of usage of the various commands in the PHP core.

The table shown next summarizes the functions that have been removed in PHP 8 and what to use in their place:

Removed Function	Suggested Replacement
`__autoload()`	`spl_autoload_register()`
`convert_cyr_string()`	`mb_convert_encoding()`
`create_function()`	`function () {}` `fn () => <expression>`
`each()`	`ArrayIterator`
`ezmlm_hash()`	none other than running an OS command
`fgetss()`	`strip_tags(fgets())`
`get_magic_quotes_gpc()` `get_magic_quotes_runtime()`	none: the magic quotes feature itself has been removed from PHP
`hebrevc()`	`hebrev()`
`is_real()`	`is_float()`
`money_format()`	`NumberFormatter::formatCurrency`
`restore_include_path()`	`ini_restore('include_path')`

Table 8.1 – PHP 8 removed functions and suggested replacements

For the remainder of this section, we cover a few of the more important removed functions and give you suggestions on how to refactor your code to achieve the same results. Let's start by examining `each()`.

Working with each()

`each()` was introduced in PHP 4 as a way of walking through an array, producing key/value pairs upon each iteration. The syntax and usage of `each()` is extremely simple and is oriented toward procedural usage. We'll show a short code example that demonstrates `each()` usage, as follows:

1. In this code example, we first open a connection to a data file containing city data from the GeoNames (https://geonames.org) project, as follows:

```
// /repo/ch08/php7_each.php
$data_src = __DIR__
    . '/../sample_data/cities15000_min.txt';
$fh       = fopen($data_src, 'r');
$pattern  = "%30s : %20s\n";
$target   = 10000000;
$data     = [];
```

2. We then use the `fgetcsv()` function to pull a row of data into `$line`, and pack latitude and longitude information into a `$data` array. Note in the following code snippet that we filter out rows of data on cities with a population less than `$target` (in this case, less than 10 million):

```
while ($line = fgetcsv($fh, '', "\t")) {
    $popNum = $line[14] ?? 0;
    if ($popNum > $target) {
        $city = $line[1] ?? 'Unknown';
        $data[$city] = $line[4] . ',' . $line[5];
    }
}
```

3. We then close the file handle and sort the array by city name. To present the output, we use `each()` to walk through the array, producing key/value pairs, where the city is the key, and latitude and longitude is the value. The code is illustrated in the following snippet:

```
fclose($fh);
ksort($data);
printf($pattern, 'City', 'Latitude/Longitude');
printf($pattern, '----', '------------------');
while ([$city, $latLon] = each($data)) {
    $city = str_pad($city, 30, ' ', STR_PAD_LEFT);
    printf($pattern, $city, $latLon);
}
```

Here is the output as it appears in PHP 7:

```
root@php8_tips_php7 [ /repo/ch08 ]# php php7_each.php
                          City : Latitude/Longitude
                          ---- : ------------------
                       Beijing : 39.9075,116.39723
                  Buenos Aires : -34.61315,-58.37723
                         Delhi : 28.65195,77.23149
                         Dhaka : 23.7104,90.40744
                     Guangzhou : 23.11667,113.25
                      Istanbul : 41.01384,28.94966
                       Karachi : 24.8608,67.0104
```

```
       Mexico City :    19.42847,-99.12766
            Moscow :    55.75222,37.61556
            Mumbai :    19.07283,72.88261
             Seoul :    37.566,126.9784
          Shanghai :    31.22222,121.45806
          Shenzhen :    22.54554,114.0683
         São Paulo :    -23.5475,-46.63611
            Tianjin :   39.14222,117.17667
```

This code example won't work in PHP 8, however, because each() has been removed. The *best practice* is to move toward an **object-oriented programming (OOP)** approach: use ArrayIterator instead of each(). The next code example produces exactly the same results as previously but uses object classes instead of procedural functions:

1. Instead of using fopen(), we instead create an SplFileObject instance. You'll also notice in the following code snippet that instead of creating an array, we create an ArrayIterator instance to hold the final data:

```
// /repo/ch08/php8_each_replacements.php
$data_src = __DIR__
          . '/../sample_data/cities15000_min.txt';
$fh       = new SplFileObject($data_src, 'r');
$pattern  = "%30s : %20s\n";
$target   = 10000000;
$data     = new ArrayIterator();
```

2. We then loop through the data file using the fgetcsv() method to retrieve a line and offsetSet() to append to the iteration, as follows:

```
while ($line = $fh->fgetcsv("\t")) {
    $popNum = $line[14] ?? 0;
    if ($popNum > $target) {
        $city = $line[1]   ?? 'Unknown';
        $data->offsetSet($city, $line[4]. ',' .
            $line[5]);
    }
}
```

3. Finally, we sort by key, rewind to the top, and loop while the iteration still has more values. We use `key()` and `current()` methods to retrieve key/value pairs, as follows:

```
$data->ksort();
$data->rewind();
printf($pattern, 'City', 'Latitude/Longitude');
printf($pattern, '----', '--------------------');
while ($data->valid()) {
    $city = str_pad($data->key(), 30, ' ', STR_PAD_LEFT);
    printf($pattern, $city, $data->current());
    $data->next();
}
```

This code example will actually work in any version of PHP, from PHP 5.1 up to and including PHP 8! The output is exactly as shown in the preceding PHP 7 output and is not duplicated here.

Let's now have a look at `create_function()`.

Working with create_function()

Prior to PHP 5.3, the only way to assign a function to a variable was to use `create_function()`. Starting with PHP 5.3, the preferred approach is to define an anonymous function. Anonymous functions, although technically part of the procedural programming **application programming interface (API)**, are actually instances of the `Closure` class, and thus also belong to the realm of OOP.

> **Tip**
> If the functionality you need can be condensed into a single expression, in PHP 8 you also have the option of using an **arrow function**.

When the function defined by `create_function()` was executed, PHP executed the `eval()` function internally. The result of this architecture, however, is awkward syntax. Anonymous functions are equivalent in performance and more intuitive to use.

The following example demonstrates `create_function()` usage. The objective of this example is to scan a web-server access log and sort the results by **Internet Protocol (IP)** address:

1. We start by recording the start time in microseconds. Later, we use this value to determine performance. Here's the code you'll need:

   ```
   // /repo/ch08/php7_create_function.php
   $start = microtime(TRUE);
   ```

2. Next, use `create_function()` to define a callback that reorganizes the IP address at the start of each line into uniform segments of exactly three digits each. We need to do this in order to perform a proper sort (defined later). The first argument to `create_function()` is a string the represents the parameters. The second argument is the actual code to be executed. The code is illustrated in the following snippet:

   ```
   $normalize = create_function(
       '&$line, $key',
       '$split = strpos($line, " ");'
       . '$ip = trim(substr($line, 0, $split));'
       . '$remainder = substr($line, $split);'
       . '$tmp = explode(".", $ip);'
       . 'if (count($tmp) === 4)'
       . '    $ip = vsprintf("%03d.%03d.%03d.%03d", $tmp);'
       . '$line = $ip . $remainder;'
   );
   ```

   Note the extensive use of strings. This awkward syntax can easily lead to syntax or logic errors, as most code editors make no effort to interpret commands embedded in a string.

3. Next, we define a sorting callback to be used with `usort()`, as follows:

   ```
   $sort_by_ip = create_function(
       '$line1, $line2',
       'return $line1 <=> $line2;' );
   ```

4. We then pull the contents of the access log into an array using the `file()` function. We also move `$sorted` to a file to hold the sorted access log entries. The code is illustrated in the following snippet:

```
$orig    = __DIR__ . '/../sample_data/access.log';
$log     = file($orig);
$sorted  = new SplFileObject(__DIR__
         . '/access_sorted_by_ip.log', 'w');
```

5. We are then able to normalize the IP address using `array_walk()` and perform a sort using `usort()`, as follows:

```
array_walk($log, $normalize);
usort($log, $sort_by_ip);
```

6. Finally, we write the sorted entries to the alternate log file and display the time difference between start and stop, as follows:

```
foreach ($log as $line) $sorted->fwrite($line);
$time = microtime(TRUE) - $start;
echo "Time Diff: $time\n";
```

We are not showing the completed alternate access log as it's far too lengthy to be included in the book. Instead, here are a dozen lines pulled out from the middle of the listing to give you an idea of the output:

```
094.198.051.136 - - [15/Mar/2021:10:05:06 -0400]        "GET /
courses HTTP/1.0" 200 21530
094.229.167.053 - - [21/Mar/2021:23:38:44 -0400]
    "GET /wp-login.php HTTP/1.0" 200 34605
095.052.077.114 - - [10/Mar/2021:22:45:55 -0500]
    "POST /career HTTP/1.0" 200 29002
095.103.103.223 - - [17/Mar/2021:15:48:39 -0400]
    "GET /images/courses/php8_logo.png HTTP/1.0" 200 9280
095.154.221.094 - - [25/Mar/2021:11:43:52 -0400]
    "POST / HTTP/1.0" 200 34546
095.154.221.094 - - [25/Mar/2021:11:43:52 -0400]
    "POST / HTTP/1.0" 200 34691
095.163.152.003 - - [14/Mar/2021:16:09:05 -0400]
    "GET /images/courses/mongodb_logo.png HTTP/1.0" 200 11084
```

```
095.163.255.032 - - [13/Apr/2021:15:09:40 -0400]
    "GET /robots.txt HTTP/1.0" 200 78
095.163.255.036 - - [18/Apr/2021:01:06:33 -0400]
    "GET /robots.txt HTTP/1.0" 200 78
```

In PHP 8, to accomplish the same task, we define anonymous functions instead of using `create_function()`. Here is how the rewritten code example might appear in PHP 8:

1. Again, we start by recording the start time, as with the PHP 7 code example just described. Here's the code you'll need to accomplish this:

    ```
    // /repo/ch08/php8_create_function.php
    $start = microtime(TRUE);
    ```

2. Next, we define a callback that normalizes the IP address into four blocks of three digits each. We use exactly the same logic as in the previous example; however, this time, we define commands in the form of an anonymous function. This takes advantage of code editor helpers, and each line is viewed by the code editor as an actual PHP command. The code is illustrated in the following snippet:

    ```
    $normalize = function (&$line, $key) {
        $split = strpos($line, ' ');
        $ip = trim(substr($line, 0, $split));
        $remainder = substr($line, $split);
        $tmp = explode(".", $ip);
        if (count($tmp) === 4)
            $ip = vsprintf("%03d.%03d.%03d.%03d", $tmp);
        $line = $ip . $remainder;
    };
    ```

    Because each line in the anonymous function is treated exactly as if you were defining a normal PHP function, you are less likely to have typos or syntax errors.

3. In a similar manner, we define the sort callback in the form of an arrow function, as follows:

    ```
    $sort_by_ip = fn ($line1, $line2) => $line1 <=> $line2;
    ```

The remainder of the code example is exactly the same as described earlier and is not shown here. Likewise, the output is exactly the same. The performance time is also approximately the same.

We now turn our attention to money_format().

Working with money_format()

The money_format() function, first introduced in PHP 4.3, is designed to display monetary values using international currencies. If you are maintaining an international PHP-based website that has any financial transactions, you might be affected by this change after a PHP 8 update.

The latter was introduced in PHP 5.3, and should thus not cause your code to break. Let's have a look at a simple example involving money_format() and how it can be rewritten to work in PHP 8, as follows:

1. We first assign an amount to a $amt variable. We then set the monetary locale to en_US (**United States**, or **US**) and echo the value using money_format(). We use the %n format code for national formatting, followed by the %i code for international rendering. In the latter case, the **International Organization for Standardization (ISO)** currency code (**US Dollars**, or **USD**) is displayed. The code is illustrated in the following snippet:

    ```
    // /repo/ch08/php7_money_format.php
    $amt = 1234567.89;
    setlocale(LC_MONETARY, 'en_US');
    echo "Natl: " . money_format('%n', $amt) . "\n";
    echo "Intl: " . money_format('%i', $amt) . "\n";
    ```

2. We then change the monetary locale to de_DE (Germany) and echo the same amount in both national and international formats, as follows:

    ```
    setlocale(LC_MONETARY, 'de_DE');
    echo "Natl: " . money_format('%n', $amt) . "\n";
    echo "Intl: " . money_format('%i', $amt) . "\n";
    ```

Here is the output in PHP 7.1:

```
root@php8_tips_php7 [ /repo/ch08 ]# php php7_money_format.php
Natl: $1,234,567.89
Intl: USD 1,234,567.89
Natl: 1.234.567,89 EUR
Intl: 1.234.567,89 EUR
```

You might note from the output that `money_format()` did not render the Euro symbol, only the ISO code (`EUR`). It did, however, properly format the amounts, using a comma for the thousands separator, a period for the decimal separator for the `en_US` locale, and the reverse for the `de_DE` locale.

A *best practice* is to replace any usage of `money_format()` with `NumberFormatter::formatCurrency()`. Here is the preceding example, rewritten to work in PHP 8. Please note that the same example will also work in any version of PHP from 5.3 onward! We'll proceed as follows:

1. First, we assign the amount to `$amt` and create a `NumberFormatter` instance. In creating this instance, we supply arguments that indicate the locale and type of number—in this case, currency. We then use the `formatCurrency()` method to produce the national representation of this amount, as illustrated in the following code snippet:

```
// /repo/ch08/php8_number_formatter_fmt_curr.php
$amt = 1234567.89;
$fmt = new NumberFormatter('en_US',
    NumberFormatter::CURRENCY );
echo "Natl: " . $fmt->formatCurrency($amt, 'USD') . "\n";
```

2. In order to produce the ISO currency code—in this case, `USD`—we need to use the `setSymbol()` method. Otherwise, the default is to produce the `$` currency symbol instead of the `USD` ISO code. We then use the `format()` method to render the output. Note the trailing space after `USD` in the following code snippet. This is to prevent the ISO code from running into the number when echoed!:

```
$fmt->setSymbol(NumberFormatter::CURRENCY_SYMBOL,'USD ');
echo "Intl: " . $fmt->format($amt) . "\n";
```

3. We then format the same amount using the de_DE locale, as follows:

```
$fmt = new NumberFormatter( 'de_DE',
    NumberFormatter::CURRENCY );
echo "Natl: " . $fmt->formatCurrency($amt, 'EUR') . "\n";
$fmt->setSymbol(NumberFormatter::CURRENCY_SYMBOL, 'EUR');
echo "Intl: " . $fmt->format($amt) . "\n";
```

Here is the output from PHP 8:

```
root@php8_tips_php8 [ /repo/ch08 ]#
php php8_number_formatter_fmt_curr.php
Natl: $1,234,567.89
Intl: USD 1,234,567.89
Natl: 1.234.567,89 €
Intl: 1.234.567,89 EUR
```

As you can see from the output, the comma decimal is reversed between the en_US and de_DE locales, as expected. You also see that both the currency symbols, as well as the ISO currency codes, are correctly rendered.

Now that you have an idea of how to replace `money_format()`, let's have a look at other programming code usage that has been removed in PHP 8.

Discovering other PHP 8 usage changes

There are a number of program code usage changes that you need to be aware of in PHP 8. We'll start with a look at two typecasts that are no longer allowed.

Removed typecasts

Developers often use forced typecasts in order to ensure the data type of a variable is appropriate for a particular usage. As an example, when processing a **HyperText Markup Language** (**HTML**) form submission, for the sake of argument, let's say one of the form elements represents a monetary amount. A quick and easy way to sanitize this data element is to typecast it to a `float` data type, as follows:

`$amount = (float) $_POST['amount'];`

However, rather than typecast to float, some developers prefer to use `real` or `double`. Interestingly, all three produce exactly the same result! In PHP 8, the typecast to `real` has been removed. If your code uses this typecast, a *best practice* is to change it to float.

The `unset` typecast has also been removed. The purpose of this typecast is to unset a variable. In the following code snippet, the value of `$obj` becomes `NULL`:

```
$obj = new ArrayObject();
/* some code (not shown) */
$obj = (unset) $obj;
```

A *best practice* in PHP 8 is to use either of the following:

```
$obj = NULL;
// or this:
unset($obj);
```

Let's now turn our attention to anonymous functions.

Changes in generating anonymous functions from class methods

In PHP 7.1, a new `Closure::fromCallable()` method was added that allows you to return a class method as a `Closure` instance (for example, an anonymous function). `ReflectionMethod::getClosure()` was also introduced and is also able to convert a class method into an anonymous function.

To illustrate this, we define a class that returns `Closure` instances able to perform hashing using different algorithms. We'll proceed as follows:

1. First, we define a class and a public `$class` property, as follows:

    ```
    // /repo/src/Services/HashGen.php
    namespace Services;
    use Closure;
    class HashGen {
        public $class = 'HashGen: ';
    ```

2. We then define a method that produces one of three callbacks, each designed to produce a different type of hash, as follows:

    ```
    public function makeHash(string $type) {
        $method = 'hashTo' . ucfirst($type);
        if (method_exists($this, $method))
            return Closure::fromCallable(
                [$this, $method]);
        else
    ```

```
        return Closure::fromCallable(
            [$this, 'doNothing']);
    }
}
```

3. Next, we define three different methods, each producing a different form of hash (not shown): `hashToMd5()`, `hashToSha256()`, and `doNothing()`.
4. In order to make use of the class, a calling program is devised that first includes the class file and creates an instance, as follows:

```
// /repo/ch08/php7_closure_from_callable.php
require __DIR__ . '/../src/Services/HashGen.php';
use Services\HashGen;
$hashGen = new HashGen();
```

5. The callback is then executed followed by `var_dump()` to view information about the `Closure` instance, as illustrated in the following code snippet:

```
$doMd5 = $hashGen->makeHash('md5');
$text  = 'The quick brown fox jumped over the fence';
echo $doMd5($text) . "\n";
var_dump($doMd5);
```

6. To end this example, we create and bind an anonymous class to the `Closure` instance, as illustrated in the following code snippet. Theoretically, the output display should start with `Anonymous` if the anonymous class were truly bound to `$this`:

```
$temp = new class() { public $class = 'Anonymous: '; };
$doMd5->bindTo($temp);
echo $doMd5($text) . "\n";
var_dump($doMd5);
```

Here is the output of this code example running in PHP 8:

```
root@php8_tips_php8 [ /repo/ch08 ]#
php php7_closure_from_callable.php
HashGen: b335d9cb00b899bc6513ecdbb2187087
object(Closure)#2 (2) {
  ["this"]=> object(Services\HashGen)#1 (1) {
```

```
    ["class"]=>    string(9) "HashGen: "
  }
  ["parameter"]=> array(1) {
    ["$text"]=>    string(10) "<required>"
  }
}
PHP Warning:  Cannot bind method Services\HashGen::hashToMd5()
to object of class class@anonymous in /repo/ch08/php7_closure_
from_callable.php on line 16
HashGen: b335d9cb00b899bc6513ecdbb2187087
object(Closure)#2 (2) {
  ["this"]=> object(Services\HashGen)#1 (1) {
    ["class"]=>    string(9) "HashGen: "
  }
  ["parameter"]=> array(1) {
    ["$text"]=>    string(10) "<required>"
  }
}
```

As you can see from the output, `Closure` simply ignored the attempt to bind another class and produced the expected output. In addition, a `Warning` message was generated, notifying you of the illegal bind attempt.

Let's now have a look at differences in comment handling.

Differences in comment handling

PHP has traditionally supported a number of symbols to denote comments. One such symbol is the hash sign (#). Due to the introduction of a new language construct known as **Attributes**, however, the hash sign immediately followed by an opening square bracket (# [) is no longer allowed to denote a comment. Support for the hash sign not immediately followed by an opening square bracket continues to serve as a comment delimiter.

Here is a brief example that works in PHP 7 and earlier, but not in PHP 8:

```
// /repo/ch08/php7_hash_bracket_comment.php
test = new class() {
    # This works as a comment
    public $works = 'OK';
    #[ This does not work in PHP 8 as a comment]
    public $worksPhp7 = 'OK';
```

```
};
var_dump($test);
```

When we run this example in PHP 7, the output is as expected, as we can see here:

```
root@php8_tips_php7 [ /repo/ch08 ]#
php php7_hash_bracket_comment.php
/repo/ch08/php7_hash_bracket_comment.php:10:
class class@anonymous#1 (2) {
  public $works => string(2) "OK"
  public $worksPhp7 => string(2) "OK"
}
```

The same example in PHP 8, however, throws a fatal `Error` message, as illustrated here:

```
root@php8_tips_php8 [ /repo/ch08 ]#
php php7_hash_bracket_comment.php
PHP Parse error:  syntax error, unexpected identifier "does",
expecting "]" in /repo/ch08/php7_hash_bracket_comment.php on
line 7
```

Note that the example might have accidentally worked in PHP 8 if we had formulated the `Attribute` instance correctly. However, since the syntax used was in line with the syntax for a comment, the code failed.

Now that you have an idea about functions and usage that have been removed from PHP 8, we now examine core deprecations.

Examining core deprecations

In this section, we examine functions and usage that are deprecated in PHP 8. As the PHP language continues to mature, the PHP community is able to suggest to the PHP core development team that certain functions, classes, or even language usage should be removed. If two-thirds of the PHP development team vote in favor of a proposal, it's adopted for inclusion in a future release of the language.

In the case of functionality to be removed, it is not immediately taken out of the language. Instead, the function, class, method, or usage generates a `Deprecation` notice. This notice serves as a means to notify developers that this function, class, method, or usage will be disallowed in an as-yet-unspecified release of PHP. Accordingly, you must pay close attention to `Deprecation` notices. Failure to do so inevitably causes a code break in the future.

> **Tip**
> Starting with PHP 5.3, an official **Request for Comments (RFC)** process was initiated. The status of any proposal can be viewed at `https://wiki.php.net/rfc`.

Let's start by examining deprecated usage in parameter order.

Deprecated usage in parameter order

The term *usage* refers to how you call functions and class methods in your application code. You will discover that in PHP 8, older usages were allowed that are now considered bad practices. Understanding how PHP 8 enforces best practices in code usage helps you to write better code.

If you define a function or method with a mixture of mandatory and optional parameters, most PHP developers agree that the optional parameters should follow the mandatory parameters. In PHP 8, this usage best practice, if not followed, will result in a `Deprecation` notice. The rationale behind the decision to deprecate this usage is to avoid potential logic errors.

This simple example demonstrates this usage difference. In the following example, we define a simple function that accepts three arguments. Note that the `$op` optional parameter is sandwiched between two mandatory parameters, `$a` and `$b`:

```
// /repo/ch08/php7_usage_param_order.php
function math(float $a, string $op = '+', float $b) {
    switch ($op) {
        // not all cases are shown
        case '+' :
        default :
            $out = "$a + $b = " . ($a + $b);
    }
    return $out . "\n";
}
```

If we echo the results of the add operation in PHP 7, there is no problem, as we can see here:

```
root@php8_tips_php7 [ /repo/ch08 ]#
php php7_usage_param_order.php
22 + 7 = 29
```

In PHP 8, however, there is a `Deprecation` notice, after which the operation is allowed to continue. Here is the output running in PHP 8:

```
root@php8_tips_php8 [ /repo/ch08 ]#
php php7_usage_param_order.php
PHP Deprecated:  Required parameter $b follows optional
parameter $op in /repo/ch08/php7_usage_param_order.php on line
4
22 + 7 = 29
```

A `Deprecation` notice is a signal to the developer that this usage is considered a bad practice. In this case, a best practice would be to modify the function signature and list all mandatory parameters first.

Here is the rewritten example, acceptable to all versions of PHP:

```
// /repo/ch08/php8_usage_param_order.php
function math(float $a, float $b, string $op = '+') {
    // remaining code is the same
}
```

It's important to note that the following usage is still allowed in PHP 8:

`function test(object $a = null, $b) {}`

However, a better way to write the same function signature and still stay within the best practice of listing mandatory parameters first would be to rewrite this signature, as follows:

`function test(?object $a, $b) {}`

You now know about features removed from the PHP 8 core. Let's now have a look at removed functionality in PHP 8 extensions.

Working with removed functionality in PHP 8 extensions

In this section, we will have a look at removed functionality in PHP 8 extensions. This information is extremely important in order to avoid writing code that does not work in PHP 8. Further, an awareness of removed functionality helps you prepare existing code for a PHP 8 migration.

The following table summarizes removed functionality in extensions:

Extension	Removed Function	Suggested Replacement
Exif	`read_exif_data()`	`exif_read_data()`
GD	`image2wbmp()` `png2wbmp()` `jpeg2wbmp()`	create the image as normal, then use `imagewbmp()`
GMP	`gmp_random()`	`gmp_random_range()` or `gmp_random_bits()`
Imap	`imap_header()`	`imap_headerinfo()`
LDAP	`ldap_sort()`	`$res = ldap_search();` and then: `usort($res);`
	`ldap_control_paged_result()` `ldap_control_paged_result_response()`	`$res = ldap_search();` and then implement pagination using `FilterIterator`
OCI8	`oci_internal_debug()` `ociinternaldebug()`	None
Zlib	`gzgetss()`	`strip_tags(gzgets())`

Table 8.2 – Functions removed from PHP 8 extensions

The preceding table provides a useful list of removed functions. Use this list to check against your existing code prior to a PHP 8 migration.

Let's now have a look at a potentially serious change to the mbstring extension.

Discovering mbstring extension changes

The `mbstring` extension has had two major changes that have massive potential for a backward-compatible code break. The first change is that a significant number of convenience aliases have been removed. The second major change is that support for the mbstring PHP function overloading capability has been removed. Let's first have a look at removed aliases.

Handling mbstring extension removed aliases

At the request of a number of developers, the PHP development team responsible for this extension graciously created a series of aliases, replacing `mb_*()` with `mb*()`. The exact rationale for granting this request has been lost in time. The burden of supporting such a massive number of aliases, however, wastes a tremendous amount of time every time the extension needs to be updated. Accordingly, the PHP development team voted to remove these aliases from the mbstring extension in PHP 8.

The following table provides a list of the aliases removed, as well as which function to use in their place:

Alias	Use Instead
mbereg	mb_ereg()
mbereg_match	mb_ereg_match()
mbereg_replace	mb_ereg_replace()
mbereg_search	mb_ereg_search()
mbereg_search_getpos	mb_ereg_search_getpos()
mbereg_search_getregs	mb_ereg_search_getregs()
mbereg_search_init	mb_ereg_search_init()
mbereg_search_pos	mb_ereg_search_pos()
mbereg_search_regs	mb_ereg_search_regs()
mbereg_search_setpos	mb_ereg_search_setpos()
mberegi	mb_eregi()
mberegi_replace	mb_eregi_replace()
mbregex_encoding	mb_regex_encoding()
mbsplit	mb_split()

Table 8.3 – Removed mbstring aliases

Let's now have a look at another major change in string handling, pertaining to function overloading.

Working with mbstring extension function overloading

The function overloading feature allows standard PHP string functions (for example, substr()) to be silently replaced with their mbstring extension equivalences (for example, mb_substr()) if the php.ini directive mbstring.func_overload is assigned a value. The value assigned to this directive takes the form of a bitwise flag. Depending on the setting of this flag, the mail(), str*(), substr(), and split() functions could be subject to overloading. This feature was deprecated in PHP 7.2 and has been removed in PHP 8.

In addition, three mbstring extension constants related to this feature have also been removed. The three constants are MB_OVERLOAD_MAIL, MB_OVERLOAD_STRING, and MB_OVERLOAD_REGEX.

> **Tip**
> For more information on this feature, visit the following link:
> https://www.php.net/manual/en/mbstring.overload.php

Any code that relies upon this functionality will break. The only way to avoid serious application failure is to rewrite the affected code and replace the silently substituted PHP core string functions with the intended `mbstring` extension functions.

In the following example, when `mbstring.func_overload` is enabled, PHP 7 reports the same values for both `strlen()` and `mb_strlen()`:

```
// /repo/ch08/php7_mbstring_func_overload.php
$str  = 'วันนี้สบายดีไหม';
$len1 = strlen($str);
$len2 = mb_strlen($str);
echo "Length of '$str' using 'strlen()' is $len1\n";
echo "Length of '$str' using 'mb_strlen()' is $len2\n";
```

Here is the output in PHP 7:

```
root@php8_tips_php7 [ /repo/ch08 ]#
php php7_mbstring_func_overload.php
Length of 'วันนี้สบายดีไหม' using 'strlen()' is 45
Length of 'วันนี้สบายดีไหม' using 'mb_strlen()' is 15

root@php8_tips_php7 [ /repo/ch08 ]#
echo "mbstring.func_overload=7" >> /etc/php.ini

root@php8_tips_php7 [ /repo/ch08 ]#
php php7_mbstring_func_overload.php
Length of 'วันนี้สบายดีไหม' using 'strlen()' is 15
Length of 'วันนี้สบายดีไหม' using 'mb_strlen()' is 15
```

As you can see from the preceding output, once the `mbstring.func_overload` setting is enabled in the `php.ini` file, the results reported by `strlen()` and `mb_strlen()` are identical. This is because calls to `strlen()` are silently diverted to `mb_strlen()` instead. In PHP 8, the output (not shown) shows the results in both cases because the `mbstring.func_overload` setting is ignored. `strlen()` reports a length of 45, and `mb_strlen()` reports a length of 15.

To determine if your code is vulnerable to this backward-compatible break, check your `php.ini` file and see if the `mbstring.func_overload` setting has a value other than zero.

You now have an idea of where to look for potential code breaks pertaining to the `mbstring` extension. At this time, we turn our attention to changes in the Reflection extension.

Reworking code that uses Reflection*::export()

In the Reflection extension, a critical difference between PHP 8 and earlier versions is that all of the `Reflection*::export()` methods have been removed! The primary reason for this change is that simply echoing the Reflection object produces exactly the same results as using `export()`.

If you have any code that currently uses any of the `Reflection*::export()` methods, you need to rewrite the code to use the `__toString()` method instead.

Discovering other deprecated PHP 8 extension functionality

In this section, we review a number of other significant deprecated functionality of note in PHP 8 extensions. First, we look at XML-RPC.

Changes to the XML-RPC extension

In versions of PHP prior to PHP 8, the XML-RPC extension was part of the core and always available. Starting with PHP 8, this extension has quietly been moved to the **PHP Extension Community Library** (**PECL**) (http://pecl.php.net/) and is no longer included in a standard PHP distribution by default. You can still install and use this extension. This change is easily confirmed by scanning the list of extensions in the PHP core here: https://github.com/php/php-src/tree/master/ext.

This will not present a backward-compatible code break. However, if you perform a standard PHP 8 installation and then migrate code that contains references to XML-RPC, your code might generate a fatal `Error` message and display a message that XML-RPC classes and/or functions are not defined. In this situation, simply install the XML-RPC extension using `pecl` or any other method normally used to install non-core extensions.

We now turn our attention to the DOM extension.

Changes made to the DOM extension

Since PHP 5, the **Document Object Model** (**DOM**) extension included a number of classes in its source code repository that were never implemented. In PHP 8, a decision was made to support DOM as a **living standard** (much like with HTML 5). A living standard is one that does not feature a set series of releases, but rather incorporates a continuous set of releases in an effort to keep up with web technology.

> **Tip**
> For more information on the proposed DOM living standard, have a look at this reference: https://dom.spec.whatwg.org/. For a good discussion on moving the PHP DOM extension onto a living standard basis, have a look at the *Working with interfaces and traits* section of *Chapter 9*, *Mastering PHP 8 Best Practices*.

Mainly due to the move toward a living standard, the following unimplemented classes have been removed from the DOM extension as of PHP 8:

- DOMNameList
- DOMImplementationList
- DOMConfiguration
- DOMError
- DOMErrorHandler
- DOMImplementationSource
- DOMLocator
- DOMUserDataHandler
- DOMTypeInfo

These classes were never implemented, which means that your source code will not suffer any backward-compatibility breaks.

Let's now have a look at deprecations in the PHP PostgreSQL extension.

Changes made to the PostgreSQL extension

Aside from the deprecated functionality indicated in *Table 8.5 – Deprecated functionality in PHP 8 extensions* (shown later), you need to be aware that a couple of dozen aliases have been deprecated in the PHP 8 PostgreSQL extension. As with the aliases removed from the `mbstring` extension, the aliases we cover in this section are without underscore characters in the latter part of the alias name.

This table summarizes the aliases removed, and which functions to call in their place:

Alias	Use Instead	Alias	Use Instead
pg_errormessage()	pg_last_error()	pg_getlastoid()	pg_last_oid()
pg_numrows()	pg_num_rows()	pg_locreate()	pg_lo_create()
pg_numfields()	pg_num_fields()	pg_lounlink()	pg_lo_unlink()
pg_cmdtuples()	pg_affected_rows()	pg_loopen()	pg_lo_open()
pg_fieldname()	pg_field_name()	pg_loclose()	pg_lo_close()
pg_fieldsize()	pg_field_size()	pg_loread()	pg_lo_read()
pg_fieldtype()	pg_field_type()	pg_lowrite()	pg_lo_write()
pg_fieldnum()	pg_field_num()	pg_loreadall()	pg_lo_read_all()
pg_result()	pg_fetch_result()	pg_loimport()	pg_lo_import()
pg_fieldprtlen()	pg_field_prtlen()	pg_loexport()	pg_lo_export()
pg_fieldisnull()	pg_field_is_null()	pg_setclientencoding()	pg_set_client_encoding()
pg_freeresult()	pg_free_result()	pg_clientencoding()	pg_client_encoding()

Table 8.4 – Deprecated functionality in PostgreSQL extension

Please note that it's often difficult to find documentation on deprecations. In this case, you can consult the PHP 7.4 to PHP 8 migration guide here: https://www.php.net/manual/en/migration80.deprecated.php#migration80.deprecated.pgsql. Otherwise, you can always look in the C source code docblocks for @deprecation annotations here: https://github.com/php/php-src/blob/master/ext/pgsql/pgsql.stub.php. Here is an example:

```
/**
 * @alias pg_last_error
 * @deprecated
 */
function pg_errormessage(
    ?PgSql\Connection $connection = null): string {}
```

In the last part of this section, we summarize deprecated functionality in PHP 8 extensions.

Deprecated functionality in PHP 8 extensions

Finally, in order to make it easier for you to identify deprecated functionality in PHP 8 extensions, we provide a summary. The following table summarizes functionality deprecated in PHP 8 extensions:

Extension	Deprecated Functionality	Suggested Replacement

Enchant	`enchant_dict_add_to_personal()`
	`enchant_dict_is_in_session()`
	`enchant_broker_free()`
	`enchant_broker_free_dict()`
	`enchant_broker_set_dict_path()`
	`enchant_broker_get_dict_path()`
		`enchant_dict_add()`
		`enchant_dict_is_added()`
		`unset(SenchantObject)`
		(same)
		None: no longer supported
		(same)

OCI8	`OCI-Lob` `OCI-Collection`	`OCILob` `OCICollection`
ODBC	`odbc_connect()` `odbc_exec()`	No longer re-uses connections The `flags` parameter is removed
PostgreSQL	`PGSQL_LIBPQ_VERSION_STR`	`PGSQL_LIBPQ_VERSION`
	`pg_connect()`	Must now use a connection string
	`pg_lo_import()`, `pg_lo_export()`	First argument is now the connection
	`pg_fetch_all()`	Now returns empty array if no results

Reflection	`ReflectionParameter::getClass()`
	`ReflectionParameter::isArray()`
	`ReflectionParameter::isCallable()`
	`ReflectionParameter::isDisabled()`
		`ReflectionParameter::getType()`
		(same)
		(same)
		None

LibXML	`libxml_disable_entity_loader()`	None: no longer needed

Table 8.5 – Deprecated functionality in PHP 8 extensions

We will use the PostgreSQL extension to illustrate deprecated functionality. Before running the code example, you need to perform a small bit of setup inside the PHP 8 Docker container. Proceed as follows:

1. Open a command shell into the PHP 8 Docker container. From the command shell start PostgreSQL running using this command:

   `/etc/init.d/postgresql start`

2. Next, switch to the `su postgres` user.

3. The prompt changes to `bash-4.3$`. From here, type `psql` to enter the PostgreSQL interactive terminal.

4. Next, from the PostgreSQL interactive terminal, issue the following set of commands to create and populate a sample database table:

```
CREATE DATABASE php8_tips;
\c php8_tips;
\i /repo/sample_data/pgsql_users_create.sql
```

5. Here is the entire chain of commands replayed:

```
root@php8_tips_php8 [ /repo/ch08 ]# su postgres
bash-4.3$ psql
psql (10.2)
Type "help" for help.
postgres=# CREATE DATABASE php8_tips;
CREATE DATABASE
postgres=# \c php8_tips;
You are now connected to database "php8_tips"
    as user "postgres".
php8_tips=# \i /repo/sample_data/pgsql_users_create.sql
CREATE TABLE
INSERT 0 4
CREATE ROLE
GRANT
php8_tips=# \q
bash-4.3$ exit
exit
root@php8_tips_php8 [ /repo/ch08 ]#
```

6. We now define a short code example to illustrate the deprecation concepts just discussed. Notice in the following code example that we create a **Structured Query Language (SQL)** statement for a non-existent user:

```
// /repo/ch08/php8_pgsql_changes.php
$usr = 'php8';
$pwd = 'password';
$dsn = 'host=localhost port=5432 dbname=php8_tips '
     . ' user=php8 password=password';
$db  = pg_connect($dsn);
$sql = "SELECT * FROM users WHERE user_name='joe'";
$stmt = pg_query($db, $sql);
echo pg_errormessage();
$result = pg_fetch_all($stmt);
var_dump($result);
```

7. Here is the output from the preceding code example:

```
root@php8_tips_php8 [ /repo/ch08 ]#
php php8_pgsql_changes.php
Deprecated: Function pg_errormessage() is
deprecated in /repo/ch08/php8_pgsql_changes.php on
line 22
array(0) {}
```

The two main things to notice from the output are the fact that `pg_errormessage()` is deprecated and that when no results are returned from a query, instead of a `FALSE` Boolean, an empty array is returned instead. Don't forget to stop the PostgreSQL database using this command:

`/etc/init.d/postgresql stop`

Now that you have an idea about deprecated functionality in the various PHP 8 extensions, we turn our attention to security-related deprecations.

Dealing with deprecated or removed security-related functionality

Any changes to functionality that affect security are extremely important to note. Ignoring these changes can very easily lead not only to breaks in your code but can also open your websites to potential attackers. In this section, we cover a variety of security-related changes in functionality present in PHP 8. Let's start the discussion by examining filters.

Examining PHP 8 stream-filter changes

PHP `input/output` (**I/O**) operations depend upon a subsystem known as **streams**. One of the interesting aspects of this architecture is the ability to append a stream filter to any given stream. The filters you can append can be either custom-defined stream filters, registered using `stream_filter_register()`, or predefined filters included with your PHP installation.

An important change of which you need to be aware is that in PHP 8, all `mcrypt.*` and `mdecrypt.*` filters have been removed, as well as the `string.strip_tags` filter. If you're not sure which filters are included in your PHP installation, you can either run `phpinfo()` or, better yet, `stream_get_filters()`.

Here's the `stream_get_filters()` output running in the PHP 7 Docker container used with this book:

```
root@php8_tips_php7 [ /repo/ch08 ]#
php -r "print_r(stream_get_filters());"
Array (
    [0] => zlib.*
    [1] => bzip2.*
    [2] => convert.iconv.*
    [3] => mcrypt.*
    [4] => mdecrypt.*
    [5] => string.rot13
    [6] => string.toupper
    [7] => string.tolower
    [8] => string.strip_tags
    [9] => convert.*
    [10] => consumed
    [11] => dechunk
)
```

Here's the same command running in the PHP 8 Docker container:

```
root@php8_tips_php8 [ /repo/ch08 ]#
php -r "print_r(stream_get_filters());"
Array (
    [0] => zlib.*
    [1] => bzip2.*
    [2] => convert.iconv.*
    [3] => string.rot13
    [4] => string.toupper
    [5] => string.tolower
    [6] => convert.*
    [7] => consumed
    [8] => dechunk
)
```

You'll notice from the PHP 8 output that the filters mentioned earlier have all been removed. Any code that uses any of the three filters listed will break after a PHP 8 migration. We now look at changes made to custom error handling.

Dealing with custom error-handling changes

Starting with PHP 7.0, most errors are now **thrown**. The exception to this are situations where the PHP engine is unaware that there is an error condition, such as running out of memory, exceeding the time limit, or if a segmentation fault occurs. Another exception is when the program deliberately triggers an error using the `trigger_error()` function.

Using the `trigger_error()` function to trap errors is not a best practice. A *best practice* would be to develop object-oriented code and place it inside a `try/catch` construct. However, if you are assigned to manage an application that does make use of this practice, there is a change in what gets passed to the custom error handler.

In versions prior to PHP 8, the data passed to the custom error handler's fifth argument, `$errorcontext`, was information about arguments passed to the function. In PHP 8, this argument is ignored. To illustrate the difference, have a look at the simple code example shown next. Here are the steps leading to this:

1. First, we define a custom error handler, as follows:

    ```php
    // /repo/ch08/php7_error_handler.php
    function handler($errno, $errstr, $errfile,
        $errline, $errcontext = NULL) {
        echo "Number : $errno\n";
        echo "String : $errstr\n";
        echo "File   : $errfile\n";
        echo "Line   : $errline\n";
        if (!empty($errcontext))
            echo "Context: \n"
                . var_export($errcontext, TRUE);
        exit;
    }
    ```

2. We then define a function that triggers an error, sets the error handler, and invokes the function, as follows:

```
function level1($a, $b, $c) {
    trigger_error("This is an error", E_USER_ERROR);
}
set_error_handler('handler');
echo level1(TRUE, 222, 'C');
```

Here's the output running in PHP 7:

```
root@php8_tips_php7 [ /repo/ch08 ]#
php php7_error_handler.php
Number  : 256
String  : This is an error
File    : /repo/ch08/php7_error_handler.php
Line    : 17
Context:
array (
  'a' => true,
  'b' => 222,
  'c' => 'C',
)
```

As you can see from the preceding output, $errorcontext provides information about the arguments received by the function. In contrast, have a look at the output produced by PHP 8, shown here:

```
root@php8_tips_php8 [ /repo/ch08 ]#
php php7_error_handler.php
Number  : 256
String  : This is an error
File    : /repo/ch08/php7_error_handler.php
Line    : 17
```

As you can see, the output is identical except for a lack of information coming into $errorcontext. Let's now have a look at generating backtraces.

Dealing with changes to backtraces

Amazingly, before PHP 8, it was possible to change function arguments through a backtrace. This was possible because traces produced by either `debug_backtrace()` or `Exception::getTrace()` provided access to function arguments by reference.

This is an extremely bad practice because it allows your program to continue to operate despite potentially being in an error state. Further, when reviewing such code, it's not clear how the argument data is being provided. Accordingly, in PHP 8, this practice is no longer allowed. Both `debug_backtrace()` or `Exception::getTrace()` still operate as before. The only difference is that they no longer pass argument variables by reference.

Let's now have a look at changes to `PDO` error handling.

PDO error-handling mode default changed

For many years, novice PHP developers were mystified when their database applications using the `PDO` extension failed to produce results. The reason for this problem, in many cases, was a simple SQL syntax error that was not reported. This was due to the fact that in PHP versions prior to PHP 8, the default `PDO` error mode was `PDO::ERRMODE_SILENT`.

SQL errors are not PHP errors. Accordingly, such errors are not captured by normal PHP error handling. Instead, PHP developers had to specifically set the `PDO` error mode to either `PDO::ERRMODE_WARNING` or `PDO::ERRMODE_EXCEPTION`. PHP developers can now breathe a sigh of relief because, as of PHP 8, the PDO default error-handling mode is now `PDO::ERRMODE_EXCEPTION`.

In the following example, PHP 7 allows the incorrect SQL statement to silently fail:

```php
// /repo/ch08/php7_pdo_err_mode.php
$dsn = 'mysql:host=localhost;dbname=php8_tips';
$pdo = new PDO($dsn, 'php8', 'password');
$sql = 'SELEK propertyKey, hotelName FUM hotels '
     . "WARE country = 'CA'";
$stm = $pdo->query($sql);
if ($stm)
    while($hotel = $stm->fetch(PDO::FETCH_OBJ))
        echo $hotel->name . ' ' . $hotel->key . "\n";
else
    echo "No Results\n";
```

In PHP 7, the only output is `No Results`, which is both deceptive and unhelpful. It might lead the developer to believe there were no results when in fact, the problem is a SQL syntax error.

The output running in PHP 8, shown here, is much more helpful:

```
root@php8_tips_php8 [ /repo/ch08 ]# php php7_pdo_err_mode.php
PHP Fatal error:  Uncaught PDOException: SQLSTATE[42000]:
Syntax error or access violation: 1064 You have an error in
your SQL syntax; check the manual that corresponds to your
MariaDB server version for the right syntax to use near 'SELEK
propertyKey, hotelName FUM hotels WARE country = 'CA'' at line
1 in /repo/ch08/php7_pdo_err_mode.php:10
```

As you can see from the preceding PHP 8 output, the actual problem is clearly identified.

> **TIP**
> For more information about this change, see this RFC:
> https://wiki.php.net/rfc/pdo_default_errmode

We next examine the `track_errors` php.ini directive.

Examining the track_errors php.ini setting

As of PHP 8, the `track_errors` php.ini directive has been removed. This means that the `$php_errormsg` automatically created variable is no longer available. For the most part, anything that caused an error prior to PHP 8 has now been converted to throw an `Error` message instead. However, for versions of PHP prior to PHP 8, you can still use the `error_get_last()` function instead.

In the following simple code example, we first set the `track_errors` directive on. We then call `strpos()` without any arguments, deliberately causing an error. We then rely on `$php_errormsg` to reveal the true error:

```
// /repo/ch08/php7_track_errors.php
ini_set('track_errors', 1);
@strpos();
echo $php_errormsg . "\n";
echo "OK\n";
```

Here is the output in PHP 7:

```
root@php8_tips_php7 [ /repo/ch08 ]# php php7_track_errors.php
strpos() expects at least 2 parameters, 0 given
OK
```

As you can see from the preceding output, `$php_errormsg` reveals the error, and the code block is allowed to continue. In PHP 8, of course, we are not allowed to call `strpos()` without any arguments. Here is the output:

```
root@php8_tips_php8 [ /repo/ch08 ]# php php7_track_errors.php
PHP Fatal error:  Uncaught ArgumentCountError: strpos() expects at least 2 arguments, 0 given in /repo/ch08/php7_track_errors.php:5
```

As you can see, PHP 8 throws an `Error` message. A best practice is to use a `try/catch` block and trap any `Error` messages that might be thrown. You can also use the `error_get_last()` function. Here is a rewritten example that works in both PHP 7 and PHP 8 (output not shown):

```php
// /repo/ch08/php8_track_errors.php
try {
    strpos();
    echo error_get_last()['message'];
    echo "\nOK\n";
} catch (Error $e) {
    echo $e->getMessage() . "\n";
}
```

You now have an idea about PHP functionality that has been deprecated or removed in PHP 8. That concludes this chapter.

Summary

In this chapter, you learned about deprecated and removed PHP functionality. The first section in this chapter dealt with core functionality that has been removed. The rationale for the change was explained, and you learned that the main reason for removing the functionality described in this chapter is not only to move you toward code that follows best practices but to have you use PHP 8 functionality that is faster and more efficient.

Summary

In the next section, you learned about deprecated functionality. The key theme in this section was to highlight how the deprecated functions, classes, and methods lead to bad practices and bug-ridden code. You also were given guidance on functionality that has been either removed or deprecated in a number of key PHP 8 extensions.

You learned how to locate and rewrite code that has been deprecated, and how to develop workarounds for functionality that has been removed. Another skill you learned in this chapter included how to refactor code using removed functionality involving extensions, and last, but not least, you learned how to improve application security by rewriting code depending on removed functions.

In the next chapter, you will learn how to gain greater efficiency and performance in your PHP 8 code by mastering best practices.

Section 3: PHP 8 Best Practices

In this section, you are introduced to PHP 8 best practices. You will learn how PHP 8 has introduced a number of additional controls that enforce certain best practices. In addition, the best ways to write code in PHP 8 are covered.

In this section, the following chapters are included:

- *Chapter 9, Mastering PHP 8 Best Practices*
- *Chapter 10, Improving Performance*
- *Chapter 11, Migrating Existing PHP Apps to PHP 8*
- *Chapter 12, Creating PHP 8 Applications Using Asynchronous Programming*

9
Mastering PHP 8 Best Practices

In this chapter, you will be introduced to the best practices that are currently enforced in PHP 8. We will cover several significant method signature changes and how their new usage continues the general PHP trend of helping you produce better code. We will also have a look at how private methods, interfaces, traits, and anonymous class usage has changed. Finally, we will discuss important changes in how namespaces are parsed.

Mastering the best practices that will be covered in this chapter will not only move you toward writing better code, but how to avoid the potential code breaks that might arise if you fail to grasp these new practices. In addition, the techniques discussed in this chapter will help you write code that's more efficient than was possible in the past.

In this chapter, we will cover the following topics:

- Discovering method signature changes
- Dealing with private methods
- Working with interfaces and traits
- Controlling anonymous class usage
- Understanding changes in namespaces

Technical requirements

To examine and run the code examples provided in this chapter, the minimum recommended hardware is as follows:

- X86_64-based desktop PC or laptop
- 1 GB free disk space
- 4 GB of RAM
- 500 Kbps or faster internet connection

In addition, you will need to install the following software:

- Docker
- Docker Compose

Please refer to the *Technical requirements* section of *Chapter 1, Introducing New PHP 8 OOP Features,* for more information on how to install Docker and Docker Compose, as well as how to build the Docker container used to demonstrate the code in this book. In this book, we will refer to the directory that you restored the sample code in as `/repo`.

The source code for this chapter is located here: `https://github.com/PacktPublishing/PHP-8-Programming-Tips-Tricks-and-Best-Practices`. We will start by examining significant method signature changes.

Discovering method signature changes

Several **method signature changes** have been introduced in PHP 8. Understanding these signature changes is important if your code extends any of the classes or implements any of the methods described in this section. As long as you are aware of these changes, your code will function correctly, resulting in fewer bugs.

The signature changes that were introduced in PHP 8 reflect the updated *best practices*. Accordingly, if you write code that uses the correct method signatures, you are following these best practices. We will begin our discussion by reviewing PHP 8 changes to magic method signatures.

Managing magic method signatures

In PHP 8, the definition and use of **magic methods** has taken a significant step toward standardization. This was accomplished by introducing precise magic method signatures in the form of strict argument and return data types. As with most of the improvements seen in PHP 8, this update was included to prevent the misuse of magic methods. The overall result is better code with fewer bugs.

The downside of this enhancement is that if you have code that provides an incorrect argument or return value type, an `Error` is thrown. On the other hand, if your code does provide the correct argument data type and return value type, or if your code does not use argument or return value data types at all, this enhancement will have no adverse effects.

The following code block summarizes the new argument and return value data types for magic methods in PHP 8 and above:

```
__call(string $name, array $arguments) : mixed;
__callStatic(string $name, array $arguments) : mixed;
__clone() : void;
__debugInfo() : ?array;
__get(string $name) : mixed;
__invoke(mixed $arguments) : mixed;
__isset(string $name) : bool;
__serialize() : array;
__set(string $name, mixed $value) : void;
__set_state(array $properties) : object;
__sleep() : array;
__unserialize(array $data) : void;
__unset(string $name) : void;
__wakeup() : void;
```

Now, let's have a look at three simple examples that illustrate the impact of the magic method signature changes:

1. The first example involves the `NoTypes` class, which defines `__call()` but does not define any data types:

   ```
   // /repo/ch09/php8_bc_break_magic.php
   class NoTypes {
       public function __call($name, $args) {
           return "Attempt made to call '$name' "
               . "with these arguments: '"
               . implode(',', $args) . "'\n";
       }
   }
   $no = new NoTypes();
   echo $no->doesNotExist('A','B','C');
   ```

2. The following example (in the same file as the preceding example) is of the `MixedTypes` class, which defines `__invoke()` but uses an `array` data type rather than a `mixed` one:

```
class MixedTypes {
    public function __invoke(array $args) : string {
        return "Arguments: '"
            . implode(',', $args) . "'\n";
    }
}
$mixed= new MixedTypes();
echo $mixed(['A','B','C']);
```

Here is the PHP 7 output for the code sample shown in the preceding steps:

```
root@php8_tips_php7 [ /repo/ch09 ]#
php php8_bc_break_magic.php
Attempt made to call 'doesNotExist' with these arguments: 'A,B,C'
Arguments: 'A,B,C'
```

And here is the same code sample but running under PHP 8:

```
root@php8_tips_php8 [ /repo/ch09 ]#
php php8_bc_break_magic.php
Attempt made to call 'doesNotExist' with these arguments: 'A,B,C'
Arguments: 'A,B,C'
```

As you can see, the two sets of output are identical. The first class shown, `NoTypes`, works because no data type hints were defined. Interestingly, the `MixedTypes` class works in both PHP 8 and below since the new `mixed` data type is actually a union of all types. Accordingly, you are safe to use any specific data type in place of `mixed`.

3. In our final example, we will define the `WrongType` class. In this class, we will define a magic method called `__isset()` using a return data type that doesn't match the PHP 8 requirement. Here, we are using `string`, whereas in PHP 8, its return type needs to be `bool`:

```php
// /repo/ch09/php8_bc_break_magic_wrong.php
class WrongType {
    public function __isset($var) : string {
        return (isset($this->$var)) ? 'Y' : '';
    }
}
$wrong = new WrongType();
echo (isset($wrong->nothing)) ? 'Set' : 'Not Set';
```

This example works in PHP 7 because it relies on the fact that the empty string is returned in this example if the variable is not set, and is then interpolated as a `FALSE` Boolean. Here is the PHP 7 output:

```
root@php8_tips_php7 [ /repo/ch09 ]#
php php8_bc_break_magic_wrong.php
Not Set
```

In PHP 8, however, because magic method signatures are now standardized, the example fails, as shown here:

```
root@php8_tips_php8 [ /repo/ch09 ]#
php php8_bc_break_magic_wrong.php
PHP Fatal error:  WrongTypes::__isset(): Return type must be bool when declared in /repo/ch09/php8_bc_break_magic_wrong.php on line 6
```

As you can see, PHP 8 strictly enforces its magic method signatures.

> **Tip**
>
> *Best Practice*: Revise any code that uses magic methods to follow the new strict method signatures. For more information on strict magic method signatures, go to https://wiki.php.net/rfc/magic-methods-signature.

You now have an idea of what to look for and how to correct potential code breaks involving magic methods. Now, let's have a look at Reflection extension method signature changes.

Examining Reflection method signature changes

Backward compatible code breaks may occur if your application is using either the `invoke()` or `newInstance()` Reflection extension method. In PHP 7 and below, all three methods listed next accepted an unlimited number of arguments. However, in the method signature, only one argument was listed, as follows:

- `ReflectionClass::newInstance($args)`
- `ReflectionFunction::invoke($args)`
- `ReflectionMethod::invoke($args)`

In PHP 8, the method signatures accurately reflect reality in that `$args` is preceded by the `variadics` operator. Here are the new method signatures:

- `ReflectionClass::newInstance(...$args)`
- `ReflectionFunction::invoke(...$args)`
- `ReflectionMethod::invoke($object, ...$args)`

This change will only break your code if you have a custom class that extends any of these three classes, and where your custom class also overrides any of the three methods listed in the previous bulleted list.

Finally, the `isBuiltin()` method has been moved from `ReflectionType` to `ReflectionNamedType`. This presents a potential code break if you are using `ReflectionType::isBuiltIn()`.

Now, let's have a look at method signature changes in the PDO extension.

Dealing with PDO extension signature changes

The PDO extension has two method signature changes that are of importance. These changes are needed to address inconsistencies in method calls when different **fetch modes** are applied. Here is the new method signature for `PDO::query()`:

```
PDO::query(string $query,
    ?int $fetchMode = null, mixed ...$fetchModeArgs)
```

This is the new signature for `PDOStatement::setFetchMode()`:

```
PDOStatement::setFetchMode(int $mode, mixed ...$args)
```

> **Tip**
> The `PDO::query()` method signature changes are referenced in the PHP 7.4 to PHP 8 migration guide, here: https://www.php.net/manual/en/migration80.incompatible.php#migration80.incompatible.pdo.

The two new method signatures are much more uniform than the old signatures, and they completely cover syntactical differences when you're using different fetch modes. A simple code example that performs `PDO::query()` using two different fetch modes illustrates why the method signature needed to be normalized:

1. Let's start by including a configuration file that contains database connection parameters. From this, we will create a PDO instance:

```
// /repo/ch09/php8_pdo_signature_change.php
$config  = include __DIR__ . '/../src/config/config.php';
$db_cfg  = $config['db-config'];
$pdo     = new PDO($db_cfg['dsn'],
    $db_cfg['usr'], $db_cfg['pwd']);
```

2. Now, let's define a SQL statement and send it so that it can be prepared:

```
$sql   = 'SELECT hotelName, city, locality, '
       . 'country, postalCode FROM hotels '
       . 'WHERE country = ? AND city = ?';
$stmt  = $pdo->prepare($sql);
```

3. Next, we will execute the prepared statement and set the fetch mode to `PDO::FETCH_ASSOC`. Notice that when we use this fetch mode, only one argument is provided to the `setFetchMode()` method:

```
$stmt->execute(['IN', 'Budhera']);
$stmt->setFetchMode(PDO::FETCH_ASSOC);
while ($row = $stmt->fetch()) var_dump($row);
```

4. Finally, we will execute the same prepared statement for a second time. This time, we will set the fetch mode to `PDO::FETCH_CLASS`. Notice that when we use this fetch mode, two arguments are provided to the `setFetchMode()` method:

```
$stmt->execute(['IN', 'Budhera']);
$stmt->setFetchMode(
    PDO::FETCH_CLASS, ArrayObject::class);
while ($row = $stmt->fetch()) var_dump($row);
```

The output in the first query is an associative array. The second query produces an `ArrayObject` instance. Here is the output:

```
root@php8_tips_php8 [ /repo/ch09 ]#
php php8_pdo_signature_change.php
array(5) {
  ["hotelName"]=> string(10) "Rose Lodge"
  ["city"]=> string(7) "Budhera"
  ["locality"]=> string(7) "Gurgaon"
  ["country"]=> string(2) "IN"
  ["postalCode"]=> string(6) "122505"
}
object(ArrayObject)#3 (6) {
  ["hotelName"]=> string(10) "Rose Lodge"
  ["city"]=> string(7) "Budhera"
  ["locality"]=> string(7) "Gurgaon"
  ["country"]=> string(2) "IN"
  ["postalCode"]=> string(6) "122505"
  ["storage":"ArrayObject":private]=> array(0) { }
}
```

It's important to observe that even though the method signatures have changed, you can keep your existing code as-is: this *does not* present a backward compatible code break!

Now, let's have a look at methods that are declared as `static`.

Dealing with newly defined static methods

Another potentially significant change seen in PHP 8 is that several methods are now declared `static`. If you are already using the classes and methods described here as direct object instances, then you do not have a problem.

The following methods are now declared as static:

- `tidy::repairString()`
- `tidy::repairFile()`
- `XMLReader::open()`
- `XMLReader::xml()`

The potential for a code break my occur if you override one of the classes mentioned previously. In this case, you *must* declare the overridden method as `static`. Here is a simple example that illustrates the potential problem:

1. First, let's define a string that has mismatched `<div>` tags:

```php
// /repo/ch08/php7_tidy_repair_str_static.php
$str = <<<EOT
<DIV>
    <Div>Some Content</div>
    <Div>Some Other Content
</div>
EOT;
```

2. Then, define an anonymous class that extends `tidy`, fixes the string, and returns the string with all HTML tags in lowercase:

```php
$class = new class() extends tidy {
    public function repairString($str) {
        $fixed = parent::repairString($str);
        return preg_replace_callback(
            '/<+?>/',
            function ($item) {
                return strtolower($item); },
            $fixed);
    }
};
```

3. Finally, echo the repaired string:

```
echo $class->repairString($str);
```

If we run this code example in PHP 7, the output will be as follows:

```
root@php8_tips_php7 [ /repo/ch09 ]#
php php7_tidy_repair_str_static.php
<!DOCTYPE html>
<html>
<head>
<title></title>
</head>
<body>
<div>
<div>Some Content</div>
<div>Some Other Content</div>
</div>
</body>
</html>
```

As you can see, the mismatched `<div>` tag has been repaired, and a properly formatted HTML document has been produced. You'll also note that all the tags are in lowercase.

In PHP 8, however, a method signature issue arises, as you can see here:

```
root@php8_tips_php8 [ /repo/ch09 ]#
php php7_tidy_repair_str_static.php
PHP Fatal error:  Cannot make static method tidy::repairString() non static in class tidy@anonymous in /repo/ch09/php7_tidy_repair_str_static.php on line 11
```

As you can see, in PHP 8, the `repairString()` method is now declared as `static`. The method signature for `repairString()` in the anonymous class we defined earlier needs to be rewritten, as follows:

```
public static function repairString(
    string $str,
    array|string|null $config = null,
    ?string $encoding = null) { // etc.
```

The output (not shown), once rewritten, is the same as the PHP 7 output shown earlier. Also, note that the last line can now also be written as follows:

```
echo $class::repairString($str);
```

Now that you know about the methods that are newly defined as static, let's look at a related topic; that is, the static return type.

Working with the static return type

The **static** keyword is used in several contexts in PHP. Its basic uses are beyond the scope of this discussion. In this section, we will focus on a new usage for `static` as a return data type.

Since `static` is considered a subtype of `self`, it can be used to widen the narrower return type of `self`. The `static` keyword cannot be used as a type hint, however, as it would violate the *Liskov Substitution Principle*. It would also confuse developers as `static` is already used in too many other contexts.

> **Tip**
>
> The following article describes the background discussion that preceded the introduction of the static return type: `https://wiki.php.net/rfc/static_return_type`. The following documentation references late static binding: `https://www.php.net/manual/en/language.oop5.late-static-bindings.php`. The *Liskov Substitution Principle* was discussed in *Chapter 5, Discovering Potential OOP Backward-Compatibility Breaks*, in the *Understanding expanded PHP 8 variance support* section.

The most common use for this new return data type would be in classes that use the **fluent interface**. The latter is a technique whereby an object method returns an instance of the current object state, thus allowing a chain of method calls to be used in a *fluent* (readable) manner. In the following example, note how the object builds a SQL SELECT statement:

1. First, we must define a `Where` class that accepts an unlimited number of arguments to form a SQL WHERE clause. Note the return data type of `static`:

```
// /src/Php8/Sql/Where.php
namespace Php8\Sql;
class Where {
    public $where = [];
    public function where(...$args) : static {
```

```
        $this->where = array_merge($this->where, $args);
        return $this;
    }
    // not all code is shown
}
```

2. Now, let's define the main class, `Select`, which provides methods for building parts of a SQL SELECT statement. Again, notice that the methods shown all return the current class instance and have a return data type of `static`:

```
// /src/Php8/Sql/Select.php
namespace Php8\Sql;
class Select extends Where {
    public $from   = '';
    public $limit  = 0;
    public $offset = 0;
    public function from(string $table) : static {
        $this->from = $table;
        return $this;
    }
    public function order(string $order) : static {
        $this->order = $order;
        return $this;
    }
    public function limit(int $num) : static {
        $this->limit = $num;
        return $this;
    }
    // not all methods and properties are shown
}
```

3. Finally, we must define a calling program that provides the values needed to build the SQL statement. Note that the `echo` statement uses the fluent interface to make programmatically creating the SQL statement much easier to follow:

```
// /repo/ch09/php8_static_return_type.php
require_once __DIR__
    . '/../src/Server/Autoload/Loader.php';
```

```
$loader = new \Server\Autoload\Loader();
use Php8\Sql\Select;
$start = "'2021-06-01'";
$end   = "'2021-12-31'";
$select = new Select();
echo $select->from('events')
        ->cols(['id', 'event_name', 'event_date'])
        ->limit(10)
        ->where('event_date', '>=', $start)
        ->where('AND', 'event_date', '<=', $end)
        ->render();
```

Here is the output of the code example running in PHP 8:

```
root@php8_tips_php8 [ /repo/ch09 ]#
php php8_static_return_type.php
SELECT id,event_name,event_date FROM events WHERE event_date >=
'2021-06-01' AND event_date <= '2021-12-31' LIMIT 10
```

This example doesn't work in PHP 7, of course, as the `static` keyword is not available as a return data type. Next, let's have a look at the extended use of the special `::class` constant.

Extending the use of the ::class constant

The special `::class` constant is an extremely useful construct in that it can silently expand into a full namespace, plus a classname string. Understanding how it is used, as well as how its use has been extended in PHP 8, can save you lots of time. Its use can also make your code much more readable, especially if you're dealing with lengthy namespaces and class names.

The special `::class` constant is a combination of the **scope resolution operator** (`::`) and the `class` keyword. Unlike `::parent`, `::self`, and `::static`, however, the `::class` construct can be used outside a class definition. In a sense, the `::class` construct is a sort of *magic constant* in that it causes the class it's associated with to magically expand into its full namespace, plus class name.

Before we get into how its use has been expanded in PHP 8, let's have a look at its conventional usage.

Conventional ::class constant usage

The special `::class` constant is frequently used in situations where you have a lengthy namespace and wish to not only save yourself a lot of unneeded typing, but also preserve the readability of your source code.

In this simple example, using the `Php7\Image\Strategy` namespace, we wish to create a list of strategy classes:

1. First, let's identify the namespace and set up the autoloader:

   ```
   // /repo/ch09/php7_class_normal.php
   namespace Php7\Image\Strategy;
   require_once __DIR__
       . '/../src/Server/Autoload/Loader.php';
   $autoload = new \Server\Autoload\Loader();
   ```

2. Before the special `::class` constant was introduced, to produce a list of full namespace class names, you had to write it all out as a string, as shown here:

   ```
   $listOld = [
       'Php7\Image\Strategy\DotFill',
       'Php7\Image\Strategy\LineFill',
       'Php7\Image\Strategy\PlainFill',
       'Php7\Image\Strategy\RotateText',
       'Php7\Image\Strategy\Shadow'
   ];
   print_r($listOld);
   ```

3. Using the special `::class` constant, you can reduce the amount of typing required, and you can also make the code more readable, as shown here:

   ```
   $listNew = [
       DotFill::class,
       LineFill::class,
       PlainFill::class,
       RotateText::class,
       Shadow::class
   ];
   print_r($listNew);
   ```

If we run this code example, we'll see that the two lists are identical in both PHP 7 and PHP 8. Here's the PHP 7 output:

```
root@php8_tips_php7 [ /repo/ch09 ]#
php php7_class_normal.php
Array (
    [0] => Php7\Image\Strategy\DotFill
    [1] => Php7\Image\Strategy\LineFill
    [2] => Php7\Image\Strategy\PlainFill
    [3] => Php7\Image\Strategy\RotateText
    [4] => Php7\Image\Strategy\Shadow
)
Array (
    [0] => Php7\Image\Strategy\DotFill
    [1] => Php7\Image\Strategy\LineFill
    [2] => Php7\Image\Strategy\PlainFill
    [3] => Php7\Image\Strategy\RotateText
    [4] => Php7\Image\Strategy\Shadow
)
```

As you can see, the special ::class constant causes class names to be expanded into their full namespace, plus class name, at compile time, causing both lists to contain identical information.

Now, let's have a look at special ::class constant usage in PHP 8.

Expanded special ::class constant usage

In line with other improvements in syntax uniformity seen in PHP 8, it's now possible to use the special ::class constant on active object instances. Although the effect is the same as using get_class(), it makes sense to use the special ::class constant as part of the general best practice of moving away from procedural and toward OOP.

In this example, the extended `::class` syntax is used to determine the type of error that's thrown:

1. When an `Error` or `Exception` is thrown, it's best practice to make an entry in the error log. In this example, which works in both PHP 7 and PHP 8, the class name of this `Error` or `Exception` is included in the log message:

   ```
   // /repo/ch09/php7_class_and_obj.php
   try {
       $pdo = new PDO();
       echo 'No problem';
   } catch (Throwable $t) {
       $msg = get_class($t) . ':' . $t->getMessage();
       error_log($msg);
   }
   ```

2. In PHP 8, you can achieve the same result by rewriting the example, as follows:

   ```
   // /repo/ch09/php8_class_and_obj.php
   try {
       $pdo = new PDO();
       echo 'No problem';
   } catch (Throwable $t) {
       $msg = $t::class . ':' . $t->getMessage();
       error_log($msg);
   }
   ```

As you can see from the second block of code, the syntax is more concise and avoids the use of a procedural function. We must stress, however, that in this example, there is no performance gain.

Now that you are aware of changes in special `::class` constant usage, let's have a quick look at commas.

Taking advantage of trailing commas

PHP has long allowed the use of trailing commas when defining arrays. For example, the syntax shown here is not uncommon:

```
$arr = [1, 2, 3, 4, 5,];
```

However, doing the same thing in a function or method signature is not allowed:

```
function xyz ($fn, $ln, $mid = '',) { /* code */ }
```

Although it's not really such a big deal, it's annoying to be able to add a trailing comma when defining an array, but not be allowed the same liberty when it comes to function or method signatures!

PHP 8 now allows you to use trailing commas in both function and method signatures. The new rule also applies to use() statements associated with anonymous functions.

To illustrate this change, consider the following example. In this example, an anonymous function is defined that renders a full name:

```
// /repo/ch09/php8_trailing_comma.php
$full = function ($fn, $ln, $mid = '',) {
    $mi = ($mid) ? strtoupper($mid[0]) . '.' : '';
    return $fn . ' ' . $mi . $ln;
};
echo $full('Fred', 'Flintstone', 'John');
```

As you can see, there's a comma following the third argument to the anonymous function. Here is the output from PHP 7:

```
root@php8_tips_php7 [ /repo/ch09 ]#
php php8_trailing_comma.php
PHP Parse error:  syntax error, unexpected ')', expecting variable (T_VARIABLE) in /repo/ch09/php8_trailing_comma.php on line 4
```

In PHP 8, the trailing comma is allowed and the expected output appears, as shown here:

```
root@php8_tips_php8 [ /repo/ch09 ]#
php php8_trailing_comma.php
Fred J. Flintstone
```

Although having a trailing comma in function or method definitions is not necessarily a best practice, it does make PHP 8 consistent in its overall treatment of trailing commas.

Now, let's turn our attention to methods that still exist but no longer have any use.

Learning about methods that are no longer required

Primarily as a result of the PHP 8 resource-to-object migration, a number of functions and methods are no longer required. They are not deprecated at the time of writing, but these functions no longer serve any practical use.

As an analogy, in versions of PHP before PHP 8, you would use `fopen()` to open a file handle resource. Once you had finished working on the file, you would normally use `fclose()` on the file handle resource to close the connection.

Now, let's assume that you are using `SplFileObject` instead of `fopen()`. When the work with the file has been completed, you can simply unset the object. This accomplishes the same thing as using `fclose()`, making `fclose()` redundant.

The following table summarizes functions that exist, and can still be used, but no longer have any practical value in PHP 8. The ones marked with an asterisk are also deprecated:

Extension	Functions No Longer Useful
cURL	curl_close() curl_multi_close() curl_share_close()
Exif	read_exif_data()
GD	imagedestroy()
OpenSSL	openssl_x509_free() *
Shared Memory	shmop_close() *
XMLParser	xml_parser_free()

Table 9.1 – Functions that are no longer useful

Now that you have an idea of what major method signature and usage changes have been made in PHP 8, let's have a look at the best practices to take into consideration when working with interfaces and traits.

Working with interfaces and traits

The PHP 8 trait implementation has been expanded in several ways. There are also several new interfaces that can potentially alter how you work with the DOM and DateTime extensions. For the most part, the changes improve the abilities of these two extensions. However, as method signatures have changed in some cases, you may run into a potential code break. Due to this, it's important to pay close attention to the discussion presented in this section to ensure that existing and future PHP code remains functional.

First, let's have a look at the new DOM extension interfaces.

Discovering new DOM extension interfaces

The *cost of living* economic statistic is issued each year by many world governments. It depicts how much it costs an average citizen to live year by year. As web technology matures, a similar principal has been applied – first to HTML, and now to DOM. The **DOM Living Standard** is maintained by the **Web Hypertext Application Technology Working Group** (**WHATWG**) (https://whatwg.org/).

The reason why this information is important to PHP developers is that in PHP 8, the decision was made to move the PHP DOM extension to the DOM Living Standard. Accordingly, starting with PHP 8, a series of incremental and continuous changes will be applied to this extension in accordance with changes to the living standard.

For the most part, the changes are backward compatible. However, since some method signatures change to maintain adherence to the standard, you may experience code breaks. The most significant change to the DOM extension in PHP 8 is the introduction of two new interfaces. Let's examine these interfaces, and then discuss their impact on PHP development.

Examining the new DOMParentNode interface

The first of the two new interfaces is **DOMParentNode**. The following classes implement this interface in PHP 8:

- DOMDocument
- DOMElement
- DOMDocumentFragment

Here is the interface definition:

```
interface DOMParentNode {
    public readonly ?DOMElement $firstElementChild;
    public readonly ?DOMElement $lastElementChild;
    public readonly int $childElementCount;
    public function append(
        ...DOMNode|string|null $nodes) : void;
    public function prepend(
        ...DOMNode|string|null $nodes) : void;
}
```

It's important to note that there is no *readonly* attribute available to PHP developers. However, the interface specification shows the properties as read only because they are internally generated and cannot be changed.

> **Tip**
> There actually was a PHP RFC that was introduced in 2014 that proposed adding a *readonly* attribute to class properties. This proposal was withdrawn, however, as the same effect can be achieved by defining a constant or simply marking a property `private`! For more information on this proposal, see https://wiki.php.net/rfc/readonly_properties.

The following table summarizes the properties and methods of the new `DOMParentNode` interface:

Method / Property	Description
`$firstElementChild`	Contains either the first `DOMElement` instance in this object, or NULL.
`$lastElementChild`	Contains either the last `DOMElement` instance in this object, or NULL.
`$elementChildCount`	Integer value representing the total number of child elements in this object.
`append()`	Appends the node to the end of the current list of child nodes.
`prepend()`	Adds the node to the beginning of the current list of child nodes.

Table 9.2 – DOMParentNode interface methods and properties

The functionality represented by the new interface doesn't add anything new to the existing DOM capabilities. Its main purpose is to bring the PHP DOM extension in line with the living standard.

> **Tip**
> There is another purpose for architecturally renovating the DOM extension in the future. In future versions of PHP, the DOM extension will have the capability of manipulating an entire branch of the DOM tree. When you issue an `append()`, for example, in the future, you will be able to append not only the one node, but all its child nodes as well. For more information, see the following RFC: https://wiki.php.net/rfc/dom_living_standard_api.

Now, let's have a look at the second new interface.

Examining the new DOMChildNode interface

The second of the two new interfaces is **DOMChildNode**. The `DOMElement` and `DOMCharacterData` classes implement this interface in PHP 8.

Here is the interface definition:

```
interface DOMChildNode {
    public readonly ?DOMElement $previousElementSibling;
    public readonly ?DOMElement $nextElementSibling;
    public function remove() : void;
    public function before(
        ...DOMNode|string|null $nodes) : void;
    public function after(
        ...DOMNode|string|null $nodes) : void;
    public function replaceWith(
        ...DOMNode|string|null $nodes) : void;
}
```

The following table summarizes the methods and properties of `DOMChildNode`:

Method / Property	Description
`$previousElementSibling`	Contains either the previous `DOMElement` instance at the same node level in this object, or NULL.
`$nextElementSibling`	Contains either the next `DOMElement` instance at the same node level in this object, or NULL.
`remove()`	Simplified way of removing this node. Alleviates the need to first acquire the parent node.
`before()`	Adds the node at the same level in this object before this node.
`after()`	Adds the node at the same level in this object after this node.
`replaceWith()`	Replaces this node with specified element.

Table 9.3 – DOMChildNode interface methods and properties

In this case, the functionality departs slightly from the existing DOM capabilities. The most significant departure is `DOMChildNode::remove()`. Before PHP 8, to remove a node, you had to access its parent. Assuming that `$topic` is a `DOMElement` instance, PHP 7 or earlier code may appear as follows:

```
$topic->parentNode->removeChild($topic);
```

In PHP 8, the same code can be written as follows:

```
$topic->remove();
```

Aside from the new methods mentioned in the two tables shown previously, DOM functionality remains the same. Now, let's have a look at how moving a child node might be rewritten in PHP 8 to take advantage of the new interfaces.

DOM usage example – comparing PHP 7 and PHP 8

To illustrate the use of the new interfaces, let's have a look at a code example. In this section, we will present a block of code that uses the DOM extension to move a node that represents `Topic X` from one document to another:

1. Here is an HTML fragment that contains a set of nested `<div>` tags:

```
<!DOCTYPE html>
<!-- /repo/ch09/dom_test_1.html -->
<div id="content">
<div id="A">Topic A</div>
```

```
<div id="B">Topic B</div>
<div id="C">Topic C</div>
<div id="X">Topic X</div>
</div>
```

2. The second HTML fragment includes topics D, E, and F:

```
<!DOCTYPE html>
<!-- /repo/ch09/dom_test_2.html -->
<div id="content">
<div id="D">Topic D</div>
<div id="E">Topic E</div>
<div id="F">Topic F</div>
</div>
```

3. To create `DOMDocument` instances from each of the two fragments, we can make a static call; that is, `loadHTMLFile`. Note that this usage is deprecated in PHP 7 and has been removed in PHP 8:

```
$doc1 = DomDocument::loadHTMLFile('dom_test_1.html');
$doc2 = DomDocument::loadHTMLFile('dom_test_2.html');
```

4. Then, we can extract `Topic X` into `$topic` and import it into the second document as `$new`. Next, retrieve the target node; that is, `content`:

```
$topic = $doc1->getElementById('X');
$new = $doc2->importNode($topic);
$new->textContent = $topic->textContent;
$main = $doc2->getElementById('content');
```

5. Here is where PHP 7 and PHP 8 start to differ. In PHP 7, to move the node, the code must be as follows:

```
// /repo/ch09/php7_dom_changes.php
$main->appendChild($new);
$topic->parentNode->removeChild($topic);
```

6. However, in PHP 8, when using the new interfaces, the code has more of an compact. To remove the topic in PHP 8, there's no need to reference the parent node:

```
// /repo/ch09/php8_dom_changes.php
$main->append($new);
$topic->remove();
```

7. For both PHP 7 and PHP 8, we can view the resulting HTML like so:

```
echo $doc1->saveHTML();
echo $doc2->saveHTML();
```

8. Another difference is how to extract the value of the new last child element of $main. Here's how it might appear in PHP 7:

```
// /repo/ch09/php7_dom_changes.php
echo $main->lastChild->textContent . "\n";
```

9. And here is the same thing in PHP 8:

```
// /repo/ch09/php8_dom_changes.php
echo $main->lastElementChild->textContent . "\n";
```

There are slight differences in the output for both code examples. In PHP 7, you will see a deprecation notice, as shown here:

```
root@php8_tips_php7 [ /repo/ch09 ]# php php7_dom_changes.php
PHP Deprecated:  Non-static method DOMDocument::loadHTMLFile() should not be called statically in /repo/ch09/php7_dom_changes.php on line 6
```

If we try to run the PHP 7 code in PHP 8, a fatal `Error` will be thrown as the `loadHTMLFile()` method's static usage is no longer allowed. Otherwise, if we run the pure PHP 8 example, the output will appear as follows:

```
root@php8_tips_php8 [ /repo/ch09 ]# php php8_dom_changes.php
<!DOCTYPE html>
<html><body><div id="content">
<div id="A">Topic A</div>
<div id="B">Topic B</div>
<div id="C">Topic C</div>
```

```
</div>
</body></html>
<!DOCTYPE html>
<html><body><div id="content">
<div id="D">Topic D</div>
<div id="E">Topic E</div>
<div id="F">Topic F</div>
<div id="X">Topic X</div></div>
</body></html>
Last Topic in Doc 2: Topic X
```

As you can see, in either case, `Topic X` was moved from the first and into the second HTML fragment.

In future versions of PHP, expect the DOM extension to continue to grow while following the living standard for DOM. Also, its usage continues to get easier, with more flexibility and efficiency being provided.

Now, let's turn our attention to changes in the `DateTime` extension.

Using new DateTime methods

When working with date and time, it's often useful to create `DateTimeImmutable` instances. `DateTimeImmutable` objects are the same as `DateTime` objects, except that their property values cannot be altered. Knowing how to switch back and forth between `DateTime` and `DateTimeImmutable` is a useful technique and can save you from many hidden logic errors.

Before we discuss the improvements that were made in PHP 8, let's have a look at the potential problem that `DateTimeImmutable` solves.

Use case for DateTimeImmutable

In this simple example, an array of three instances will be created representing 30, 60, and 90 days from today. These will be used to form the basis of a 30-60-90-day accounts receivable aging report:

1. First, let's initialize a few key variables that represent the interval, date format, and array to hold the final values:

```
// /repo/ch09/php7_date_time_30-60-90.php
$days = [0, 30, 60, 90];
```

```
$fmt    = 'Y-m-d';
$aging  = [];
```

2. Now, let's define a loop that adds the intervals to a `DateTime` instance to produce (hopefully!) an array representing days 0, 30, 60, and 90. Veteran developers have most likely already spotted the problem!

```
$dti = new DateTime('now');
foreach ($days as $span) {
    $interval = new DateInterval('P' . $span . 'D');
    $item = $dti->add($interval);
    $aging[$span] = clone $item;
}
```

3. Next, display the set of dates that have been produced:

```
echo "Day\tDate\n";
foreach ($aging as $key => $obj)
    echo "$key\t" . $obj->format($fmt) . "\n";
```

4. The output, which is a complete disaster, is shown here:

```
root@php8_tips_php7 [ /repo/ch09 ]#
php php7_date_time_30-60-90.php
Day    Date
0      2021-11-20
30     2021-06-23
60     2021-08-22
90     2021-11-20
```

As you can see, the problem is that the `DateTime` class is not immutable. Thus, every time we add a `DateInterval`, the original value is altered, resulting in the inaccurate dates shown.

5. By making one simple alteration, however, we can correct this problem. Instead of originally creating a `DateTime` instance, all we need to do is create a `DateTimeImmutable` instance instead:

```
$dti = new DateTimeImmutable('now');
```

6. To populate the array with `DateTime` instances, however, we need to convert from `DateTimeImmutable` into `DateTime`. In PHP 7.3, the `DateTime::createFromImmutable()` method was introduced. Accordingly, when the value is assigned to `$aging`, the revised code might appear as follows:

```
$aging[$span] = DateTime::createFromImmutable($item);
```

7. Otherwise, you're stuck with creating a new `DateTime` instance, as shown here:

```
$aging[$span] = new DateTime($item->format($fmt));
```

With this one change, the correct output will look as follows:

Day	Date
0	2021-05-24
30	2021-06-23
60	2021-07-23
90	2021-08-22

You now know how `DateTimeImmutable` might be used, and you also have an idea of how to convert into `DateTime`. You'll be pleased to know that in PHP 8, the conversion between the two object types has been made much easier with the introduction of the `createFromInterface()` method.

Examining the createFromInterface() method

In PHP 8, it's much easier to convert between `DateTime` and `DateTimeImmutable`, and back again. A new method called `createFromInterface()` has been added to both classes. The method signature simply calls for a `DateTimeInterface` instance, which means that instances of either `DateTime` or `DateTimeImmutable` are acceptable arguments for this method.

The following brief code example demonstrates how easy it is to convert from one type into another in PHP 8:

1. First, let's define a `DateTimeImmutable` instance and `echo` its class and date:

```
// /repo/ch09/php8_date_time.php
$fmt = 'l, d M Y';
$dti = new DateTimeImmutable('last day of next month');
echo $dti::class . ':' . $dti->format($fmt) . "\n";
```

2. Then, create a `DateTime` instance from `$dti` and add an interval of 90 days, displaying its class and current date:

```
$dtt = DateTime::createFromInterface($dti);
$dtt->add(new DateInterval('P90D'));
echo $dtt::class . ':' . $dtt->format($fmt) . "\n";
```

3. Finally, create a `DateTimeImmutable` instance from `$dtt` and display its class and date:

```
$dtx = DateTimeImmutable::createFromInterface($dtt);
echo $dtx::class . ':' . $dtx->format($fmt) . "\n";
```

Here is the output of this code example, running in PHP 8:

```
root@php8_tips_php8 [ /repo/ch09 ]# php php8_date_time.php
DateTimeImmutable:Wednesday, 30 Jun 2021
DateTime:Tuesday, 28 Sep 2021
DateTimeImmutable:Tuesday, 28 Sep 2021
```

As you can see, we used the same `createFromInterface()` method to create instances. Bear in mind, of course, that we are not actually *converting* the class instance into another. Instead, we are creating cloned instances, but of a different class type.

You now know why you may want `DateTimeImmutable` instead of `DateTime`. You also know that in PHP 8, a new method called `createFromInterface()` provides a uniform way to create instances of one from the other. Next, we'll have a look at how handling traits has been refined in PHP 8.

Understanding PHP 8 trait handling refinements

The implementation of **traits** was first introduced in PHP version 5.4. Since that time, a continuous stream of refinements has been made. PHP 8 continues that trend by providing a means to clearly identify which methods are used when multiple traits have conflicting methods. Also, in addition to removing inconsistencies in visibility declarations, PHP 8 irons out problems in how traits handled (or did not handle!) abstract methods.

As a developer, having a complete mastery of the use of traits enables you to write code that is both more efficient and easier to maintain. Traits can help you avoid producing redundant code. They solve the problem of needing the same logic available across namespaces, or across different class inheritance structures. The information presented in this section enables you to make proper use of traits in code running under PHP 8.

First, let's examine how conflicts between traits are resolved in PHP 8.

Resolving method conflicts between traits

Multiple traits can be used by simply listing the trait names separated by commas. A potential problem can arise, however, if two traits define the same method. To resolve such conflicts, PHP offers the `as` keyword. In PHP 7 and below, to avoid a conflict between two methods of the same name, you could simply rename one of the methods. The code to perform the renaming might appear as follows:

```
use Trait1, Trait2 { <METHOD> as <NEW_NAME>; }
```

The problem with this approach, however, is that PHP is making a silent assumption: METHOD is assumed to come from `Trait1`! In its continuing efforts to enforce good coding practices, PHP 8 no longer allows this assumption. The solution in PHP 8 is to be more specific by using `insteadof` rather than `as`.

Here is a trivial example that illustrates this problem:

1. First, let's define two traits that define the same method, `test()`, but return a different result:

```
// /repo/ch09/php7_trait_conflict_as.php
trait Test1 {
    public function test() {
        return '111111';
    }
}
trait Test2 {
    public function test() {
        return '222222';
    }
}
```

2. Then, define an anonymous class that uses both traits and specifies `test()` as `otherTest()` to avoid a naming collision:

```
$main = new class () {
    use Test1, Test2 { test as otherTest; }
    public function test() { return 'TEST'; }
};
```

3. Next, define a block of code to `echo` the return value of both methods:

```
echo $main->test() . "\n";
echo $main->otherTest() . "\n";
```

Here is the output in PHP 7:

```
root@php8_tips_php7 [ /repo/ch09 ]#
php php7_trait_conflict_as.php
TEST
111111
```

As you can see, PHP 7 silently assumes that we mean to rename `Trait1::test()` as `otherTest()`. From the example code, however, it's not at all clear that this is the programmer's intention!

Running the same code example in PHP 8, we get a different result:

```
root@php8_tips_php8 [ /repo/ch09 ]#
php php7_trait_conflict_as.php
PHP Fatal error:  An alias was defined for method test(), which
exists in both Test1 and Test2. Use Test1::test or Test2::test
to resolve the ambiguity in /repo/ch09/php7_trait_conflict_
as.php on line 6
```

Clearly, PHP 8 does not make such silent assumptions as they can easily lead to unexpected behavior. In this example, the best practice would be to use the scope resolution (`::`) operator. Here is the rewritten code:

```
$main = new class () {
    use Test1, Test2 { Test1::test as otherTest; }
    public function test() { return 'TEST'; }
};
```

If we were to rerun the code in PHP 8, the output would be the same as the output shown for PHP 7. The scope resolution operator affirms that `Trait1` is the source trait for the `test()` method, thus avoiding any ambiguity. Now, let's have a look at how PHP 8 traits handle abstract method signatures.

Working with trait abstract signature checking

As API developers are well aware, marking a method as `abstract` is how you can signal to API users that a method is mandatory, but has yet to be defined. This technique allows the API developer to dictate not only the method name, but its signature as well.

In PHP 7 and below, however, abstract methods defined in a trait ignored the signature, defeating part of the purpose of using an abstract method in the first place! When you use a trait with an abstract method in PHP 8, its signature is checked against the implementation in the class using the trait.

The following example works in PHP 7 but fails in PHP 8 as the method signature is different:

1. First, let's declare strict type checking and define a trait with an abstract method; that is, `add()`. Note the method signature calls for integer data types all around:

    ```
    // /repo/ch09/php7_trait_abstract_signature.php
    declare(strict_types=1);
    trait Test1 {
        public abstract function add(int $a, int $b) : int;
    }
    ```

2. Next, define an anonymous class that uses the trait and defines `add()`. Note that the data types for the class are `float` all around:

    ```
    $main = new class () {
        use Test1;
        public function add(float $a, float $b) : float {
            return $a + $b;
        }
    };
    ```

3. Then, echo the results of adding `111.111` and `222.222`:

    ```
    echo $main->add(111.111, 222.222) . "\n";
    ```

The results of this small code example running in PHP 7 are surprising:

```
root@php8_tips_php7 [ /repo/ch09 ]#
php php7_trait_abstract_signature.php
333.333
```

As you can see from the results, the method signature of the abstract definition in the trait is completely ignored! In PHP 8, however, the outcome is much different. Here is the code's output running in PHP 8:

```
root@php8_tips_php8 [ /repo/ch09 ]#
php php7_trait_abstract_signature.php
PHP Fatal error:  Declaration of class@anonymous::add(float $a, float $b): float must be compatible with Test1::add(int $a, int $b): int in /repo/ch09/php7_trait_abstract_signature.php on line 9
```

The preceding PHP 8 output shows us that good coding practices are enforced, regardless of the source of the abstract method definition.

The last topic in this section will show you how to handle abstract private methods in traits.

Handling private abstract methods in traits

Generally, in PHP, you can't enforce control over an **abstract private method** in an abstract super class as it will not be inherited. In PHP 8, however, you can define an abstract private method in a trait! This can be used as a use-of-code enforcement mechanism when you're doing API development where the using class is required to define a specified private method.

Please note that although you can designate an abstract method as private in a PHP 8 trait, trait method visibility can easily be overridden in the class that uses the trait. Accordingly, we will not show any code examples in this section as the effect of a private abstract trait method is exactly the same as using an abstract trait method at other visibility levels.

> **Tip**
> For more information on trait abstract method handling in PHP 8, have a look at this RFC: https://wiki.php.net/rfc/abstract_trait_method_validation.

Now, let's have a look at general usage changes in private methods.

Dealing with private methods

One of the reasons why developers create a super class is to exert a certain degree of control over the method signatures of subclasses. During the parsing phase, PHP normally confirms that the method signatures match. This leads to proper use of your code by other developers.

In the same vein, it does not make sense to have PHP perform the same rigorous method signature check if a method is marked as `private`. The purpose of a private method is that it is invisible to the extending class. If you define a method of the same name in the extending class, you should be free to define it at will.

To illustrate this problem, let's define a class called `Cipher` with a private method called `encrypt()`. The `OpenCipher` subclass redefines this method, causing a fatal error when running under PHP 7:

1. First, let's define a `Cipher` class whose constructor generates random values for `$key` and `$salt`. It also defines a public method called `encode()` that makes a call to the private `encrypt()` method:

```php
// /repo/src/Php7/Encrypt/Cipher.php
namespace Php7\Encrypt;
class Cipher {
    public $key  = '';
    public $salt = 0;
    public function __construct() {
        $this->salt = rand(1,255);
        $this->key  = bin2hex(random_bytes(8));
    }
    public function encode(string $plain) {
        return $this->encrypt($plain);
    }
}
```

2. Next, let's define a private method called `encrypt()` that produces encrypted text using `str_rot13()`. Note that the method is marked as `final`. Although this does not make any sense, for the purposes of this illustration, assume that this is intended:

```
    final private function encrypt(string $plain) {
        return base64_encode(str_rot13($plain));
    }
}
```

3. Finally, let's define a brief calling program that creates class instances and calls the methods that have been defined:

```
// /repo/ch09/php7_oop_diffs_private_method.php
include __DIR__ . '/../src/Server/Autoload/Loader.php';
$loader = new \Server\Autoload\Loader();
use Php7\Encrypt\{Cipher,OpenCipher};
$text = 'Super secret message';
$cipher1 = new Cipher();
echo $cipher1->encode($text) . "\n";
$cipher2 = new OpenCipher();
var_dump($cipher2->encode($text));
```

If we run the calling program in PHP 7, we'll get the following output:

```
oot@php8_tips_php7 [ /repo/ch09 ]#
php php7_oop_diffs_private_method.php
RmhjcmUgZnJwZXJnIHpyZmZudHI=
PHP Fatal error:  Cannot override final method Php7\Encrypt\Cipher::encrypt() in /repo/src/Php7/Encrypt/OpenCipher.php on line 21
```

Here, you can see that the output from `Cipher` was correctly produced. However, a fatal `Error` has been thrown, along with a message stating that we are unable to override a `final` method. Theoretically, a private method should be completely invisible to the subclass. However, as you can clearly see from the output, this is not the case. The method signature of a private method of the `Cipher` superclass affects our ability to redefine the same method in the subclass.

In PHP 8, however, this paradox has been resolved. Here is the output of the same code running in PHP 8:

```
root@php8_tips_php8 [ /repo/ch09 ]#
php php7_oop_diffs_private_method.php
PHP Warning:  Private methods cannot be final as they are never
overridden by other classes in /repo/src/Php7/Encrypt/Cipher.
php on line 17
RmhjcmUgZnJwZXJnIHpyZmZudHI=
array(2) {
  ["tag"]=> string(24) "woD6Vi73/IXLaKHFGUC3aA=="
  ["cipher"]=> string(28) "+vd+jWKqo8WFPd7SakSvszkoIX0="
```

As you can see from the preceding output, the application succeeded, and output from both the parent and child classes is being displayed. We can also see a `Warning`, informing us that the private methods cannot be marked as `final`.

> **Tip**
>
> For more information on the background discussion on private method signatures, have a look at this documentation reference:
>
> https://wiki.php.net/rfc/inheritance_private_methods.

Now that you have an idea of how PHP 8 prevents subclasses from seeing private methods in the superclass, let's turn our attention to differences in anonymous classes in PHP 8.

Controlling anonymous class usage

Anonymous classes, by their very definition, do not have a name. However, for the purposes of information, PHP informational functions such as `var_dump()`, `var_export()`, `get_class()`, and other classes in the Reflection extension will report the anonymous class simply as `class@anonymous`. However, when an anonymous class extends another class or implements an interface, it might be of some use to have PHP informational functions reflect this fact.

In PHP 8, anonymous classes that extend a class or implement an interface now reflect that fact by changing the label that's assigned to the anonymous class to `Xyz@anonymous`, where `Xyz` is the name of the class or interface. If the anonymous class implements more than one interface, only the first interface will appear. If the anonymous class extends a class and also implements one or more interfaces, the name of the class it extends will appear in its label. The following table summarizes these possibilities:

Context	New Name
`extends Xyz`	`Xyz@anonymous`
`implements Abc`	`Abc@anonymous`
`implements Abc, Def`	`Abc@anonymous`
`extends Xyz implements Abc`	`Xyz@anonymous`

Table 9.4 – Anonymous class promotion

Bear in mind that PHP can already test the anonymous class to see if it falls under a certain line of inheritance. The `instanceof` operator, for example, can be used for this purpose. The following example illustrates how to test the anonymous class for inheritance, as well as how to view its new name:

1. For this example, we will define a `DirectoryIterator` instance that grabs a list of files from the current directory:

```
// /repo/ch09/php8_oop_diff_anon_class_renaming.php
$iter = new DirectoryIterator(__DIR__);
```

2. Then, we will define an anonymous class that extends `FilterIterator`. In this class, we will define the `accept()` method, which produces a Boolean result. If the result is `TRUE`, then that item will appear in the final iteration:

```
$anon = new class ($iter) extends FilterIterator {
    public $search = '';
    public function accept() {
        return str_contains(
            $this->current(), $this->search);
    }
};
```

3. Next, we will produce a list of files that contain `bc_break` in their name:

```
$anon->search = 'bc_break';
foreach ($anon as $fn) echo $fn . "\n";
```

4. In the next two lines, we will use `instanceof` to test whether the anonymous class implements `OuterIterface`:

```
if ($anon instanceof OuterIterator)
    echo "This object implements OuterIterator\n";
```

5. Finally, we will simply dump the contents of the anonymous class using `var_dump()`:

```
echo var_dump($anon);
```

Here is the output running under PHP 8. We cannot run this example in PHP 7 as that version lacks the `str_contains()` function!

```
root@php8_tips_php8 [ /repo/ch09 ]#
php php8_oop_diff_anon_class_renaming.php
php8_bc_break_construct.php
php8_bc_break_serialization.php
php8_bc_break_destruct.php
php8_bc_break_sleep.php
php8_bc_break_scanner.php
php8_bc_break_serializable.php
php8_bc_break_magic_wrong.php
php8_bc_break_magic.php
php8_bc_break_magic_to_string.php
This object implements OuterIterator
object(FilterIterator@anonymous)#2 (1) {
    ["search"]=> string(8) "bc_break"
}
```

As you can see, `instanceof` correctly reports that the anonymous class implements `OuterInterface` (because it extends `FilterIterator`, which, in turn, implements `OuterInterface`). You can also see that `var_dump()` reports the name of the anonymous class as `FilterIterator@anonymous`.

Now that you have an idea of how anonymous class naming has changed in PHP 8, let's have a look at changes in namespace handling.

Understanding changes in namespaces

The concept of a **namespace** was introduced in PHP 5.3 as a means of isolating hierarchies of classes. Unfortunately, the original algorithm that was used to parse namespace names had several flaws. In addition to being overly complicated, the way in which namespace and class names were **tokenized** internally was performed in an inconsistent manner, leading to unexpected errors.

Before we get into the benefits and potential backward compatible breaks, let's have a look at how the namespace tokenization process has changed.

Discovering differences in tokenization

The tokenization process is an important part of the interpretation process and takes place when your PHP code is executed. In the process of producing byte code, the PHP program code is broken down into tokens by the PHP parsing engine.

The following table summarizes namespace tokenization changes:

Namespace + Class	Old Tokenization	New Tokenization
JustClass	T_STRING	T_STRING
\AbsoluteClass	T_NS_SEPARATOR + T_STRING	T_NAME_FULLY_QUALIFIED
Some\Thing\Class	T_STRING + T_NS_SEPARATOR + T_STRING	T_NAME_QUALIFIED
<namespace>\Class	T_NAMESPACE + T_NS_SEPARATOR + T_STRING	T_NAME_RELATIVE

Table 9.5 – Namespace tokenization differences in PHP 8

As you can see, PHP 8 namespace tokenization is much simpler and streamlined.

> **Tip**
> For more information on parser tokens, have a look at the following documentation reference: `https://www.php.net/manual/en/tokens`.

The impact of this change produces extremely positive results. For one, you can now use reserved key words as part of a namespace. Also, in the future, as new keywords are introduced into the language, PHP will not force you to change namespaces in your applications. The new tokenization process also facilitates the use of `Attributes` with namespaces.

First, let's have a look at using keywords in a namespace.

Using reserved keywords in a namespace

The namespace tokenization process in PHP 7 produced a series of string (`T_STRING`) and backslash (`T_NS_SEPARATOR`) tokens. The problem with this approach is that if one of the strings happened to be a PHP keyword, a syntax error was immediately thrown during the parsing process. PHP 8, however, produces just a single token, as shown earlier, in *Table 9.5*. Ultimately, this means that you can put pretty much anything in a namespace and don't have to worry about reserved keyword conflicts.

The following code example illustrates the difference in namespace handling between PHP 8 and earlier versions. In this example, a PHP keyword is being used as part of the namespace. In PHP 7, due to its inaccurate tokenization process, `List` is seen as a keyword rather than part of the namespace:

```
// /repo/ch09/php8_namespace_reserved.php
namespace List\Works\Only\In\PHP8;
class Test {
    public const TEST = 'TEST';
}
echo Test::TEST . "\n";
```

Here is the output from PHP 7:

```
root@php8_tips_php7 [ /repo/ch09 ]#
php php8_namespace_reserved.php
PHP Parse error:  syntax error, unexpected 'List' (T_LIST), expecting '{' in /repo/ch09/php8_namespace_reserved.php on line 3
```

In PHP 8, the program code snippet works as expected, as shown here:

```
root@php8_tips_php8 [ /repo/ch09 ]#
php php8_namespace_reserved.php
TEST
```

Now that you have an idea of how the tokenization process differs between PHP 8 and earlier PHP versions, as well as its potential benefits, let's have a look at potential backward compatible code breaks.

Exposing bad namespace naming practices

The same PHP 8 tokenization process that releases you from having to worry about keyword conflicts may also end up exposing bad namespace naming practices. Any namespaces with white space in them are now considered invalid. However, it's a bad practice to include whitespace in a namespace anyhow!

The following simple code example illustrates this principle. In this example, you'll notice that the namespace includes white space:

```
// /repo/ch09/php7_namespace_bad.php
namespace Doesnt \Work \In \PHP8;
class Test {
    public const TEST = 'TEST';
}
echo Test::TEST . "\n";
```

If we run this code in PHP 7, it works OK. Here's the PHP 7 output:

```
root@php8_tips_php7 [ /repo/ch09 ]#
php php7_namespace_bad.php
TEST
```

In PHP 8, however, a `ParseError` is thrown, as shown here:

```
root@php8_tips_php8 [ /repo/ch09 ]#
php php7_namespace_bad.php
PHP Parse error:  syntax error, unexpected fully qualified name "\Work", expecting "{" in /repo/ch09/php7_namespace_bad.php on line 3
```

The space serves as a delimiter that's used by the parser during the tokenization process. In this code example, PHP 8 assumes that the namespace is `Doesnt`. The next token is `\Work`, which marks a fully qualified class name. However, it's not expected at this point, which is why an error was thrown.

This concludes our discussion on the changes that have been made to namespace handling in PHP 8. You are now in a better position to create namespace names in PHP 8 that not only follow best practices, but also take advantage of its independence from keyword naming conflicts.

Summary

PHP 8, as you learned, is much stricter in terms of how it defines magic methods. In this chapter, you learned about method signature changes and how to reduce potential bugs by using magic methods properly. You also learned about the method signature changes in both the Reflection and PDO extensions. With the knowledge you've gained in this chapter, you can avoid potential problems when migrating to PHP 8. In addition, you learned about changes in how static methods can be called, as well as a new static return type.

Then, you learned how to make the best use of private methods, as well as how to exert greater control over anonymous classes. You also picked up a few tips on new syntax possibilities and which methods are now obsolete due to changes in the language.

You also learned how to correctly use interfaces and traits to facilitate efficient use of your code. You learned about the new interfaces that were introduced to bring the DOM extension up to the new DOM Living Standard. In addition, you gained insights into using new methods introduced in the DateTime extension.

Finally, you learned how to clean up namespace usage and produce tighter code. You now have a better understanding of how the namespace tokenization process was inaccurate and how it's been improved in PHP 8.

The next chapter will present you with something every developer strives for: tips, tricks, and techniques to improve performance.

10
Improving Performance

PHP 8.x introduces a number of new features that have a positive effect on performance. Also, a number of internal improvements, especially in array handling and managing object references, lead to a substantive performance increase over earlier PHP versions. In addition, many of the PHP 8 best practices covered in this chapter lead to greater efficiency and lower memory usage. In this chapter, you'll discover how to optimize your PHP 8 code to achieve maximum performance.

PHP 8 includes a technology referred to as weak references. By mastering this technology, discussed in the last section of this chapter, your applications will use far less memory. By carefully reviewing the material covered in this chapter and by studying the code examples, you will be able to write faster and more efficient code. Such mastery will vastly improve your standing as a PHP developer and result in satisfied customers, as well as improving your career potential.

Topics covered in this chapter include the following:

- Working with the **Just-In-Time (JIT)** compiler
- Speeding up array handling
- Implementing stable sort
- Using weak references to improve efficiency

Technical requirements

To examine and run the code examples provided in this chapter, the minimum recommended hardware is the following:

- x86_64 based desktop PC or laptop
- 1 gigabyte (GB) free disk space
- 4 GB of RAM
- 500 kilobits per second (Kbps) or faster internet connection

In addition, you will need to install the following software:

- Docker
- Docker Compose

Please refer to the *Technical requirements* section of *Chapter 1, Introducing New PHP 8 OOP Features*, for more information on Docker and Docker Compose installation, as well as how to build the Docker container used to demonstrate the code explained in this book. In this book, we refer to the directory in which you stored the sample code for this book as `/repo`.

The source code for this chapter is located here: `https://github.com/PacktPublishing/PHP-8-Programming-Tips-Tricks-and-Best-Practices`. We can now begin our discussion by having a look at the long-awaited JIT compiler.

Working with the JIT compiler

PHP 8 introduces the long-awaited **JIT compiler**. This is an important step and has important ramifications for the long-term viability of the PHP language. Although PHP already had the ability to produce and cache **bytecode**, before the introduction of the JIT compiler, PHP did not have the ability to directly cache **machine code**.

There have actually been several attempts to add JIT compiler capabilities to PHP, dating back to 2011. The performance boost seen in PHP 7 was a direct result of these early efforts. None of the earlier JIT compiler efforts were proposed as **RFCs** (**Requests for Comments**) as they didn't significantly improve performance. The core team now feels that any further performance gains can now only be achieved using JIT. As a side benefit, this opens the possibility of PHP being used as a language for non-web environments. Another benefit is that the JIT compiler opens the possibility to develop PHP extensions in languages other than C.

It's extremely important to pay close attention to the details given in this chapter as proper use of the new JIT compiler has the potential to greatly improve the performance of your PHP applications. Before we get into implementation details, it's first necessary to explain how PHP executes bytecode without the JIT compiler. We'll then show you how the JIT compiler works. After this, you will be in a better position to understand the various settings and how they can be fine-tuned to produce the best possible performance for your application code.

Let's now turn our attention to how PHP works without the JIT compiler.

Discovering how PHP works without JIT

When PHP is installed on a server (or in a Docker container), in addition to the core extensions, the main component installed is actually a **virtual machine** (**VM**) often referred to as the **Zend Engine**. This VM operates in a manner quite different from virtualization technologies such as *VMware* or *Docker*. The Zend Engine is closer in nature to the **Java Virtual Machine** (**JVM**) in that it accepts *bytecode* and produces *machine code*.

This begs the question: *what is bytecode* and *what is machine code*? Let's have a look at this question now.

Understanding bytecode and machine code

Machine code, or **machine language**, is a set of hardware instructions understood by the CPU directly. Each piece of machine code is an instruction that causes the CPU to perform a specific operation. These low-level operations include moving information between registers, moving a given number of bytes in or out of memory, adding, subtracting, and so forth.

Machine code is often rendered somewhat human-readable by using **assembly language**. Here is an example of machine code rendered in assembly language:

```
JIT$Mandelbrot::iterate: ;
        sub $0x10, %esp
        cmp $0x1, 0x1c(%esi)
        jb .L14
        jmp .L1
.ENTRY1:
        sub $0x10, %esp
.L1:
        cmp $0x2, 0x1c(%esi)
```

```
            jb .)L15
            mov $0xec3800f0, %edi
            jmp .L2
.ENTRY2:
            sub $0x10, %esp
.L2:
            cmp $0x5, 0x48(%esi)
            jnz .L16
            vmovsd 0x40(%esi), %xmm1
            vsubsd 0xec380068, %xmm1, %xmm1
```

Although, for the most part, the commands are not easily understood, you can see from the assembly language representation that the instructions include commands to compare (`cmp`), move information between registers and/or memory (`mov`), and jump to another point in the instruction set (`jmp`).

Bytecode, also called **opcode**, is a greatly reduced symbolic representation of the original program code. Bytecode is produced by a parsing process (often called the **interpreter**) that breaks human-readable program code into symbols known as **tokens**, along with values. Values would be any string, integer, float, and Boolean data used in the program code.

Here is an example of a fragment of the bytecode produced based upon the example code (shown later) used to create a Mandelbrot:

```
00000840  ff ff ff ff 00 00 00 00  ff ff ff ff ff ff ff ff  |................|
00000850  40 02 00 00 00 00 00 00  0d 00 00 00 ff ff ff ff  |@...............|
00000860  1d aa 83 9f 7a c3 f4 d5  20 08 00 00 00 00 00 00  |....z... .......|
00000870  01 00 00 00 56 00 00 00  1d aa 83 9f 7a c3 f4 d5  |....V.......z...|
00000880  39 00 00 00 00 00 00 00  00 70 68 70 38 5c 6a 69  |9........php8\ji|
00000890  74 5c 6d 61 6e 64 65 6c  62 72 6f 74 2f 72 65 70  |t\mandelbrot/rep|
000008a0  6f 2f 73 72 63 2f 50 68  70 38 2f 4a 69 74 2f 4d  |o/src/Php8/Jit/M|
000008b0  61 6e 64 65 6c 62 72 6f  74 2e 70 68 70 3a 35 24  |andelbrot.php:5$|
000008c0  30 00 00 00 00 00 00 00  01 00 00 00 56 00 00 00  |0...........V...|
000008d0  8c 06 62 77 f6 61 07 b3  13 00 00 00 00 00 00 00  |..bw.a..........|
000008e0  50 68 70 38 5c 4a 69 74  5c 4d 61 6e 64 65 6c 62  |Php8\Jit\Mandelb|
000008f0  72 6f 74 00 00 00 00 00  ff ff ff ff ff ff ff ff  |rot.............|
```

Figure 10.1 – Bytecode fragment produced by the PHP parsing process

Let's now have a look at the conventional execution flow of a PHP program.

Understanding conventional PHP program execution

In a conventional PHP program run cycle, the PHP program code is evaluated and broken down into bytecode by an operation known as **parsing**. The bytecode is then passed to the Zend Engine, which in turn converts the bytecode into machine code.

When PHP is first installed on a server, the installation process kicks in the necessary logic that tailors the Zend Engine to the specific CPU and hardware (or virtual CPU and hardware) for that particular server. Thus, when you write PHP code, you have no awareness of the particulars of the actual CPU that eventually runs your code. It is the Zend Engine that provides hardware-specific awareness.

Figure 10.2, shown next, illustrates conventional PHP execution:

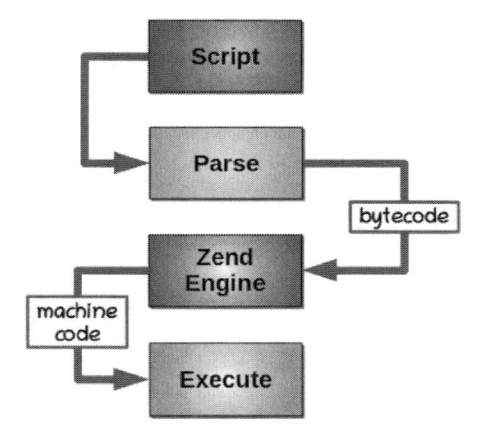

Figure 10.2 – Conventional PHP program execution flow

Although PHP, especially PHP 7, is quite fast, it's still of interest to gain additional speed. For this purpose, most installations also enable the PHP **OPcache** extension. Let's have a quick look at OPcache before moving on to the JIT compiler.

Understanding the operation of PHP OPcache

As the name implies, the PHP OPcache extension *caches* opcode (bytecode) the first time a PHP program is run. On subsequent program runs, the bytecode is drawn from the cache, eliminating the parsing phase. This saves a significant amount of time and is a highly desirable feature to enable on a production site. The PHP OPcache extension is part of the set of core extensions; however, it's not enabled by default.

Before enabling this extension, you must first confirm that your version of PHP has been compiled with the `--enable-opcache` configure option. You can check this by executing the `phpinfo()` command from inside PHP code running on your web server. From the command line, enter the `php -i` command. Here is an example running `php -i` from the Docker container used for this book:

```
root@php8_tips_php8 [ /repo/ch10 ]# php -i
phpinfo()
PHP Version => 8.1.0-dev
System => Linux php8_tips_php8 5.8.0-53-generic #60~20.04.1-Ubuntu SMP Thu May 6 09:52:46 UTC 2021 x86_64
Build Date => Dec 24 2020 00:11:29
Build System => Linux 9244ac997bc1 3.16.0-4-amd64 #1 SMP Debian 3.16.7-ckt11-1 (2015-05-24) x86_64 GNU/Linux
Configure Command =>  './configure'  '--prefix=/usr' '--sysconfdir=/etc' '--localstatedir=/var' '--datadir=/usr/share/php' '--mandir=/usr/share/man' '--enable-fpm' '--with-fpm-user=apache' '--with-fpm-group=apache'
// not all options shown
'--with-jpeg' '--with-png' '--with-sodium=/usr' '--enable-opcache-jit' '--with-pcre-jit' '--enable-opcache'
```

As you can see from the output, OPcache was included in the configuration for this PHP installation. To enable OPcache, add or uncomment the following `php.ini` file settings:

- `zend_extension=opcache`
- `opcache.enable=1`
- `opcache.enable_cli=1`

The last setting is optional. It determines whether or not PHP commands executed from the command line are also processed by OPcache. Once enabled, there are a number of other `php.ini` file settings that affect performance, however, these are beyond the scope of this discussion.

> **Tip**
>
> For more information on PHP `php.ini` file settings that affect OPcache, have a look here: `https://www.php.net/manual/en/cpcache.configuration.php`.

Let's now have a look at how the JIT compiler operates, and how it differs from OPcache.

Discovering PHP program execution with the JIT compiler

The problem with the current approach is that whether or not the bytecode is cached, it's still necessary for the Zend Engine to convert the bytecode into machine code each and every time the program request is made. What the JIT compiler offers is the ability to not only compile bytecode into machine code but to *cache machine code* as well. The process is facilitated by a tracing mechanism that creates traces of requests. The trace allows the JIT compiler to determine which blocks of machine code need to be optimized and cached. The execution flow using the JIT compiler is summarized in *Figure 10.3*:

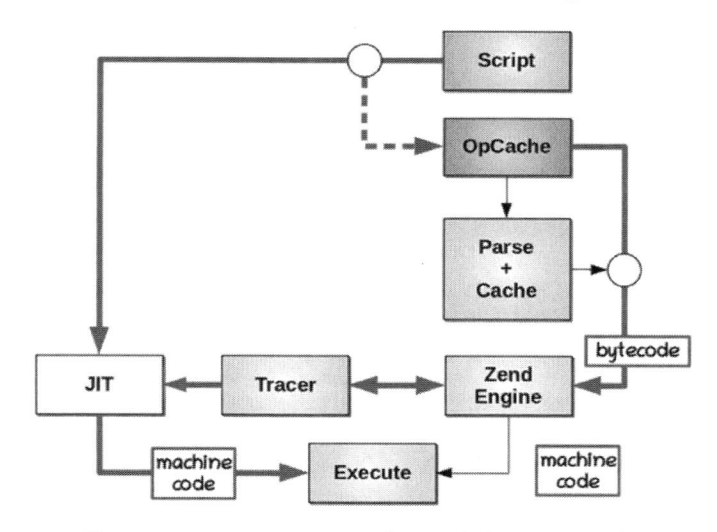

Figure 10.3 – PHP execution flow with the JIT compiler

As you can see from the diagram, the normal execution flow incorporating OPcache is still present. The main difference is that a request might invoke a trace, causing the program flow to shift immediately to the JIT compiler, effectively bypassing not only the parsing process but the Zend Engine as well. Both the JIT compiler and the Zend Engine can produce machine code ready for direct execution.

The JIT compiler did not evolve out of thin air. The PHP core team elected to port the highly performant and well-tested **DynASM** preprocessing assembler. Although DynASM was primarily developed for the JIT compiler used by the **Lua** programming language, its design is such that it's perfectly suited to form the basis of a JIT compiler for any C-based language (such as PHP!).

Another favorable aspect of the PHP JIT implementation is that it doesn't produce any **Intermediate Representation (IR)** code. In contrast, the **PyPy VM** used to run Python code using JIT compiler technology, has to first produce IR code in a **graph structure**, used for flow analysis and optimization, before the actual machine code is produced. The DynASM core in the PHP JIT doesn't require this extra step, resulting in greater performance than is possible in other interpreted programming languages.

> **Tip**
>
> For more information on DynASM, have a look at this website: `https://luajit.org/dynasm.html`. Here's an excellent overview of how the PHP 8 JIT operates: `https://www.zend.com/blog/exploring-new-php-jit-compiler`. You can also read the official JIT RFC here: `https://wiki.php.net/rfc/jit`.

Now that you have an idea of how the JIT compiler fits into the general flow of a PHP program execution cycle, it's time to learn how to enable it.

Enabling the JIT compiler

Because the primary function of the JIT compiler is to cache machine code, it operates as an independent part of the OPcache extension. OPcache serves as a gateway to both enable JIT functionality as well as to allocate memory to the JIT compiler from its own allotment. Therefore, in order to enable the JIT compiler, you must first enable OPcache (see the previous section, *Understanding the operation of PHP OPcache*).

In order to enable the JIT compiler, you must first confirm that PHP has been compiled with the `--enable-opcache-jit` configuration option. You are then in a position to enable or disable the JIT compiler by simply assigning a non-zero value to the `php.ini` file's `opcache.jit_buffer_size` directive.

Values are specified either as an integer – in which case, the value represents the number of bytes; a value of zero (the default), which disables the JIT compiler; or you can assign a number followed by any of the following letters:

- `K`: Kilobytes
- `M`: Megabytes
- `G`: Gigabytes

The value you specify for the JIT compiler buffer size must be less than the memory allocation you assigned to OPcache because the JIT buffer is taken out of the OPcache buffer.

Here is an example that sets the OPcache memory consumption to 256 M and the JIT buffer to 64 M. These values can be placed anywhere in the `php.ini` file:

```
opcache.memory_consumption=256
opcache.jit_buffer_size=64M
```

Now that you have an idea of how the JIT compiler works, and how it can be enabled, it's extremely important that you know how to properly set the tracing mode.

Configuring the tracing mode

The `php.ini` setting `opcache.jit` controls the JIT tracer operation. For convenience, one of the following four preset strings can be used:

- `opcache.jit=disable`

  Completely disables the JIT compiler (regardless of other settings).

- `opcache.jit=off`

  Disables the JIT compiler but (in most cases) you can enable it at runtime using `ini_set()`.

- `opcache.jit=function`

  Sets the JIT compiler tracer to function mode. This mode corresponds to the **CPU Register Trigger Optimization (CRTO)** digits 1205 (explained next).

- `opcache.jit=tracing`

  Sets the JIT compiler tracer to tracing mode. This mode corresponds to the CRTO digits 1254 (explained next). In most cases, this setting gives you the best performance.

- `opcache.jit=on`

  This is an alias for tracing mode.

> **Tip**
> Relying upon runtime JIT activation is risky and can produce inconsistent application behavior. The best practice is to use either the `tracing` or the `function` setting.

The four convenience strings actually resolve into a four-digit number. Each digit corresponds to a different aspect of the JIT compiler tracer. The four digits are not bitmasks unlike other `php.ini` file settings and are specified in this order: CRTO. Here is a summary of each of the four digits.

C (CPU opt flags)

The first digit represents CPU optimization settings. If you set this digit to 0, no CPU optimization takes place. A value of 1 enables the generation of **Advanced Vector Extensions (AVX) instructions**. AVX are extensions to the x86 instruction set architecture for microprocessors from Intel and AMD. AVX has been supported on Intel and AMD processors since 2011. AVX2 is available on most server-type processors such as Intel Xeon.

R (register allocation)

The second digit controls how the JIT compiler deals with **registers**. Registers are like RAM, except that they reside directly inside the CPU itself. The CPU constantly moves information in and out of registers in order to perform operations (for example, adding, subtracting, performing logical AND, OR, and NOT operations, and so forth). The options associated with this setting allow you to disable register allocation optimization or allow it at either the local or global level.

T (JIT trigger)

The third digit dictates when the JIT compiler should trigger. Options include having the JIT compiler operate the first time a script is loaded or upon first execution. Alternatively, you can instruct the JIT when to compile **hot functions**. Hot functions are ones that are called the most frequently. There is also a setting that tells JIT to only compile functions marked with the `@jit docblock` annotation.

O (optimization level)

The fourth digit corresponds to the optimization level. Options include disabling optimization, minimal, and selective. You can also instruct the JIT compiler to optimize based upon individual functions, call trees, or the results of inner procedure analysis.

> **Tip**
> For a complete breakdown of the four JIT compiler tracer settings, have a look at this documentation reference page: https://www.php.net/manual/en/opcache.configuration.php#ini.opcache.jit.

Let's now have a look at the JIT compiler in action.

Using the JIT compiler

In this example, we use a classic benchmark program that produces a **Mandelbrot**. This is an excellent test as it's extremely computation-intensive. The implementation we use here is drawn from the implementation code produced by **Dmitry Stogov**, one of the PHP core development team members. You can view the original implementation here: https://gist.github.com/dstogov/12323ad13d3240aee8f1:

1. We first define the Mandelbrot parameters. Especially important is the number of iterations (`MAX_LOOPS`). A large number spawns more calculations and slows down overall production. We also capture the start time:

    ```
    // /repo/ch10/php8_jit_mandelbrot.php
    define('BAILOUT',    16);
    define('MAX_LOOPS', 10000);
    define('EDGE',       40.0);
    $d1  = microtime(1);
    ```

2. In order to facilitate multiple program runs, we add an option to capture a command line param, `-n`. If this parameter is present, the Mandelbrot output is suppressed:

    ```
    $time_only = (bool) ($argv[1] ?? $_GET['time'] ?? FALSE);
    ```

3. We then define a function, `iterate()`, drawn directly from the Mandelbrot implementation by Dmitry Stogov. The actual code, not shown here, can be viewed at the URL mentioned earlier.

4. Next, we produce the ASCII image by running through the X/Y coordinates determined by `EDGE`:

    ```
    $out = '';
    $f   = EDGE - 1;
    for ($y = -$f; $y < $f; $y++) {
    ```

```
        for ($x = -$f; $x < $f; $x++) {
            $out .= (iterate($x/EDGE,$y/EDGE) == 0)
                    ? '*' : ' ';
        }
        $out .= "\n";
    }
```

5. Finally, we produce output. If running through a web request, the output is wrapped in `<pre>` tags. If the `-n` flag is present, only the elapsed time is shown:

```
if (!empty($_SERVER['REQUEST_URI'])) {
    $out = '<pre>' . $out . '</pre>';
}
if (!$time_only) echo $out;
$d2 = microtime(1);
$diff = $d2 - $d1;
printf("\nPHP Elapsed %0.3f\n", $diff);
```

6. We first run the program in the PHP 7 Docker container three times using the `-n` flag. Here is the result. Please note that the elapsed time was easily over 10 seconds in the demo Docker container used in conjunction with this book:

```
root@php8_tips_php7 [ /repo/ch10 ]#
php php8_jit_mandelbrot.php -n
PHP Elapsed 10.320
root@php8_tips_php7 [ /repo/ch10 ]#
php php8_jit_mandelbrot.php -n
PHP Elapsed 10.134
root@php8_tips_php7 [ /repo/ch10 ]#
php php8_jit_mandelbrot.php -n
PHP Elapsed 11.806
```

7. We now turn to the PHP 8 Docker container. To start, we adjust the `php.ini` file to disable the JIT compiler. Here are the settings:

```
opcache.jit=off
opcache.jit_buffer_size=0
```

8. Here is the result of running the program three times in PHP 8 using the -n flag:

```
root@php8_tips_php8 [ /repo/ch10 ]#
php php8_jit_mandelbrot.php -n
PHP Elapsed 1.183
root@php8_tips_php8 [ /repo/ch10 ]#
php php8_jit_mandelbrot.php -n
PHP Elapsed 1.192
root@php8_tips_php8 [ /repo/ch10 ]#
php php8_jit_mandelbrot.php -n
PHP Elapsed 1.210
```

9. Right away, you can see a great reason to switch to PHP 8! Even without the JIT compiler, PHP 8 was able to perform the same program in a little over 1 second: 1/10 of the amount of time!

10. Next, we modify the php.ini file settings to use the JIT compiler `function` tracer mode. Here are the settings used:

```
opcache.jit=function
opcache.jit_buffer_size=64M
```

11. We then run the same program again using the -n flag. Here are the results running in PHP 8 using the JIT compiler `function` tracer mode:

```
root@php8_tips_php8 [ /repo/ch10 ]#
php php8_jit_mandelbrot.php -n
PHP Elapsed 0.323
root@php8_tips_php8 [ /repo/ch10 ]#
php php8_jit_mandelbrot.php -n
PHP Elapsed 0.322
root@php8_tips_php8 [ /repo/ch10 ]#
php php8_jit_mandelbrot.php -n
PHP Elapsed 0.324
```

12. Wow! We managed to speed up processing by a factor of 3. The speed is now less than 1/3 of a second! But what happens if we try the recommended JIT compiler `tracing` mode? Here are the settings to invoke that mode:

```
opcache.jit=tracing
opcache.jit_buffer_size=64M
```

13. Here are the results of our last set of program runs:

```
root@php8_tips_php8 [ /repo/ch10 ]#
php php8_jit_mandelbrot.php -n
PHP Elapsed 0.132
root@php8_tips_php8 [ /repo/ch10 ]#
php php8_jit_mandelbrot.php -n
PHP Elapsed 0.132
root@php8_tips_php8 [ /repo/ch10 ]#
php php8_jit_mandelbrot.php -n
PHP Elapsed 0.131
```

The last result, as shown in the output, is truly staggering. Not only can we run the same program 10x faster than PHP 8 without the JIT compiler, but we are running *100x faster* than PHP 7!

> **Important note**
> It's important to note that times will vary depending on the host computer you are using to run the Docker containers associated with this book. You will not see exactly the same times as shown here.

Let's now have a look at JIT compiler debugging.

Debugging with the JIT compiler

Normal debugging using **XDebug** or other tools will not work effectively when using the JIT compiler. Accordingly, the PHP core team added an additional `php.ini` file option, `opcache.jit_debug`, which produces additional debugging information. In this case, the settings available take the form of bit flags, which means you can combine them using bitwise operators such as AND, OR, XOR, and so forth.

Table 10.1 summarizes values that can be assigned as an `opcache.jit_debug` setting. Please note that the column labeled **Internal Constant** does not show PHP predefined constants. These values are internal C code references:

Internal Constant	Value	Meaning
ZEND_JIT_DEBUG_ASM	1	Dump assembler code
ZEND_JIT_DEBUG_SSA	2	Dump static single assignments
ZEND_JIT_DEBUG_REG_ALLOC	4	Register allocation info
ZEND_JIT_DEBUG_ASM_STUBS	8	Assembler stubs
ZEND_JIT_DEBUG_PERF	16	Create perf.map for Linux perf
ZEND_JIT_DEBUG_PERF_DUMP	32	Create perf.dump for Linux perf
ZEND_JIT_DEBUG_OPROFILE	64	Debug info for Linux Oprofile
ZEND_JIT_DEBUG_VTUNE	128	Debug info for Intel VTune
ZEND_JIT_DEBUG_GDB	256	Debug using GNU debugger
ZEND_JIT_DEBUG_SIZE	512	Memory sizing
ZEND_JIT_DEBUG_ASM_ADDR	1024	Assembler addressing
ZEND_JIT_DEBUG_TRACE_START	4096	Trace start
ZEND_JIT_DEBUG_TRACE_STOP	8192	Trace stop
ZEND_JIT_DEBUG_TRACE_COMPILED	16384	Trace compiled
ZEND_JIT_DEBUG_TRACE_EXIT	32768	Trace exit
ZEND_JIT_DEBUG_TRACE_ABORT	65536	Trace abort
ZEND_JIT_DEBUG_TRACE_BLACKLIST	131072	Trace blacklist
ZEND_JIT_DEBUG_TRACE_BYTECODE	262144	Trace bytecode reference
ZEND_JIT_DEBUG_TRACE_TSSA	524288	Trace static single assignment
ZEND_JIT_DEBUG_TRACE_EXIT_INFO	1048576	Trace exit information

Table 10.1 – opcache.jit_debug settings

So, for example, if you wish to enable debugging for ZEND_JIT_DEBUG_ASM, ZEND_JIT_DEBUG_PERF, and ZEND_JIT_DEBUG_EXIT, you could make the assignment in the php.ini file as follows:

1. First, you need to add up the values you wish to set. In this example, we would add:

   1 + 16 + 32768

2. You then apply the sum to the php.ini setting:

   opcache.jit_debug=32725

3. Or, alternatively, represent the values using bitwise OR:

   opcache.jit_debug=1|16|32768

Depending on the debug setting, you are now in a position to debug the JIT compiler using tools such as the Linux perf command, or Intel VTune.

Here is a partial example of debug output when running the Mandelbrot test program discussed in the previous section. For the purposes of illustration, we are using the `php.ini` file setting `opcache.jit_debug=32725`:

```
root@php8_tips_php8 [ /repo/ch10 ]#
php php8_jit_mandelbrot.php -n
---- TRACE 1 start (loop) iterate()
/repo/ch10/php8_jit_mandelbrot.php:34
---- TRACE 1 stop (loop)
---- TRACE 1 Live Ranges
#15.CV6($i): 0-0 last_use
#19.CV6($i): 0-20 hint=#15.CV6($i)
... not all output is shown
---- TRACE 1 compiled
---- TRACE 2 start (side trace 1/7) iterate()
/repo/ch10/php8_jit_mandelbrot.php:41
---- TRACE 2 stop (return)
TRACE-2$iterate$41: ; (unknown)
    mov $0x2, EG(jit_trace_num)
    mov 0x10(%r14), %rcx
    test %rcx, %rcx
    jz .L1
    mov 0xb0(%r14), %rdx
    mov %rdx, (%rcx)
    mov $0x4, 0x8(%rcx)
... not all output is shown
```

What the output shows you is machine code rendered in assembly language. If you experience problems with your program code when using the JIT compiler, the assembly language dump might assist you in locating the source of the error.

However, please be aware that assembly language is not portable, and is completely oriented toward the CPU being used. Accordingly, you might have to obtain the hardware reference manual for that CPU and look up the assembly language code being used.

Let's now have a look at the other `php.ini` file settings that affect the operation of the JIT compiler.

Discovering additional JIT compiler settings

Table 10.2 provides a summary of all other `opcache.jit*` settings in the `php.ini` file that have not already been covered:

opcache.* Setting	Type	Description
jit_bisect_limit	int	Much like a break point, this tells JIT to stop after this limit has been reached. Use this to isolate the process causing the break.
jit_prof_threshold	float	If your "P" value is set to 2, this setting sets the level at which a function is considered "hot". (# calls to this func) divided by the (# calls to all funcs) must be > the value set here. For example, 0.1 means that functions that comprise more than 10% of all calls will be compiled
jit_max_root_traces	int	Maximum number of root traces.
jit_max_side_traces	int	Maximum number of side traces.
jit_max_exit_counters	int	Maximum number of side trace exit counters. Puts a limit on the total number of side traces.
jit_hot_loop	int	A loop is considered "hot" after this many iterations.
jit_hot_func	int	A function is considered "hot" after this many iterations.
jit_hot_return	int	A return is considered "hot" after this many iterations.
jit_hot_side_exit	int	An exit is considered "hot" after this many iterations.
jit_blacklist_root_trace	int	Maximum times a root trace compilation can fail before being blacklisted.
jit_blacklist_side_trace	int	Maximum times a side trace compilation can fail before being blacklisted.
jit_max_loop_unrolls	int	Maximum times a an attempt to close the loop on a side trace compilation can fail before being blacklisted.
jit_max_recursive_calls	int	Maximum number of times recursive call loops closings can fail.
jit_max_recursive_returns	int	Maximum number of times recursive return loops closings can fail.
jit_max_polymorphic_calls	int	Maximum number of times polymorphic (dynamic or method) calls can be inlined. Any call above this limit is classed as megamorphic and is not inlined.

Table 10.2 – Additional opcache.jit* php.ini file settings

As you can see from the table, you have a high degree of control over how the JIT compiler operates. Collectively, these settings represent thresholds that control decisions the JIT compiler makes. These settings, if properly configured, allow the JIT compiler to ignore infrequently used loops and function calls. We'll now leave the exciting world of the JIT compiler and have a look at how to improve array performance.

Speeding up array handling

Arrays are a vital part of any PHP program. Indeed, dealing with arrays is unavoidable as much of the real-world data your program handles day to day arrives in the form of an array. One example is data from an HTML form posting. The data ends up in either `$_GET` or `$_POST` as an array.

In this section, we'll introduce you to a little-known class included with the SPL: the `SplFixedArray` class. Migrating your data from a standard array over to a `SplFixedArray` instance will not only improve performance but requires significantly less memory as well. Learning how to take advantage of the techniques covered in this chapter can have a substantial impact on the speed and efficiency of any program code currently using arrays with a massive amount of data.

Working with SplFixedArray in PHP 8

The `SplFixedArray` class, introduced in PHP 5.3, is literally an object that acts like an array. Unlike `ArrayObject`, however, this class requires you to place a hard limit on the array size, and only allows integer indices. The reason why you might want to use `SplFixedArray` rather than `ArrayObject` is `SplFixedArray` takes significantly less memory and is highly performant. In fact, `SplFixedArray` actually takes *less memory* than a standard array with the same data!

Comparing SplFixedArray with array and ArrayObject

A simple benchmark program illustrates the differences between a standard array, `ArrayObject`, and `SplFixedArray`:

1. First, we define a couple of constants used later in the code:

    ```
    // /repo/ch10/php7_spl_fixed_arr_size.php
    define('MAX_SIZE', 1000000);
    define('PATTERN', "%14s : %8.8f : %12s\n");
    ```

2. Next, we define a function that adds 1 million elements comprised of a string 64 bytes long:

    ```
    function testArr($list, $label) {
        $alpha = new InfiniteIterator(
            new ArrayIterator(range('A','Z')));
        $start_mem = memory_get_usage();
        $start_time = microtime(TRUE);
        for ($x = 0; $x < MAX_SIZE; $x++) {
            $letter = $alpha->current();
            $alpha->next();
            $list[$x] = str_repeat($letter, 64);
        }
        $mem_diff = memory_get_usage() - $start_mem;
    ```

Speeding up array handling

```
            return [$label, (microtime(TRUE) - $start_time),
                number_format($mem_diff)];
        }
```

3. We then call the function three times, supplying `array`, `ArrayObject`, and `SplFixedArray` respectively as arguments:

```
printf("%14s : %10s : %12s\n", '', 'Time', 'Memory');
$result = testArr([], 'Array');
vprintf(PATTERN, $result);
$result = testArr(new ArrayObject(), 'ArrayObject');
vprintf(PATTERN, $result);
$result = testArr(
    new SplFixedArray(MAX_SIZE), 'SplFixedArray');
vprintf(PATTERN, $result);
```

4. Here are the results from our PHP 7.1 Docker container:

```
root@php8_tips_php7 [ /repo/ch10 ]#
php php7_spl_fixed_arr_size.php
                :       Time :       Memory
          Array : 1.19430900 :  129,558,888
    ArrayObject : 1.20231009 :  129,558,832
  SplFixedArray : 1.19744802 :   96,000,280
```

5. In PHP 8, the amount of time taken is significantly less, as shown here:

```
root@php8_tips_php8 [ /repo/ch10 ]#
php php7_spl_fixed_arr_size.php
                :       Time :       Memory
          Array : 0.13694692 :  129,558,888
    ArrayObject : 0.11058593 :  129,558,832
  SplFixedArray : 0.09748793 :   96,000,280
```

As you can see from the results, PHP 8 handles arrays 10 times faster than PHP 7.1. The amount of memory used is identical between the two versions. What stands out, using either version of PHP, is that `SplFixedArray` uses significantly less memory than either a standard array or `ArrayObject`. Let's now have a look at how `SplFixedArray` usage has changed in PHP 8.

Working with SplFixedArray changes in PHP 8

You might recall a brief discussion on the `Traversable` interface in *Chapter 7, Avoiding Traps When Using PHP 8 Extensions*, in the *Traversable to IteratorAggregate migration* section. The same considerations brought out in that section also apply to `SplFixedArray`. Although `SplFixedArray` does not implement `Traversable`, it does implement `Iterator`, which in turn extends `Traversable`.

In PHP 8, `SplFixedArray` no longer implements `Iterator`. Instead, it implements `IteratorAggregate`. The benefit of this change is that `SplFixedArray` in PHP 8 is faster, more efficient, and also safe to use in nested loops. The downside, and also a potential code break, is if you are using `SplFixedArray` along with any of these methods: `current()`, `key()`, `next()`, `rewind()`, or `valid()`.

If you need access to array navigation methods, you now must use the `SplFixedArray::getIterator()` method to access the inner iterator, from which all of the navigation methods are available. A simple code example, shown here, illustrates the potential code break:

1. We start by building an `SplFixedArray` instance from an array:

```
// /repo/ch10/php7_spl_fixed_arr_iter.php
$arr    = ['Person', 'Woman', 'Man', 'Camera',
'TV'];$fixed = SplFixedArray::fromArray($arr);
```

2. We then use array navigation methods to iterate through the array:

```
while ($fixed->valid()) {
    echo $fixed->current() . '. ';
    $fixed->next();
}
```

In PHP 7, the output is the five words in the array:

```
root@php8_tips_php7 [ /repo/ch10 ]#
php php7_spl_fixed_arr_iter.php
Person. Woman. Man. Camera. TV.
```

In PHP 8, however, the result is quite different, as seen here:

```
root@php8_tips_php8 [ /repo/ch10 ]#
php php7_spl_fixed_arr_iter.php
```

```
PHP Fatal error:  Uncaught Error:  Call to undefined method
SplFixedArray::valid() in /repo/ch10/php7_spl_fixed_arr_iter.
php:5
```

In order to get the example working in PHP 8, all you need to do is to use the `SplFixedArray::getIterator()` method to access the inner iterator. The remainder of the code does not need to be rewritten. Here is the revised code example rewritten for PHP 8:

```php
// /repo/ch10/php8_spl_fixed_arr_iter.php
$arr   = ['Person', 'Woman', 'Man', 'Camera', 'TV'];
$obj   = SplFixedArray::fromArray($arr);
$fixed = $obj->getIterator();
while ($fixed->valid()) {
    echo $fixed->current() . '. ';
    $fixed->next();
}
```

The output is now the five words, without any errors:

```
root@php8_tips_php8 [ /repo/ch10 ]#
php php8_spl_fixed_arr_iter.php
Person. Woman. Man. Camera. TV.
```

Now that you have an idea of how to improve array handling performance, we'll turn our attention to yet another aspect of array performance: sorting.

Implementing stable sort

When designing the logic for array sorting, the original PHP developers sacrificed stability for speed. At the time, this was considered a reasonable sacrifice. However, if complex objects are involved in the sorting process, a **stable sort** is needed.

In this section, we discuss what stable sort is, and why it's important. If you can ensure that data is stably sorted, your application code will produce more accurate output, which results in greater customer satisfaction. Before we get into the details of how PHP 8 enables stable sorting, we first need to define what a stable sort is.

Understanding stable sorts

When the values of properties used for the purposes of a sort are equal, in a *stable sort* the original order of elements is guaranteed. Such a result is closer to user expectations. Let's have a look at a simple dataset and determine what would comprise a stable sort. For the sake of illustration, let's assume our dataset includes entries for access time and username:

2021-06-01 11:11:11	Betty
2021-06-03 03:33:33	Betty
2021-06-01 11:11:11	Barney
2021-06-02 02:22:22	Wilma
2021-06-01 11:11:11	Wilma
2021-06-03 03:33:33	Barney
2021-06-01 11:11:11	Fred

If we wish to sort by time, you will note right away that there are duplications for `2021-06-01 11:11:11`. If we were to perform a stable sort on this dataset, the expected outcome would appear as follows:

2021-06-01 11:11:11	Betty
2021-06-01 11:11:11	Barney
2021-06-01 11:11:11	Wilma
2021-06-01 11:11:11	Fred
2021-06-02 02:22:22	Wilma
2021-06-03 03:33:33	Betty
2021-06-03 03:33:33	Barney

You'll notice from the sorted dataset that entries for the duplicate time of `2021-06-01 11:11:11` appear in the order they were originally entered. Thus, we can say that this result represents a stable sort.

In an ideal world, the same principle should also apply to a sort that retains the key/value association. One additional criterion for a stable sort is that it should offer no difference in performance compared to an unregulated sort.

> **Tip**
> For more information on PHP 8 stable sorts, have a look at the official RFC here: `https://wiki.php.net/rfc/stable_sorting`.

In PHP 8, the core *sort*() functions and ArrayObject::*sort*() methods have been rewritten to achieve a stable sort. Let's have a look at a code example that illustrates the issue that may arise in earlier versions of PHP.

Contrasting stable and non-stable sorting

In this example, we wish to sort an array of Access instances by time. Each Access instance has two properties, $name and $time. The sample dataset contains duplicate access times, but with different usernames:

1. First, we define the Access class:

   ```
   // /repo/src/Php8/Sort/Access.php
   namespace Php8\Sort;
   class Access {
       public $name, $time;
       public function __construct($name, $time) {
           $this->name = $name;
           $this->time = $time;
       }
   }
   ```

2. Next, we define a sample dataset that consists of a CSV file, /repo/sample_data/access.csv, with 21 rows. Each row represents a different name and access time combination:

   ```
   "Fred",   "2021-06-01 11:11:11"
   "Fred",   "2021-06-01 02:22:22"
   "Betty",  "2021-06-03 03:33:33"
   "Fred",   "2021-06-11 11:11:11"
   "Barney", "2021-06-03 03:33:33"
   "Betty",  "2021-06-01 11:11:11"
   "Betty",  "2021-06-11 11:11:11"
   "Barney", "2021-06-01 11:11:11"
   "Fred",   "2021-06-11 02:22:22"
   "Wilma",  "2021-06-01 11:11:11"
   "Betty",  "2021-06-13 03:33:33"
   "Fred",   "2021-06-21 11:11:11"
   "Betty",  "2021-06-21 11:11:11"
   ```

```
"Barney","2021-06-13 03:33:33"
"Betty", "2021-06-23 03:33:33"
"Barney","2021-06-11 11:11:11"
"Barney","2021-06-21 11:11:11"
"Fred",  "2021-06-21 02:22:22"
"Barney","2021-06-23 03:33:33"
"Wilma", "2021-06-21 11:11:11"
"Wilma", "2021-06-11 11:11:11"
```

You will note, scanning the sample data, that all of the dates that have `11:11:11` as an entry time are duplicates, however, you will also note that the original order for any given date is always users `Fred`, `Betty`, `Barney`, and `Wilma`. Additionally, note that for dates with a time of `03:33:33`, entries for `Betty` always precede `Barney`.

3. We then define a calling program. The first thing to do in this program is to configure autoloading and use the `Access` class:

```
// /repo/ch010/php8_sort_stable_simple.php
require __DIR__ .
'/../src/Server/Autoload/Loader.php';
$loader = new \Server\Autoload\Loader();
use Php8\Sort\Access;
```

4. Next, we load the sample data into the `$access` array:

```
$access = [];
$data = new SplFileObject(__DIR__
    . '/../sample_data/access.csv');
while ($row = $data->fgetcsv())
    if (!empty($row) && count($row) === 2)
        $access[] = new Access($row[0], $row[1]);
```

5. We then execute `usort()`. Note that the user-defined callback function performs a comparison of the `time` properties of each instance:

```
usort($access,
    function($a, $b) { return $a->time <=> $b->time; });
```

6. Finally, we loop through the newly sorted array and display the result:

```
foreach ($access as $entry)
    echo $entry->time . "\t" . $entry->name . "\n";
```

In PHP 7, note that although the times are in order, the names do not reflect the expected order Fred, Betty, Barney, and Wilma. Here is the PHP 7 output:

```
root@php8_tips_php7 [ /repo/ch10 ]#
php php8_sort_stable_simple.php
2021-06-01 02:22:22    Fred
2021-06-01 11:11:11    Fred
2021-06-01 11:11:11    Wilma
2021-06-01 11:11:11    Betty
2021-06-01 11:11:11    Barney
2021-06-03 03:33:33    Betty
2021-06-03 03:33:33    Barney
2021-06-11 02:22:22    Fred
2021-06-11 11:11:11    Barney
2021-06-11 11:11:11    Wilma
2021-06-11 11:11:11    Betty
2021-06-11 11:11:11    Fred
2021-06-13 03:33:33    Barney
2021-06-13 03:33:33    Betty
2021-06-21 02:22:22    Fred
2021-06-21 11:11:11    Fred
2021-06-21 11:11:11    Betty
2021-06-21 11:11:11    Barney
2021-06-21 11:11:11    Wilma
2021-06-23 03:33:33    Betty
2021-06-23 03:33:33    Barney
```

As you can see from the output, in the first set of 11:11:11 dates, the final order is Fred, Wilma, Betty, and Barney, whereas the original order of entry was Fred, Betty, Barney, and Wilma. You'll also notice that for the date and time 2021-06-13 03:33:33, Barney precedes Betty whereas the original order of entry is the reverse. According to our definition, PHP 7 does not implement a stable sort!

Let's now have a look at the same code example running in PHP 8. Here is the PHP 8 output:

```
root@php8_tips_php8 [ /repo/ch10 ]#
php php8_sort_stable_simple.php
2021-06-01 02:22:22    Fred
2021-06-01 11:11:11    Fred
2021-06-01 11:11:11    Betty
2021-06-01 11:11:11    Barney
2021-06-01 11:11:11    Wilma
2021-06-03 03:33:33    Betty
2021-06-03 03:33:33    Barney
2021-06-11 02:22:22    Fred
2021-06-11 11:11:11    Fred
2021-06-11 11:11:11    Betty
2021-06-11 11:11:11    Barney
2021-06-11 11:11:11    Wilma
2021-06-13 03:33:33    Betty
2021-06-13 03:33:33    Barney
2021-06-21 02:22:22    Fred
2021-06-21 11:11:11    Fred
2021-06-21 11:11:11    Betty
2021-06-21 11:11:11    Barney
2021-06-21 11:11:11    Wilma
2021-06-23 03:33:33    Betty
2021-06-23 03:33:33    Barney
```

As you can see from the PHP 8 output, for all of the `11:11:11` entries, the original order of entry `Fred`, `Betty`, `Barney`, and `Wilma` is respected. You'll also notice that for the date and time `2021-06-13 03:33:33`, `Betty` precedes `Barney` consistently. Thus, we can conclude that PHP 8 performs a stable sort.

Now that you can see the issue in PHP 7, and are now aware that PHP 8 addresses and resolves this issue, let's have a look at the effect on keys in stable sorting.

Examining the effect of stable sorting on keys

The concept of stable sorting also affects key/value pairs when using `asort()`, `uasort()`, or the equivalent `ArrayIterator` methods. In the example shown next, `ArrayIterator` is populated with 20 elements, every other element being a duplicate. The key is a hexadecimal number that increments sequentially:

1. First, we define a function to produce random 3-letter combinations:

   ```
   // /repo/ch010/php8_sort_stable_keys.php
   $randVal = function () {
       $alpha = 'ABCDEFGHIJKLMNOPQRSTUVWXYZ';
       return $alpha[rand(0,25)] . $alpha[rand(0,25)]
           . $alpha[rand(0,25)];};
   ```

2. Next, we load an `ArrayIterator` instance with sample data. Every other element is a duplicate. We also capture the starting time:

   ```
   $start = microtime(TRUE);
   $max   = 20;
   $iter  = new ArrayIterator;
   for ($x = 256; $x < $max + 256; $x += 2) {
       $key = sprintf('%04X', $x);
       $iter->offsetSet($key, $randVal());
       $key = sprintf('%04X', $x + 1);
       $iter->offsetSet($key, 'AAA'); // <-- duplicate
   }
   ```

3. We then perform `ArrayIterator::asort()` and display the resulting order along with the elapsed time:

   ```
   // not all code is shown
   $iter->asort();
   foreach ($iter as $key => $value) echo "$key\t$value\n";
   echo "\nElapsed Time: " . (microtime(TRUE) - $start);
   ```

Here is the result of this code example running in PHP 7:

```
root@php8_tips_php7 [ /repo/ch10 ]#
php php8_sort_stable_keys.php
0113    AAA
```

010D	AAA
0103	AAA
0105	AAA
0111	AAA
0107	AAA
010F	AAA
0109	AAA
0101	AAA
010B	AAA
0104	CBC
... some output omitted ...	
010C	ZJW
Elapsed Time: 0.00017094612121582	

As you can see from the output, although the values are in order, in the case of duplicate values, the keys appear in chaotic order. In contrast, have a look at the output from the same program code running in PHP 8:

root@php8_tips_php8 [/repo/ch10]#	
php php8_sort_stable_keys.php	
0101	AAA
0103	AAA
0105	AAA
0107	AAA
0109	AAA
010B	AAA
010D	AAA
010F	AAA
0111	AAA
0113	AAA
0100	BAU
... some output omitted ...	
0104	QEE
Elapsed Time: 0.00010395050048828	

The output shows that the keys for any duplicate entries appear in the output in their original order. The output demonstrates that PHP 8 implements stable sorting for not only values but for keys as well. Further, as the elapsed time results show, PHP 8 has managed to retain the same (or better) performance as before. Let's now turn our attention to another difference in PHP 8 that directly affects array sorting: the handling of illegal sort functions.

Handling illegal sort functions

PHP 7 and earlier allows developers to get away with an **illegal function** when using `usort()` or `uasort()` (or the equivalent `ArrayIterator` methods). It's extremely important for you to be aware of this bad practice. Otherwise, when you migrate your code to PHP 8, a potential backward-compatibility break exists.

In the example shown next, the same array is created as in the example described in the *Contrasting stable and non-stable sorting* section. The *illegal* sort function returns a Boolean value, whereas the `u*sort()` callback needs to return the *relative position* between the two elements. In literal terms, the user-defined function, or callback, needs to return -1 if the first operand is less than the second, 0 if equal, and 1 if the first operand is greater than the second. If we rewrite the line of code the defines the `usort()` callback, an illegal function might appear as follows:

```
usort($access, function($a, $b) {
    return $a->time < $b->time; });
```

In this code snippet, instead of using the spaceship operator (<=>), which would return -1, 0, or 1, we use a less-than symbol (<). In PHP 7 and below, a callback that returns a boolean return value is acceptable and produces the desired results. But what actually happens is that the PHP interpreter needs to add an additional operation to make up the missing operation. Thus, if the callback only performs this comparison:

`op1 > op2`

The PHP interpreter adds an additional operation:

`op1 <= op2`

In PHP 8, illegal sort functions spawn a deprecation notice. Here is the rewritten code running in PHP 8:

```
root@php8_tips_php8 [ /repo/ch10 ]#
php php8_sort_illegal_func.php
PHP Deprecated:  usort(): Returning bool from comparison
function is deprecated, return an integer less than, equal to,
```

```
or greater than zero in /repo/ch10/php8_sort_illegal_func.php
on line 30
2021-06-01 02:22:22      Fred
2021-06-01 11:11:11      Fred
2021-06-01 11:11:11      Betty
2021-06-01 11:11:11      Barney
... not all output is shown
```

As you can see from the output, PHP 8 allows the operation to continue, and the results are consistent when using the proper callback. However, you can also see that a `Deprecation` notice is issued.

> **Tip**
> You can also use the arrow function in PHP 8. The callback shown previously might be rewritten as follows:
> `usort($array, fn($a, $b) => $a <=> $b)`.

You now have a greater understanding of what a stable sort is, and why it's important. You also are able to spot potential problems due to differences in handling between PHP 8 and earlier versions. We'll now have a look at other performance improvements introduced in PHP 8.

Using weak references to improve efficiency

As PHP continues to grow and mature, more and more developers are turning to PHP frameworks to facilitate rapid application development. A necessary by-product of this practice, however, is ever larger and more complex objects occupying memory. Large objects that contain many properties, other objects, or sizeable arrays are often referred to as **expensive objects**.

Compounding the potential memory issues caused by this trend is the fact that all PHP object assignments are automatically made by reference. Without references, the use of third-party frameworks would become cumbersome in the extreme. When you assign an object by reference, however, the object must remain in memory, in its entirety, until all references are destroyed. Only then, after unsetting or overwriting the object, is it entirely destroyed.

In PHP 7.4, a potential solution to this problem was introduced in the form of weak reference support. PHP 8 expanded upon this new ability by adding a weak map class. In this section, you'll learn how this new technology works, and how it can prove advantageous to development. Let's first have a look at weak references.

Taking advantage of weak references

Weak references were first introduced in PHP 7.4, and have been refined in PHP 8. This class serves as a wrapper for object creation that allows the developer to use references to objects in such a manner whereby out-of-scope (for example, `unset()`) objects are not protected from garbage collection.

There are a number of PHP extensions currently residing on `pecl.php.net` that provide support for weak references. Most of the implementations hack into the C language structures of the PHP language core, and either overload object handlers, or manipulate the stack and various C pointers. The net result, in most cases, is a loss of portability and lots of segmentation faults. The PHP 8 implementation avoids these problems.

It's important to master the use of PHP 8 weak references if you are working on program code that involves large objects and where the program code might run for a long time. Before getting into usage details, let's have a look at the class definition.

Reviewing the WeakReference class definition

The formal definition for the `WeakReference` class is as follows:

```
WeakReference {
    public __construct() : void
    public static create (object $object) : WeakReference
    public get() : object|null
}
```

As you can see, the class definition is quite simple. The class can be used to provide a wrapper around any object. The wrapper makes it easier to completely destroy an object without fear there may be a lingering reference causing the object to still reside in memory.

> **Tip**
>
> For more information on the background and nature of weak references, have a look here: https://wiki.php.net/rfc/weakrefs. The documentation reference is here: https://www.php.net/manual/en/class.weakreference.php.

Let's now have a look at a simple example to help your understanding.

Using weak references

This example demonstrates how weak references could be used. You will see in this example that when a normal object assignment by reference is made, even if the original object is unset, it still remains loaded in memory. On the other hand, if you assign the object reference using `WeakReference`, once the original object is unset, it's completely removed from memory:

1. First, we define four objects. Note that `$obj2` is a normal reference to `$obj1`, whereas `$obj4` is a weak reference to `$obj3`:

   ```
   // /repo/ch010/php8_weak_reference.php
   $obj1 = new class () { public $name = 'Fred'; };
   $obj2 = $obj1;  // normal reference
   $obj3 = new class () { public $name = 'Fred'; };
   $obj4 = WeakReference::create($obj3); // weak ref
   ```

2. We then display the contents of `$obj2` before and after `$obj1` is unset. Because the connection between `$obj1` and `$obj2` is a normal PHP reference, `$obj1` remains in memory due to the strong reference created:

   ```
   var_dump($obj2);
   unset($obj1);
   var_dump($obj2);  // $obj1 still loaded in memory
   ```

3. We then do the same for `$obj3` and `$obj4`. Note that we need to use `WeakReference::get()` to obtain the associated object. Once `$obj3` is unset, all information pertaining to both `$obj3` and `$obj4` is removed from memory:

   ```
   var_dump($obj4->get());
   unset($obj3);
   var_dump($obj4->get()); // both $obj3 and $obj4 are gone
   ```

Here is the output from this code example running in PHP 8:

```
root@php8_tips_php8 [ /repo/ch10 ]#
php php8_weak_reference.php
object(class@anonymous)#1 (1) {
  ["name"]=> string(4) "Fred"
}
object(class@anonymous)#1 (1) {
  ["name"]=> string(4) "Fred"
}
object(class@anonymous)#2 (1) {
  ["name"]=> string(4) "Fred"
}
NULL
```

The output tells us an interesting story! The second `var_dump()` operation shows us that even though `$obj1` has been unset, it still lives on like a zombie because of the strong reference created with `$obj2`. If you are dealing with expensive objects and complex application code, in order to free up memory, you'll need to first hunt down and destroy all the references before memory is freed!

On the other hand, if you really need the memory, instead of making a direct object assignment, which in PHP is automatically by reference, create the reference using the `WeakReference::create()` method. A weak reference has all the power of a normal reference. The only difference is that if the object it refers to is destroyed or goes out of scope, the weak reference is automatically destroyed as well.

As you can see from the output, the result of the last `var_dump()` operation was `NULL`. This tells us that the object has truly been destroyed. When the main object is unset, all of its weak references go away automatically. Now that you have an idea of how to use weak references, and the potential problem they solve, it's time to take a look at a new class, `WeakMap`.

Working with WeakMap

In PHP 8, a new class, `WeakMap`, has been added that leverages weak reference support. The new class is similar to `SplObjectStorage` in functionality. Here is the official class definition:

```
final WeakMap implements Countable,
    ArrayAccess, IteratorAggregate {
```

```
public __construct ( )
public count ( ) : int
abstract public getIterator ( ) : Traversable
public offsetExists ( object $object ) : bool
public offsetGet ( object $object ) : mixed
public offsetSet ( object $object , mixed $value ) : void
public offsetUnset ( object $object ) : void
}
```

Just like `SplObjectStorage`, this new class appears as an array of objects. Because it implements `IteratorAggregate`, you can use the `getIterator()` method, to gain access to the inner iterator. Thus, the new class offers not only traditional array access, but OOP iterator access as well, the best of both worlds! Before getting into the details of how to use `WeakMap`, it's important for you to understand typical usage for `SplObjectStorage`.

Implementing a container class using SplObjectStorage

A potential use for the `SplObjectStorage` class is to use it to form the basis of a **dependency injection** (**DI**) container (also referred to as a **service locator** or **inversion of control** container). DI container classes are designed to create and hold instances of objects for easy retrieval.

In this example, we load a container class with an array of expensive objects drawn from the `Laminas\Filter\*` classes. We then use the container to sanitize sample data, after which we unset the array of filters:

1. First, we define a container class based on `SplObjectStorage`. (Later, in the next section, we develop another container class that does the same thing and is based upon `WeakMap`.) Here is the `UsesSplObjectStorage` class. In the `__construct()` method, we attach configured filters to the `SplObjectStorage` instance:

```
// /repo/src/Php7/Container/UsesSplObjectStorage.php
namespace Php7\Container;
use SplObjectStorage;
class UsesSplObjectStorage {
    public $container;
```

```
    public $default;
    public function __construct(array $config = []) {
        $this->container = new SplObjectStorage();
        if ($config) foreach ($config as $obj)
            $this->container->attach(
                $obj, get_class($obj));
        $this->default = new class () {
            public function filter($value) {
                return $value; }};
    }
```

2. We then define a `get()` method that iterates through the `SplObjectStorage` container and returns the filter if found. If not found, a default class that simply passes the data straight through is returned:

```
    public function get(string $key) {
        foreach ($this->container as $idx => $obj)
            if ($obj instanceof $key) return $obj;
        return $this->default;
    }
}
```

Note that when using a `foreach()` loop to iterate a `SplObjectStorage` instance, we return the *value* (`$obj`), not the key. If we're using a `WeakMap` instance, on the other hand, we need to return the *key* and not the value!

We then define a calling program that uses our newly created `UsesSplObjectStorage` class to contain the filter set:

1. First, we define autoloading and use the appropriate classes:

```
// /repo/ch010/php7_weak_map_problem.php
require __DIR__ .
    '/../src/Server/Autoload/Loader.php';
loader = new \Server\Autoload\Loader();
use Laminas\Filter\ {StringTrim, StripNewlines,
    StripTags, ToInt, Whitelist, UriNormalize};
use Php7\Container\UsesSplObjectStorage;
```

2. Next, we define an array of sample data:

```
$data = [
    'name'    => '<script>bad JavaScript</script>name',
    'status'  => 'should only contain digits 9999',
    'gender'  => 'FMZ only allowed M, F or X',
    'space'   => "  leading/trailing whitespace or\n",
    'url'     => 'unlikelysource.com/about',
];
```

3. We then assign filters that are required for all fields (`$required`) and filters specific to certain fields (`$added`):

```
$required = [StringTrim::class,
             StripNewlines::class, StripTags::class];
$added = ['status'  => ToInt::class,
          'gender'  => Whitelist::class,
          'url'     => UriNormalize::class ];
```

4. After that, we create an array of filter instances, used to populate our service container, `UseSplObjectStorage`. Please bear in mind that each filter class carries a lot of overhead and can be considered an *expensive* object:

```
$filters = [
    new StringTrim(),
    new StripNewlines(),
    new StripTags(),
    new ToInt(),
    new Whitelist(['list' => ['M','F','X']]),
    new UriNormalize(['enforcedScheme' => 'https']),
];
$container = new UsesSplObjectStorage($filters);
```

5. We now cycle through the data files using our container class to retrieve filter instances. The `filter()` method produces a sanitized value specific to that filter:

```
foreach ($data as $key => &$value) {
    foreach ($required as $class) {
        $value = $container->get($class)->filter($value);
    }
```

```
            if (isset($added[$key])) {
                $value = $container->get($added[$key])
                                   ->filter($value);
            }
        }
        var_dump($data);
```

6. Finally, we grab memory statistics to form the basis of comparison between `SplObjectStorage` and `WeakMap` usage. We also unset `$filters`, which should theoretically release a sizeable amount of memory. We run `gc_collect_cycles()` to force the PHP garbage collection process, releasing freed memory back into the pool:

```
$mem = memory_get_usage();
unset($filters);
gc_collect_cycles();
$end = memory_get_usage();
echo "\nMemory Before Unset: $mem\n";
echo "Memory After  Unset: $end\n";
echo 'Difference          : ' . ($end - $mem) . "\n";
echo 'Peak Memory Usage   : ' . memory_get_peak_usage();
```

Here is the result, running in PHP 8, of the calling program just shown:

```
root@php8_tips_php8 [ /repo/ch10 ]#
php php7_weak_map_problem.php
array(5) {
  ["name"]=> string(18) "bad JavaScriptname"
  ["status"]=> int(0)
  ["gender"]=> NULL
  ["space"]=> string(30) "leading/trailing whitespace or"
  ["url"]=> &string(32) "https://unlikelysource.com/about"
}
Memory Before Unset: 518936
Memory After  Unset: 518672
Difference          :    264
Peak Memory Usage   : 780168
```

As you can see from the output, our container class works perfectly, giving us access to any of the stored filter classes. What is also of interest is that the memory released following the `unset($filters)` command is 264 bytes: not very much!

You now have an idea of the typical usage of the `SplObjectStorage` class. Let's now have a look at a potential problem with the `SplObjectStorage` class, and how `WeakMap` solves it.

Understanding the benefits of WeakMap over SplObjectStorage

The main problem with `SplObjectStorage` is that when an assigned object gets unset or otherwise goes out of scope, it still remains in memory. The reason for this is when the object is attached to the `SplObjectStorage` instance, it's done by reference.

If you're only dealing with a small number of objects, you'll probably not experience any serious issues. If you use `SplObjectStorage` and assign a large number of expensive objects for storage, this could eventually cause memory leaks in long-running programs. If, on the other hand, you use a `WeakMap` instance for storage, garbage collection is allowed to remove the object, which in turn frees up memory. When you start to integrate `WeakMap` instances into your regular programming practice, you end up with more efficient code that takes up much less memory.

> **Tip**
>
> For more information about `WeakMap`, have a look at the original RFC here: https://wiki.php.net/rfc/weak_maps. Also have a look at the documentation: https://www.php.net/weakMap.

Let's now rewrite the example from the previous section (`/repo/ch010/php7_weak_map_problem.php`), but this time using `WeakMap`:

1. As described in the previous code example, we define a container class called `UsesWeakMap` that holds our expensive filter classes. The main difference between this class and the one shown in the previous section is that `UsesWeakMap` uses `WeakMap` instead of `SplObjectStorage` for storage. Here is the class setup and `__construct()` method:

```
// /repo/src/Php7/Container/UsesWeakMap.php
namespace Php8\Container;
use WeakMap;
class UsesWeakMap {
```

```php
        public $container;
        public $default;
        public function __construct(array $config = []) {
            $this->container = new WeakMap();
            if ($config)
                foreach ($config as $obj)
                    $this->container->offsetSet(
                        $obj, get_class($obj));
            $this->default = new class () {
                public function filter($value) {
                    return $value; }};
        }
```

2. Another difference between the two classes is that `WeakMap` implements `IteratorAggregate`. However, this still allows us to use a simple `foreach()` loop in the `get()` method:

```php
        public function get(string $key) {
            foreach ($this->container as $idx => $obj)
                if ($idx instanceof $key) return $idx;
            return $this->default;
        }
    }
```

Note that when using a `foreach()` loop to iterate a `WeakMap` instance, we return the *key* (`$idx`) and not the value!

3. We then define a calling program that invokes the autoloader and uses the appropriate filter classes. The biggest difference between this calling program and the one from the previous section is that we use our new container class that's based upon `WeakMap`:

```php
// /repo/ch010/php8_weak_map_problem.php
require __DIR__ .
    '/../src/Server/Autoload/Loader.php';
$loader = new \Server\Autoload\Loader();
use Laminas\Filter\ {StringTrim, StripNewlines,
    StripTags, ToInt, Whitelist, UriNormalize};
use Php8\Container\**UsesWeakMap**;
```

4. As in the previous example, we define an array of sample data and assign filters. This code is not shown as it's identical to *steps 2* and *3* of the previous example.

5. We then create filter instances in an array that serves as an argument to our new container class. We use the array of filters as an argument to create the container class instance:

```
$filters = [
    new StringTrim(),
    new StripNewlines(),
    new StripTags(),
    new ToInt(),
    new Whitelist(['list' => ['M','F','X']]),
    new UriNormalize(['enforcedScheme' => 'https']),
];
$container = new UsesWeakMap($filters);
```

6. Finally, exactly as shown in *step 6* from the previous example, we cycle through the data and apply filters from the container class. We also collect and display memory statistics.

Here is the output, running in PHP 8, for the revised program using `WeakMap`:

```
root@php8_tips_php8 [ /repo/ch10 ]#
php php8_weak_map_problem.php
array(5) {
  ["name"]=> string(18) "bad JavaScriptname"
  ["status"]=> int(0)
  ["gender"]=> NULL
  ["space"]=> string(30) "leading/trailing whitespace or"
  ["url"]=> &string(32) "https://unlikelysource.com/about"
}
Memory Before Unset: 518712
Memory After Unset: 517912
Difference         :    800
Peak Memory Usage  : 779944
```

As you might expect, overall memory usage is slightly lower. The biggest difference, however, is the difference in memory after unsetting `$filters`. In the previous example, the difference was `264` bytes. In this example, using `WeakMap` produced a difference of `800` bytes. This means that using `WeakMap` has the potential to free up more than three times the amount of memory compared with using `SplObjectStorage`!

This ends our discussion of weak references and weak maps. You are now in a position to write code that is more efficient and uses less memory. The larger the objects being stored, the greater the potential for memory saving.

Summary

In this chapter, you learned not only how the new JIT compiler works, but you gained an understanding of the traditional PHP interpret-compile-execute cycle. Using PHP 8 and enabling the JIT compiler has the potential to speed up your PHP application anywhere from three times faster and up.

In the next section, you learned what a stable sort is, and how PHP 8 implements this vital technology. By mastering the stable sort, your code will produce data in a rational manner, resulting in greater customer satisfaction.

The section following introduced you to a technique that can vastly improve performance and reduce memory consumption by taking advantage of the `SplFixedArray` class. After that, you learned about PHP 8 support for weak references as well as the new `WeakMap` class. Using the techniques covered in this chapter will cause your applications to execute much quicker, run more efficiently, and use less memory.

In the next chapter, you'll learn how to perform a successful migration to PHP 8.

11
Migrating Existing PHP Apps to PHP 8

Throughout the book, you have been warned of potential code breaks. Unfortunately, there are not really any good tools available that can scan your existing code and check for potential code breaks. In this chapter, we take you through the development of a set of classes that form the basis of a PHP 8 **backward-compatible** (**BC**) break scanner. In addition, you learn the recommended process to migrate an existing customer PHP application to PHP 8.

After reading through this chapter and carefully studying the examples, you are much better equipped to handle a PHP 8 migration. With knowledge of the overall migration procedure, you gain confidence and are able to perform PHP 8 migrations with a minimal number of problems.

The topics covered in this chapter include the following:

- Understanding development, staging, and production environments
- Learning how to spot BC breaks before a migration
- Performing the migration
- Testing and troubleshooting the migration

Technical requirements

To examine and run the code examples provided in this chapter, the minimum recommended hardware is the following:

- An x86_64-based desktop PC or laptop
- 1 **gigabyte** (**GB**) free disk space
- 4 GB of RAM
- 500 **kilobits per second** (**Kbps**) or faster internet connection

In addition, you will need to install the following software:

- Docker
- Docker Compose

Please refer to the *Technical requirements* section of *Chapter 1, Introducing New PHP 8 OOP Features*, for more information on Docker and Docker Compose installation, as well as how to build the Docker container used to demonstrate the code explained in this book. In this book, we refer to the directory in which you restored the sample code for this book as `/repo`.

The source code for this chapter is located at `https://github.com/PacktPublishing/PHP-8-Programming-Tips-Tricks-and-Best-Practices`. We can now begin our discussion by having a look at environments used as part of the overall migration process.

Understanding development, staging, and production environments

The ultimate goal for a website update is to move the updated application code from development to production in as seamless a manner as possible. This movement of application code is referred to as **deployment**. Movement, in this context, involves copying application code and configuration files from one **environment** to another.

Before we get into the details of migrating an application to PHP 8, let's first have a look at what these environments are. Gaining an understanding of what form the different environments might take is critical to your role as a developer. With this understanding, you are in a better position to deploy your code to production with a minimal amount of errors.

Defining an environment

We use the word *environment* to describe a combination of software stacks that include the operating system, web server, database server, and PHP installation. In the past, the environment equated to a *server*. In this modern age, however, the term *server* is deceptive in that it implies a physical computer in a metal box sitting on a rack in some unseen server room. Today, this is more likely not going to be the case, given the abundance of cloud service providers and highly performant virtualization technologies (for example, Docker). Accordingly, when we use the term *environment*, understand this to mean either a physical or virtual server.

Environments are generally classified into three distinct categories: **development**, **staging**, and **production**. Some organizations also provide a separate **testing** environment. Let's first have a look at what is common across all environments.

Common components

It's important to note that what goes into all environments is driven by what is in the production environment. The production environment is the final destination of your application code. Accordingly, all other environments should match the operating system, database, web server, and PHP installation as closely as possible. Thus, for example, if the production environment enables the PHP OPCache extension, all other environments must enable this extension as well.

All environments, including the production environment, need to have an operating system and PHP installation at a minimum. Depending on the needs of your application, it's also quite common to have a web server and database server installed. The type and version of the web and database server should match that of the production environment as closely as possible.

As a general rule, the closer your development environment matches that of the production environment, the less chance there is of a bug cropping up after deployment.

We now look at what goes into a development environment.

Development environment

The development environment is where you initially develop and test your code. It is unique in that it has the tools needed for application maintenance and development. This would include housing a source code repository (for example, Git), as well as various scripts needed to start, stop, and reset the environment.

Often the development environment will have scripts to trigger an automated deployment procedure. Such scripts could take the place of **commit hooks**, designed to activate when you issue a commit to your source code repository. One example of this is **Git Hooks**, script files that can be placed in the `.git/hooks` directory.

> **Tip**
> For more information on Git Hooks, have a look at the documentation here: `https://git-scm.com/book/en/v2/Customizing-Git-Git-Hooks`.

The traditional development environment consisted of a personal computer with a database server, web server, and PHP. This conventional paradigm fails to take into account the variations that might be present in the target production environment. If you have 12 customers that you work with regularly, for example, it's highly unlikely that all 12 customers have exactly the same OS, database server, web server, and version of PHP! The *best practice* is to model the production environment as closely as possible in the form of a virtual machine or Docker container.

The code editor or **IDE (Integrated Development Environment)** is thus not located inside the development environment. Rather, you perform code creation and editing outside of the development environment. You would then push your changes locally either by directly copying files into the virtual development environment via a shared directory, or by committing changes to the source code repository, and then pulling the changes from inside the development environment virtual machine.

It's also appropriate to perform unit testing in the development environment. Developing unit tests will not only give you greater assurance that your code works in production, but is also a great way to spot bugs in the early stages of application development. And, of course, you need to do as much debugging as possible in the local environment! Catching and fixing a bug in development generally takes a tenth of the time you might spend fixing a bug found in production!

Let's now examine the staging environment.

Staging environment

It's quite common for large application development projects to have multiple developers all working on the same code base. In this situation, using version control repositories is critical. The *staging* environment is where all of the developers upload their code after development environment testing and debugging phases are complete.

The staging environment must be an *exact copy* of the production environment. You can visualize the staging environment as the last step on an assembly line in a car plant. This is where all of the various pieces coming from one or more development environments are fit into place. The staging environment is a prototype of how production should appear.

It's important to note that often the staging server has direct internet access; however, it's usually located in a secure area that requires a password before you can gain access.

Finally, let's have a look at the production environment.

Production environment

The production environment is often maintained and hosted by the client directly. This environment is also referred to as the **live environment**. To make an analogy to a Bollywood production, if the development environment is practice, the staging environment is the dress rehearsal, and the production environment is the live show (perhaps minus the singing and dancing!).

The production environment has direct internet access but is protected by a firewall, and is often further protected by an intrusion detection and prevention system (for example, `https://snort.org/`). In addition, the production environment may be hidden behind a reverse proxy configuration that runs on an internet-facing web server. Otherwise, at least theoretically, the production environment should be an *exact clone* of the staging environment.

Now that you have an idea about the environments through which the application code moves on its way from development to production, let's have a look at a critical first step in a PHP 8 migration: spotting potential BC code breaks.

Learning how to spot BC breaks before a migration

Ideally, you should go into the PHP 8 migration with an action plan in hand. A critical part of this action plan includes getting an idea of how many potential BC breaks exist in your current code base. In this section, we show you how to develop a BC break sniffer that automates the process of looking through hundreds of code files for potential BC breaks.

First, we'll step back and review what we've learned so far about BC issues that might arise in PHP 8.

Gaining an overview of BC breaks

You already know, having read the previous chapters in this book, that potential code breaks originate from several sources. Let's briefly summarize the general trends that might lead to code failure after a migration. Please note that we do not cover these topics in this chapter as these are the topics that have all been covered in earlier chapters in this book:

- Resource-to-object migration
- Minimum versions for supporting OS libraries
- `Iterator` to `IteratorAggregate` migration
- Removed functions
- Usage changes
- Magic method signature enforcement

Many of the changes can be detected by adding a simple callback based upon `preg_match()` or `strpos()`. Usage changes are much more difficult to detect as at a glance there's no way for an automated break scanner to detect the result of usage without making extensive use of `eval()`.

Let's now have a look at how a break scan configuration file might appear.

Creating a BC break scan configuration file

A configuration file allows us to develop a set of search patterns independently of the BC break scanner class. Using this approach, the BC break scanner class defines the actual logic used to conduct the search whereas the configuration file provides a list of specific conditions along with a warning and suggested remedial actions.

Quite a few potential code breaks can be detected by simply looking for the presence of the functions that have been removed in PHP 8. For this purpose, a simple `strpos()` search will suffice. On the other hand, a more complex search might require that we develop a series of callbacks. Let's first have a look at how configuration might be developed based on a simple `strpos()` search.

Defining a simple strpos() search configuration

In the case of a simple `strpos()` search, all we need to do is to provide an array of key/value pairs, where the key is the name of the removed function, and the value is its suggested replacement. The search logic in the BC break scanner class can then do this:

```
$contents = file_get_contents(FILE_TO_SEARCH);
foreach ($config['removed'] as $key => $value)
    if (str_pos($contents, $key) !== FALSE) echo $value;
```

We will cover the full BC break scanner class implementation in the next section. For now, we just focus on the configuration file. Here's how the first few `strpos()` search entries might appear:

```
// /repo/ch11/bc_break_scanner.config.php
use Migration\BreakScan;
return [
    // not all keys are shown
    BreakScan::KEY_REMOVED => [
        '__autoload' => 'spl_autoload_register(callable)',
        'each' => 'Use "foreach()" or ArrayIterator',
        'fgetss' => 'strip_tags(fgets($fh))',
        'png2wbmp' => 'imagebmp',
        // not all entries are shown
    ],
];
```

Unfortunately, some PHP 8 backward incompatibilities might prove beyond the abilities of a simple `strpos()` search. We now turn our attention toward detecting potential breaks caused by the PHP 8 resource-to-object migration.

Detecting BC breaks associated with is_resource()

In *Chapter 7, Avoiding Traps When Using PHP 8 Extensions*, in the *PHP 8 extension resource to object migration* section, you learned that there is a general trend in PHP away from resources and toward objects. As you may recall, this trend in and of itself does not pose any threat of a BC break. However, if, in confirming that the connection has been made, your code uses `is_resource()`, there is a potential for a BC break.

In order to account for this BC break potential, our BC break scan configuration file needs to list any of the functions that formerly produced a resource but now produce an object. We then need to add a method in the BC break scan class (discussed next) that makes use of this list.

This is how the potential configuration key of affected functions might appear:

```
// /repo/ch11/bc_break_scanner.config.php
return [     // not all keys are shown
    BreakScan::KEY_RESOURCE => [
        'curl_init',
        'xml_parser_create',
        // not all entries are shown
    ],
];
```

In the break scan class, all we need to do is to first confirm that `is_resource()` is called, and then check to see if any of the functions listed under the `BreakScan::KEY_RESOURCE` array are present.

We now turn out attention to **magic method signature** violations.

Detecting magic method signature violations

PHP 8 strictly enforces magic method signatures. If your classes use loose definitions where you do not perform method signature data typing, and if you do not define a return value data type for magic methods, you are safe from a potential code break. On the other hand, if your magic method signatures do contain data types, and those data types do not match the strictly defined set enforced in PHP 8, you have a potential code break on your hands!

Accordingly, we need to create a set of regular expressions needed to detect magic method signature violations. In addition, our configuration should include the correct signature. In this manner, if a violation is detected, we can present the correct signature in the resulting message, speeding up the update process.

This is how a magic method signature configuration might appear:

```
// /repo/ch11/bc_break_scanner.config.php
use Php8\Migration\BreakScan;
return [
    BreakScan::KEY_MAGIC => [
```

```
    '__call' => [ 'signature' =>
        '__call(string $name, array $arguments): mixed',
        'regex' => '/__call\s*\((string\s)?'
            . '\$.+?(array\s)?\$.+?\)(\s*:\s*mixed)?/',
        'types' => ['string', 'array', 'mixed']],
    // other configuration keys not shown
    '__wakeup' => ['signature' => '__wakeup(): void',
        'regex' => '/__wakeup\s*\(\)(\s*:\s*void)?/',
        'types' => ['void']],
    ]
    // other configuration keys not shown
];
```

You might notice that we included an extra option, `types`. This is included in order to automatically generate a regular expression. The code that does this is not shown. If you are interested, have a look at /path/to/repo/ch11/php7_build_magic_signature_regex.php.

Let's have a look at how you might handle complex break detection where a simple `strpos()` search is not sufficient.

Addressing complex BC break detection

In the case where a simple `strpos()` search proves insufficient, we can develop another set of key/value pairs where the value is a callback. As an example, take the potential BC break where a class defines a `__destruct()` method, but also uses `die()` or `exit()` in the `__construct()` method. In PHP 8 it's possible the `__destruct()` method might not get called under these circumstances.

In such a situation, a simple `strpos()` search is insufficient. Instead, we must develop logic that does the following:

- Checks to see if a `__destruct()` method is defined. If so, no need to continue further as there is no danger of a break in PHP 8.
- Checks to see if `die()` or `exit()` is used in the `__construct()` method. If so, issue a warning of a potential BC break.

In our BC break scan configuration array, the callback takes the form of an anonymous function. It accepts the file contents as an argument. We then assign the callback to an array configuration key and include the warning message to be delivered if the callback returns TRUE:

```php
// /repo/ch11/bc_break_scanner.config.php
return [
    // not all keys are shown
    BreakScan::KEY_CALLBACK => [
      'ERR_CONST_EXIT' => [
        'callback' => function ($contents) {
            $ptn = '/__construct.*?\{.*?(die|exit).*?}/im';
            return (preg_match($ptn, $contents)
                && strpos('__destruct', $contents)); },
        'msg' => 'WARNING: __destruct() might not get '
            . 'called if "die()" or "exit()" used '
            . 'in __construct()'],
    ], // etc.
    // not all entries are shown
];
```

In our BC break scanner class (discussed next), the logic needed to invoke the callbacks might appear as follows:

```php
$contents = file_get_contents(FILE_TO_SEARCH);
$className = 'SOME_CLASS';
foreach ($config['callbacks'] as $key => $value)
    if ($value['callback']($contents)) echo $value['msg'];
```

If the requirements to detect additional potential BC breaks are beyond the capabilities of a callback, we would then define a separate method directly inside the BC break scan class.

As you can see, it's possible to develop a configuration array that supports not only simple `strpos()` searches, but also searches of greater complexity using an array of callbacks.

Now that you have an idea of what would go into a configuration array, it's time to define the main class that performs the break scanning.

Developing a BC break scan class

The `BreakScan` class is oriented toward a single file. In this class, we define methods that utilize the various break scan configuration just covered. If we need to scan multiple files, the calling program produces a list of files and passes them to `BreakScan` one at a time.

The `BreakScan` class can be broken down into two main parts: methods that define infrastructure, and methods that define how to conduct given scans. The latter is primarily dictated by the structure of the configuration file. For each configuration file section, we'll need a `BreakScan` class method.

Let's have a look at the infrastructural methods first.

Defining BreakScan class infrastructural methods

In this section, we have a look at the initial part of the `BreakScan` class. We also cover methods that perform infrastructure-related activities:

1. First, we set up the class infrastructure, placing it in the `/repo/src/Php8/Migration` directory:

   ```php
   // /repo/src/Php8/Migration/BreakScan.php
   declare(strict_types=1);
   namespace Php8\Migration;
   use InvalidArgumentException;
   use UnexpectedValueException;
   class BreakScan {
   ```

2. Next, we define a set of class constants to render messages indicating the nature of any given post-scan failure:

   ```php
   const ERR_MAGIC_SIGNATURE = 'WARNING: magic method '
       . 'signature for %s does not appear to match '
       . 'required signature';
   const ERR_NAMESPACE = 'WARNING: namespaces can no '
       . 'longer contain spaces in PHP 8.';
   const ERR_REMOVED = 'WARNING: the following function'
       . 'has been removed: %s.  Use this instead: %s';
   // not all constants are shown
   ```

3. We also define a set of constants that represent configuration array keys. We do this to maintain consistency between key definitions in the configuration file and calling program (discussed later):

```php
const KEY_REMOVED  = 'removed';
const KEY_CALLBACK = 'callbacks';
const KEY_MAGIC    = 'magic';
const KEY_RESOURCE = 'resource';
```

4. We then initialize key properties, representing the configuration, the contents of the file to be scanned, and any messages:

```php
public $config = [];
public $contents = '';
public $messages = [];
```

5. The `__construct()` method accepts our break scan configuration file as an argument, and cycles through all of the keys to ensure they exist:

```php
public function __construct(array $config) {
    $this->config = $config;
    $required = [self::KEY_CALLBACK,
        self::KEY_REMOVED,
        self::KEY_MAGIC,
        self::KEY_RESOURCE];
    foreach ($required as $key) {
        if (!isset($this->config[$key])) {
            $message = sprintf(
                self::ERR_MISSING_KEY, $key);
            throw new Exception($message);
        }
    }
}
```

6. We then define a method that reads in the contents of the file to be scanned. Note that we remove carriage returns (`"\r"`) and linefeeds (`"\n"`) in order to make scanning via regular expression easier to process:

```php
public function getFileContents(string $fn) {
    if (!file_exists($fn)) {
```

```
            self::$className = '';
            $this->contents  = '';
            throw new Exception(
                sprintf(self::ERR_FILE_NOT_FOUND, $fn));
        }
        $this->contents = file_get_contents($fn);
        $this->contents = str_replace(["\r","\n"],
            ['', ' '], $this->contents);
        return $this->contents;
    }
```

7. Some of the callbacks need a way to extract just the class name, or just the namespace. For that purpose, we define the static `getKeyValue()` method:

```
public static function getKeyValue(
    string $contents, string $key, string $end) {
    $pos = strpos($contents, $key);
    $end = strpos($contents, $end,
        $pos + strlen($key) + 1);
    return trim(substr($contents,
        $pos + strlen($key),
        $end - $pos - strlen($key)));
}
```

This method looks for the keyword (for example, `class`). It then finds whatever follows the keyword up to the delimiter (for example, `';'`). So, if you want to get the class name, you would execute the following: `$name = BreakScan::geyKeyValue($contents,'class',';')`.

8. We also need a way to retrieve and reset `$this->messages`. Here are the two methods to do that:

```
public function clearMessages() : void {
    $this->messages = [];
}
public function getMessages(bool $clear = FALSE) {
    $messages = $this->messages;
    if ($clear) $this->clearMessages();
    return $messages;
}
```

9. We then define a method that runs all scans (covered in the next section). This method also collects the number of potential BC breaks detected and reports back the total:

```
public function runAllScans() : int {
    $found = 0;
    $found += $this->scanRemovedFunctions();
    $found += $this->scanIsResource();
    $found += $this->scanMagicSignatures();
    $found += $this->scanFromCallbacks();
    return $found;
}
```

Now that you have an idea of how the basic `BreakScan` class infrastructure might appear, let's have a look at the individual scan methods.

Examining individual scan methods

The four individual scan methods correspond directly to the top-level keys in the break scan configuration file. Each method is expected to accumulate messages about potential BC breaks in `$this->messages`. In addition, each method is expected to return an integer representing the total number of potential BC breaks detected.

Let's now examine these methods in order:

1. The first method we examine is `scanRemovedFunctions()`. In this method, we search for the function name followed either directly by an open parenthesis, `'('`, or by a space and open parenthesis, `' ('`. If the function is found, we increment `$found`, and add the appropriate warning and suggested replacement to `$this-> messages`. If no potential breaks are found, we add a success message and return 0:

```
public function scanRemovedFunctions() : int {
    $found = 0;
    $config = $this->config[self::KEY_REMOVED];
    foreach ($config as $func => $replace) {
        $search1 = '' . $func . '(';
        $search2 = '' . $func . ' (';
        if (
            strpos($this->contents, $search1) !== FALSE
            ||
```

```
                strpos($this->contents, $search2) !== FALSE)
            {
                $this->messages[] = sprintf(
                    self::ERR_REMOVED, $func, $replace);
                $found++;
            }
        }
        if ($found === 0)
            $this->messages[] = sprintf(
                self::OK_PASSED, __FUNCTION__);
        return $found;
    }
```

The main problem with this approach is that if the function is not preceded by a space, its use would not be detected. However, if we do not include the leading space in the search, we could end up with a false positive. For example, without the leading space, every single instance of `foreach()` would trigger a warning by the break scanner when looking for `each()`!

2. Next we have a look at a method that scans for `is_resource()` usage. If a reference is located, this method runs through the list of functions that no longer produce a resource. If both `is_resource()` and one of these methods is located, a potential BC break is flagged:

```
    public function scanIsResource() : int {
        $found = 0;
        $search = 'is_resource';
        if (strpos($this->contents, $search) === FALSE)
            return 0;
        $config = $this->config[self::KEY_RESOURCE];
        foreach ($config as $func) {
            if ((strpos($this->contents, $func) !== FALSE)) {
                $this->messages[] =
                    sprintf(self::ERR_IS_RESOURCE, $func);
                $found++;
            }
        }
        if ($found === 0)
            $this->messages[] =
```

```php
            sprintf(self::OK_PASSED, __FUNCTION__);
        return $found;
}
```

3. We then have a look at what's required to go through our list of callbacks. As you recall, we need to employ callbacks in situations where a simple `strpos()` is insufficient. Accordingly, we first collect all the callback subkeys and loop through each one in turn. If there is no bottom-level key *callback*, we throw an `Exception`. Otherwise, we run the callback, supplying `$this->contents` as an argument. If any potential BC breaks are found, we add the appropriate error message, and increment `$found`:

```php
public function scanFromCallbacks() {
    $found = 0;
    $list = array_keys($this-config[self::KEY_CALLBACK]);
    foreach ($list as $key) {
        $config = $this->config[self::KEY_CALLBACK][$key]
            ?? NULL;
        if (empty($config['callback'])
            || !is_callable($config['callback'])) {
            $message = sprintf(self::ERR_INVALID_KEY,
                self::KEY_CALLBACK . ' => '
                . $key . ' => callback');
            throw new Exception($message);
        }
        if ($config['callback']($this->contents)) {
            $this->messages[] = $config['msg'];
            $found++;
        }
    }
    return $found;
}
```

4. Finally, we turn to by far the most complex method, which scans for invalid magic method signatures. The primary problem is that the method signatures vary widely, thus we need to build separate regular expressions to properly test validity. The regular expressions are stored in the BC break configuration file. If a magic method is detected, we retrieve its correct signature and add that to $this->messages.

5. First, we check to see if there are any magic methods by looking for anything that matches function __:

```
public function scanMagicSignatures() : int {
    $found   = 0;
    $matches = [];
    $result  = preg_match_all(
        '/function __(.+?)\b/',
        $this->contents, $matches);
```

6. If the array of matches is not empty, we loop through the set of matches and assign to $key the magic method name:

```
if (!empty($matches[1])) {
    $config = $this->config[self::KEY_MAGIC] ?? NULL;
    foreach ($matches[1] as $name) {
        $key = '__' . $name;
```

7. If the configuration key matching this presumed magic method is not set, we assume it's either not a magic method, or is a method not in the configuration file, and thus nothing to worry about. Otherwise, if a key is present, we extract a substring representing the method call that is assigned to $sub:

```
if (empty($config[$key])) continue;
if ($pos = strpos($this->contents, $key)) {
    $end = strpos($this->contents,
        '{', $pos);
    $sub = (empty($sub) || !is_string($sub))
        ? '' : trim($sub);
```

8. We then pull the regular expression from the configuration and match it against the substring. The pattern represents a proper signature for that particular magic method. If preg_match() returns FALSE, we know the actual signature is incorrect and flag it as a potential BC break. We retrieve and store the warning message and increment $found:

```
            $ptn = $config[$key]['regex'] ?? '/.*/';
            if (!preg_match($ptn, $sub)) {
                $this->messages[] = sprintf(
                    self::ERR_MAGIC_SIGNATURE, $key);
                $this->messages[] =
                    $config[$key]['signature']
                    ?? 'Check signature'
                $found++;
}}}}
    if ($found === 0)
        $this->messages[] = sprintf(
            self::OK_PASSED, __FUNCTION__);
    return $found;
}
```

This concludes our examination of the BreakScan class. Now we turn our attention to defining the calling program needed to run the scans programmed into the BreakScan class.

Building a BreakScan class calling program

The main job of the program that calls the BreakScan class is to accept a path argument and to recursively build a list of PHP files located in that path. We then loop through the list, extracting the contents of each file in turn, and run BC break scans. At the end, we present a report that can be either sparse or verbose, depending on the verbosity level selected.

Bear in mind that both the `BreakScan` class and the calling program we are about to discuss are designed to run under PHP 7. The reason we do not use PHP 8 is because we assume that a developer would wish to run the BC break scanner *before* they do a PHP 8 update:

1. We start by configuring the autoloader and getting the path and verbosity levels either from the command line (`$argv`) or from the URL (`$_GET`). In addition, we present an option to write the results to a CSV file and accept as a parameter the name of such a file. You might note that we also perform a degree of input sanitization, although theoretically the BC break scanner will only be used on a development server, directly by a developer:

```php
// /repo/ch11/php7_bc_break_scanner.php
define('DEMO_PATH', __DIR__);
require __DIR__ . '/../src/Server/Autoload/Loader.php';
$loader = new \Server\Autoload\Loader();
use Php8\Migration\BreakScan;
// some code not shown
$path = $_GET['path'] ?? $argv[1] ?? NULL;
$show = $_GET['show'] ?? $argv[2] ?? 0;
$show = (int) $show;
$csv  = $_GET['csv']  ?? $argv[3] ?? '';
$csv  = basename($csv);
```

2. We next confirm the path. If it's not found, we exit and display usage information (`$usage` is not shown):

```php
if (empty($path)) {
    if (!empty($_SERVER['REQUEST_URI']))
        echo '<pre>' . $usage . '</pre>';
    else
        echo $usage;
    exit;
}
```

3. We then grab the BC break configuration file and create a `BreakScan` instance:

```
$config = include __DIR__
    . '/php8_bc_break_scanner_config.php';
$scanner = new BreakScan($config);
```

4. To build a list of files we use a `RecursiveDirectoryIterator`, wrapped inside a `RecursiveIteratorIterator`, starting from the given path. This list is then filtered by `FilterIterator`, limiting the scan to PHP files only:

```
$iter = new RecursiveIteratorIterator(
    new RecursiveDirectoryIterator($path));
$filter = new class ($iter) extends FilterIterator {
    public function accept() {
        $obj = $this->current();
        return ($obj->getExtension() === 'php');
    }
};
```

5. If the developer chooses the CSV option, an `SplFileObject` instance is created. At the same time, we write out an array of headers. Further, we define an anonymous function that writes to the CSV file:

```
if ($csv) {
    $csv_file = new SplFileObject($csv, 'w');
    $csv_file->fputcsv(
        ['Directory','File','OK','Messages']);
}
$write = function ($dir, $fn, $found, $messages)
    use ($csv_file) {
    $ok = ($found === 0) ? 1 : 0;
    $csv_file->fputcsv([$dir, $fn, $ok, $messages]);
    return TRUE;
};
```

6. We launch the scan by looping through the list of files presented by the `FilterIterator` instance. As we are scanning file by file, on each pass `$found` is zeroed out. We do maintain `$total`, however, to give a total count of potential BC breaks at the end. You might also note that we distinguish files from directories. If the directory changes, its name is displayed as a header:

```
$dir   = '';
$total = 0;
foreach ($filter as $name => $obj) {
    $found = 0;
    $scanner->clearMessages();
    if (dirname($name) !== $dir) {
        $dir = dirname($name);
        echo "Processing Directory: $name\n";
    }
```

7. We use `SplFileObject::isDir()` to determine if the item in the file list is a directory. If so, we continue with the next item on the list. We then push the file contents into `$scanner` and run all scans. Messages are then retrieved in the form of a string:

```
    if ($obj->isDir()) continue;
    $fn = basename($name);
    $scanner->getFileContents($name);
    $found    = $scanner->runAllScans();
    $messages = implode("\n", $scanner->getMessages());
```

8. We use a `switch()` block to take action based on the display level represented by `$show`. Level 0 only shows files where potential BC breaks are found. Level 1 shows that plus messages. Level 2 shows all possible output, including success messages:

```
    switch ($show) {
        case 2 :
            echo "Processing: $fn\n";
            echo "$messages\n";
            if ($csv)
                $write($dir, $fn, $found, $messages);
            break;
        case 1 :
            if (!$found) break;
```

```php
            echo "Processing: $fn\n";
            echo BreakScan::WARN_BC_BREAKS . "\n";
            printf(BreakScan::TOTAL_BREAKS, $found);
            echo "$messages\n";
            if ($csv)
                $write($dir, $fn, $found, $messages);
            break;
        case 0 :
        default :
            if (!$found) break;
            echo "Processing: $fn\n";
            echo BreakScan::WARN_BC_BREAKS . "\n";
            if ($csv)
                $write($dir, $fn, $found, $messages);
    }
```

9. Finally, we accumulate the totals and display the final results:

```php
    $total += $found;
}
echo "\n" . str_repeat('-', 40) . "\n";
echo "\nTotal number of possible BC breaks: $total\n";
```

Now that you have an idea how the calling might appear, let's have a look at the results of a test scan.

Scanning application files

For demonstration purposes, in the source code associated with this book, we have included an older version of **phpLdapAdmin**. You can find the source code at /path/to/repo/sample_data/phpldapadmin-1.2.3. For this demonstration, we opened a shell into the PHP 7 container and ran the following command:

```
root@php8_tips_php7 [ /repo ]#
php ch11/php7_bc_break_scanner.php \
    sample_data/phpldapadmin-1.2.3/ 1 |less
```

Here is a partial result from running this command:

```
Processing: functions.php
WARNING: the code in this file might not be
compatible with PHP 8
Total potential BC breaks: 4
WARNING: the following function has been removed: function
  __autoload.
Use this instead: spl_autoload_register(callable)
WARNING: the following function has been removed: create_
function.  Use this instead: Use either "function () {}" or "fn
() => <expression>"
WARNING: the following function has been removed: each.
  Use this instead: Use "foreach()" or ArrayIterator
PASSED this scan: scanIsResource
PASSED this scan: scanMagicSignatures
WARNING: using the "@" operator to suppress warnings
no longer works in PHP 8.
```

As you can see from the output, although `functions.php` passed the `scanMagicSignatures` and `scanIsResource` scans, this code file used three functions that have been removed in PHP 8: `__autoload()`, `create_function()`, and `each()`. You'll also note that this file uses the `@` symbol to suppress errors, which is no longer effective in PHP 8.

If you specified the CSV file option, you can open it in any spreadsheet program. Here's how it appears in Libre Office Calc:

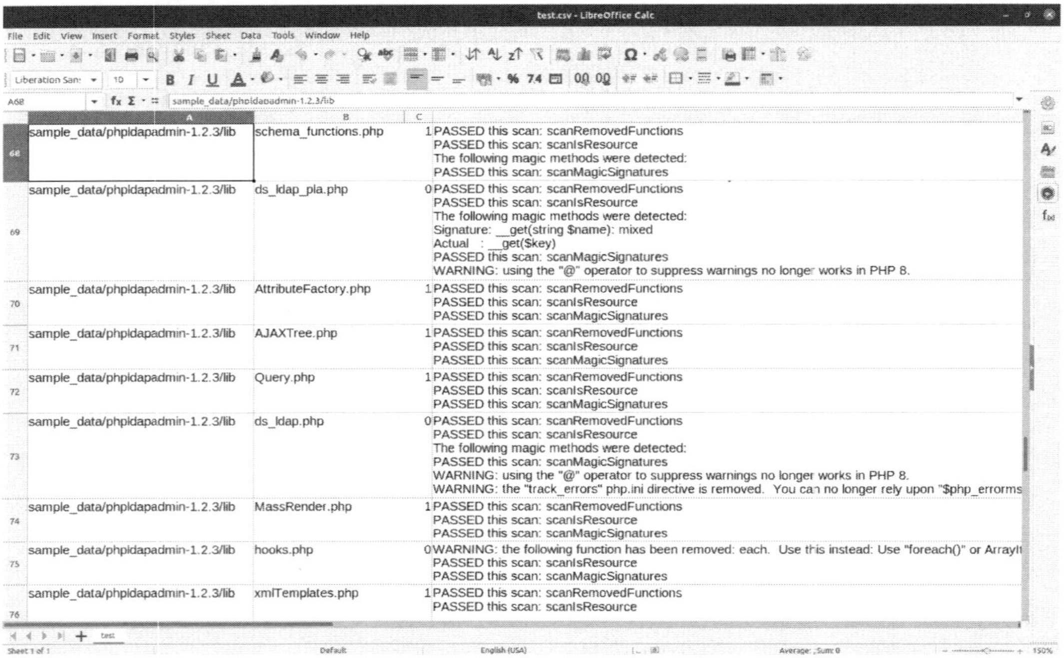

Figure 11.1 – CSV file open in Libre Office Calc

You now have an idea of how to create an automated procedure to detect potential BC breaks. Please bear in mind that the code is far from perfect and doesn't cover every single possible code break. For that, you must rely upon your own judgment after having carefully reviewed the material in this book.

It's now time to turn our attention to the actual migration itself.

Performing the migration

Performing the actual migration from your current version to PHP version 8 is much like the process of deploying a new set of features to an existing application. If possible, you might consider running two websites in parallel until such time as you are confident the new version works as expected. Many organizations run the staging environment in parallel with the production environment for this purpose.

In this section, we present a **twelve-step guide** to perform a successful migration. Although we are focused on migrating to PHP 8, these twelve steps can apply to any PHP update you may wish to perform. Understanding and following these steps carefully is critical to the success of your production website. Included in the twelve steps are plenty of places where you can revert to an earlier version if you encounter problems.

Before we get into details, here is a general overview of a twelve-step migration process going from an older version of PHP to PHP 8:

1. Carefully review the appropriate migration guide located in the PHP documentation appendices. In our case, we choose *Migrating from PHP 7.4x to PHP 8.0x*. (`https://www.php.net/manual/en/appendices.php`).
2. Make sure your current code works on the current version of PHP.
3. Back up the database (if any), all source code, and any associated files and assets (for example, CSS, JavaScript, or graphics images).
4. Create a new branch for the soon-to-be-updated application code in your version control software.
5. Scan for BC breaks (possibly using the `BreakScan` class discussed in the previous section).
6. Update any incompatible code.
7. Repeat *steps* 5 and 6 as needed.
8. Upload your source code to the repository.
9. Test the source code in a virtual environment updated to PHP 8 that closely simulates the production server.
10. If the virtualized simulation is not successful, return to *step 5*.
11. Update the staging server (or equivalent virtual environment) to PHP 8, making sure you can switch back to the old version.
12. Run every test you can imagine. If not successful, switch back to the master branch and return to *step 5*. If successful, clone the staging environment to production.

Let's now look at each step in turn.

Step 1 – Review the migration guide

With every major release of PHP, the PHP core team posts a **migration guide**. The guide we are mainly concerned with in this book is *Migrating from PHP 7.4.x to PHP 8.0.x*, located at `https://www.php.net/manual/en/migration80.php`. This migration guide is broken down into four sections:

- New Features
- Backward Incompatible Changes
- Deprecated Features
- Other Changes

If you are migrating to PHP 8.0 from a version other than PHP 7.4, you should also review all of the past migration guides from your current PHP version, up to PHP 8. We'll now have a look at other recommended steps in the migration process.

Step 2 – Make sure the current code works

Before you start to make changes to the current code base to ensure it works in PHP 8, it's absolutely critical for you to make sure it's working. If the code isn't working now, it surely will not work once you migrate to PHP 8! Run any unit tests along with any **black-box tests** to ensure the code is functioning correctly in the current version of PHP.

If you make any changes to the current code before migration, be sure these changes are reflected in the main branch (often called the **master branch**) of your version control software.

Step 3 – Back up everything

The next step is to back up everything. This includes the database, source code, JavaScript, CSS, images, and so forth. Also, please do not forget to back up important configuration files such as the `php.ini` file, the webserver configuration, and any other configuration file associated with PHP and web communications.

Step 4 – Create a version control branch

In this step, you should create a new branch in your version control system and check out that branch. In the main branch, you should only have code that currently works.

This is how such a command might work using Git:

```
$ git branch php8_migration
$ git checkout php8_migration
Switched to branch 'php8_migration'
```

The first command shown creates a branch called `php8_migration`. The second command causes `git` to switch to the new branch. In the process, all of your existing code gets ported to the new branch. The main branch is now safe and preserved from any changes made while in the new branch.

For more information on version control using Git, have a look here: https://git-scm.com/.

Step 5 – Scan for BC breaks

Now it's time to put the `BreakScan` class to good use. Run the calling program and supply as arguments the starting directory path for your project as well as a verbosity level (0, 1, or 2). You can also specify a CSV file as a third option, as shown earlier in *Figure 11.1*.

Step 6 – Fix incompatibilities

In this step, knowing where the breaks reside, you can proceed to fix the incompatibilities. You should be able to do so in such a way that the code continues to run in the current version of PHP but can also run in PHP 8. As we've pointed out consistently throughout this book, BC breaks, for the most part, stem from bad coding practices. By fixing the incompatibilities, you improve your code at the same time.

Step 7 – Repeat steps 5 and 6 as needed

There's a famous line, repeated in many Hollywood movies, where the doctor says to the anxious patient, *take two aspirin and call me in the morning*. The same advice applies to the process of addressing BC breaks. You must be patient, and continue to fix and scan, fix and scan. Keep on doing this until the scan reveals no more potential BC breaks.

Step 8 – Commit changes to the repository

Once you are relatively confident there are no further BC breaks, it's time to commit changes to the new PHP 8 migration branch you created in your version control software. Go ahead and push the changes at this point. You are then in a position to retrieve the updated code from this branch once you've sorted out the PHP update on the production server.

Remember this important point: your current working code is safely stored in the main branch. You are only saving to the PHP 8 migration branch at this stage, so you can always switch back.

Step 9 – Test in a simulated virtual environment

Think of this step as a dress rehearsal for the real thing. In this step, you create a virtual environment (for example, using a Docker container) that most closely simulates the production server. In this virtual environment, you then install PHP 8. Once the virtual environment has been created, you can open a command shell into it, and download your source code from the PHP 8 migration branch.

You can then run unit tests, and any other tests you deem necessary in order to test the updated code. Hopefully, this is where you'll trap any additional errors.

Step 10 – Return to step 5 if the test is unsuccessful

If the unit tests, black-box tests, or other testing performed in the virtual environment show that your application code fails, you must return to *step 5*. To proceed to the live production site in the face of certain failure would be extremely ill-advised!

Step 11 – Install PHP 8 on the staging environment

The next step is to install PHP 8 in the staging environment. As you might recall from our discussion in the first part of this chapter, the traditional flow is from the development environment, to staging, and then on to production. Once all testing has been completed on the staging environment, you can then clone staging to production.

PHP installation is well documented on the main `php.net` website, so there is no need for further detail here. Instead, in this section we give you a light overview of PHP installation, with a focus on the ability to switch between PHP 8 and your current PHP version.

> **Tip**
> For information on installing PHP in various environments, consult this documentation page: https://www.php.net/manual/en/install.php.

For the purpose of illustration, we choose to discuss PHP 8 installation on two of the main branches of Linux: Debian/Ubuntu and Red Hat/CentOS/Fedora. Let's start with Debian/Ubuntu Linux.

Installing PHP 8 on Debian/Ubuntu Linux

The best way to install PHP 8 is via the available set of pre-compiled binaries. Newer PHP versions tend to be made available much later than their release date, and PHP 8 is no exception. In this case, it's recommended that you resort to using a (**Personal Package Archive(PPA)**). The PPA hosted at https://launchpad.net/~ondrej is the most extensive and widely used.

If you want to simulate the following steps on your own computer, run an Ubuntu Docker image with PHP 7.4 pre-installed using this command:

```
docker run -it \
    unlikelysource/ubuntu_focal_with_php_7_4:latest /bin/bash
```

In order to install PHP 8 on Debian or Ubuntu Linux, open a command shell onto the production server (or demo container), and, as the *root* user, proceed as follows. Alternatively, if *root* user access isn't available, preface each command shown with `sudo`.

From the command shell, to install PHP 8, proceed as follows:

1. Update and upgrade the current set of packages using the **apt** utility. Any package manager can be used; however, we show the use of `apt` to maintain consistency between the installation steps covered here:

    ```
    apt update
    apt upgrade
    ```

2. Add the `Ondrej PPA` repository to your `apt` sources:

    ```
    add-apt-repository ppa:ondrej/php
    ```

3. Install PHP 8. This installs only the PHP 8 core and basic extensions:

    ```
    apt install php8.0
    ```

4. Use the following command to scan the repository for additional extensions and use `apt` to install them as needed:

```
apt search php8.0-*
```

5. Do a PHP version check to ensure you're now running PHP 8:

```
php --version
```

Here is the version check output:

```
root@ec873e16ee93:/# php --version
PHP 8.0.7 (cli) (built: Jun  4 2021 21:26:10) ( NTS )
Copyright (c) The PHP Group
Zend Engine v4.0.7, Copyright (c) Zend Technologies
    with Zend OPcache v8.0.7, Copyright (c), by Zend Technologies
```

Now that you have a basic idea of how a PHP 8 installation might proceed, let's have a look at how to switch between the current version and PHP 8. For the purposes of illustration, we assume that PHP 7.4 is the current PHP version prior to the PHP 8 installation.

Switching between PHP versions in Debian and Ubuntu Linux

If you check to see where PHP is located, you will note that PHP 7.4, the earlier version, still exists following the PHP 8 installation. You can use `whereis php` for this purpose. The output on our simulation Docker Ubuntu container appears as follows:

```
root@ec873e16ee93:/# whereis php
php: /usr/bin/php /usr/bin/php8.0 /usr/bin/php7.4 /usr/lib/php
/etc/php /usr/share/php7.4-opcache /usr/share/php8.0-opcache
/usr/share/php8.0-readline /usr/share/php7.4-readline /usr/
share/php7.4-json /usr/share/php8.0-common /usr/share/php7.4-
common
```

As you can see, we now have both the 7.4 and 8.0 versions of PHP installed. To switch between the two, use this command:

```
update-alternatives --config php
```

You are then presented with an option screen allowing you to choose which PHP version should be active. Here is how the output screen appears on the Ubuntu Docker image:

```
root@ec873e16ee93:/# update-alternatives --config php
There are 2 choices for the alternative php
(providing /usr/bin/php).

  Selection    Path              Priority   Status
------------------------------------------------------------
* 0            /usr/bin/php8.0    80        auto mode
  1            /usr/bin/php7.4    74        manual mode
  2            /usr/bin/php8.0    80        manual mode
Press <enter> to keep the current choice[*], or type selection number:
```

After switching, you can execute `php --version` again to confirm that the other version of PHP is active.

Let's now turn our attention to PHP 8 installation on Red Hat Linux and its derivatives.

Installing PHP 8 on Red Hat, CentOS, or Fedora Linux

PHP installation on Red Hat, CentOS, or Fedora Linux follows a sequence of commands that are similar to the Debian/Ubuntu installation procedure. The main difference is that you would most likely use a combination of `dnf` and `yum` to install the pre-compiled PHP binaries.

If you care to follow along with the installation we outline in this section, you can use a Fedora Docker container with PHP 7.4 already installed. Here is the command to run the simulation:

```
docker run -it unlikelysource/fedora_34_with_php_7_4 /bin/bash
```

Much like the PPA environment described in the previous section, in the Red Hat world, the **Remi's RPM Repository** project (http://rpms.remirepo.net/) provides pre-compiled binaries in **Red Hat Package Management** (**RPM**) format.

To install PHP 8 on Red Hat, CentOS, or Fedora, open a command shell onto the production server (or demo environment) and, as the *root* user, and proceed as follows:

1. First of all, it's a good idea to confirm the OS version and release you're using. For that purpose, the `uname` command is used, along with a simple `cat` command to view the release (stored as a text file in the `/etc` directory):

   ```
   [root@9d4e8c93d7b6 /]# uname -a
   Linux 9d4e8c93d7b6 5.8.0-55-generic #62~20.04.1-Ubuntu
   SMP Wed Jun 2 08:55:04 UTC 2021 x86_64 x86_64 x86_64
   GNU/Linux
   [root@9d4e8c93d7b6 /]# cat /etc/fedora-release
   Fedora release 34 (Thirty Four)
   ```

2. Before getting started, be sure to update `dnf` and install the configuration manager:

   ```
   dnf upgrade
   dnf install 'dnf-command(config-manager)'
   ```

3. You would then add Remi's repository to your package sources, using the version number you prefer in place of NN:

   ```
   dnf install \
       https://rpms.remirepo.net/fedora/remi-release-NN.rpm
   ```

4. At this point, you can confirm the versions of PHP installed using `dnf module list`. We also use `grep` to limit the list of modules shown to PHP only. The `[e]` designation indicates *enabled*:

   ```
   [root@56b9fbf499d6 /]# dnf module list |grep php
   php                    remi-7.4 [e]    common [d] [i],
   devel, minimal         PHP scripting language
   php                    remi-8.0        common [d],
   devel, minimal         PHP scripting language
   ```

5. We then check the current version of PHP:

   ```
   [root@d044cbe477c8 /]# php --version
   PHP 7.4.20 (cli) (built: Jun 1 2021 15:41:56) (NTS)
   Copyright (c) The PHP Group
   Zend Engine v3.4.0, Copyright (c) Zend Technologies
   ```

6. Next, we reset the PHP module, and install PHP 8:

   ```
   dnf -y module reset php
   dnf -y module install php:remi-8.0
   ```

7. Another quick PHP version check shows us that we are now using PHP 8 instead of PHP 7:

   ```
   [root@56b9fbf499d6 /]# php -v
   PHP 8.0.7 (cli) (built: Jun  1 2021 18:43:05)
   ( NTS gcc x86_64 ) Copyright (c) The PHP Group
   Zend Engine v4.0.7, Copyright (c) Zend Technologies
   ```

8. To switch back to the earlier version of PHP, proceed as follows, where X.Y is the version you plan to use:

   ```
   dnf -y module reset php
   dnf -y module install php:remi-X.Y
   ```

This completes the PHP installation instructions for Red Hat, CentOS, or Fedora. For this demonstration, we only showed you the PHP command-line installation. If you plan to use PHP with a web server, you also need to install either the appropriate PHP web server package, and/or install the PHP-FPM (FastCGI Processing Module) package.

Let's now have a look at the last step.

Step 12 – Test and clone the staging environment to production

In the last step, you download the source code from your PHP 8 migration branch onto the staging environment and run every imaginable test to make sure everything's working. Once you are assured of success, you then clone the staging environment onto the production environment.

If you are using virtualization, the clone procedure might simply involve creating an identical Docker container or virtual disk file. Otherwise, if actual hardware is involved, you will probably end up cloning the hard drive, or whatever method is appropriate for your setup.

This concludes our discussion of how to perform the migration. Let's now have a look at testing and troubleshooting.

Testing and troubleshooting the migration

In an ideal world, the migration troubleshooting will take place on the staging server, or simulated virtual environment, well before the actual move to production. However, as the seasoned developer well knows, we need to hope for the best, but prepare for the worst! In this section, we cover additional aspects of testing and troubleshooting that can be easily overlooked.

For the purposes of this section, you can exit the temporary shell if you were following the Debian/Ubuntu or the Red Hat/CentOS/Fedora installation process. Return to the Docker container used for this course and open a command shell into the PHP 8 container. Please refer to the *Technical requirements* section of *Chapter 1, Introducing New PHP 8 OOP Features*, for more information on how to do this if you are unsure.

Testing and troubleshooting tools

There are too many fine testing and troubleshooting tools available to document here, so we focus on a few open source tools to help with testing and troubleshooting.

Working with Xdebug

Xdebug is a tool that provides diagnostics, profiling, tracing, and step-debugging, among other features. It's a PHP extension, and is thus able to give you detailed information in case you run into problems that you cannot easily solve. The main website is `https://xdebug.org/`.

To enable the Xdebug extension, you can install it just as you would any other PHP extension: using the `pecl` command, or by downloading and compiling the source code from `https://pecl.php.net/package/xdebug`.

Also, the following `/etc/php.ini` settings should be set, at a minimum:

```
zend_extension=xdebug.so
xdebug.log=/repo/xdebug.log
xdebug.log_level=7
xdebug.mode=develop,profile
```

Figure 11.2 shows the output using the `xdebug_info()` command called from `/repo/ch11/php8_xdebug.php`:

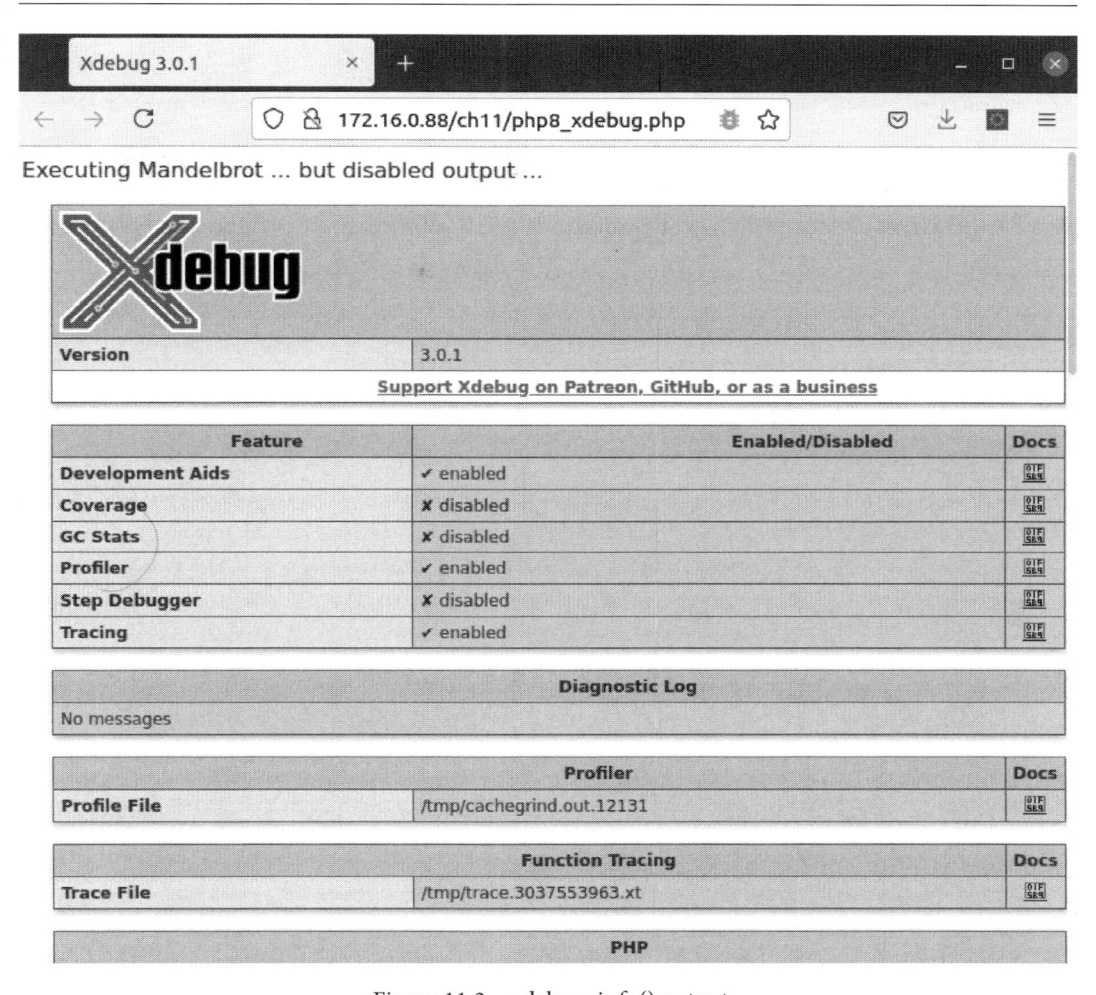

Figure 11.2 – xdebug_info() output

Let's now have a look at another tool that checks your application from an outside perspective.

Using Apache JMeter

An extremely useful open source tool for testing web applications is **Apache JMeter** (https://jmeter.apache.org/). It allows you to develop a series of test plans that simulate requests from a browser. You can simulate hundreds of user requests, each with their own cookies and session. Although mainly designed for HTTP or HTTPS, it's also capable of a dozen other protocols as well. In addition to an excellent graphical UI, it also has a command-line mode that makes it possible to incorporate JMeter in an automated deployment process.

Installation is quite simple, involving a single download from `https://jmeter.apache.org/download_jmeter.cgi`. You must have the **Java Virtual Machine (JVM)** installed before JMeter will run. Test plan execution is beyond the scope of this book, but the documentation is quite extensive. Also, please bear in mind that JMeter is designed to be run from a client, not on the server. Accordingly, if you wish to test the website in the Docker container for this book, you'll need to install Apache JMeter on your local computer, and then build a test plan that points to the Docker container. Normally the IP address for the PHP 8 container is `172.16.0.88`.

Figure 11.3 shows the opening screen for Apache JMeter running on a local computer:

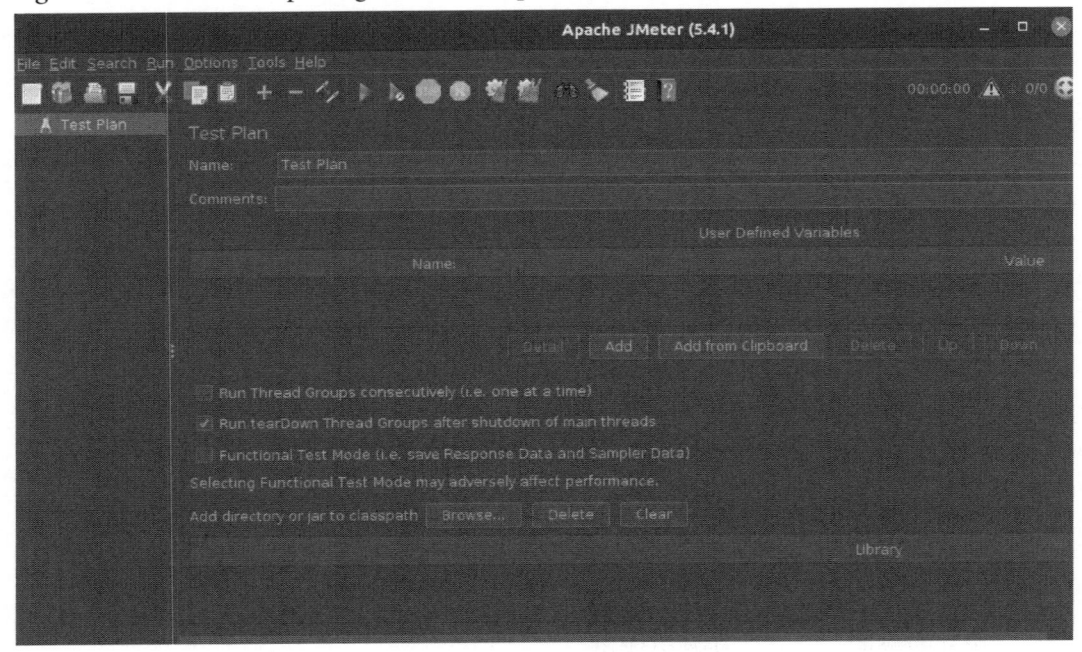

Figure 11.3 – Apache JMeter

From this screen you can develop one or more test plans, indicating the URL(s) to access, simulate `GET` and `POST` requests, set the number of users, and so forth.

> **Tip**
> If you encounter this error while trying to run `jmeter: Can't load library: /usr/lib/jvm/java-11-openjdk-amd64/lib/ libawt_xawt.so`, try installing *OpenJDK 8*. You can then use the techniques mentioned in the earlier section to switch between versions of Java.

Let's now have a look at potential issues with Composer following a PHP 8 upgrade.

Handling issues with Composer

One common issue developers face after the migration to PHP 8 has concluded is with third-party software. In this section, we discuss potential issues surrounding the use of the popular *Composer* package manager for PHP.

The first issue you might encounter has to do with versions of Composer itself. In the year 2020, Composer version 2 was released. Not all of the 300,000+ packages residing on the main packaging website (https://packagist.org/) have been updated to version 2, however. Accordingly, in order to install a given package, you might find yourself having to switch between Composer 2 and Composer 1. The latest releases of each version are available here:

- Version 1: https://getcomposer.org/download/latest-1.x/composer.phar
- Version 2: https://getcomposer.org/download/latest-2.x/composer.phar

Another, more serious, issue has to do with platform requirements of the various Composer packages you might be using. Each package has its own composer.json file, with its own requirements. In many cases, the package provider might add a PHP version requirement.

The problem is that while most Composer packages now work on PHP 7, the requirements were specified in such a manner as to exclude PHP 8. After a PHP 8 update, when you use Composer to update your third-party packages, an error occurs and the update fails. Ironically, most PHP 7 packages will also work on PHP 8!

As an example, we install a Composer project called laminas-api-tools. At the time of writing, although the package itself is ready for PHP 8, a number of its dependent packages are not. When running the command to install the API tools, the following error is encountered:

```
root@php8_tips_php8 [ /srv ]#
composer create-project laminas-api-tools/api-tools-skeleton
Creating a "laminas-api-tools/api-tools-skeleton" project at
"./api-tools-skeleton"
Installing laminas-api-tools/api-tools-skeleton (1.3.1p1)
  - Downloading laminas-api-tools/api-tools-skeleton (1.3.1p1)
  - Installing laminas-api-tools/api-tools-skeleton (1.3.1p1):
Extracting archiveCreated project in /srv/api-tools-skeleton
Loading composer repositories with package information
```

```
Updating dependencies
Your requirements could not be resolved to an installable set
of packages.
  Problem 1
    - Root composer.json requires laminas/laminas-developer-
tools dev-master, found laminas/laminas-developer-tools[dev-
release-1.3, 0.0.1, 0.0.2, 1.0.0alpha1, ..., 1.3.x-dev, 2.0.0,
..., 2.2.x-dev] but it does not match the constraint.
  Problem 2
    - zendframework/zendframework 2.5.3 requires php ^5.5
   || ^7.0 -> your php version (8.1.0-dev) does not satisfy
    that requirement.
```

The core problem, highlighted in the last portion of the output just shown, is that one of the dependent packages requires PHP `^7.0`. In the `composer.json` file, this indicates a range of versions from PHP 7.0 through to and including PHP 8.0. In this particular example, the Docker container used runs PHP 8.1, so we have a problem.

Fortunately, in such cases, we are confident that if this package runs in PHP 8.0, it should also run in PHP 8.1. Accordingly, all we need to do is to add the `--ignore-platform-reqs` flag. When we retry the installation, as you can see from the following output, it is successful:

```
root@php8_tips_php8 [ /srv ]#
composer create-project --ignore-platform-reqs \
    laminas-api-tools/api-tools-skeleton
Creating a "laminas-api-tools/api-tools-skeleton" project at
"./api-tools-skeleton"
Installing laminas-api-tools/api-tools-skeleton (1.6.0)
  - Downloading laminas-api-tools/api-tools-skeleton (1.6.0)
  - Installing laminas-api-tools/api-tools-skeleton (1.6.0):
Extracting archive
Created project in /srv/api-tools-skeleton
Installing dependencies from lock file (including require-dev)
Verifying lock file contents can be installed on current
platform.
Package operations: 109 installs, 0 updates, 0 removals
  - Downloading laminas/laminas-zendframework-bridge (1.3.0)
  - Downloading laminas-api-tools/api-tools-asset-manager
(1.4.0)
```

```
- Downloading squizlabs/php_codesniffer (3.6.0)
- Downloading dealerdirect/phpcodesniffer-composer-installer
(v0.7.1)
- Downloading laminas/laminas-component-installer (2.5.0)
... not all output is shown
```

In the output just shown, no platform requirement errors appear and we are able to continue working with the application.

Let's now turn our attention to unit testing.

Working with unit tests

Unit testing using **PHPUnit** is a critical factor in the process of ensuring that an application will run after a new feature has been added, or after a PHP update. Most developers create a set of unit tests to at least perform the bare minimum required to prove that an application performs as expected. Tests are methods in a class that extends `PHPUnit\Framework\TestCase`. The core of the test is what is referred to as an **assertion**.

> **Tip**
> Instructions on how to create and run tests are beyond the scope of this book. However, you can go through the excellent documentation with plenty of examples at the main PHPUnit website: `https://phpunit.de/`.

The problem you might encounter after a PHP migration is that **PHPUnit** (`https://phpunit.de/`) itself might fail! The reason for this is because PHPUnit has a new release each year that corresponds to the version of PHP that is current for that year. The older versions of PHPUnit are based upon what versions of PHP are officially supported. Accordingly, it's entirely possible that the version of PHPUnit currently installed for your application is an older version that doesn't support PHP 8. The simplest solution is to use Composer to perform an update.

To illustrate the possible problem, let's assume that the testing directory for an application currently includes PHP unit 5. If we run a test in the Docker container that runs PHP 7.1, everything works as expected. Here is the output:

```
root@php8_tips_php7 [ /repo/test/phpunit5 ]# php --version
PHP 7.1.33 (cli) (built: May 16 2020 12:47:37) (NTS)
Copyright (c) 1997-2018 The PHP Group
Zend Engine v3.1.0, Copyright (c) 1998-2018 Zend Technologies
```

```
            with Xdebug v2.9.1, Copyright (c) 2002-2020, by Derick
Rethans
root@php8_tips_php7 [ /repo/test/phpunit5 ]#
vendor/bin/phpunit
PHPUnit 5.7.27 by Sebastian Bergmann and contributors.

........
8 / 8 (100%)
Time: 27 ms, Memory: 4.00MB
OK (8 tests, 8 assertions)
```

However, if we run the same version but in the Docker container that's running PHP 8, the results are quite different:

```
root@php8_tips_php8 [ /repo/test/phpunit5 ]# php --version
PHP 8.1.0-dev (cli) (built: Dec 24 2020 00:13:50) (NTS)
Copyright (c) The PHP Group
Zend Engine v4.1.0-dev, Copyright (c) Zend Technologies
    with Zend OPcache v8.1.0-dev, Copyright (c),
    by Zend Technologies
root@php8_tips_php8 [ /repo/test/phpunit5 ]#
vendor/bin/phpunit
PHP Warning:  Private methods cannot be final as they are never overridden by other classes in /repo/test/phpunit5/vendor/phpunit/phpunit/src/Util/Configuration.php on line 162
PHPUnit 5.7.27 by Sebastian Bergmann and contributors.

........
8 / 8 (100%)
Time: 33 ms, Memory: 2.00MB
OK (8 tests, 8 assertions)
```

As you can see from the output, PHPUnit itself reports an error. The simple solution, of course, is that after a PHP 8 upgrade, you also need to re-run Composer and update all third-party packages you use along with your application.

This concludes our discussion of testing and troubleshooting. You now have an idea of what additional tools can be brought to bear to assist you in testing and troubleshooting. Please note, however, that this is by no means a comprehensive list of all testing and troubleshooting tools. There are many many more, some free and open source, others that offer a free trial period, and still more that are only available by purchase.

Summary

In this chapter, you learned how the term *environment* is used rather than *server* because many websites these days use virtualized services. You then learned about three distinct environments used during the deployment phase: development, staging, and production.

An automated tool that is able to scan your application code for potential code breaks was introduced next. As you learned in that section, a break-scanning application might consist of a configuration file that addresses removed functionality, changes to method signatures, functions that no longer produce resources, and a set of callbacks for complex usage detection, a scanning class, and a calling program that gathers filenames.

Next, you were shown a typical twelve-step PHP 8 migration procedure that ensures a greater chance of success when you are finally ready to upgrade the production environment. Each step is designed to spot potential code breaks, with fallback procedures in case something goes wrong. You also learned how to install PHP 8 on two common platforms as well as how to easily revert to the older version. Finally, you learned about a number of free open source tools that can assist in testing and troubleshooting.

All in all, after carefully reading this chapter and studying the examples, you are now in a position to not only use existing testing and troubleshooting tools, but now have an idea of how to develop your own scanning tool that greatly reduces the risk of a potential code break after a PHP 8 migration. You also now have an excellent idea what is involved in a migration to PHP 8, and can carry out smoother transitions without fear of failure. Your new ability to anticipate and fix migration problems will ease any anxiety you might otherwise have experienced. You can also look forward to having happy and satisfied customers.

The next chapter introduces you to new and exciting trends in PHP programming that can improve performance even further.

12
Creating PHP 8 Applications Using Asynchronous Programming

In recent years, an exciting new technology has taken the **PHP: Hypertext Preprocessor** (**PHP**) community by storm: **asynchronous programming**, also known as **PHP async**. The asynchronous programming model addresses an issue present in any application code written using the traditional synchronous mode of programming: your application is forced to wait for certain tasks to complete before providing results. The **central processing unit** (**CPU**) (or CPUs) of the server upon which your application is running sits idle while mundane **input/output** (**I/O**) tasks are performed. PHP async allows your application to take full advantage of hardware resources by suspending blocking I/O tasks until later. The net effect is a massive increase in performance, as well as the ability to handle a geometrically larger number of user requests.

After reading through this chapter and carefully studying the examples, you will be able to develop PHP async applications. In addition, you will be able to take advantage of the async capabilities of selected PHP extensions and frameworks. By the time you are done working through this chapter, you will be in a position to improve the performance of your applications, from 5 times up to a staggering *40 times faster*!

Topics covered in this chapter include the following:

- Understanding the PHP async programming model
- Using the Swoole extension
- Using selected PHP frameworks in async mode
- Learning about PHP 8.1 fibers

Technical requirements

The minimum hardware required to examine and run the code examples provided in this chapter is listed here:

- x86_64 based desktop PC or laptop
- 1 **gigabyte** (**GB**) free disk space
- 4 GB of **random-access memory** (**RAM**)
- 500 **kilobits per second** (**Kbps**) or faster internet connection

In addition, you will need to install the following software:

- Docker
- Docker Compose

Please refer to the *Technical requirements* section of *Chapter 1, Introducing New PHP 8 OOP Features,* for more information on the Docker and Docker Compose installation, as well as how to build the Docker container used to demonstrate the code explained in this book. In this book, we refer to the directory in which you restored the sample code for the book as `/repo`.

The source code for this chapter is located here: `https://github.com/PacktPublishing/PHP-8-Programming-Tips-Tricks-and-Best-Practices`.

We can now begin our discussion by having a look at PHP async.

Understanding the PHP async programming model

Before we get into the details of how to develop PHP applications using asynchronous libraries, it's important to step back and have a look at the PHP **asynchronous programming model**. Understanding the difference between this and the conventional **synchronous programming model** opens a new world of high performance for you to utilize when developing PHP applications. Let's first have a look at the synchronous programming model, after which we'll dive into async.

Developing synchronous programming code

In traditional PHP programming, code executes in a linear fashion. Once the code has been compiled into machine code, the CPU executes the code one line after another in a sequential manner until the code ends. This is certainly true of PHP *procedural programming*. Surprising to some, this is also true for **object-oriented programming** (**OOP**) as well! Regardless of whether or not you use objects as part of your code, the OOP code gets compiled into first-byte code and then machine code, and is processed in a synchronous manner in exactly the same manner as is procedural code.

Using OPcache and the **Just-in-Time** (**JIT**) compiler has no bearing on whether or not the code operates in a synchronous manner. The only thing that OPcache and the JIT compiler bring to the table is the ability to operate synchronous code faster than was otherwise possible.

> **Important note**
>
> Please do not get the impression that there is something wrong with writing code using the synchronous programming model! This approach is not only tried and true but also quite successful. Furthermore, synchronous code is supported by many ancillary tools such as PHPUnit, Xdebug, numerous frameworks, and many others.

There is a major drawback to the synchronous programming model, however. Using this model, the CPU has to constantly wait for certain tasks to complete before the program is allowed to move along. To a large extent, such tasks include access to an external resource, such as making a database query, writing to a log file, or sending an email. Such tasks are referred to as **blocking operations** (operations that block progress).

The following diagram gives you a visual representation of an application flow, which involves the blocking operations of writing to a log file and sending an email notification:

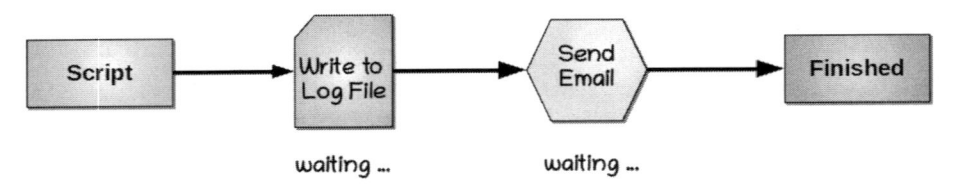

Figure 12.1 – Synchronous programming model

As you can see from *Figure 12.1*, when an application writes to a log file, the CPU puts a hold on program code execution until the **operating system** (**OS**) signals that the log file's write operation has finished. Later, the code might send out an email notification. Again, the CPU puts a hold on code execution until the email send operation has concluded. Although each waiting interval may be insignificant in and of itself, when you add together the waiting intervals for all such blocking operations—especially if lengthy loops are involved—performance starts to degrade.

One solution is to liberally implement a caching solution. Another solution, as you may have guessed, is to write your application using the asynchronous programming model. Let's have a look at that right now.

Understanding the asynchronous programming model

The idea behind asynchronous operations has been around for quite some time. One extremely well-known example is Apache Web Server, with its **Multi-Processing Modules** (**MPMs**). The MaxRequestWorkers directive allows you to specify how many simultaneous requests the web server can handle (see https://httpd.apache.org/docs/current/mod/mpm_common.html#maxrequestworkers for more information).

The asynchronous programming model usually involves setting up management nodes, referred to as **workers**. This allows program execution to continue without having to wait for any given task to complete. The gain in performance can be quite dramatic, especially in situations where a large number of blocking operations (for example, filesystem access or database queries) occur.

The following diagram visualizes how the tasks of writing to a log file and sending an email might be accomplished using the asynchronous programming model:

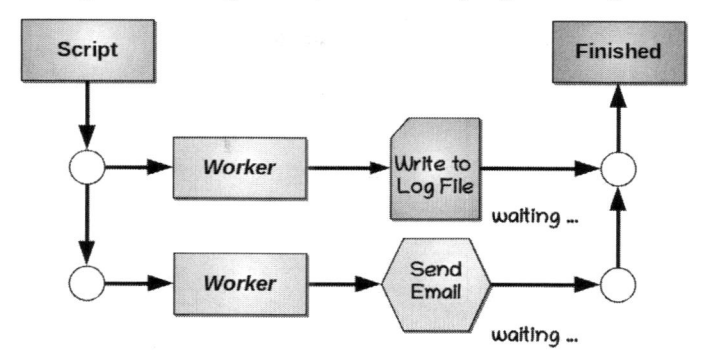

Figure 12.2 – Asynchronous programming model

The total waiting time is reduced by a factor of how many workers are assigned. The program flow shown in *Figure 12.2* would involve half the waiting time as that shown in *Figure 12.1*. Overall performance improves as the number of workers assigned to handle blocking operations increases.

> **Important note**
> The asynchronous programming model is *not to be confused* with **parallel programming**. In parallel programming, tasks are literally executed simultaneously, often being assigned to different CPUs or CPU cores. Asynchronous programming, on the other hand, operates sequentially but allows the sequential code to continue while waiting for the results of a blocking operation (for example, a filesystem request or a database query).

Now that you have an idea of how the PHP async programming model works, let's have a look at coroutine support.

Working with async coroutine support

Coroutines are similar to **threads** but operate in user space, not kernel space, and thus do not need to involve the OS. If this support is available, the coroutine support component detects blocking operations (such as reading or writing to a file) and effectively suspends that operation until results are received. This frees up the CPU to proceed with other tasks until the results have been returned from the blocking process. This process operates at the machine-code level and is thus undetectable to us, other than the fact that our code runs faster.

Theoretically, using an extension or framework that provides **coroutine support** might boost performance, even if your code is written using the synchronous programming model. Please note that not all PHP async frameworks or extensions offer this support, which might, in turn, influence your choice of framework or extension to use for future development.

The **Swoole extension** (https://www.swoole.co.uk/) offers coroutine support. On the other hand, ReactPHP (https://reactphp.org/), one of the most popular PHP async frameworks, does not offer coroutine support unless used with the Swoole extension (discussed next) or with PHP fibers (discussed in the *Learning about PHP 8.1 fibers* section). One of the reasons why ReactPHP is so popular, however, is the very fact that the Swoole extension is not required. If you are operating in a hosting environment where you do not have control over the PHP installation, you can still use ReactPHP and achieve a substantial performance gain, without having to touch the PHP installation.

We now turn our attention to writing code for the async model.

Creating a PHP async application

Now comes the hard part! Unfortunately, an application written using the synchronous programming model does not take advantage of what the async model has to offer. Even if you are using a framework and/or extension that provides coroutine support, you do not realize maximum performance gain unless you refactor your code to follow the async programming model.

Most PHP async frameworks and extensions offer a number of ways for you to separate tasks. Here is a brief summary of the more commonly used approaches.

Event loops

In a certain sense, an **event loop** is a repetitive block of code that runs continuously until a specified event occurs. All of the PHP async extensions and frameworks offer this feature in one form or another. Listeners that take the form of a callback are added to an event loop. When an event is triggered, the listener's logic is invoked.

The Swoole event loop leverages Linux `epoll_wait` (https://linux.die.net/man/2/epoll_wait) functionality. Because hardware-based events report to Linux through pseudo file handles, the Swoole event loop allows the developer to base the starting and stopping of the event loop not only on attributes of actual files but also of any hardware process that produces a **file descriptor** (**FD**).

The ReactPHP framework offers the same functionality, but uses the PHP `stream_select()` function by default, in place of the OS `epoll_wait` functionality. This makes the ReactPHP event loop **application programming interface** (**API**) portable between servers, although reaction time will be slower. ReactPHP also offers the ability to define an event loop based on the `ext-event`, `ext-ev`, `ext-uv`, or `ext-libevent` PHP extensions. Leveraging these extensions gives ReactPHP access to the hardware, much as does Swoole.

Promises

A **promise** is a software construct that allows you to defer the processing of a task until later. The concept was first proposed as part of the **CommonJS** project (`http://wiki.commonjs.org/wiki/Promises/A`). It was designed as a bridge between the synchronous and asynchronous programming worlds.

In synchronous programming, a function (or class method) generally either *succeeds* or *fails*. In PHP, a failure is handled as either a deliberately thrown exception or a fatal error. In the asynchronous model, three states are identified as part of a *promise*: **fulfilled**, **failed**, and **unfulfilled**. Accordingly, when a *promise* instance is created, you need to supply three handlers that take action based upon the state they represent.

In the case of ReactPHP, when you create a `React\Promise\Promise` instance, you supply a **resolver** as the first constructor argument. The resolver itself requires three callbacks labeled `$resolve`, `$reject`, and `$notify`. These three correspond to the three possible states of a promise: fulfilled, failed, or unfulfilled.

Streams

Many async frameworks provide a wrapper for PHP **streams**. PHP streams are most often used to handle operations involving the filesystem. File access is a blocking operation that causes program execution to pause until the OS returns the results.

In order to avoid having file access block the progress of an async application, a `streams` component is used. ReactPHP, for example, provides classes under the `React\Stream` namespace that implement `ReadableStreamInterface` or `WritableStreamInterface`. These classes serve as a wrapper for ordinary PHP stream functions such as `fopen()`, `fread()`, and `fwrite()`, as well as `file_get_contents()` and `file_put_contents()`. The ReactPHP classes use memory to avoid blocking and defer the actual read or write until later, thus allowing asynchronous activities to continue.

Timers

Timers are separate tasks that can be set to run after a given interval. In this respect, timers resemble the JavaScript `setTimeout()` function. Tasks scheduled using timers can be set to run one time only, or continuously at specified intervals.

The timer implementation in most PHP async frameworks or extensions generally avoids using the PHP `pcntl_alarm()` function. The latter function allows a developer to send a `SIGALRM` signal to a process after a certain number of seconds. The `pcntl_alarm()` function only allows you to set one at a time, however, and the lowest time interval is measured in seconds. In contrast, PHP async frameworks and extensions allow you to set multiple timers accurately, to the millisecond. Another difference in PHP async timer implementation is that it is not dependent upon the `declare(ticks=1)` statement.

There are many potential uses for timers—for example, a timer could check a directory that contains **Completely Automated Public Turing test to tell Computers and Humans Apart** (**CAPTCHA**) images and can remove old ones. Another potential use would be to refresh the cache periodically.

Channels

Channels are a means of communicating between concurrent processes. The current implementation of channels is based upon an algebraic model proposed in 1978 by Sir Charles Antony Hoare. His proposal was refined over the years and evolved into the model described in his book *Communicating Sequential Processes*, published in 1985. Channels and the **communicating sequential processes** (**CSP**) model are a feature of many currently popular languages such as **Go**.

In contrast to other more complicated approaches, when using channels the CSP processes are anonymous, whereas the channel is explicitly named. Another aspect of the channel approach is that the sender is prevented from sending until the receiver is ready to receive. This simple principle alleviates having to implement an excessive amount of shared locking logic. In the Swoole extension, for example, channels are used to implement connection pools or as a means of scheduling concurrent tasks.

Now that you have a basic understanding of PHP async theory, it's time to put the theory into practice. We start by examining how to use the Swoole extension.

Using the Swoole extension

The PHP **Swoole extension** was first made available on the PHP extension C library website (https://pecl.php.net/) in December 2013. Since that time, it's gained considerable attention. With the introduction of the JIT compiler in PHP 8, there has been a considerable amount of renewed interest in the Swoole extension as it's fast and stable and is in a position to make PHP applications run even faster. The total number of downloads is close to 6 million, and the average number per month is around 50,000.

In this section, you will learn about the extension, how it's installed, and how it's used. Let's first get an overview of the extension.

Examining the Swoole extension

Because the extension is written in the C language, once it's compiled, installed, and enabled, a set of functions and classes are added to your current PHP installation. The extension leverages certain low-level features that are only available in OSes derived from UNIX, however. This means that if you are running a Windows server, the only way you can get a PHP async application that uses the Swoole extension running is by installing **Windows Services for Linux** (**WSL**) or by setting up your application to run in a Docker container on the Windows server.

> **Tip**
> If you want to experiment with PHP async on a Windows server, consider using ReactPHP (discussed in the *Working with ReactPHP* section), which does not have the OS dependencies required by the Swoole extension.

One of the big advantages of PHP async is that the initial block of code gets loaded immediately and stays in memory until the asynchronous server instance stops. This is the case when using the Swoole extension. In your code, you create an asynchronous server instance that effectively turns PHP into a continuously running daemon listening on the designated port. This is also a disadvantage, however, in that if you make changes to your program code, the changes are not recognized by the async server instance until you reload it.

One of the great features of the Swoole extension is its **coroutine support**. What this means, in real-life terms, is that we don't have to perform major surgery on applications written using the synchronous programming model. Swoole will automatically pick out blocking operations such as filesystem access and database queries and allow these operations to be placed on hold while the rest of the application proceeds. Because of this support, you can often simply run the synchronous application using Swoole, resulting in an immediate performance boost.

Another really great feature of the Swoole extension is `Swoole\Table`. This feature lets you create, entirely in memory, the equivalent of a database table that can be shared between multiple processes. There are many possible uses for such a construct, and the potential performance gain is truly staggering.

The Swoole extension has the ability to listen for **User Datagram Protocol** (**UDP**) transmissions rather than **Transmission Control Protocol** (**TDP**) ones. This is an extremely interesting possibility as UDP is much faster than TCP. Swoole also includes a timer implementation accurate to the millisecond, as well as async clients for MySQL, PostgreSQL, Redis, and cURL. The Swoole extension also gives you the ability to set up **inter-process communication** (**IPC**) using **Golang** style channels. Let's now have a look at installing Swoole.

Installing the Swoole extension

The Swoole extension can be installed using the same techniques you would deploy to install any PHP extension written in the C language. One approach is to simply use your OS package manager. Examples include `apt` (or its less friendly cousin, `apt-get`) for Debian or Ubuntu Linux, and `yum` or `dnf` for Red Hat, CentOS, or Fedora. When using an OS package manager, the Swoole extension is made available in the form of precompiled binaries.

The recommended approach, however, is to use the `pecl` command. If this command is not available on your installation, the `pecl` command can be installed (logged in as a root user) as follows on an Ubuntu or Debian OS: `apt install php-pear`. For a Red Hat, CentOS, or Fedora installation, the following works: `yum install php-pear`.

When installing the Swoole extension using `pecl`, you can specify a number of options. These options are summarized here:

Option	Description
--enable-openssl	Set this to allows Swoole to use OpenSSL. There's a hard dependency on the OS library `libssl.so`.
--with-openssl-dir	This tells Swoole where to find the OpenSSL library. An example for the Docker container used for this book would be `--with-openssl-dir=/usr/include/openssl`.
--enable-http2	This is especially important when you are using Swoole directly from the comand line. This option allows Swoole to process HTTP2 requests using its own built-in library `nghttp2`.
--enable-swoole-json	Makes Swoole JSON functions available. PHP ext/json must also be present, however this is already a default extension.
--enable-swoole-curl	Provides native support for cURL. For this to work properly you must also have the `libcurl4` OpenSSL development library installed on your OS.
--enable-mysqlnd	This option provides support for the PHP `mysqlnd` (MySQL Native Driver) module. The recommended option is to use PDO MySQL instead, in which case you do not need to enable `mysqlnd` support.
--enable-sockets	Use this option is you rely upon the PHP Sockets extension. Once enabled, connections created by the Sockets extension can be processed by `Swoole\Event::add()`. The best practice, however, is to use `Coroutine\Socket` instead.
--enable-debug	If you have `gdb` (the GNU debugger) installed, enable this option for Swoole debugging.
--enable-debug-log	For the development environment only, enable this option to gain access to Swoole debug logs.
--enable-trace-log	Enable this option to add kernel level tracing to the debug log.

Table 12.1 – Swoole extension pecl installation options

For more information on these options and for an overview of the installation procedure, have a look here:

https://www.swoole.co.uk/docs/get-started/installation

Let's now take a look at a sample installation that includes Swoole support for sockets, **JavaScript Object Notation (JSON)**, and cURL, as follows:

1. The first thing we need to do is to update the `pecl` **channel**. This is a list of PHP extension source code repositories and functions, much like the `sources` list used by the `apt` or `yum` package managers. Here's the code to do this:

   ```
   pecl channel-update pecl.php.net
   ```

2. Next, we specify the installation command and use the `-D` flag to add options, as follows:

   ```
   pecl install -D \
       'enable-sockets="yes" \
       enable-openssl="no" \
       enable-http2="no" \
       enable-mysqlnd="no" \
   ```

```
        enable-swoole-json="yes" \
        enable-swoole-curl="yes"' \
        swoole
```

3. This starts the extension installation process. You now see the various C language code files and header files downloaded, after which your local C compiler is used to compile the extension. Here is a partial view of the compile process:

```
root@php8_tips_php8 [ / ]# pecl install swoole
downloading swoole-4.6.7.tgz ...
Starting to download swoole-4.6.7.tgz (1,649,407 bytes)
................................................................
................................................................
................................................................
................................................................
................................................................
.......................................done: 1,649,407
bytes
364 source files, building
running: phpize
Configuring for:
PHP Api Version:          20200930
Zend Module Api No:       20200930
Zend Extension Api No:    420200930
building in /tmp/pear/temp/pear-build-defaultuserQakGt8/
swoole-4.6.7
running: /tmp/pear/temp/swoole/configure --with-php-
config=/usr/bin/php-config --enable-sockets=no --enable-
openssl=no --enable-http2=no --enable-mysqlnd=yes
--enable-swoole-json=yes --enable-swoole-curl=yes
...
Build process completed successfully
Installing '/usr/include/php/ext/swoole/config.h'
Installing '/usr/lib/php/extensions/no-debug-non-
zts-20200930/swoole.so'
install ok: channel://pecl.php.net/swoole-4.6.7
configuration option "php_ini" is not set to php.ini
location
You should add "extension=swoole.so" to php.ini
```

4. If a C compiler is not found, you will be warned. Also, you might need to install the PHP development library for your OS. The warning messages give you further guidance if this is the case.

5. Once completed, you then need to enable the extension. This is accomplished by adding `extension=swoole` to the `php.ini` file. If you are unsure of its location, use the `php -i` command and look for the location of the `php.ini` file. Here is a command you can issue from the command line that adds this directive:

```
echo "extension=swoole" >>/etc/php.ini
```

6. You can then use the following command to confirm the availability of the Swoole extension:

```
php --ri swoole
```

This concludes the installation of the Swoole extension. If you are custom-compiling PHP, you can also add the `--enable-swoole` option when running `configure` prior to compilation. This causes the Swoole extension to be compiled and enabled along with your core PHP installation (and allows you to bypass the installation steps just outlined). We will now have a look at a brief *Hello World* example taken from the documentation to test the installation.

Testing the installation

The Swoole documentation provides a simple example you can use for a quick test to see if the installation was successful. The sample code is shown on the main Swoole documentation page (`https://www.swoole.co.uk/docs/`). We do not reproduce it here for copyright reasons. Here are the steps taken to run the *Hello World* test:

1. First, we copied the *Hello World* example from `https://www.swoole.co.uk/docs/` to `/path/to/repo/ch12/php8_swoole_hello_world.php` file.

   Next, we modified the demo program and changed `$server = new Swoole\HTTP\Server("127.0.0.1", 9501);` to `$server = new Swoole\HTTP\Server("0.0.0.0", 9501);`.

   This change allows the Swoole server to listen on port `9501` for any **Internet Protocol** (**IP**) address.

2. We then modified the `/repo/ch12/docker-compose.yml` file to make port 9501 available outside the Docker container, as follows:

```
version: "3"
services:
  ...
  php8-tips-php8:
    ...
    ports:
      - 8888:80
      - 9501:9501
    ...
```

3. To make this change effective, we had to bring the service down and back up again. From a command prompt/terminal window on your local computer, use these two commands:

```
/path/to/repo/init.sh down
/path/to/repo/init.sh up
```

4. Please note that if you are running Windows, remove `.sh`.

5. We then opened a shell into the PHP 8 Docker container and ran the *Hello World* program, as follows:

```
$ docker exec -it php8_tips_php8 /bin/bash
# cd /repo/ch12
# php php8_swoole_hello_world.php
```

6. Finally, from outside the Docker container, we opened a browser to this IP address and port: `http://172.16.0.88:9501`.

The following screenshot shows the result from the Swoole *Hello World* program:

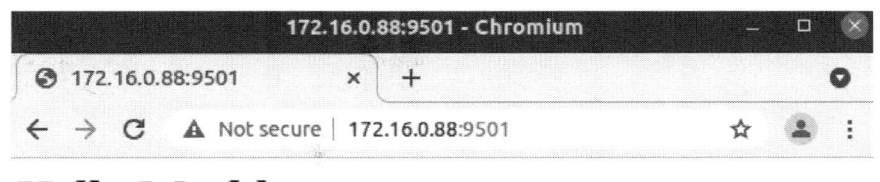

Figure 12.3 – The Swoole demo Hello World program output

Before getting into details on how the Swoole extension can be used to improve application performance, we need to examine a sample application that's a prime candidate for the PHP async model.

Examining a sample I/O-intensive application

For the sake of illustration, we have created a sample application written as a **REpresentational State Transfer** (**REST**) API, designed to run in PHP 8. The sample application presents a chat or instant messaging API with the following simple features:

- Use a **HyperText Transfer Protocol** (**HTTP**) `POST` method to post a message either to a specific user or to all users. After a successful posting, the API returns the message just posted.

- An HTTP `GET` method with a `from=username` parameter returns all messages to and from that username and messages to all users. If the `all=1` parameter is set, it returns a list of all usernames.

- An HTTP `DELETE` method removes all messages from the `messages` table.

Only parts of the application code are shown in this section. If you are interested in the entire `Chat` application, the source code is located under `/path/to/repo/src/Chat`. The primary API endpoint is provided here: `http://172.16.0.81/ch12/php8_chat_ajax.php`.

The examples that follow are executed in a PHP 8.1 Docker container. Be sure to bring down the existing containers as follows, from a command prompt on your local computer on a Windows computer: `C:\path\to\repo\init` down. For Linux or Mac, from a terminal window: `/path/to/repo/init.sh` down. To bring up the PHP 8.1 container from a Windows computer: `C:\path\to\repo\ch12\init` up. From a Linux or Mac terminal window: `/path/to/repo/ch12/init.sh` up.

The examples that follow are executed in a PHP 8.1 Docker container. Be sure to bring down the existing containers as follows from a command prompt on your local computer on a Windows computer: C:\path\to\repo\init down

For Linux or Mac, from a terminal window:

`/path/to/repo/init.sh down`

To bring up the PHP 8.1 container from a Windows computer:

`C:\path\to\repo\ch12\init up`

From a Linux or Mac terminal window:

`/path/to/repo/ch12/init.sh up`

We now look at the source code for the core API program itself, as follows:

1. First, we define a `Chat\Message\Pipe` class, identifying all of the external classes we need to use, like this:

```php
// /repo/src/Chat/Messsage/Api.php;
namespace Chat\Message;
use Chat\Handler\ {GetHandler, PostHandler,
    NextHandler,GetAllNamesHandler,DeleteHandler};
use Chat\Middleware\ {Access,Validate,ValidatePost};
use Chat\Message\Render;
use Psr\Http\Message\ServerRequestInterface;
class Pipe {
```

2. We then define an `exec()` static method that invokes a set of **PHP Standard Recommendation 15 (PSR-15)**-compliant handlers. We also invoke the first stage of the pipe by calling the `process` method of the `Chat\Middleware\Access` middleware class. The return value of `NextHandler` is ignored:

```php
public static function exec(
    ServerRequestInterface $request) {
    $params   = $request->getQueryParams();
```

```
    $method    = strtolower($request->getMethod());
    $dontcare  = (new Access())
        ->process($request, new NextHandler());
```

3. Still in the same method, we use a `match()` construct to check for HTTP GET, POST, and DELETE method calls. If the method is POST, we use the `Chat\Middleware\ValidatePost` validation middleware class to validate the POST arguments. If validation succeeds, the sanitized data is then passed to `Chat\Handler\PostHandler`. If the HTTP method is DELETE, we directly call `Chat\Handler\DeleteHandler`:

```
    $response = match ($method) {
        'post' => (new ValidatePost())
            ->process($request, new PostHandler()),
        'delete' => (new DeleteHandler())
            ->handle($request),
```

4. If the HTTP method is GET, we first check to see if the `all` parameter is set. If so, we invoke `Chat\Handler\GetAllNamesHandler`. Otherwise, the *default* clause passes data through `Chat\MiddleWare\Validate`. If validation succeeds, the sanitized data is passed to `Chat\Handler\GetHandler`:

```
        'get'    => (!empty($params['all'])
            ? (new GetAllNamesHandler())->handle($request)
            : (new Validate())->process($request,
                new GetHandler())),
        default => (new Validate())
            ->process($request, new GetHandler()) };
        return Render::output($request, $response);
    }
}
```

5. The core API class can then be called using a short conventional program, as shown here. In this calling program, we build a PSR-7 compliant `Psr\Http\Message\ServerRequestInterface` instance using `Laminas\Diactoros\ServerRequestFactory`. The request is then passed through the `Pipe` class and a response is produced:

```
// /repo/ch12/php8_chat_ajax.php
include __DIR__ . '/vendor/autoload.php';
```

```
use Laminas\Diactoros\ServerRequestFactory;
use Chat\Message\Pipe;
$request  = ServerRequestFactory::fromGlobals();
$response = Pipe::exec($request);
echo $response;
```

We also created a test program (`/repo/ch12/php8_chat_test.php`—not shown) that calls the API endpoint a set number of times (the default is 100). On each iteration, the test program posts a random message consisting of a random recipient username, a random date, and a sequential entry from the `/repo/sample_data/geonames.db` database. The test program takes two arguments. The first argument is a URL that represents the API. The second (optional) argument represents the number of iterations.

Here are example results running `/ch12/php8_chat_test.php` from a command shell into the PHP 8.1 Docker container:

```
root@php8_tips_php8_1 [ /repo/ch12 ]# php php8_chat_test.php \
    http://localhost/ch12/php8_chat_ajax.php 10000   bboyer  :
         Dubai:AE:2956587 : 2021-01-01 00:00:00
1 fcompton :         Sharjah:AE:1324473 : 2022-02-02 01:01:01
...
998 hrivas : Caloocan City:PH:1500000 : 2023-03-19 09:54:54
999 lpena  :         Budta:PH:1273715 : 2021-04-20 10:55:55
From User: dwallace
Elapsed Time: 3.3177478313446
```

From the output, take note of the elapsed time. In the next section, using Swoole, we are able to cut this time in half! Before using Swoole, however, it is only fair to incorporate the JIT compiler. We enable JIT using the following command:

```
# php /repo/ch10/php8_jit_reset.php on
```

In PHP 8.0.0, it's possible you might encounter a few errors and possibly a segmentation fault. In PHP 8.1, however, the API should work as expected with the JIT compiler enabled. However, it's highly doubtful the JIT compiler would improve performance, as the frequent API calls cause the application to wait. Any application with frequent blocking I/O operations is an excellent candidate for the asynchronous programming model. Before we proceed, however, we need to turn off JIT, using the same utility program as before, as follows:

```
# php /repo/ch10/php8_jit_reset.php off
```

Let's now have a look at how the Swoole extension might be used to improve the performance of this I/O-intensive application.

Using the Swoole extension to improve application performance

Given that Swoole provides coroutine support, all we really need to do in order to improve the Chat application performance is to rewrite the `/repo/ch12/php8_chat_ajax.php` calling program, turning it into an API that listens on port `9501` as a Swoole server instance. Here are the steps to rewrite the main API calling program:

1. First, we enable autoloading and identify the external classes needed:

    ```
    // /repo/ch12/php8_chat_swoole.php
    include __DIR__ . '/vendor/autoload.php';
    use Chat\Message\Pipe;
    use Chat\Http\SwooleToPsr7;
    use Swoole\Http\Server;
    use Swoole\Http\Request;
    use Swoole\Http\Response;
    ```

2. Next, we start a PHP session and create a `Swoole\HTTP\Server` instance that listens for any IP address on port `9501`:

    ```
    session_start();
    $server = new Swoole\HTTP\Server('0.0.0.0', 9501);
    ```

3. We then invoke the `on()` method and associate it with the `start` event. In this case, we make a log entry to identify when the Swoole server started. Other server events are documented here: https://www.swoole.co.uk/docs/modules/swoole-http-server-doc:

    ```
    $server->on("start", function (Server $server) {
        error_log('Swoole http server is started at '
            . 'http://0.0.0.0:9501');
    });
    ```

4. Finally, we define a main server event, `$server->on('request', function () {})`, which handles incoming requests. Here's the code to accomplish this:

```
$server->on("request", function (
    Request $swoole_request, Response $swoole_response) {
    $request  = SwooleToPsr7::
        swooleRequestToServerRequest($swoole_request);
    $swoole_response->header(
        "Content-Type", "text/plain");
    $response = Pipe::exec($request);
    $swoole_response->end($response);
});
$server->start();
```

Unfortunately, a `Swoole\Http\Request` instance passed to the callback associated with the `on()` method is not PSR-7-compliant! Accordingly, we need to define a `Chat\Http\SwooleToPsr7` class and a `swooleRequestToServerRequest()` method that performs the conversion using a static call. We then set headers on the `Swoole\Http|Response` instance and return a value from the pipe to complete the circuit.

It's extremely important for you to note that the standard PHP superglobals, such as `$_GET` and `$_POST`, do not work as expected from a running Swoole server instance. The main point of entry is the initial program you use to start the Swoole server from the command line. The only incoming request parameter is the actual initial program filename. Any subsequent input must be captured through the `Swoole\Http\Request` instance that's passed to the `on()` function.

The documentation found at `https://php.net/swoole` does not show all of the methods available for the `Swoole\HTTP\Request` and `Swoole\HTTP\Response` classes. However, on the Swoole website itself, you can find the relevant documentation, which is also listed here:

- https://www.swoole.co.uk/docs/modules/swoole-http-request
- https://www.swoole.co.uk/docs/modules/swoole-http-response

It's also worth noting that the `Swoole\HTTP\Request` object properties roughly correspond to the PHP superglobals, as shown here:

Swoole\HTTP\Request Property	Equivalent PHP Super Global
`Request::header`	`$_SERVER['HTTP_*']`
`Request::server`	`$_SERVER[*]`
`Request::get`	`$_GET`
`Request::post`	`$_POST`
`Request::cookie`	`$_COOKIE`
`Request::files`	`$_FILES`

Table 12.2 – Swoole request mapping to PHP superglobals

Another consideration is that using Xdebug in Swoole coroutines can lead to segmentation faults and other issues, up to and including a **core dump**. A best practice is to enable Swoole debugging with the `--enable-debug` flag when first installing Swoole using `pecl`. To test the application, we proceed as follows:

1. From a command shell into the PHP 8.1 Docker container, we run the Swoole version of our Chat API, as follows. The message immediately displayed is a result of `$server->on("start", function() {})`:

```
# cd /repo/ch12
# php php8_chat_swoole.php
Swoole http server is started at http://0.0.0.0:9501
```

2. We then open another terminal window on our host computer and open another shell into the PHP 8.1 Docker container. From there, we are able to run the `/repo/ch12/php8_chat_test.php` test program, as follows:

```
# cd /repo/ch12
# php php8_chat_test.php http://localhost:9501 1000
```

3. Note the two additional arguments. The first argument tells the test program to use the Swoole version of the API rather than the old version that uses the Apache Web Server. The last arguments tell the test program to run through 1,000 iterations.

Let's now have a look at the output, as follows:

```
root@php8_tips_php8_1 [ /repo/ch12 ]# php php8_chat_test.php \
        http://localhost:9501 1000
0       coconnel :      Dubai:AE:2956587 :      2021-01-01 00:00:00
1        htyler :       Sharjah:AE:1324473 :    2022-02-02 01:01:01
...
998     cvalenci : Caloocan City:PH:1500 :      2023-03-19 09:54:54
```

```
999    smccormi :           Budta:PH:1273715 :    2021-04-20 10:55:55
From User: ajenkins
Elapsed Time: 1.8595671653748
```

The most notable feature of the output is the elapsed time. If you look back at the previous section, you'll note that the API running as a traditional PHP application using Apache took about 3.35 seconds to complete 1,000 iterations, whereas the same API, running under Swoole, completes in approximately 1.86 seconds: almost half the time!

Please note that this is without any additional optimization. Swoole has many other features we could use, including the ability to define in-memory tables, spawn tasks off additional worker threads, and use event loops to facilitate caching, among other possibilities. As you can see, Swoole immediately provides a performance boost and is well worth investigating as a possible way to gain even more performance out of your existing applications.

Now that you have an idea of how Swoole might be used to improve application performance, let's have a look at other potential PHP async solutions.

Using selected PHP frameworks in async mode

There are a number of other PHP frameworks that implement the asynchronous programming model. In this section, we cover ReactPHP, the most popular of the PHP async frameworks, as well as Amp, another popular PHP async framework. In addition, we show you how selected PHP frameworks can be used in async mode.

It's important to note that many of the PHP frameworks able to operate in asynchronous mode have a dependency on the Swoole extension. The one that does not have this dependency is ReactPHP, covered next.

Working with ReactPHP

ReactPHP (https://reactphp.org/) is an implementation of the **Reactor software design pattern** and was inspired by the non-blocking asynchronous **Node.js** framework (https://nodejs.org/en/), among others.

Although ReactPHP does not give you the automatic performance increase seen with the Swoole extension, it has a big advantage in that it does not rely upon features of UNIX or Linux, and can thus run on a Windows server. The other advantage of ReactPHP is that it has no specific dependency on PHP extensions, other than those already included as standard extensions.

The core of any ReactPHP application is the `React\EventLoop\Loop` class. As the name implies, a `Loop` instance starts up effectively as an **infinite loop**. Most PHP infinite loops spell disaster for your application! In this case, however, the loop is used with a server instance that continuously listens to requests on a given port.

Another key component of ReactPHP is `React\Socket\Server`. This class opens a socket on the given port, enabling a ReactPHP application to listen for HTTP requests directly without having to involve a web server.

Other features of ReactPHP include the ability to listen for UDP requests, a non-blocking cache, and the implementation of async promises. ReactPHP also features a `Stream` component that allows you to defer filesystem reads and writes, greatly speeding up performance because your application no longer has to wait for such file I/O requests to finish.

One final advantage to using ReactPHP is that it's fully compliant with PSR-7 (HTTP messaging). We'll now look at the example program that runs the `Chat` API described earlier, rewritten using ReactPHP. Here are the steps to rewrite the program:

1. From Command Prompt into the Docker PHP 8 container, using Composer, we install the necessary ReactPHP components:

   ```
   cd /repo/ch12
   composer require --ignore-platform-reqs react/event-loop
   composer require --ignore-platform-reqs react/http
   composer require --ignore-platform-reqs react/socket
   ```

2. We then rewrite /repo/ch12/php8_chat_swoole.php and rename it as /repo/ch12/php8_chat_react.php. The first thing we need to change are the `use` statements:

   ```
   // /repo/ch12/php8_chat_react.php
   include __DIR__ . '/vendor/autoload.php';
   use Chat\Message\Pipe;
   use React\EventLoop\Factory;
   use React\Http\Server;
   use React\Http\Message\Response as ReactResponse;
   use Psr\Http\Message\ServerRequestInterface;
   ```

3. We then start a session and create a `React\EventLoop\Locp` instance, as follows:

```
session_start();
$loop = Factory::create();
```

4. We now define a handler that accepts a PSR-7 `ServerRequestInterface` instance as an argument and returns a `React\Http\Message\Response` instance:

```
$server = new Server($loop,
function (ServerRequestInterface $request) {
    return new ReactResponse(200,
        ['Content-Type' => 'text/plain'],
        Pipe::exec($request)
    );
});
```

5. We then set up a `React\Socker\Server` instance to listen on port `9501` and execute a loop, like this:

```
$socket = new React\Socket\Server(9501, $loop);
$server->listen($socket);
echo "Server running at http://locahost:9501\n";
$loop->run();
```

We then open a separate command shell into the PHP 8.1 container and start the ReactPHP server as follows:

`root@php8_tips_php8_1 [ /repo/ch12 ]# php php8_chat_react.php`

From another command shell into the PHP 8.1 container, we can then run the test program as follows:
`root@php8_tips_php8_1 [ /repo/ch12 ]# php php8_chat_test.php \`

`http://localhost:9501`

The output (not shown) is similar to that shown when using the Swoole extension.

Next, we have a look at another popular PHP async framework: Amp.

Implementing PHP async using Amp

The **Amp framework** (https://amphp.org/), much like ReactPHP, provides implementations of timers, promises, and streams. Amp also provides coroutine support, as well as an asynchronous iterator component. The latter is extremely intriguing, as iteration is essential to most PHP applications. If you can move iteration into an asynchronous mode of processing, while potentially involving a lot of refactoring, it might provide an immense boost to your application's performance. Another interesting twist is that Amp can directly use any ReactPHP components!

To install Amp, use Composer. The various Amp components are available in discrete repositories, so you don't have to install the entire framework—only what you need. The actual implementation of a PHP Amp server is much like the example shown for ReactPHP.

Let's now have a look at another framework that can operate in PHP async mode: **Mezzio**, formerly called **Zend Expressive**.

Using Mezzio with Swoole

The **Mezzio** framework (https://docs.mezzio.dev/) is the brainchild of Matthew Weier O'Phinney (https://mwop.net/) and represents a continuation of an older framework, **Zend Framework**, and a later one, **Zend Expressive**. Mezzio falls into the relatively new category of a **micro framework**. Micro frameworks do not have any reliance on the aging **Model-View-Controller** (**MVC**) software design pattern and are mainly oriented toward **RESTful API development**. In practical terms, micro frameworks support the principle of PHP middleware and operate with much less overhead and correspondingly greater speed.

In order to use a Mezzio application with Swoole, just the following three things are needed:

1. Install the Swoole extension (described earlier in this chapter).
2. Install the `mezzio-swoole` component, like this:

    ```
    composer require mezzio/mezzio-swoole
    ```

3. You would then need to run Mezzio using a Swoole server instance. This can be accomplished with the following command:

    ```
    /path/to/project/vendor/bin/laminas mezzio:swoole:start
    ```

4. In the configuration file for your Mezzio application, you would need to add the following key:

```
return [
    'mezzio-swoole' => [
        'swoole-http-server' => [
            'host' => '0.0.0.0',    // all IP addresses
            'port' => 9501,
        ]
    ],
];
```

To gain further performance improvements, you should of course also rewrite the appropriate portions of your code to take advantage of PHP async functionality. Next, we have a look at a PHP extension that goes beyond async.

Working with the parallel extension

The `parallel` extension (https://www.php.net/parallel) was introduced to work with PHP 7.2 and above. Its purpose is to go the next step beyond PHP async and into the world of full-blown parallel processing. The `parallel` extension provides five key low-level classes that can form the basis for a parallel-processing application. Using this extension allows PHP developers to write parallel code much like the **Go** language. Let's start with `parallel\Runtime`.

The parallel\Runtime class

Each `parallel\Runtime` instance spawns a new PHP thread. You can then use `parallel\Runtime::run()` to schedule a task. The first argument to `run()` is `Closure` (an anonymous function). The optional second argument is `$argv`, representing input arguments passed to the task at runtime. `parallel\Runtime::close()` is used to gracefully shut down a thread. When an error condition arises, a thread can be immediately exited using `parallel\Runtime::kill()`.

The parallel\Future class

A `parallel\Future` instance is created as a return value from `parallel\Runtime::run()`. It acts much like a PHP async *promise* (described earlier in this chapter). This class has three methods, listed here, that perform the following actions:

- `parallel\Future::value()`

  Returns the fulfilled value of the task

- `parallel\Future::cancel()`

  Cancels the task that represents a promise *failed* state

- `parallel\Future::cancelled()|done()`

  Returns task state if it's still unfulfilled

The parallel\Channel class

The `parallel\Channel` class allows developers to share information between tasks. Use the `__construct()` method or `make()` to create a channel. If no argument is supplied to `__construct()` or if a second argument to `make()` is not supplied, the channel is considered unbuffered. If an integer is supplied to `__construct()` or as a second argument to `make()`, the value represents the channel's **capacity**. You can then use the `parallel\Channel::send()` and `parallel\Channel::recv()` methods to send and receive data through the channel.

Unbuffered channels block calls to `send()` until there is a receiver and vice versa. Buffered channels, on the other hand, do not block until the capacity has been reached.

The parallel\Events class

The `parallel\Events` class is similar to the *event loop* described in the first section of this chapter. This class has `addChannel()` and `addFuture()` methods to add channels and/or future instances to monitor. The `setBlocking()` method allows the event loop to monitor events in either blocking or non-blocking modes. Use the `setTimeout()` method to set an overall control period (in milliseconds) for how long the loop is allowed to continue. Finally, the `poll()` method causes the event loop to poll for the next event.

Installing the parallel extension

The `parallel` extension can be installed with the `pecl` command or using precompiled binaries, just as any other non-standard PHP extension. It's extremely important to note, however, that this extension only works on **Zend Thread Safety** (**ZTS**) PHP installations. Accordingly, if using Docker, you would need to obtain a PHP ZTS image, or, if custom-compiling PHP, you would need to use either the `--enable-zts` (Windows) or `--enable-maintainer-zts` (non-Windows) `configure` utility flag.

Now that you have an idea of how to use a number of selected PHP extensions and frameworks in async mode, we'll look into the future and discuss PHP 8.1 fibers.

Learning about PHP 8.1 fibers

A **Request for Comments** (**RFC**) was published in March 2021 by Aaron Piotrowski and Niklas Keller, both PHP core team developers, outlining the case for including support for **fibers** in the PHP language core. The RFC was ratified at the end of the month and has now been implemented in the upcoming 8.1 version of PHP.

The fiber implementation is low-level, meaning that it is mainly designed to be used as part of a PHP async framework such as ReactPHP or Amp, or an extension such as the Swoole extension. Because this will, as of PHP 8.1 and beyond, be a core part of the language, developers will not have to worry so much about which extensions are loaded. Also, this greatly enhances PHP async frameworks as they now have low-level support, directly in the language core, greatly improving performance. Let's now have a look at the `Fiber` class itself.

Discovering the Fiber class

The PHP 8.1 `Fiber` class offers a bare-bones implementation upon which async framework and extension developers can build timers, event loops, promises, and other async artifacts.

Here is the formal class definition:

```
final class Fiber {
    public function __construct(callable $callback) {}
    public function start(mixed ...$args): mixed {}
    public function resume(mixed $value = null): mixed {}
    public function throw(Throwable $exception): mixed {}
    public function isStarted(): bool {}
    public function isSuspended(): bool {}
```

```
    public function isRunning(): bool {}
    public function isTerminated(): bool {}
    public function getReturn(): mixed {}
    public static function this(): ?self {}
    public static function suspend(
        mixed $value = null): mixed {}
}
```

Here is a summary of the `Fiber` class methods:

Fiber method	Description
`Fiber::start()`	Starts fiber execution. The callback associated with the fiber can then be suspended, canceled and resumed at will. Any arguments are passed to the callback. Suspend the fiber by making a static call `$fiber::suspend()`. Cancel the fiber by having it throw an exception using `$fiber->throw()`.
`Fiber::resume()`	Restarts fiber execution. Returns the value provided by `Fiber::suspend()`.
`Fiber::suspend()`	This method is made via a static call from inside the callback assigned to the fiber. You can then resume or cancel the fiber using `suspend()` or `throw()`.
`Fiber::throw()`	When calling this method, provide an instance of `Throwable`. The fiber is then canceled.

`Fiber::isStarted()`
`Fiber::isSuspended()`
`Fiber::isRunning()`
`Fiber::isTerminated()`
	These four methods return a `boolean` and are used to display the state of the fiber.

`Fiber::getReturn()`	Much like a PHP `Generator`, you can use this method to get the value provided by the callback's `return` (if any).
`Fiber::this()`	Returns the currently running fiber instance.

Table 12.3 – Fiber class method summary

As you can see from *Table 12.3*, after creating a `Fiber` instance, use `start()` to run the callback associated with the fiber. After that, you are free to suspend, resume, or cause the fiber to fail, using `throw()`. You can also just let the callback run in its own fiber, and use `getReturn()` to retrieve the returned information. You might also note that the `is*()` methods can be used to determine the fiber's state at any given moment.

> **Tip**
> For more information on the PHP 8.1 fibers implementation, please have a look at the following RFC: https://wiki.php.net/rfc/fibers.

Let's now have a look at an example that illustrates the use of fibers.

Using fibers

PHP 8.1 fibers form the basis of a PHP async application. Although the primary audience for fibers is framework and extension developers, any PHP developer can benefit from this class. To illustrate the problem PHP fibers can solve, let's have a look at a simple example.

Defining a sample program that performs blocking operations

In this example, written using the synchronous programming model, we perform three actions, as follows:

- Execute an HTTP `GET` request.
- Perform a database query.
- Write information to an access log.

Already having some knowledge of async programming, you realize that all three tasks represent *blocking* operations. Here are the steps we'll take:

1. First, we define a PHP file to be included that defines the callbacks:

```php
// /repo/ch12/php8_fibers_include.php
define('WAR_AND_PEACE',
    'https://www.gutenberg.org/files/2600/2500-0.txt');
define('DB_FILE', __DIR__
    . '/../sample_data/geonames.db');
define('ACCESS_LOG', __DIR__ . '/access.log');
$callbacks = [
    'read_url' => function (string $url) {
        return file_get_contents($url); },
    'db_query' => function (string $iso2) {
        $pdo = new PDO('sqlite:' . DB_FILE);
        $sql = 'SELECT * FROM geonames '
            . 'WHERE country_code = ?';
        $stmt = $pdo->prepare($sql);
        $stmt->execute([$iso2]);
        return var_export(
            $stmt->fetchAll(PDO::FETCH_ASSOC), TRUE);
    },
    'access_log' => function (string $info) {
        $info = date('Y-m-d H:i:s') . ": $info\n";
```

```
            return file_put_contents(
                ACCESS_LOG, $info, FILE_APPEND);
        },
    ];
    return $callbacks;
```

2. Next, we define a PHP program that includes the callbacks' definition and executes them sequentially. We use a PHP 8 `match  { }` construct to assign different arguments to pass to the appropriate callback. Finally, we return the number of bytes generated by the callback by simply returning a string and running `strlen()`:

```
// /repo/ch12/php8_fibers_blocked.php
$start = microtime(TRUE);
$callbacks = include __DIR__ . '/php8_fibers_include.php';
foreach ($callbacks as $key => $exec) {
    $info = match ($key) {
        'read_url' => WAR_AND_PEACE,
        'db_query' => 'IN',
        'access_log' => __FILE__,
        default => ''
    };
    $result = $exec($info);
    echo "Executing $key" . strlen($result) . "\n";
}
echo "Elapsed Time:" . (microtime(TRUE) - $start) . "\n";
```

If we then run the program as is, the results are predictably abysmal, as we can see here:

```
root@php8_tips_php8_1 [ /repo/ch12 ]#
php php8_fibers_blocked.php
Executing read_url:      3359408
Executing db_query:      23194
Executing access_log:    2
Elapsed Time:6.0914640426636
```

The **Uniform Resource Locator** (**URL**) request to download Tolstoy's *War and Peace* took the most time and produced a byte count of over 3 million. The total elapsed time was a fraction over 6 seconds.

Let's now look at how the calling program could be rewritten using fibers.

Example program using fibers

From the PHP 8.1 Docker container, we can define a calling program that uses fibers. Here are the steps to do this:

1. First, we include the callbacks, as we did earlier, like this:

    ```
    // /repo/ch12/php8_fibers_unblocked.php
    $start = microtime(TRUE);
    $callbacks = include __DIR__
        . '/php8_fibers_include.php';
    ```

2. Next, we create a `Fiber` instance to wrap each callback. We then use `start()` to start the callback, supplying the appropriate information:

    ```
    $fibers = [];
    foreach ($callbacks as $key => $exec) {
        $info = match ($key) {
            'read_url'   => WAR_AND_PEACE,
            'db_query'   => 'IN',
            'access_log' => __FILE__,
            default      => ''
        };
        $fibers[$key] = new Fiber($exec);
        $fibers[$key]->start($info);
    }
    ```

3. We then set up a loop and check in on each callback to see if it's finished. If so, we echo the results from `getReturn()` and unset the fiber:

    ```
    $count = count($fibers);
    $names = array_keys($fibers);
    while ($count) {
        $count = 0;
        foreach ($names as $name) {
    ```

```
            if ($fibers[$name]->isTerminated()) {
                $result = $fibers[$name]->getReturn();
                echo "Executing $name: \t"
                    . strlen($result) . "\n";
                unset($names[$name]);
            } else {
                $count++;
            }
        }
    }
    echo "Elapsed Time:" . (microtime(TRUE) - $start) . "\n";
```

Please note that this example is for illustration only. It's far more likely that you would use an existing framework such as ReactPHP or Amp, both of which have been rewritten to take advantage of PHP 8.1 fibers. It's also important to note that even if multiple fibers are running simultaneously, the shortest runtime you can achieve is directly proportionate to the amount of time taken by the longest-running task. Let's now have a look at the effect of fibers on ReactPHP and Swoole.

Examining the effect of fibers on ReactPHP and Swoole

For this illustration, you need to open two separate command shells into the PHP 8.1 Docker container. Follow the directions given in the previous section, but open two command shells instead of one. We will then use the `/repo/ch12/php8_chat_test.php` program to test the effect of fibers. Let's run the first test, using the built-in PHP web server as a control.

Testing using the built-in PHP web server

In the first test, we use the built-in PHP web server and the conventional `/repo/ch12/php8_chat_ajax.php` implementation. Here are the steps we'll take:

1. In both command shells, change to the `/repo/ch12` directory, like this:

    ```
    # cd /repo/ch12
    ```

2. In the first command shell, run a standard HTTP server using the built-in PHP web server, with this command:

    ```
    # php -S localhost:9501 php8_chat_ajax.php
    ```

3. In the second command shell, execute the test program, as shown:

```
php php8_chat_test.php http://localhost:9501 1000 --no
```

The resulting output should look something like this:

```
root@php8_tips_php8_1 [ /repo/ch12 ]#
php php8_chat_test.php http://localhost:9501 1000 --no
From User: pduarte
Elapsed Time: 1.687940120697
```

As you can see, the conventional code, written using synchronous programming, came in at around 1.7 seconds for 1,000 iterations. Let's now have a look at running the same test using ReactPHP.

Testing using ReactPHP

In the second test, we use our `/repo/ch12/php8_chat_react.php` ReactPHP implementation. Here are the steps we'll take:

1. In the first command shell, hit *Ctrl + C* to exit the built-in PHP web server.
2. Exit and re-enter the first command shell using `exit`, followed by either `init shell` for Windows or `./init.sh shell` for Linux or Mac.
3. Start the ReactPHP server using this command:

```
# php php8_chat_react.php
```

4. In the second command shell, execute the test program, like this:

```
php php8_chat_test.php http://localhost:9501 1000 --no
```

The resulting output should look something like this:

```
root@php8_tips_php8_1 [ /repo/ch12 ]#
php php8_chat_test.php http://localhost:9501 1000 --no
From User: klang
Elapsed Time: 1.2330160140991
```

From the output, you can see that ReactPHP benefits greatly from fibers. The total elapsed time was an impressive 1.2 seconds for 1,000 iterations!

This concludes our discussion of PHP 8.1 fibers. You now have an idea of what fibers are and how they can be used directly in your program code, as well as how they benefit external PHP async frameworks.

Summary

In this chapter, you learned the difference between conventional synchronous programming and asynchronous programming. Key terms such as event loops, timers, promises, and channels were covered. This knowledge gives you the ability to determine when a block of code is written using the asynchronous programming model, and how to rewrite portions of existing synchronous model applications to take advantage of asynchronous features.

You then learned about the Swoole extension and how it can be applied to existing application code to achieve performance improvements. You also learned about a number of other frameworks and extensions that operate in an asynchronous manner. You reviewed concrete code examples and now have a headstart on writing asynchronous code.

In the last section, you were introduced to PHP 8.1 fibers. You then reviewed a code example showing you how to create cooperative multitasking functions and class methods using PHP 8.1 fibers. You also saw how selected PHP async frameworks are able to benefit from PHP 8.1 fiber support, providing even more performance improvements.

This is the last chapter in the book. We hope you have enjoyed reviewing the vast array of new features and benefits made available in PHP 8. You also now have a deeper understanding of potential traps to avoid in object-oriented and procedural code, as well as various changes to PHP 8 extensions. With this knowledge, not only are you now in a position to write better code, but you also have a solid plan of action that minimizes the chance of application code failure following a PHP 8 migration.

Packt.com

Subscribe to our online digital library for full access to over 7,000 books and videos, as well as industry leading tools to help you plan your personal development and advance your career. For more information, please visit our website.

Why subscribe?

- Spend less time learning and more time coding with practical eBooks and Videos from over 4,000 industry professionals
- Improve your learning with Skill Plans built especially for you
- Get a free eBook or video every month
- Fully searchable for easy access to vital information
- Copy and paste, print, and bookmark content

Did you know that Packt offers eBook versions of every book published, with PDF and ePub files available? You can upgrade to the eBook version at packt.com and as a print book customer, you are entitled to a discount on the eBook copy. Get in touch with us at customercare@packtpub.com for more details.

At www.packt.com, you can also read a collection of free technical articles, sign up for a range of free newsletters, and receive exclusive discounts and offers on Packt books and eBooks.

Other Books You May Enjoy

If you enjoyed this book, you may be interested in these other books by Packt:

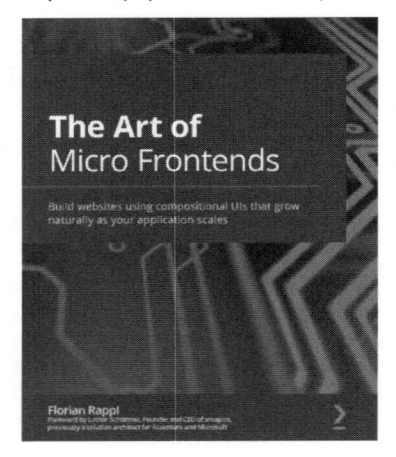

The Art of Micro Frontends

Florian Rappl

ISBN: 978-1-80056-356-8

- Understand how to choose the right micro frontend architecture
- Design screens for compositional UIs
- Create a great developer experience for micro frontend solutions
- Achieve enhanced user experiences with micro frontends
- Introduce governance and boundary checks for managing distributed frontends
- Build scalable modular web applications from scratch or by migrating an existing monolith

Responsive Web Design with HTML5 and CSS - Third Edition

Ben Frain

ISBN: 978-1-83921-156-0

- Integrate CSS media queries into your designs; apply different styles to different devices
- Load different sets of images depending upon screen size or resolution
- Leverage the speed, semantics, and clean markup of accessible HTML patterns
- Implement SVGs into your designs to provide resolution-independent images
- Apply the latest features of CSS like custom properties, variable fonts, and CSS Grid
- Add validation and interface elements like date and color pickers to HTML forms
- Understand the multitude of ways to enhance interface elements with filters, shadows, animations, and more

Packt is searching for authors like you

If you're interested in becoming an author for Packt, please visit `authors.packtpub.com` and apply today. We have worked with thousands of developers and tech professionals, just like you, to help them share their insight with the global tech community. You can make a general application, apply for a specific hot topic that we are recruiting an author for, or submit your own idea.

Share Your Thoughts

Now you've finished *PHP 8 Programming Tips, Tricks and Best Practices*, we'd love to hear your thoughts! Scan the QR code below to go straight to the Amazon review page for this book and share your feedback or leave a review on the site that you purchased it from.

`https://packt.link/r/180107187X`

Your review is important to us and the tech community and will help us make sure we're delivering excellent quality content.

Index

Symbols

__autoload() function
  disadvantages 150
  using, in PHP 8 150-152
@ error control operator
  handling 106
@ operator
  about 107-109
  usage 106, 107
__sleep() magic method
  about 166, 167
  code break 167-169
__toString() magic method
  working with 162-164
__wakeup() magic method
  using, to reopen file handle 169-171

A

abstract private method
  about 354
  handling, in traits 354
abstract private method, in PHP 8
  reference link 354
access control list (ACL) 78
action code 76
addGlob()
  options 277
addPattern()
  options 277, 278
addr()
  FFI data, working with 132-134
Advanced Vector Extensions
    (AVX) instructions 374
alignof()
  FFI data, working with 129-131
ambiguous string offset cast 104, 105
American Standard Code for Information
    Interchange (ASCII) 132, 258
Amp framework
  PHP async, implementing with 473
  URL 473
anonymous classes
  about 357
  usage, controlling 357-359
anonymous functions
  versus arrow functions 56
anonymous functions, generating
    from class methods
  changes 298-300

490   Index

Apache JMeter tool
  URL 441
  using 441, 442
application programming interface
    (API) 118, 247, 291, 455
Argon2i 232
Argon2id 232
arithmetic operations
  differences, handling 214
  non-scalar data types, handling 215-217
array
  handling, curly brace usage
    changes 225-227
  handling, in PHP 8 223
  handling, negative array offset 223-225
  versus SplFixedArray 382, 383
array handling
  array, unpacking 94-96
  element 92
  illegal offset types 96, 97
  offsets, in non-array variables 93, 94
  promoted warnings 91
  speeding up 381, 382
  techniques 67
ArrayObject
  versus SplFixedArray 382, 383
array_slice() function
  using 69, 70
array_splice() function
  working with 67, 68
arrow functions
  about 56
  generic syntax 56
  reference link 61
  using 56-60
  variable inheritance 57
  versus anonymous functions 56
assembly language 367

assert() function
  changes, handling 233
assert() function, usage
  changes, handling 234, 235
assertion 445
associative array 96
async coroutine support
  working with 453
attributes
  about 10, 300
  syntax 13-15
  viewing, with Reflection
    extension 15-17
  working with 10
Attributes class 10-13
attributes v2
  reference link 17
authorization callback 76
authorizer
  usage example 77-82
  used, for securing SQLite databases 75

B

backtraces changes
  examining 316
backward-compatible breaks
  detecting, with numeric strings 210, 211
BC breaks
  reviewing 412
  spotting, before migration 411
BC BreakScan class
  application files, scanning 428-430
  developing 417
  individual scan methods,
    examining 420-424
  infrastructural methods,
    defining 417-420

Index   491

scanFromCallbacks(), examining 422
scanIsResource(), examining 421
scanMagicSignatures(), examining 423
scanRemovedFunctions(),
    examining 420, 421
BC break scan configuration file
  creating 412
  magic method signature violations,
      detecting 414, 415
  strpos() search configuration,
      defining 413
BC breaks, with is_resource()
  detecting 413
bcrypt 232
Beginners' All-purpose Symbolic
    Instruction Code (BASIC) 112
bitwise operations
  differences, handling 214
  non-scalar data types, handling 215-217
black-box tests 432
blocking operations 451
  performing, with PHP 8.1
      fibers 478, 479
BreakScan class calling program
  building 424-428
bubble sort
  about 137
  reference link 137
built-in PHP web server
  used, for testing PHP 8.1 fibers 481
bytecode 366-368

C

cast()
  FFI data, working with 134-136
CentOS Linux
  PHP 8 installation 437-439

changes, to mb_ereg*() functions
  examining 260
changes, to mb_ereg_replace()
  examining 261, 262
channels
  implementing 456
C language
  relationship, with PHP 113
class constant
  conventional class constant,
      using 336, 337
  special class constant, using 337, 338
  using 335
class constructor
  about 156
  inconsistencies, addressing in 158-162
client Uniform Resource Locator
    (URL) (cURL) 239
code
  improving, with typed properties 33
code reduction
  with constructor property
      promotion 8, 9
COM extension changes
  reviewing 282
comment handling
  differences 300, 301
commit hooks 410
communicating sequential
    processes (CSP) 456
comparison changes
  in PHP 8 213
compile flag changes
  GD extension 264, 265
Completely Automated Public Turing
    test to tell Computers and Humans
    Apart (CAPTCHA) 456

complex BC break detection
  addressing 415, 416
complex match expressions
  example 21-23
Component Object Model (COM) 282
Composer
  issues, handling with 443-445
Computer Science 101 (CS101) 137
concatenation operations
  differences, handling 214
concatenation operator 51
constants
  using, in PHP 8 206, 207
constructor changes
  handling, in method and class
    of same name 156-158
  inconsistencies, addressing in
    class constructor 158-162
  working with 156
constructor property promotion
  about 33
  reference link 10
  syntax 7, 8
  using 7
  using, for code reduction 8, 9
container class
  implementing, with SplObjectStorage
    class 398-402
contravariant parameters
  using 180-182
conventional class constant
  using 336, 337
core deprecations
  examining 301
  in parameter order 302, 303
core functionality, removed in PHP 8
  examining 287

core functions
  calling, with named arguments 24
coroutine support 458
counter-intuitive results
  dealing with 52
covariant returns 177-180
createFromInterface() method
  about 349
  examining 349, 350
create_function()
  working with 291-295
crypt() function
  changes, handling 230, 231
cURL extension changes 282
curly brace usage changes
  handling 225-227
custom error-handling changes
  examining 314, 315

D

data
  comparing, with Foreign Function
    Interface (FFI) 124-127
database extension changes
  operating system library
    requirements 274
data type checking
  mb_str*() function 258
data types
  exploring 27
  mixed type 30
  union types 27
DateTimeImmutable
  use case 347-349
DateTime methods
  createFromInterface() method,
    examining 349, 350

Index   493

DateTimeImmutable, use case 347-349
  using 347
Debian/Ubuntu Linux
  PHP 8 installation 435, 436
  PHP versions, switching
      between 436, 437
Defense Encryption Standard (DES) 230
dependency injection (DI) 398
deprecated functionality
  in PHP 8 extensions 310-312
deprecated PHP 8 extension functionality
  discovering 307
  DOM extension changes 308
  PostgreSQL extension changes 309
  XML-RPC extension changes 307
deprecated security-related
      functionality, in PHP 8
  backtraces changes 316
  custom error-handling changes 314, 315
  examining 312
  PDO error handling changes 316, 317
  PHP 8 stream-filter changes 312-314
  track_errors php.ini setting 317, 318
de-referencing 62
development environment
  examining 409, 410
disable_functions
  changes, handling 228
disable_functions, handling differences
  examining 228-230
docblocks 267
Doctrine ORM
  reference link 17
Document Object Model (DOM) 308
DOMChildNode interface
  about 343
  examining 343, 344

DOM extension changes 308
DOM extension interfaces
  discovering 341
  DOMChildNode interface,
      examining 343, 344
  DOMParentNode interface,
      examining 341-343
  DOM usage, example 344-347
DOM Living Standard
  about 308, 341
  reference link 308
DOMParentNode interface
  about 341
  examining 341-343
DOM usage
  example 344-347
DynASM
  about 371
  reference link 372

E

each() function
  working with 288-291
empty() function, documentation
  reference link 256
empty needle-argument handling
  mb_str*() function 256-258
empty needle arguments
  handling 197-199
engineering notation 208
environment
  about 408
  components 409
  defining 409
error-level defaults 89
error_reporting() function 108, 109

errors
  dealing with 89
event loop
  implementing 454
Expat
  reference link 253
Expat C library 253
expensive objects 394
Extended Markup Language (XML) 46
Extensible Markup Language (XML) 12
extension changes
  examining 283
extension gotchas
  working with 274
external C library
  integrating, into PHP script 137-139

F

Fedora Linux
  PHP 8 installation 437-439
fetch modes 328
FFI class
  comparison methods 124-127
  creational methods 119
  examining 118
  infrastructural methods 131
  methods 118
  reference link 118
FFI creational methods
  working with 119
FFI\CType instances
  creating 119-121
  using 120, 121
FFI data
  working, with addr() 132-134
  working, with alignof() 129-131
  working, with cast() 134-136

working, with free() 132-134
working, with memcpy() 132-134
working, with memset() 132-134
working, with sizeof() 129-131
working, with typeof() 128
FFI extension
  need for 117, 118
FFI extension data
  information, extracting from 127
FFI infrastructural methods
  using 131
FFI instances
  creating 122, 123
  using 122, 123
Fiber class
  discovering 476
  methods 477
file descriptor (FD) 454
First-In, First-Out (FIFO) 188
fluent interface 333
Foreign Function Interface (FFI)
  about 112
  adding, into PHP 116
  data, comparing with 124-127
  usage, avoiding for speed 117
  usage scenarios 115, 116
  using, in application 137
free()
  FFI data, working with 132-134
functions
  affected, by locale
    independence 220-223
functions, removed in PHP 8
  create_function(), working with 291-295
  each() function, working with 288-291
  examining 287, 288
  money_format() function,
    working with 295-297

G

GD extension changes
  about 265, 266
  compile flag changes 264, 265
  dealing with 262
  resource-to-object migration 263, 264
GD library
  reference link 263
generic syntax 56
GeoNames
  reference link 74, 288
getters 35
Git Hooks
  reference link 410
Golang 458
Go language 456, 474
Graphics Interchange Format (GIF) 262

H

haystack argument
  versus needle argument 195
hot functions 374
HyperText Markup Language
  (HTML) 59, 246, 297
HyperText Transfer Protocol
  (HTTP) 242, 463

I

illegal offset 96
illegal sort functions
  handling 393, 394
imagesetinterpolation() function
  reference link 266
implode()
  changes, examining to 204, 205

inconsistent string-to-numeric
  comparison results
  dealing with 212, 213
indices 96
InfiniteIterator
  reference link 61
infinite loop 471
initialization vector (IV) 230
Integrated Development
  Environment (IDE) 410
interfaces
  working with 341
Intermediate Representation (IR) 372
International Organization for
  Standardization (ISO) 20, 295
interpreter 368
inter-process communication (IPC) 458
Intl extension changes
  working with 281, 282
inversion of control container 398
I/O-intensive application
  examining 463-467
is_resource() function
  code break, involving 240-242
IteratorAggregate migration
  implementing, instead of
    Traversable 245, 246

J

JavaScript Object Notation
  (JSON) 27, 64, 164, 459
Java Virtual Machine (JVM) 367, 442
JIT compiler
  debugging with 378-380
  enabling 372, 373
  PHP program execution,
    discovering with 371, 372

496   Index

tracing mode, configuring 373, 374
using 375-378
working with 366, 367
JIT compiler settings
   discovering 381
JIT tracer operation
   configuring 373, 374
   CPU opt flags 374
   JIT trigger 374
   optimization level 374
   register allocation 374
Just-in-Time (JIT) compiler 7, 451

K

keys
   stable sorting effect, examining 391-393

L

Last-In, First-Out (LIFO) 188
leading-numeric string 208
libxml extension
   changes to 253
Liskov Substitution Principle 177
locale independence
   about 219
   functions, affected 220-223
   operations, affected 220-223
   side effects 220
Lua programming language 371

M

machine code 366-368
machine language 367

magic methods
   about 324
   reference link 164
   using, to control PHP
      serialization 174-176
magic method signature violations
   detecting 414, 415
Mandelbrot 375
master branch 432
match expressions
   example 19, 20
   general syntax 18, 19
   incorporating, into program code 18
   reference link 23
match function 291
mb_str*() function
   data type checking 258
   empty needle-argument
      handling 256-258
   needle-argument differences,
      discovering 256
mbstring extension changes
   discovering 304
mbstring extension function overloading
   reference link 305
   working with 305-307
mbstring extension functions
   reference link 257
mbstring extension removed aliases
   handling 304
mb_strrpos()
   differences 259, 260
memcpy()
   FFI data, working with 132-134
memory leaks 140
memset()
   FFI data, working with 132-134

Index   497

merge sort 137
method and class, of same name
   changes, handling 156-158
method conflicts
   resolving, between traits 351-353
method signature 182
method signature changes
   about 324
   class constant, using 335
   discovering 324
   learning 340
   magic method signatures,
      managing 324-328
   PDO extension signature
      changes, dealing 328-330
   Reflection method signature
      changes, examining 328
   static methods, dealing with 330-333
   static return type, working with 333-335
   trailing commas, using 339
Mezzio framework
   URL 473
   using, with Swoole 473, 474
micro framework 473
migration
   performing 430-439
   testing 440
   testing and troubleshooting tools 440
   troubleshooting 440
mixed type
   about 30
   effect, on inheritance 31, 32
   need for 30
   reference link 32
Model-View-Controller (MVC) 473
modification time 277
money_format() function
   working with 295-297

Multi-Processing Modules (MPMs) 452
MySQL Improved (MySQLi) 274

N

named arguments
   about 24, 67
   generic syntax 24
   reference link 27
   used, for calling core functions 24
named arguments, usage
   documentation 25, 26
   order independence 25, 26
namespace
   about 360
   naming practices, exposing 362, 363
   reserved keywords, using 361
   tokenization process,
      discovering 360, 361
needle argument
   changes, handling 195
   empty needle arguments 197-199
   non-string needle arguments 195-197
   versus haystack argument 195
needle-argument differences
   discovering, in mb_str*() functions 256
needle-argument handling 256
negative array offset
   handling 223-225
nested serialization calls 173
nested ternary operators
   using 53-55
Node.js framework
   URL 470
non-scalar data types
   handling, in arithmetic
      operations 215-217
   handling, in bitwise operations 215-217

non-stable sort
  versus stable sort 387-390
non-strict comparison 208
non-string needle arguments
  dealing with 195-197
Notice-to-Warning promotion
  about 100
  ambiguous string offset cast 104, 105
  non-existent object property,
    access handling 101, 102
  non-existent offset handling 102, 103
  non-existent string offset 105
  resource IDs, misusing as
    array offset 103, 104
  uninitialized string offset 105
null length arguments
  working with, in PHP 8 203, 204
nullsafe operator
  about 46
  using 46-48
  using, to short-circuit chain 48-51
numeric array 96
numeric strings
  detecting, backward-compatible
    breaks 210, 211
  examining 208-210
  reference link 210

O

object error handling
  promoted warnings 90, 91
object-oriented programming
  (OOP) 44, 113, 247, 290, 451
object properties
  dealing with 148, 149
Object-Relational Mapper (ORM) 11
offsets 96

OOP coding differences
  dealing, with object properties 148, 149
  discovering 147
  static calls, handling in PHP 8 147, 148
  working, with PHP 8
    autoloading 149, 150
opcode 368
Open Web Application Security
    Project (OWASP)
  reference link 254
operations
  affected, by locale
    independence 220-223
order of precedence
  changes, examining 217-219

P

parallel\Channel class
  parallel\Events class 475
  using 475
parallel extension
  installing 476
  parallel\Channel class 475
  parallel\Events class 475
  parallel\Future class 475
  parallel\Runtime class 474
  URL 474
  working with 474
parallel\Future class
  using 475
parallel programming 453
parallel\Runtime class
  using 474
parameter order
  deprecated usage 302, 303
parser tokens
  reference link 360

parsing 369
password_hash() function
   changes, handling 232, 233
PCRE extension changes
   examining 279, 280
PDO error handling changes
   examining 316, 317
PECL website
   URL 116
Personal Package Archive (PPA) 435
PHP
   bytecode 367, 368
   Foreign Function Interface
      (FFI), adding into 116
   machine code 367, 368
   relationship, with C language 113
   working, without JIT 367
PHP 8
   arrays, handling 223
   comparison changes 213
   constants, using 206, 207
   installing, on CentOS Linux 437-439
   installing, on Debian/Ubuntu
      Linux 435, 436
   installing, on Fedora Linux 437-439
   installing, on Red Hat Linux 437-439
   null length arguments,
      working with 204
   Oniguruma library 260
   removed core functionality,
      examining 287
   removed functions, examining 287, 288
   resource-to-object migration 239, 240
   SplFixedArray changes,
      working with 384, 385
   SplFixedArray, working with 382
   static calls, handling in 147, 148

uniform variable syntax, impact on 62
upgrade issues, avoiding 213, 214
versus PHP 7 344
PHP 8.1 fibers
   about 476
   blocking operations, performing
      with 478, 479
   examining, on ReactPHP 481
   examining, on Swoole 481
   example 480, 481
   testing, with built-in PHP
      web server 481
   testing, with ReactPHP 482
   using 478
PHP 8 autoloading
   __autoload() function 150-152
   spl_autoload_register()
      function, using 153, 154
   spl_auto_register() function,
      running 154, 155
   working with 149, 150
PHP 8 error handling
   about 86
   error-level defaults 89
   undefined variable, handling 87
PHP 8 expanded variance support
   about 177
   contravariant parameters, using 180-182
   covariant returns, using 177-180
PHP 8 extensions
   deprecated functionality 310-312
   removed functionality,
      working with 303, 304
PHP 8 operators
   working with 40
PHP 8 stream-filter changes
   examining 312-314

PHP 8 string-to-numeric comparison
　about 207
　numeric strings, examining 208-210
PHP 8 trait handling refinements
　about 350
　abstract private method,
　　handling in traits 354
　method conflicts, resolving
　　between traits 351-353
　trait abstract signature check,
　　working with 353, 354
PHP 8, usage changes
　anonymous functions, generating
　　from class methods 298-300
　comment handling, differences 300, 301
　discovering 297
　removed typecasts 297
PHP async application
　channels, implementing 456
　creating 454
　event loop, implementing 454
　implementing, with Amp
　　framework 473
　promise, implementing 455
　streams, implementing 455
　timers, implementing 456
PHP asynchronous programming model
　about 451, 452
　working 453
PHP async solutions
　Amp framework 473
　Mezzio framework 473, 474
　ReactPHP 470-472
　using 470
PHP callback
　implementing 140-142
　usage issues 140
　working with 139

PHP comments 10, 11
PHP core extensions
　accessing 114
PHP DocBlocks
　considerations 11, 12
　misusing, drawbacks 12
　URL 17
PHP Extension Community
　　Library (PECL)
　about 115
　reference link 307
PHP extension prototyping 117
PHP extensions 113
php.ini documentation
　reference link 17
PHP magic methods
　changes, navigating 156
PHP magic methods, changes
　about 156
　dealing, with constructor changes 156
　working, with __toString() 162, 164
PHP non-core extensions
　examining 114, 115
　finding 115
PHP OPcache
　operation 369-371
PHP program execution
　about 369
　discovering, with JIT compiler 371, 372
PHP Reflection
　reference link 17
PHP script
　external C library, integrating
　　into 137-139
PHP serialization
　__sleep() magic method 166, 167
　__wakeup() magic method 169-171

Index 501

about 164
code break, in __sleep()
   method 167-169
controlling 164
controlling, with magic
   methods 174-176
example 165, 166
interface 171-173
interface issues, examining 173
PHP Standard Recommendation
   15 (PSR-15) 464
PHP synchronous programming code
   developing 451, 452
PHPUnit
   about 445
   URL 445
PHP versions
   switching, between in Debian/
      Ubuntu Linux 436, 437
Portable Network Graphics (PNG) 23
PostgreSQL extension changes 309
preg_last_error()
   reference link 279
private methods
   dealing with 355-357
production environment
   examining 411
promise
   implementing 455
PyPy VM 372

Q

quick sort 137

R

ReactPHP
   PHP 8.1 fibers, examining 481
   URL 454, 470
   used, for testing PHP 8.1 fibers 482
ReactPHP framework
   working with 470-472
Red Hat Linux
   PHP 8 installation 437-439
Red Hat Package Management (RPM) 437
Reflection*::export()
   reworking code, using 307
Reflection extension
   usage 267-270
   used, for viewing attributes 15-17
Reflection extension changes
   about 273, 274
   discovering 266
Reflection extension, class and method
   reference link 266
Reflection extension, improvements
   about 270
   ReflectionParameter::*DefaultValue*
      methods 271-273
   ReflectionType modifications 270
registers 374
regular expression (regex) 260, 279
Remi's RPM Repository
   URL 437
removed functionality, in
      PHP 8 extensions
   mbstring extension changes,
      discovering 304
   working with 303, 304
removed typecasts 297
REpresentational State Transfer
      (REST) 463

Index

Requests for Comments
   (RFCs) 302, 366, 476
resolver 455
resource-to-object migration
  about 239
  advantages 242-244
  code break, involving is_
     resource() 240-242
  GD extension 263, 264
  PHP 8 extension 239
  Traversable, to IteratorAggregate
     migration 245, 246
RESTful API development 473
reworking code
  using, Reflection*::export() 307

S

scanFromCallbacks()
  examining 422
scanIsResource()
  examining 421
scanMagicSignatures()
  examining 423
scanRemovedFunctions()
  examining 420, 421
scientific notation 208
scope resolution operator 335
Secure Hash Algorithm (SHA-1) 230
security functions
  assert() function 233
  changes, handling 227
  crypt() function 230, 231
  password_hash() function 232, 233
service locator container 398
setters 35
shell sort 137

SimpleXML extension
  changes, working with 248-252
sizeof()
  FFI data, working with 129-131
spaceship operator 124
special class constant
  using 337, 338
spl_autoload_register() function
  using, in PHP 8 153, 154
spl_auto_register() function
  running, in PHP 8 154, 155
SplDoublyLinkedList class
  Standard PHP Library (SPL)
     changes, handling in 188-191
SplFileObject class
  Standard PHP Library (SPL) changes,
     examining to 183-185
SplFixedArray
  versus array 382, 383
  versus ArrayObject 382, 383
  working with, in PHP 8 382
SplFixedArray changes
  working with, in PHP 8 384, 385
SplHeap class
  Standard PHP Library (SPL) changes,
     examining to 185-188
SplObjectStorage class
  container class, implementing
     with 398-402
SQLite
  about 75
  reference link 75
SQLite databases
  authorization callback 76
  callback function 76, 77
  no security 75, 76
  securing, with authorizer 75

Index 503

stable sort
  about 386, 387
  implementing 385
  reference link 386
  versus non-stable sort 387-390
stable sorting effect
  examining, on keys 391-393
staging environment
  examining 410, 411
Standard PHP Library (SPL) 59, 249
Standard PHP Library (SPL) changes
  handling 183
static calls
  handling, in PHP 8 147, 148
static keyword 333
strategy software design pattern 242
str_contains() function
  about 72-74
  using 199, 200
streams
  about 312
  implementing 455
str_ends_with() function 72
strict comparison 208
string function
  detecting 71
  str_contains() function 72-74
  str_ends_with() function 72
  str_starts_with() function 71
string handling
  empty string offset 99
  offset 98, 99
  promoted warnings 98
string handling differences
  constants, using in PHP 8 206, 207
  dealing, with v*printf() changes 200-203
  examining, changes to
    implode() 204, 205

handling, changes to needle
    argument 195
  learning 194
  working, with null length arguments
    in PHP 8 203, 204
string handling techniques 67
strpos() search configuration
  defining 413
str_starts_with() function 71
Structured Query Language (SQL) 42, 311
super-globals 208
switch statements
  example 19, 20
Swoole
  Mezzio framework, using 473, 474
  PHP 8.1 fibers, examining 481
Swoole extension
  examining 457, 458
  installing 458-461
  URL 454
  using 457
  using, to improve application
    performance 467-470
Swoole extension, installation
  testing 461-463

T

TensorFlow
  about 115
  reference link 116
ternary operators 53
testing and troubleshooting
  tools, migration
  about 440
  Apache JMeter, working with 441, 442
  Xdebug, working with 440, 441

threads 453
timers
  implementing 456
tokenization process 360
tokens 368
track_errors php.ini setting
  examining 317, 318
trailing commas
  using 339
trait abstract signature check
  working with 353, 354
traits
  working with 341
Transmission Control Protocol (TDP) 458
Traversable, to IteratorAggregate
    migration 245, 246
type casting 134
type coercion 28
typed properties
  about 33
  drawback 35-38
  need for 34, 35
  used, for improving code 33
type juggling
  about 207
  reference link 210
typeof()
  FFI data, working with 128

U

undefined constant
  about 88
  handling 88
undefined variable
  about 87
  handling 87

Uniform Resource Locator
    (URL) 80, 93, 115, 480
uniform variable syntax
  about 61
  defining 61
  reference link 61
uniform variable syntax, impact on PHP 8
  about 62
  class-constant de-referencing 64, 65
  constants, inconsistent
      de-referencing 63, 64
  de-referencing, definition 62
  enhanced expression 66
  interpolated strings, de-referencing 63
union types
  about 15, 27
  example 29, 30
  generic syntax 28
union types documentation
  reference link 32
unit tests
  working with 445, 446
updated mbstring extension
  problems, avoiding with 255, 256
User Datagram Protocol (UDP) 458
UTF-8 260

V

variadics operator
  about 41
  arguments, vacuuming up 42-44
  unknown number of arguments 41
  using, as replacement 44-46
variance 177
virtual machine (VM) 367
v*printf() changes
  dealing with 200-203

Index 505

W

WeakMap class
  advantages, over SplObjectStorage
    class 402-405
  reference link 402
  working with 397, 398
WeakReference class definition
  reviewing 395
weak references
  advantages 395
  using 396, 397
  using, to improve efficiency 394, 395
Web Hypertext Application Technology
    Working Group (WHATWG) 341
widening 31
Windows Services for Linux (WSL) 457
workers 452
World Wide Web Consortium (W3C) 246

X

XDebug
  about 378
  URL 440
Xdebug tool
  working with 440, 441
XML extensions, changes
  about 246, 253
  changes to SimpleXML extension,
    working with 252
  libxml extension 253
  SimpleXML extension changes,
    working with 248-252
  XMLParser extension 254
  XMLReader extension 254
  XMLWriter extension differences,
    examining 247, 248

XML external entity (XXE) 253
XMLParser extension
  changes 254
XMLReader extension
  changes 254
XML-RPC extension
  changes 307
XMLWriter extension differences
  examining 247, 248

Y

YAML Ain't Markup Language
    (YAML) 27

Z

Zend Engine 367
Zend Expressive 473
Zend Framework 473
Zend Thread Safety (ZTS) 476
Zip extension changes
  addGlob(), options 277, 278
  addPattern(), options 277, 278
  OOP migration, dealing 275-277
  reviewing 275
  ZipArchive class methods 277
  ZipArchive method changes 278
Zip extension OOP migration
  dealing 275-277

Printed in Great Britain
by Amazon